kare kano

his and her circumstances

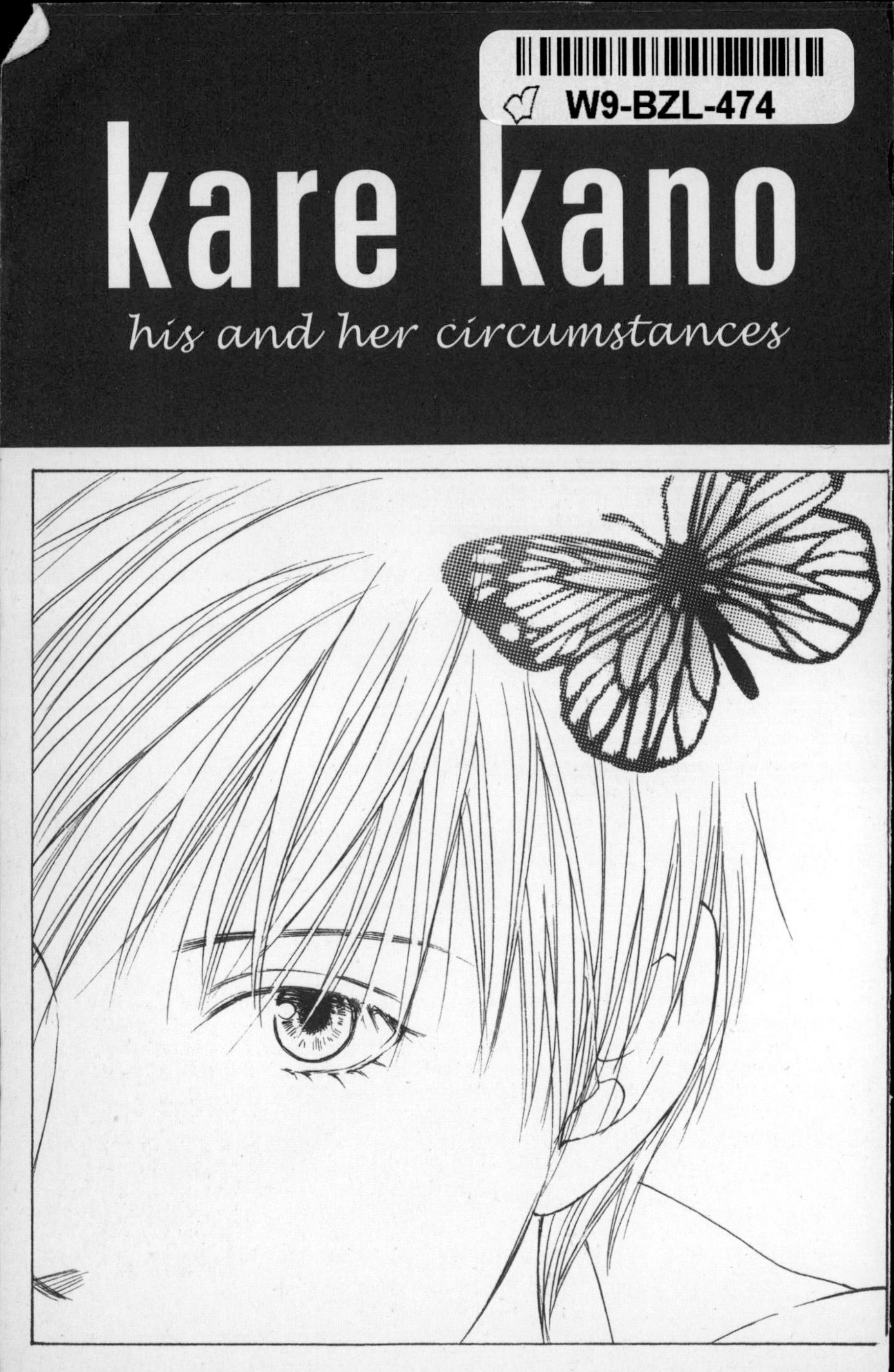

Kare Kano Vol. 17
Created by Masami Tsuda

Translation - Michelle Kobayashi
Copy Editor - Suzanne Waldman
Retouch and Lettering - Bowen Park
Production Artist - Chris Anderson
Cover Design - Gary Shum

Editor - Carol Fox
Digital Imaging Manager - Chris Buford
Production Managers - Jennifer Miller and Mutsumi Miyazaki
Managing Editor - Jill Freshney
VP of Production - Ron Klamert
Publisher and E.I.C. - Mike Kiley
President and C.O.O. - John Parker
C.E.O. - Stuart Levy

A  Manga

TOKYOPOP Inc.
5900 Wilshire Blvd. Suite 2000
Los Angeles, CA 90036

E-mail: info@TOKYOPOP.com
Come visit us online at www.TOKYOPOP.com

KARESHI KANOJO NO JIJOU by Masami Tsuda © 2003 Masami Tsuda. All rights reserved. First published in Japan in 2003 by HAKUSENSHA, INC., Tokyo. English language translation rights in the United States of America and Canada arranged with HAKUSENSHA, INC., Tokyo through Tuttle-Mori Agency Inc., Tokyo. English text copyright © 2005 TOKYOPOP Inc.

ISBN: 1-59532-591-3

First TOKYOPOP printing: September 2005
10 9 8 7 6 5 4 3 2 1
Printed in the USA

kare kano

his and her circumstances

volume seventeen

by Masami Tsuda

HAMBURG // LONDON // LOS ANGELES // TOKYO

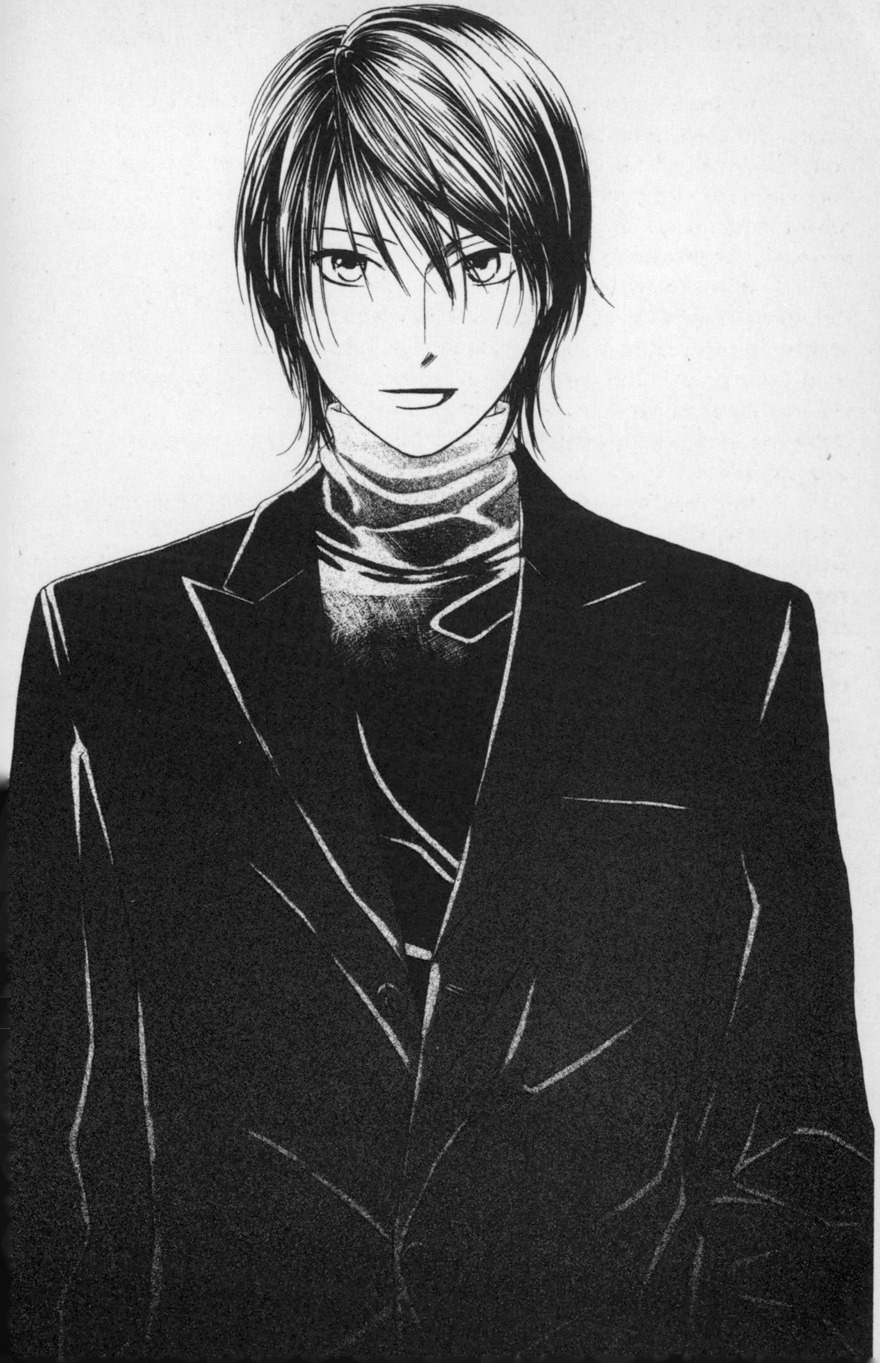

KARE KANO: THE STORY SO FAR

   Yukino Miyazawa is the perfect student: kind, athletic and smart. But she's not all she seems. She is really the self-professed "queen of vanity," and her only goal in life is winning the praise and admiration of everyone around her. Therefore, she makes it her business to always look and act perfect during school hours. At home, however, she lets her guard down and lets her true self show.

   When Yukino enters high school, she finally meets her match: Soichiro Arima, a handsome, popular, ultra-intelligent guy. Once he steals the top seat in class away from her, Yukino sees him as a bitter rival. Over time, her anger turns to amazement, when she discovers she and Soichiro have more in common than she ever imagined. As their love blossoms, they promise to stop pretending to be perfect and just be true to themselves.

   But they have plenty of obstacles. First, Hideaki, the school's token pretty boy, tries to come between them. Then Yukino and Soichiro's grades drop because they've been spending so much time together, and their teacher pressures them to break up. Once that's resolved, two more speed bumps are encountered on their road to romance. Maho, a jealous classmate, is convinced that Yukino is deceiving everyone, and vows to turn everyone against her. Then an old friend of Soichiro's from junior high tries to steal Soichiro's affections. Somehow, Yukino and Soichiro's love manages to persevere—even after Soichiro spends the summer away at a kendo tournament.

   Or has it? What Yukino doesn't realize is that although Soichiro's life with his adoptive family seems perfect, he endured a very traumatic childhood. And now Soichiro's success has attracted the attention of his birth mother, who suddenly wants him back in his life. Soichiro begins to meet with her in secret, to learn more about the family that abandoned him...until he realizes she has nothing for him but more lies and abuse. But try as he might to cut off contact, she won't be dismissed so easily.

   All the while, Soichiro keeps pushing the concerned Yukino further and further away. But she persists...and finally breaks down his walls. Now it's finally time for Yukino to learn the whole truth about who Soichiro really is...

kare kano
volume seventeen

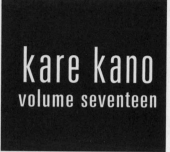

TABLE OF CONTENTS

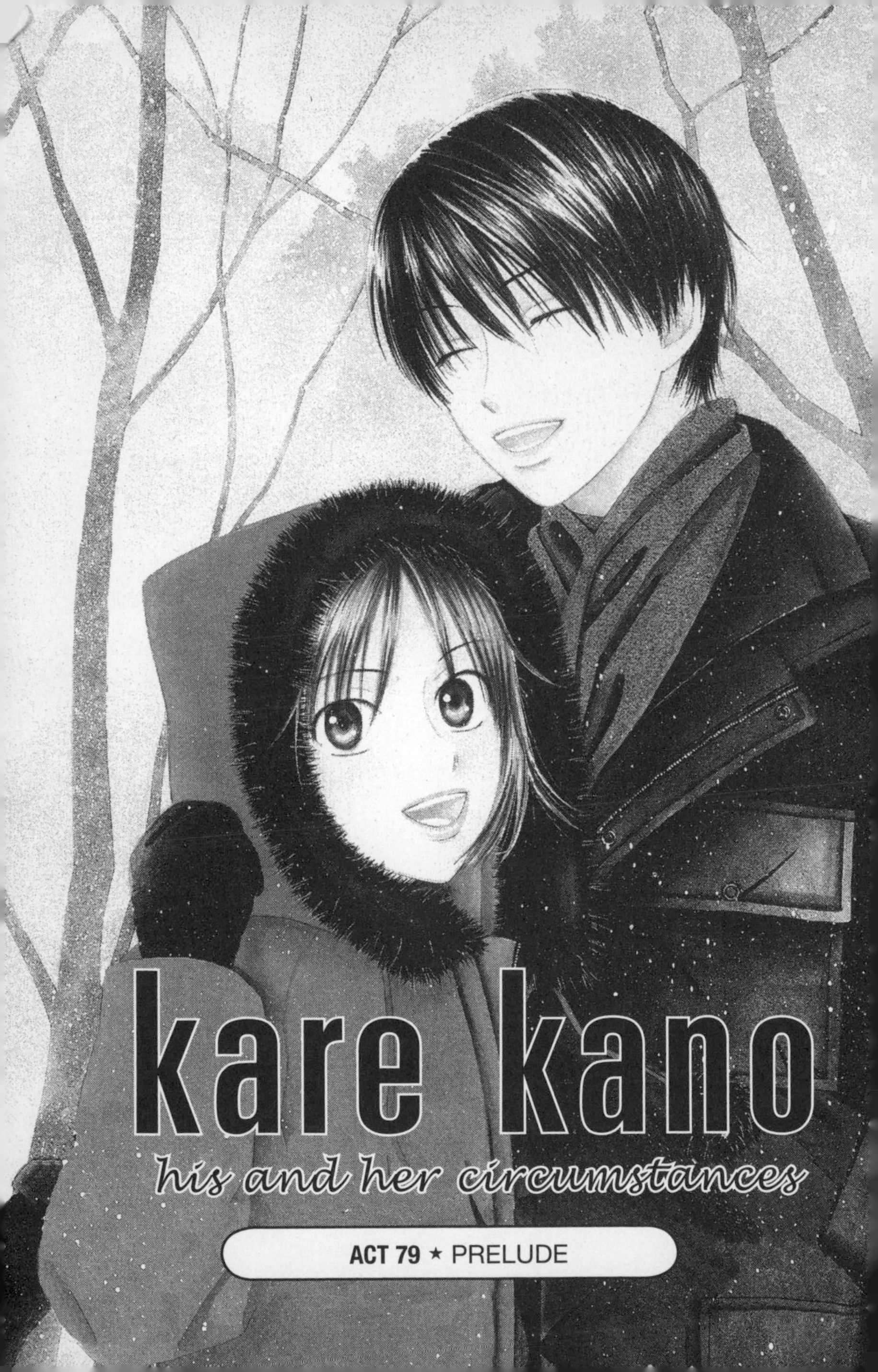
kare kano
his and her circumstances
ACT 79 ★ PRELUDE

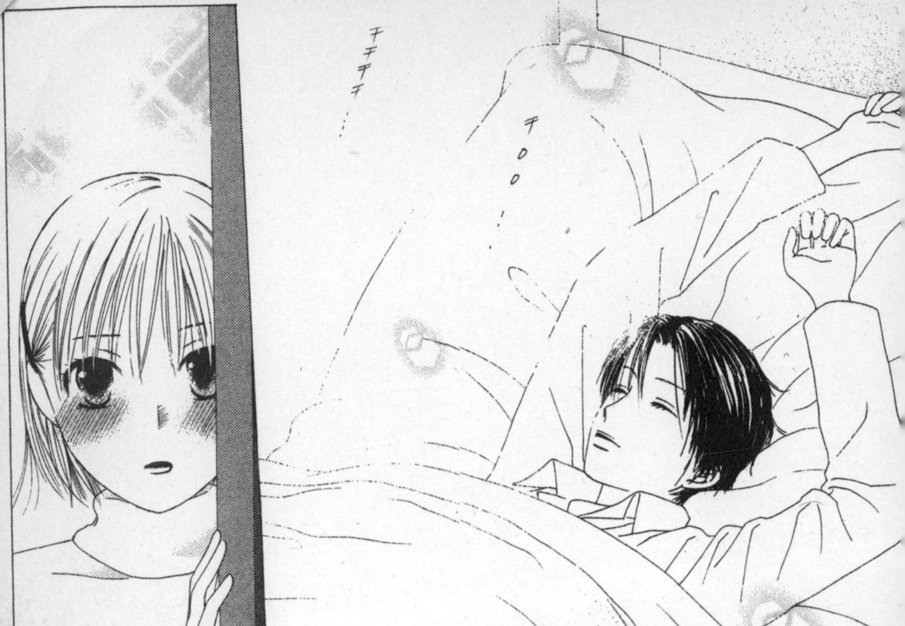
チチチチ…

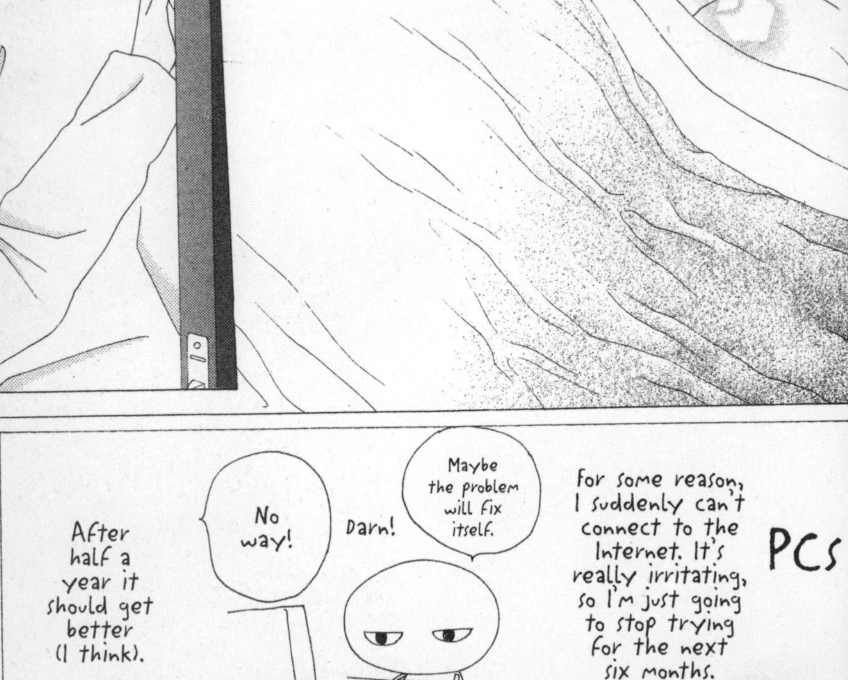
PCs
For some reason, I suddenly can't connect to the Internet. It's really irritating, so I'm just going to stop trying for the next six months.
Maybe the problem will fix itself.
Darn!
No way!
After half a year it should get better (I think).

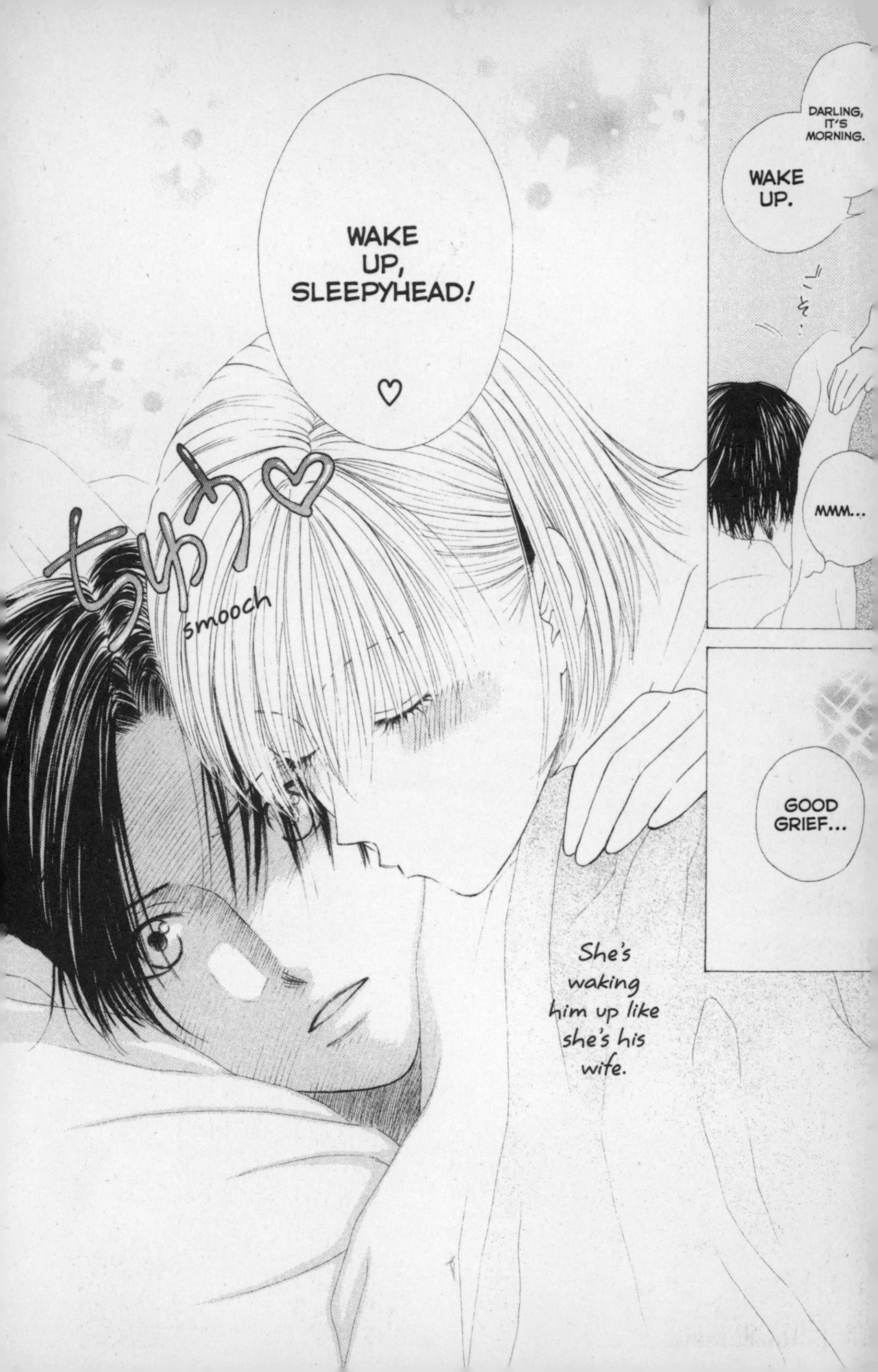
DARLING, IT'S MORNING.
WAKE UP.
MMM...
GOOD GRIEF...
WAKE UP, SLEEPYHEAD! ♡
smooch
She's waking him up like she's his wife.

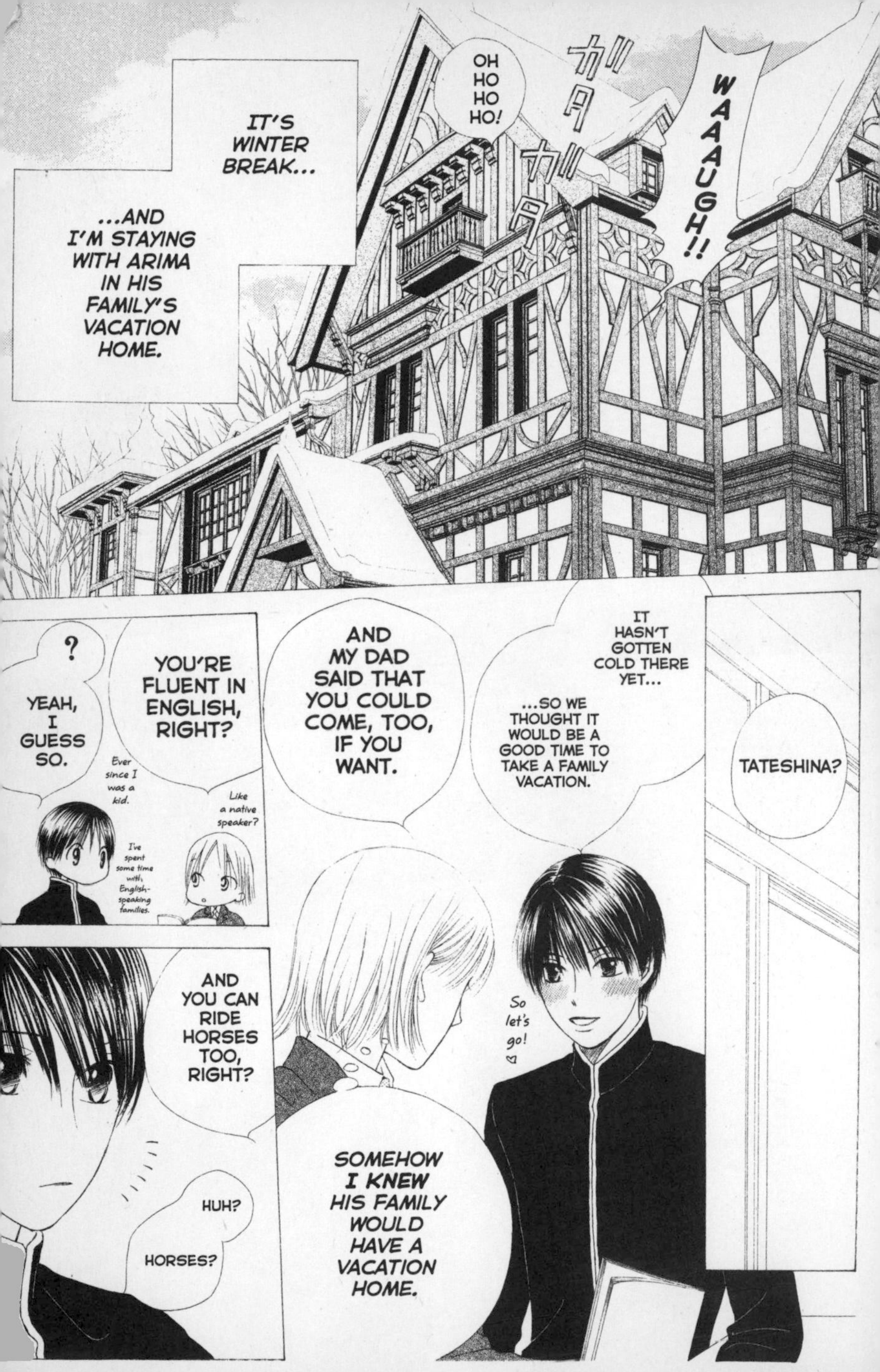
WAAAUGH!!
OH HO HO HO!
IT'S WINTER BREAK...
...AND I'M STAYING WITH ARIMA IN HIS FAMILY'S VACATION HOME.
TATESHINA?
IT HASN'T GOTTEN COLD THERE YET...
...SO WE THOUGHT IT WOULD BE A GOOD TIME TO TAKE A FAMILY VACATION.
AND MY DAD SAID THAT YOU COULD COME, TOO, IF YOU WANT.
YOU'RE FLUENT IN ENGLISH, RIGHT?
Like a native speaker?
?
YEAH, I GUESS SO.
Ever since I was a kid.
I've spent some time with English-speaking families.
So let's go! ♡
SOMEHOW I KNEW HIS FAMILY WOULD HAVE A VACATION HOME.
AND YOU CAN RIDE HORSES TOO, RIGHT?
HUH?
HORSES?

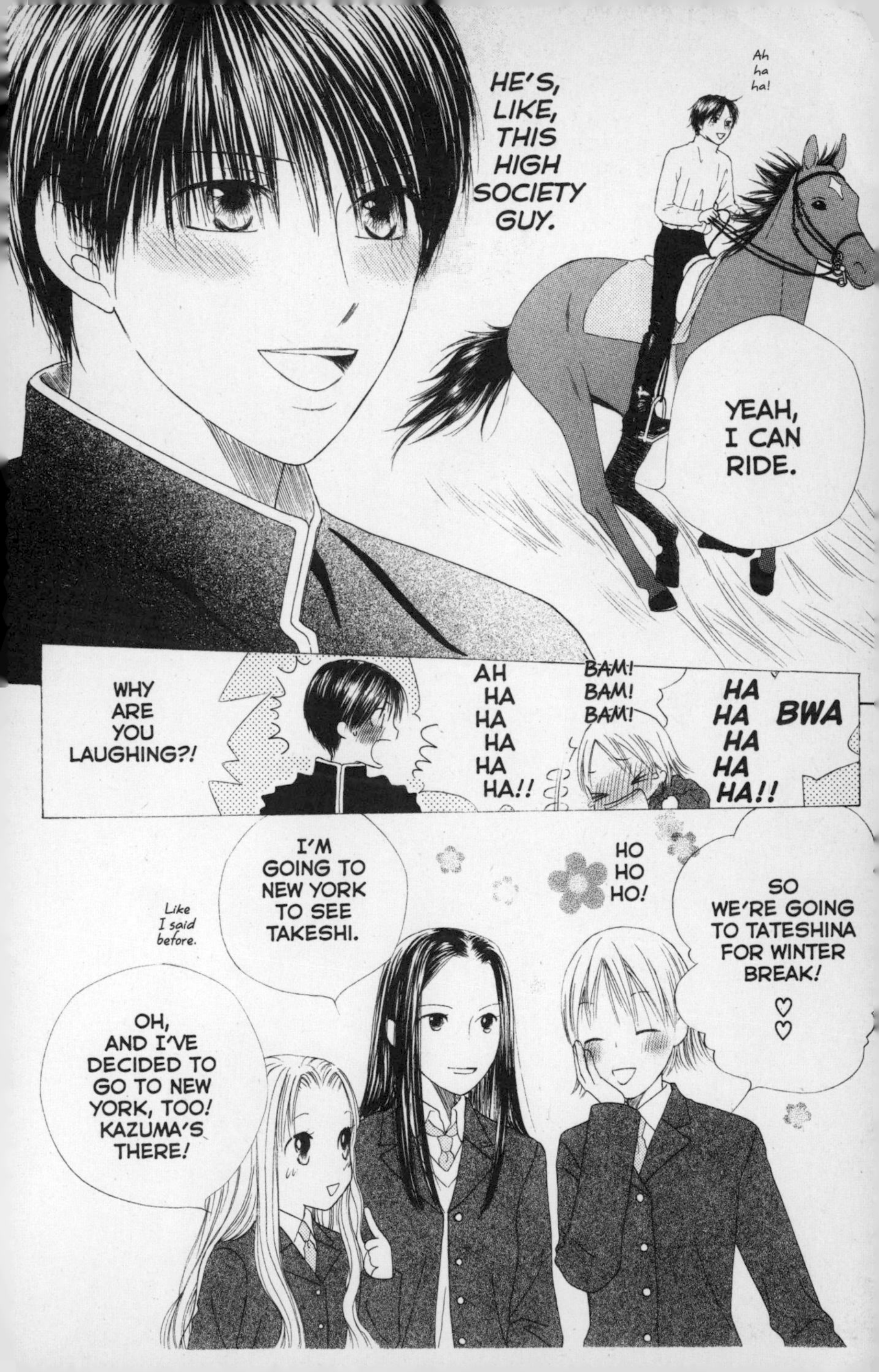

Ah ha ha!
HE'S, LIKE, THIS HIGH SOCIETY GUY.
YEAH, I CAN RIDE.
BWA HA HA HA HA HA!!
BAM! BAM! BAM!
AH HA HA HA HA HA!!
WHY ARE YOU LAUGHING?!
SO WE'RE GOING TO TATESHINA FOR WINTER BREAK! ♡ ♡
HO HO HO!
I'M GOING TO NEW YORK TO SEE TAKESHI.
Like I said before.
OH, AND I'VE DECIDED TO GO TO NEW YORK, TOO! KAZUMA'S THERE!

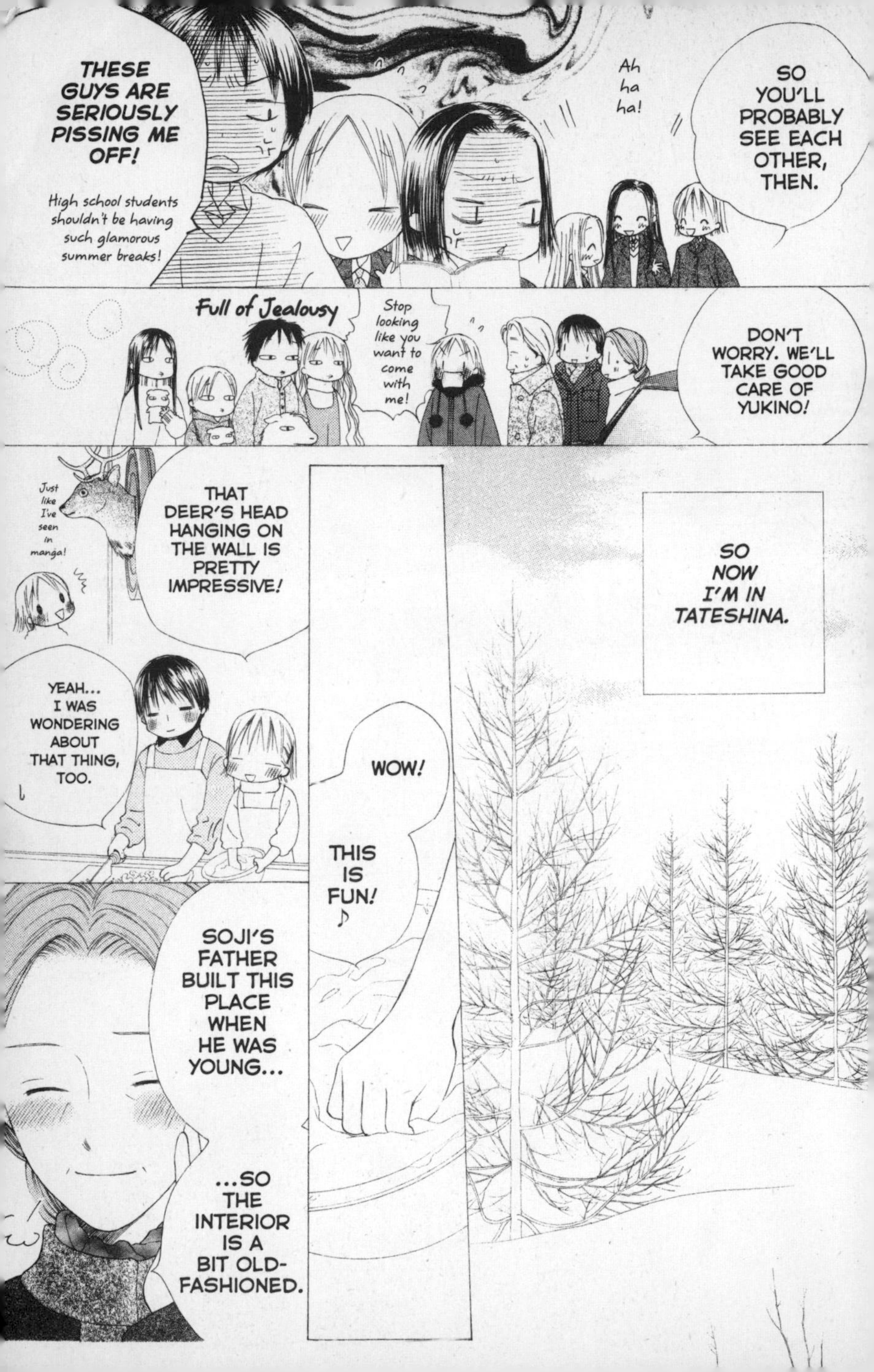
SO YOU'LL PROBABLY SEE EACH OTHER, THEN.
Ah ha ha!
THESE GUYS ARE SERIOUSLY PISSING ME OFF!
High school students shouldn't be having such glamorous summer breaks!
DON'T WORRY. WE'LL TAKE GOOD CARE OF YUKINO!
Stop looking like you want to come with me!
Full of Jealousy
SO NOW I'M IN TATESHINA.
WOW!
THIS IS FUN! ♪
THAT DEER'S HEAD HANGING ON THE WALL IS PRETTY IMPRESSIVE!
Just like I've seen in manga!
YEAH... I WAS WONDERING ABOUT THAT THING, TOO.
SOJI'S FATHER BUILT THIS PLACE WHEN HE WAS YOUNG...
...SO THE INTERIOR IS A BIT OLD-FASHIONED.

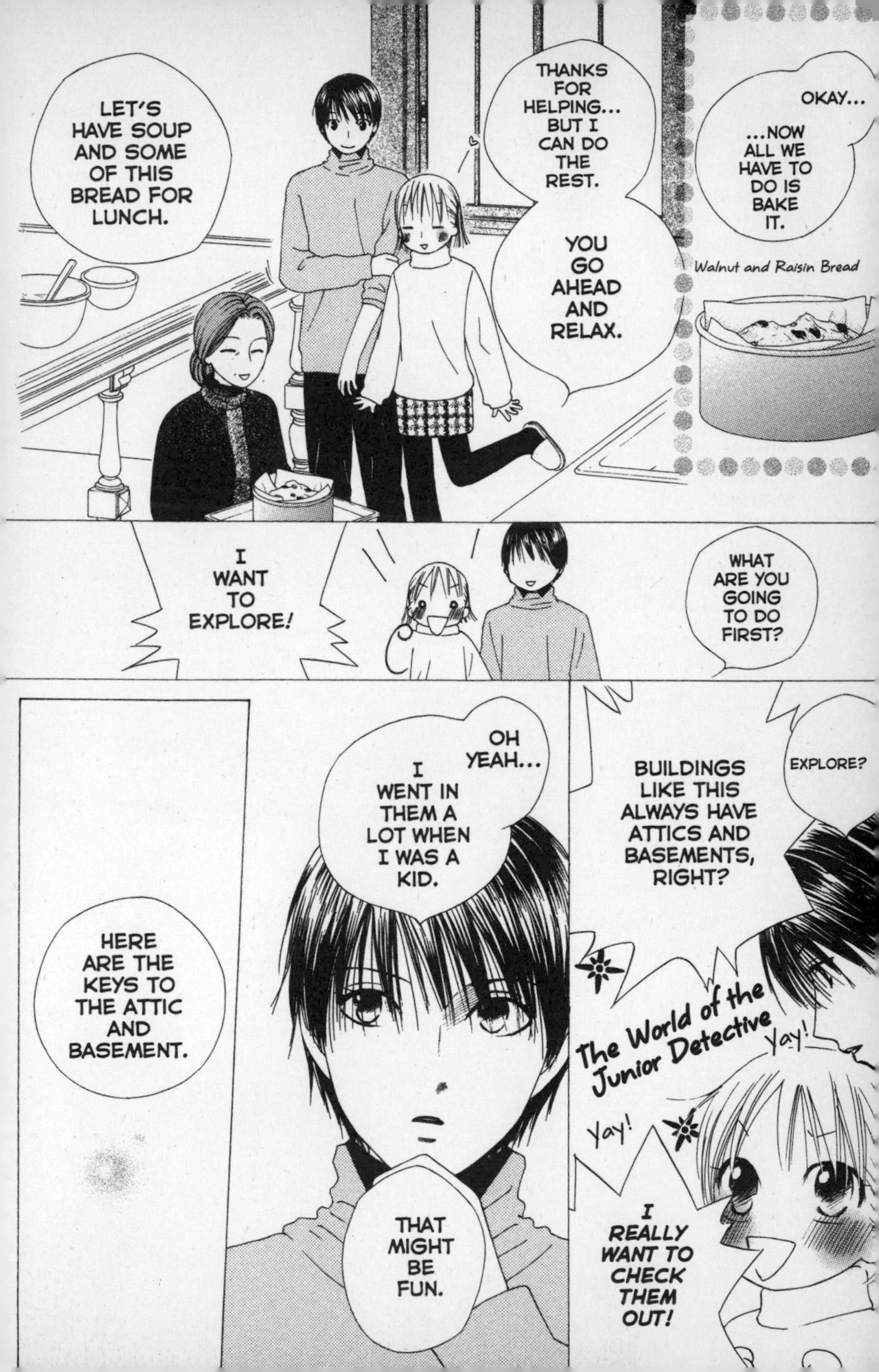
OKAY... ...NOW ALL WE HAVE TO DO IS BAKE IT.
Walnut and Raisin Bread
THANKS FOR HELPING... BUT I CAN DO THE REST.
YOU GO AHEAD AND RELAX.
LET'S HAVE SOUP AND SOME OF THIS BREAD FOR LUNCH.
WHAT ARE YOU GOING TO DO FIRST?
I WANT TO EXPLORE!
EXPLORE?
BUILDINGS LIKE THIS ALWAYS HAVE ATTICS AND BASEMENTS, RIGHT?
The World of the Junior Detective
Yay!
Yay!
I REALLY WANT TO CHECK THEM OUT!
OH YEAH...
I WENT IN THEM A LOT WHEN I WAS A KID.
THAT MIGHT BE FUN.
HERE ARE THE KEYS TO THE ATTIC AND BASEMENT.

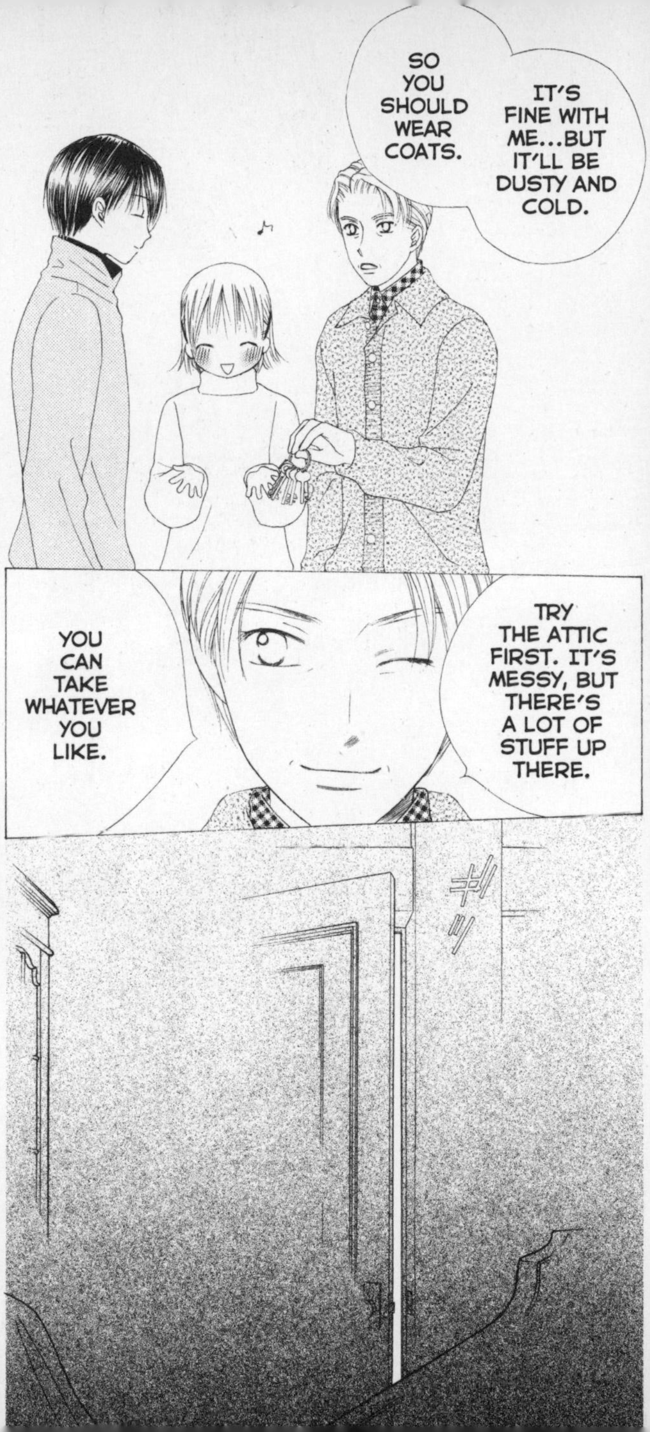
IT'S FINE WITH ME...BUT IT'LL BE DUSTY AND COLD.
SO YOU SHOULD WEAR COATS.
TRY THE ATTIC FIRST. IT'S MESSY, BUT THERE'S A LOT OF STUFF UP THERE.
YOU CAN TAKE WHATEVER YOU LIKE.

1

Hello. This is my twenty-first comic, Kare Kano Volume 17.

It was really hard researching this volume. I had to get materials from many different sources. But then I started to take an interest in it, so it was fun, too.

♡

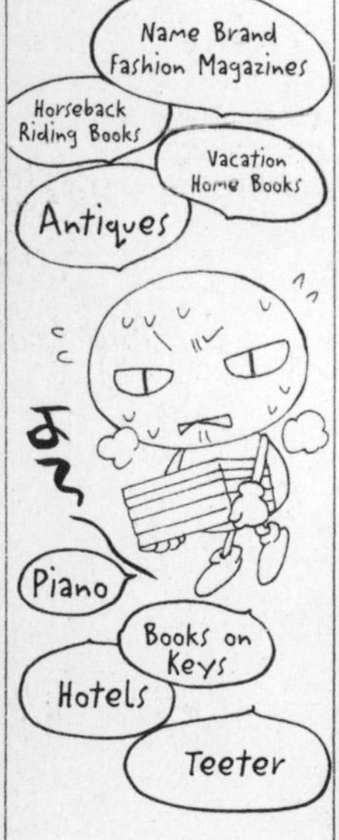
Name Brand Fashion Magazines
Horseback Riding Books
Vacation Home Books
Antiques
Piano
Books on Keys
Hotels
Teeter

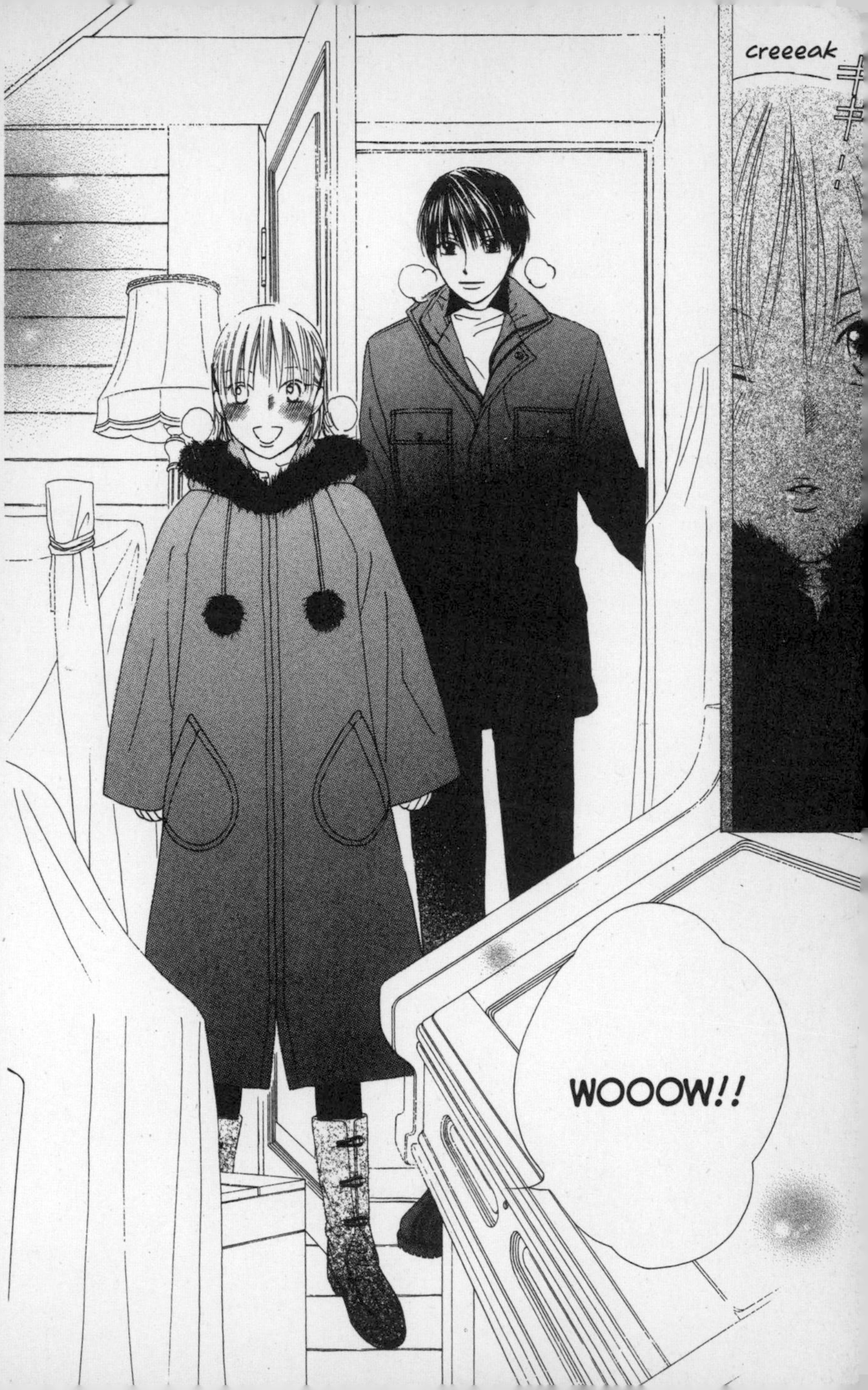
creeeak
WOOOW!!

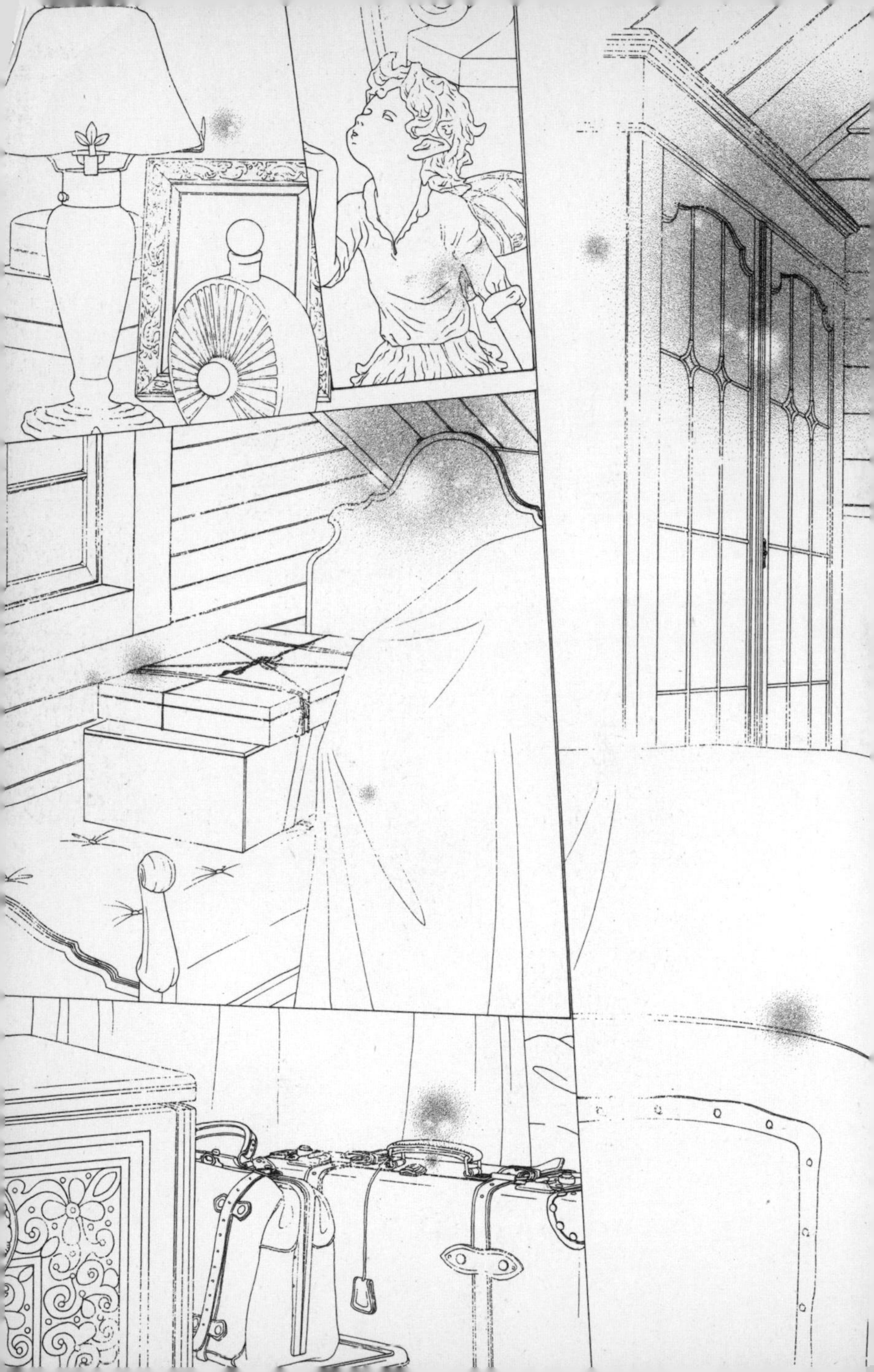

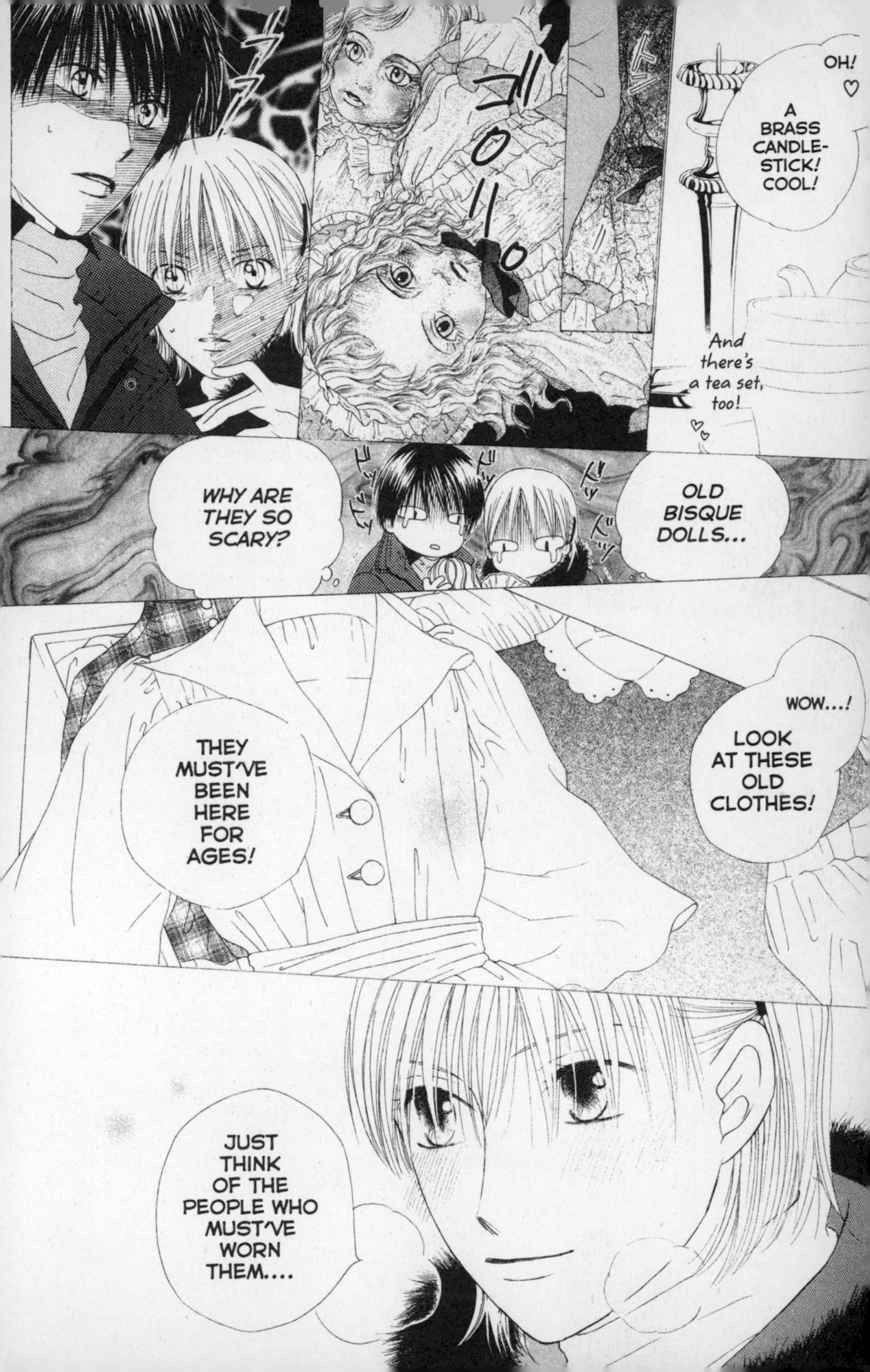
OH! ♡ A BRASS CANDLE-STICK! COOL!
And there's a tea set, too!
OLD BISQUE DOLLS...
WHY ARE THEY SO SCARY?
WOW...! LOOK AT THESE OLD CLOTHES!
THEY MUST'VE BEEN HERE FOR AGES!
JUST THINK OF THE PEOPLE WHO MUST'VE WORN THEM....

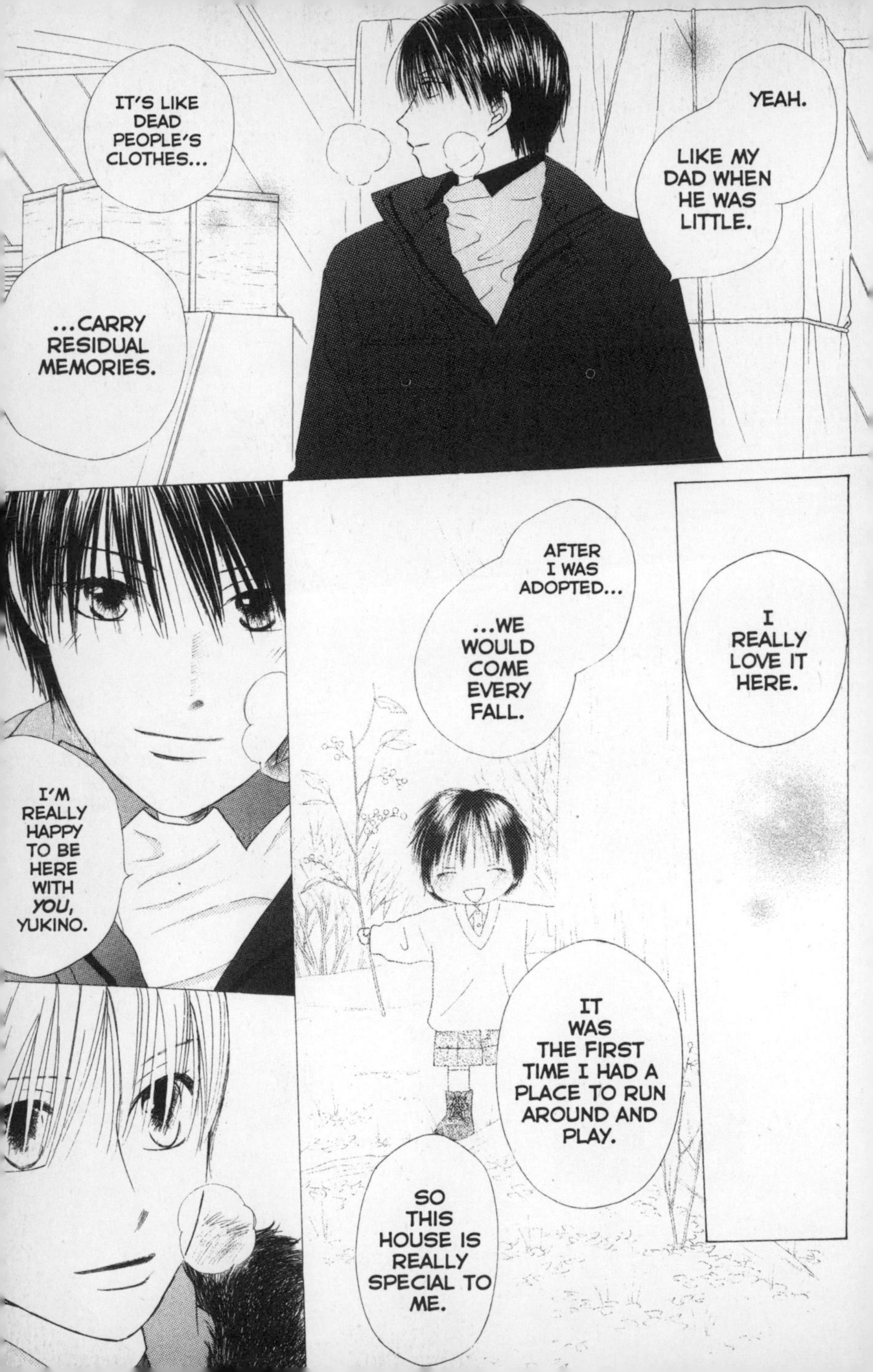
YEAH.
LIKE MY DAD WHEN HE WAS LITTLE.
IT'S LIKE DEAD PEOPLE'S CLOTHES...
...CARRY RESIDUAL MEMORIES.
I REALLY LOVE IT HERE.
AFTER I WAS ADOPTED...
...WE WOULD COME EVERY FALL.
IT WAS THE FIRST TIME I HAD A PLACE TO RUN AROUND AND PLAY.
SO THIS HOUSE IS REALLY SPECIAL TO ME.
I'M REALLY HAPPY TO BE HERE WITH *YOU*, YUKINO.

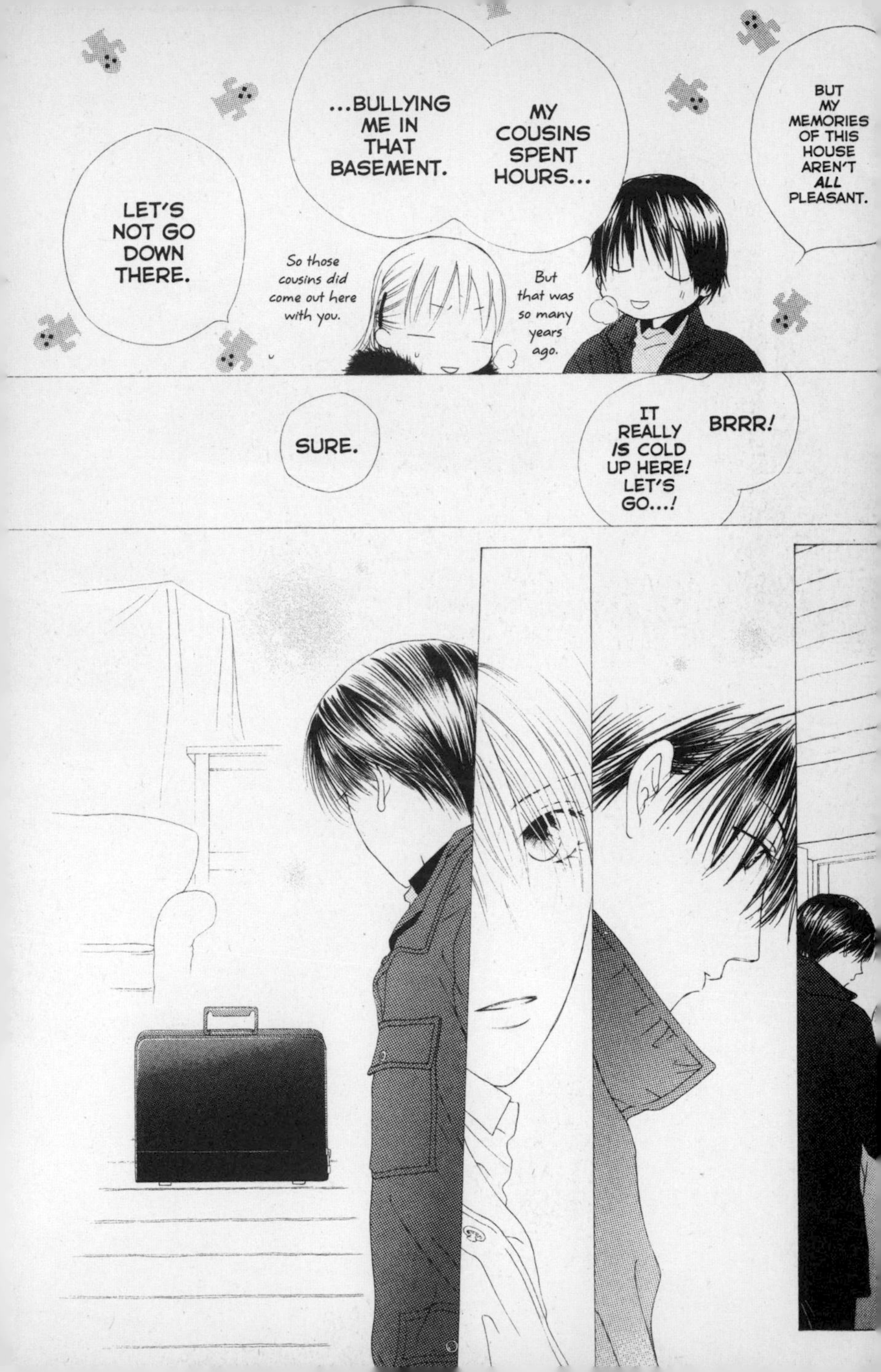
BUT MY MEMORIES OF THIS HOUSE AREN'T ALL PLEASANT.
MY COUSINS SPENT HOURS...
...BULLYING ME IN THAT BASEMENT.
But that was so many years ago.
So those cousins did come out here with you.
LET'S NOT GO DOWN THERE.
BRRR!
IT REALLY IS COLD UP HERE! LET'S GO...!
SURE.

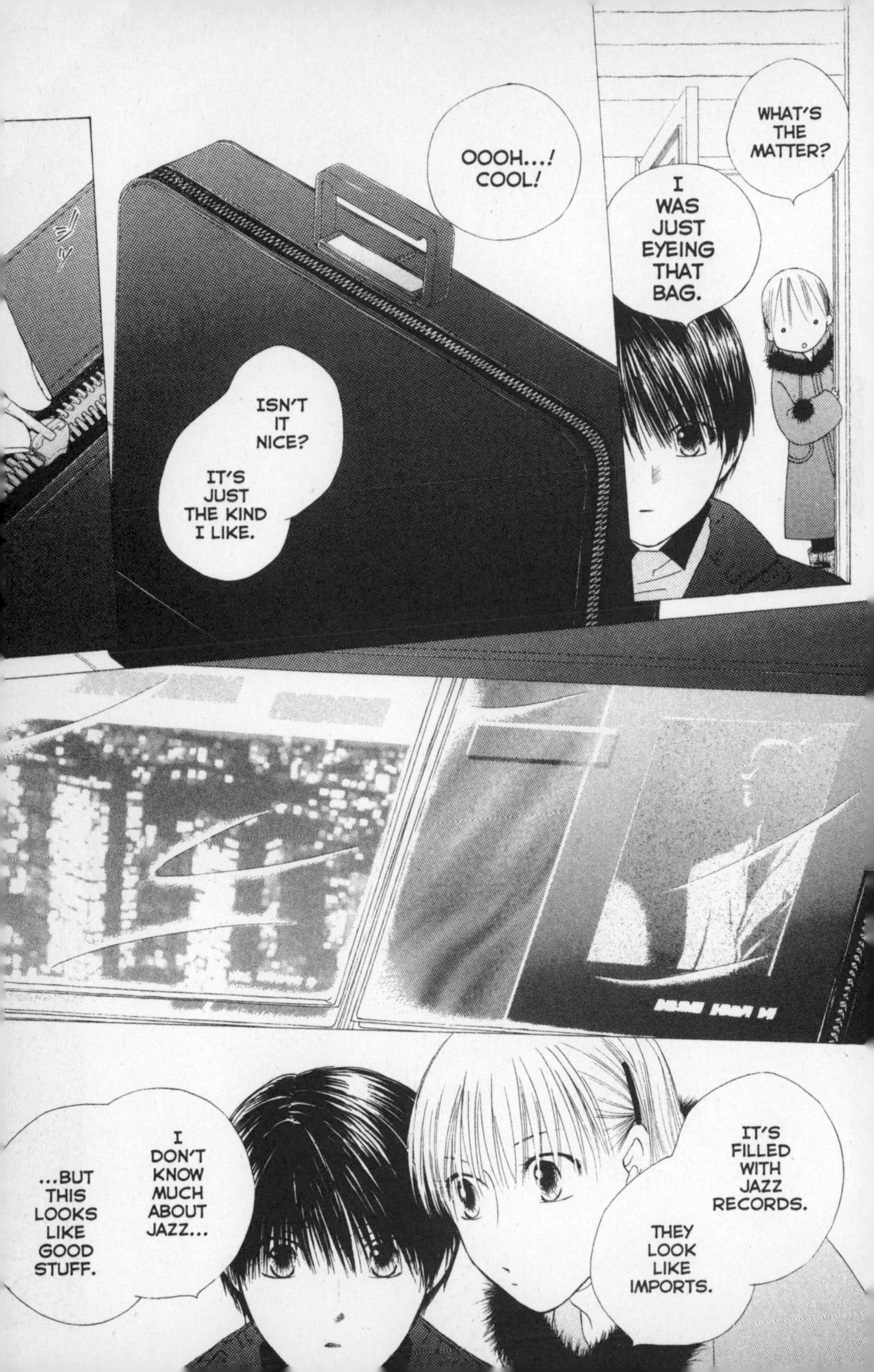
WHAT'S THE MATTER?
I WAS JUST EYEING THAT BAG.
OOOH...! COOL!
ISN'T IT NICE?
IT'S JUST THE KIND I LIKE.
IT'S FILLED WITH JAZZ RECORDS.
THEY LOOK LIKE IMPORTS.
I DON'T KNOW MUCH ABOUT JAZZ...
...BUT THIS LOOKS LIKE GOOD STUFF.

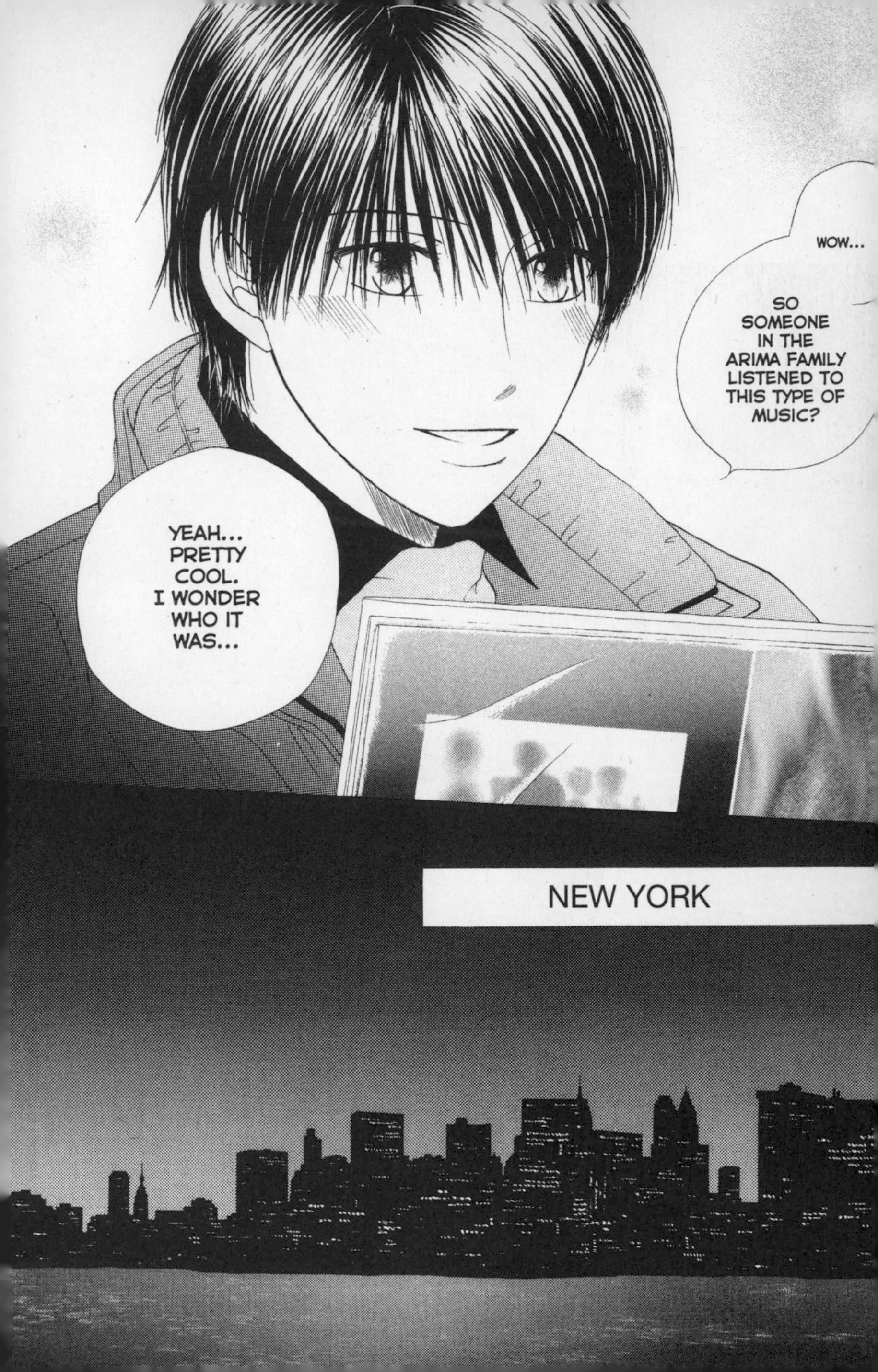
WOW...
SO SOMEONE IN THE ARIMA FAMILY LISTENED TO THIS TYPE OF MUSIC?
YEAH... PRETTY COOL. I WONDER WHO IT WAS...
NEW YORK

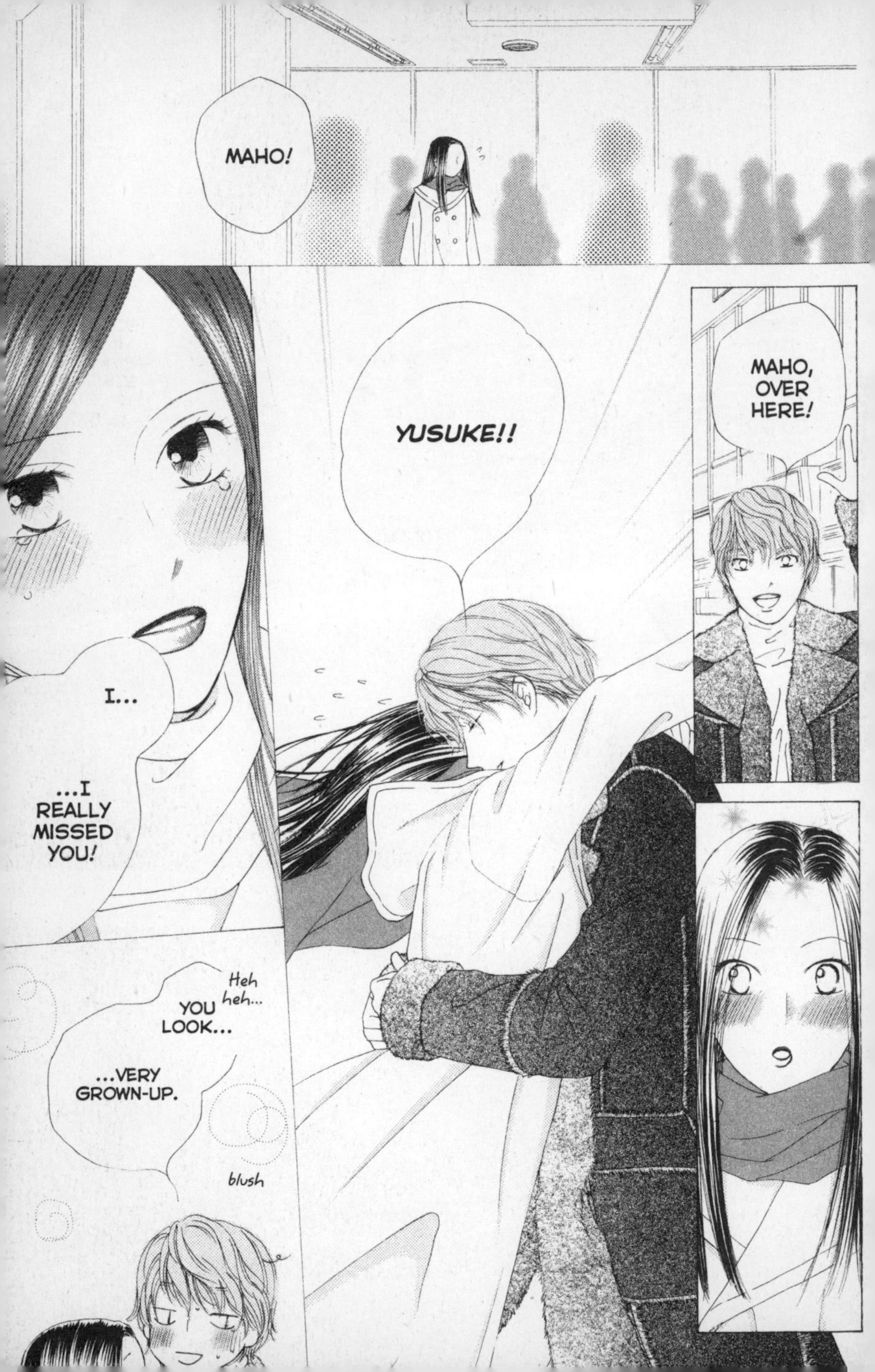
MAHO!
MAHO, OVER HERE!
YUSUKE!!
I...
...I REALLY MISSED YOU!
Heh heh...
YOU LOOK...
...VERY GROWN-UP.
blush

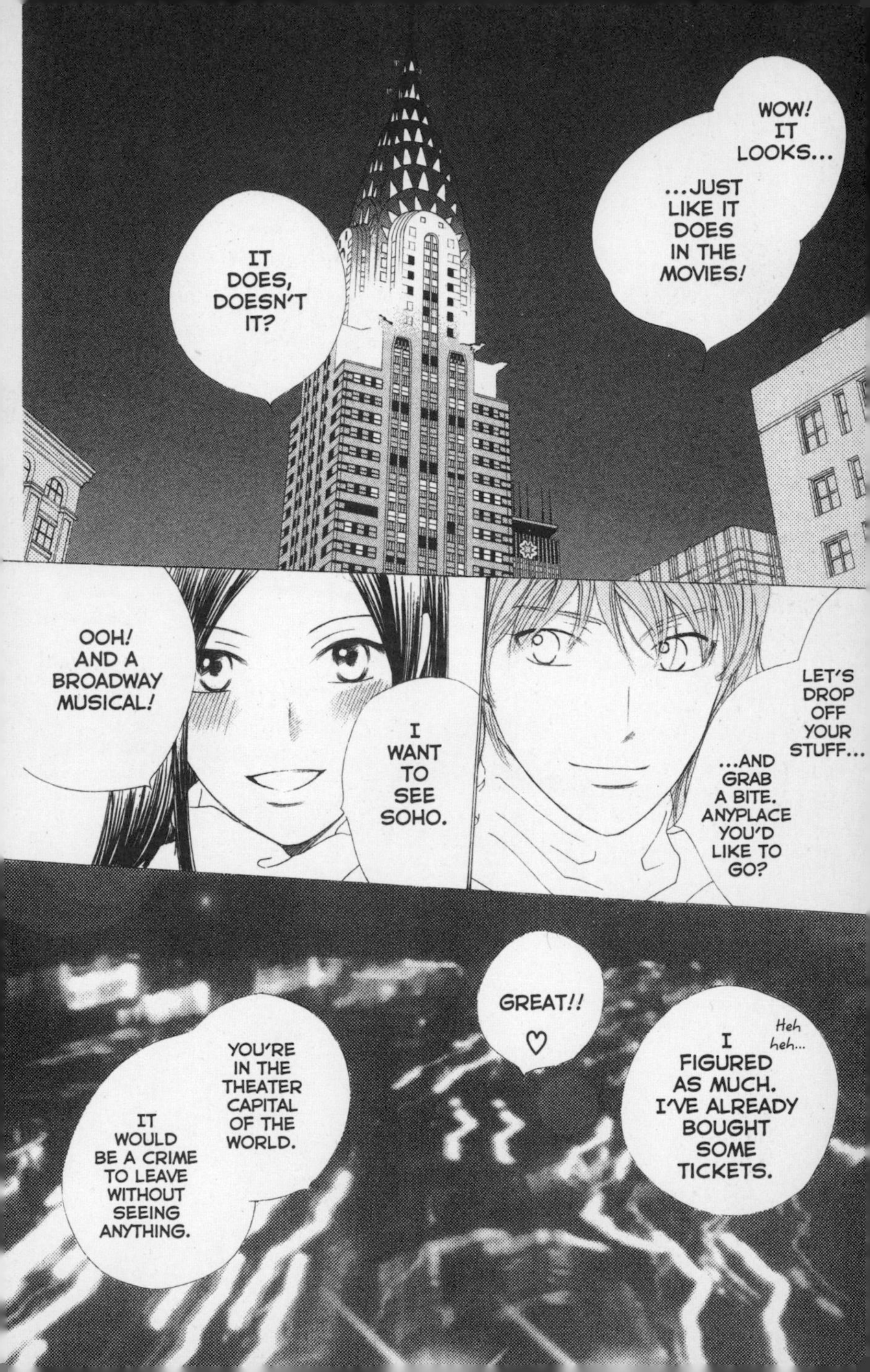
WOW! IT LOOKS...
...JUST LIKE IT DOES IN THE MOVIES!
IT DOES, DOESN'T IT?
LET'S DROP OFF YOUR STUFF...
...AND GRAB A BITE. ANYPLACE YOU'D LIKE TO GO?
I WANT TO SEE SOHO.
OOH! AND A BROADWAY MUSICAL!
Heh heh...
I FIGURED AS MUCH. I'VE ALREADY BOUGHT SOME TICKETS.
GREAT!! ♡
YOU'RE IN THE THEATER CAPITAL OF THE WORLD.
IT WOULD BE A CRIME TO LEAVE WITHOUT SEEING ANYTHING.

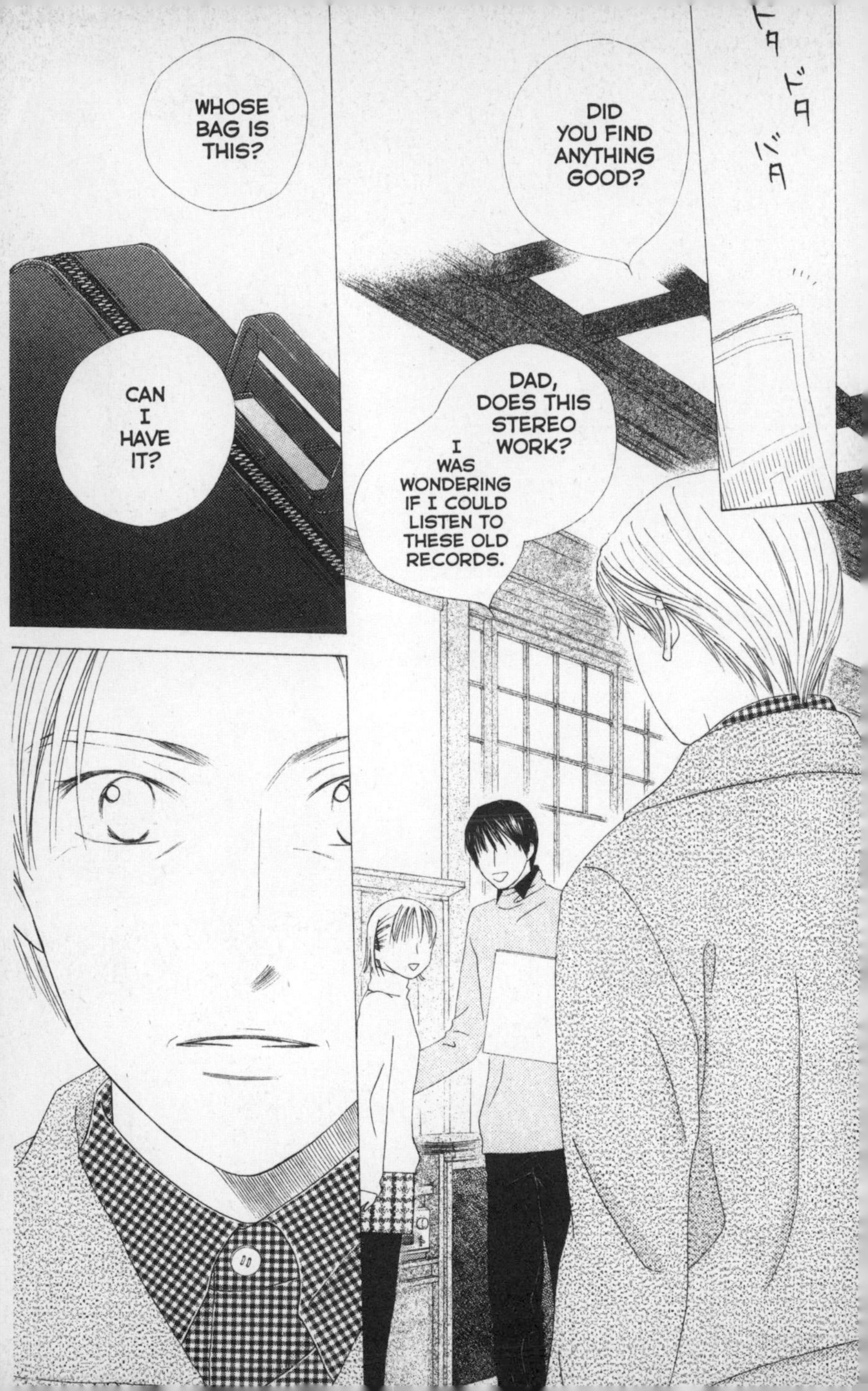
DID YOU FIND ANYTHING GOOD?
DAD, DOES THIS STEREO WORK?
I WAS WONDERING IF I COULD LISTEN TO THESE OLD RECORDS.
WHOSE BAG IS THIS?
CAN I HAVE IT?

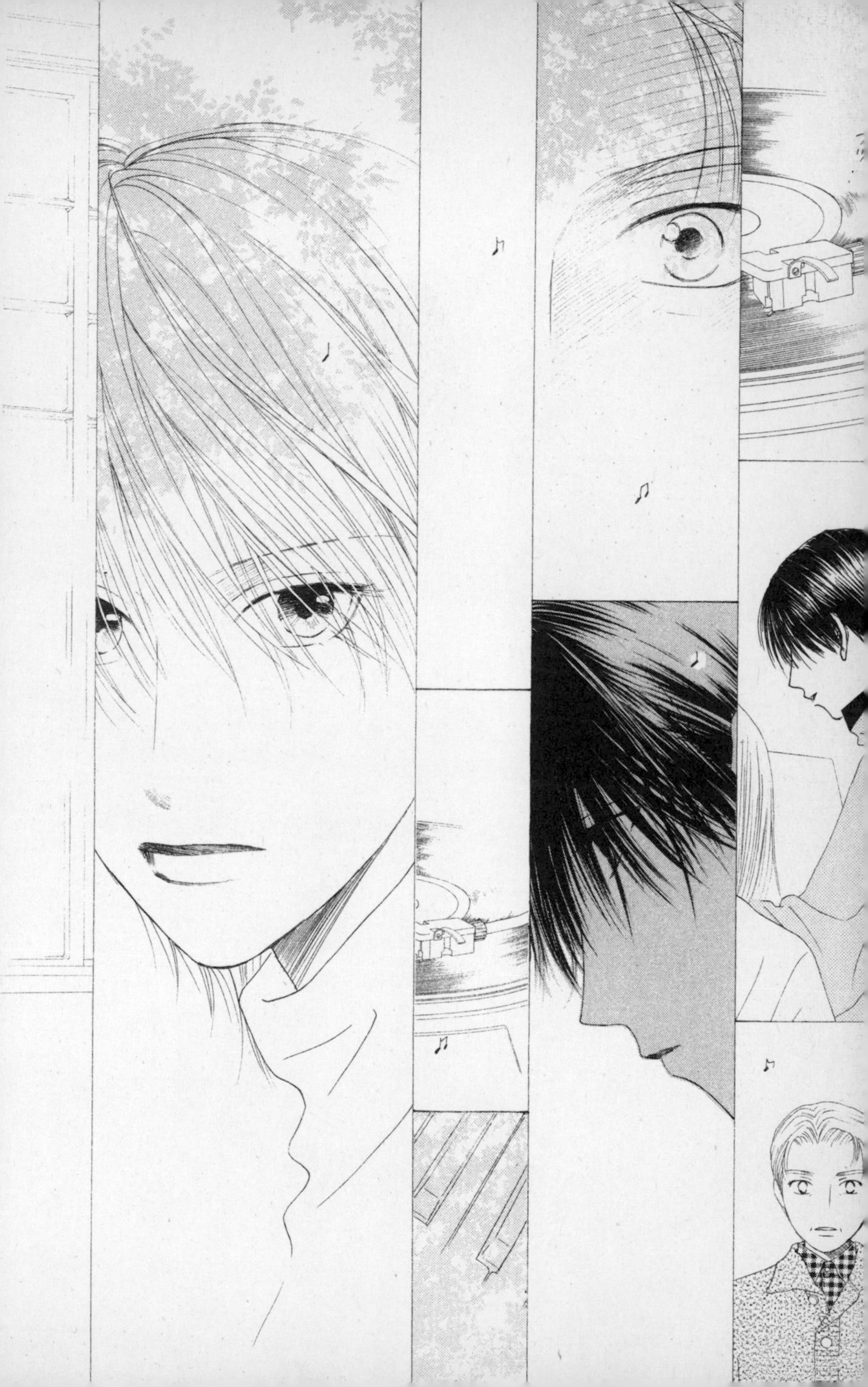

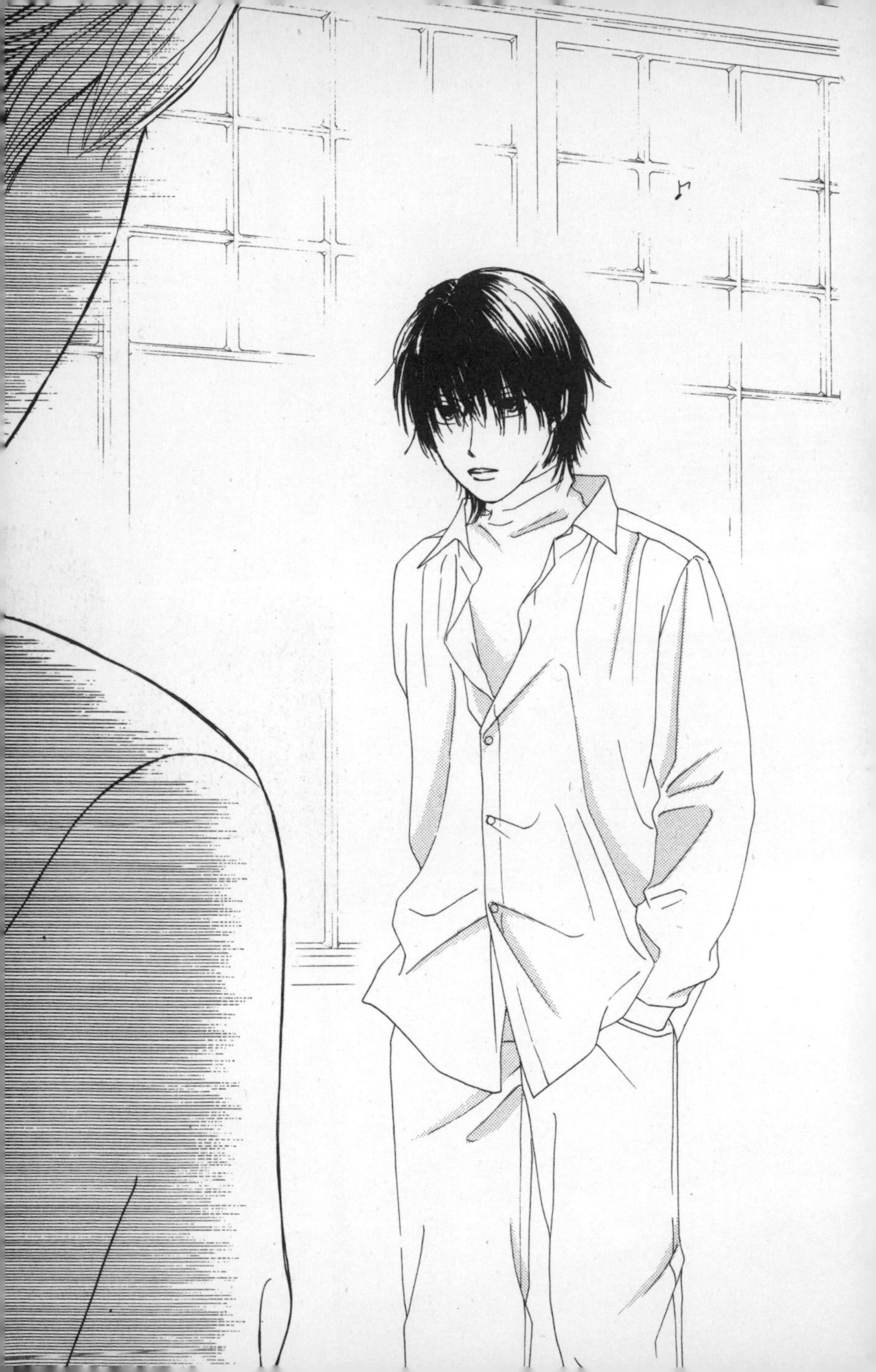

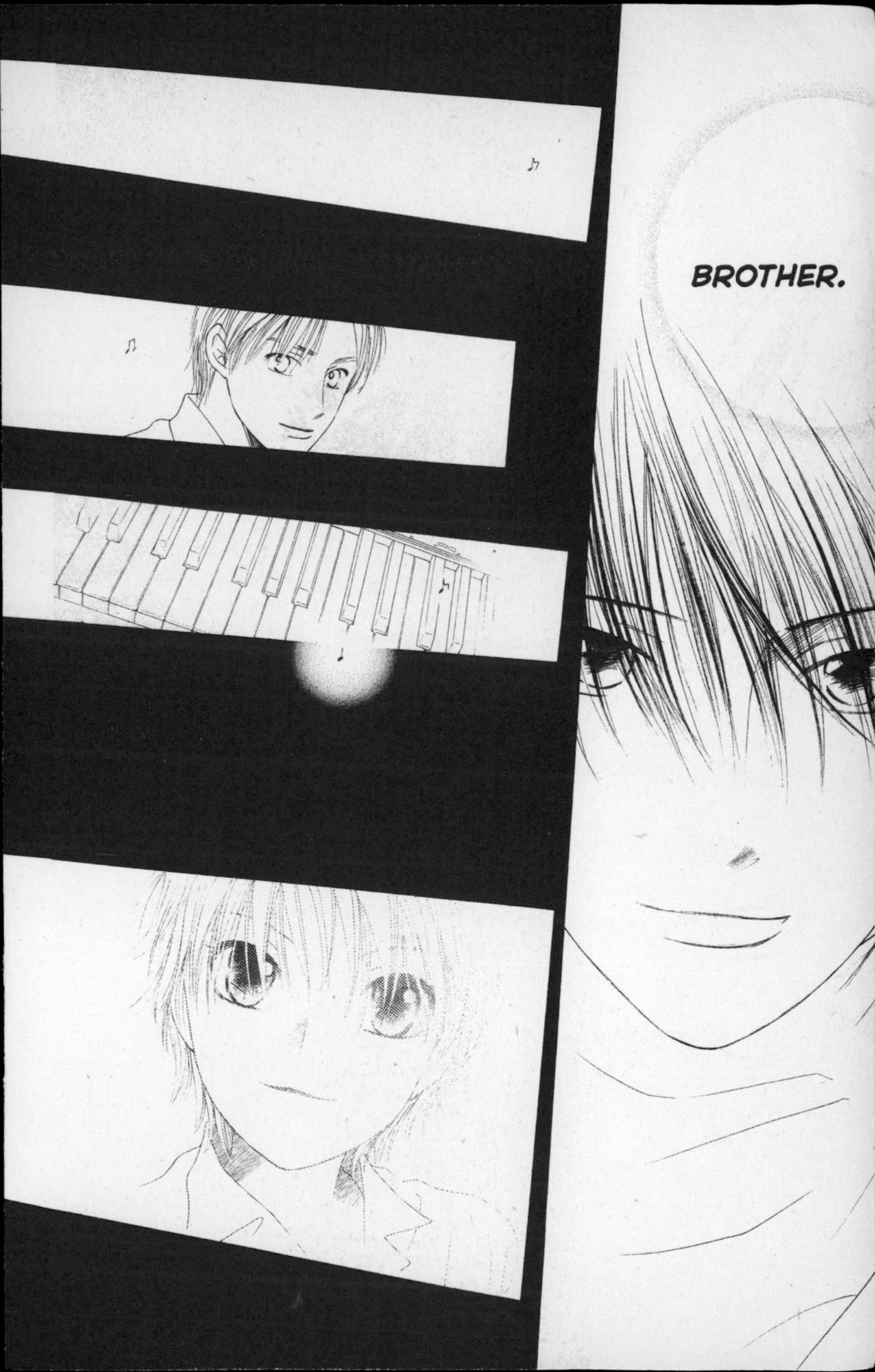
BROTHER.

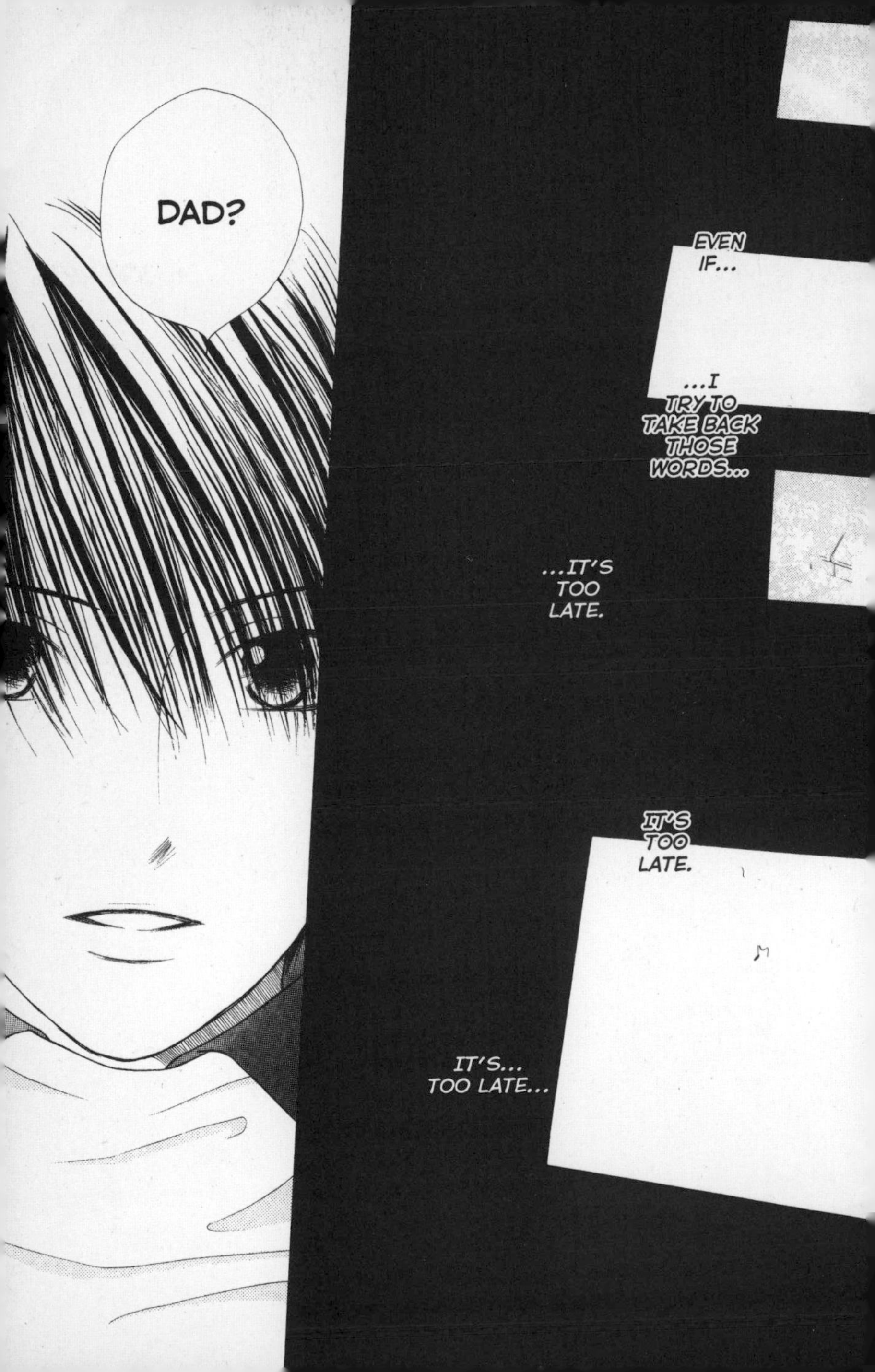
EVEN IF...
...I TRY TO TAKE BACK THOSE WORDS...
...IT'S TOO LATE.
IT'S TOO LATE.
IT'S... TOO LATE...
DAD?

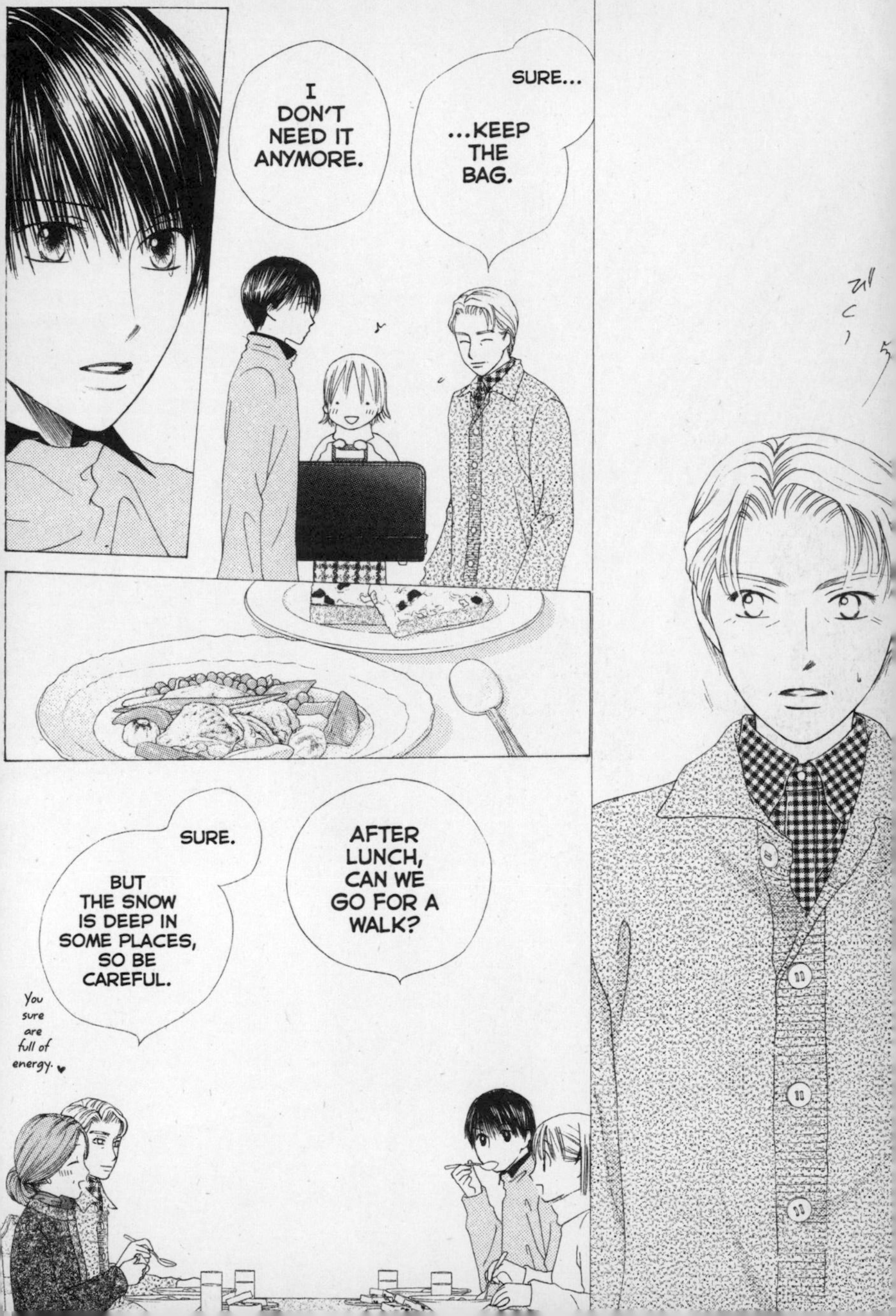
びくっ
SURE... ...KEEP THE BAG.
I DON'T NEED IT ANYMORE.
AFTER LUNCH, CAN WE GO FOR A WALK?
SURE. BUT THE SNOW IS DEEP IN SOME PLACES, SO BE CAREFUL.
You sure are full of energy.

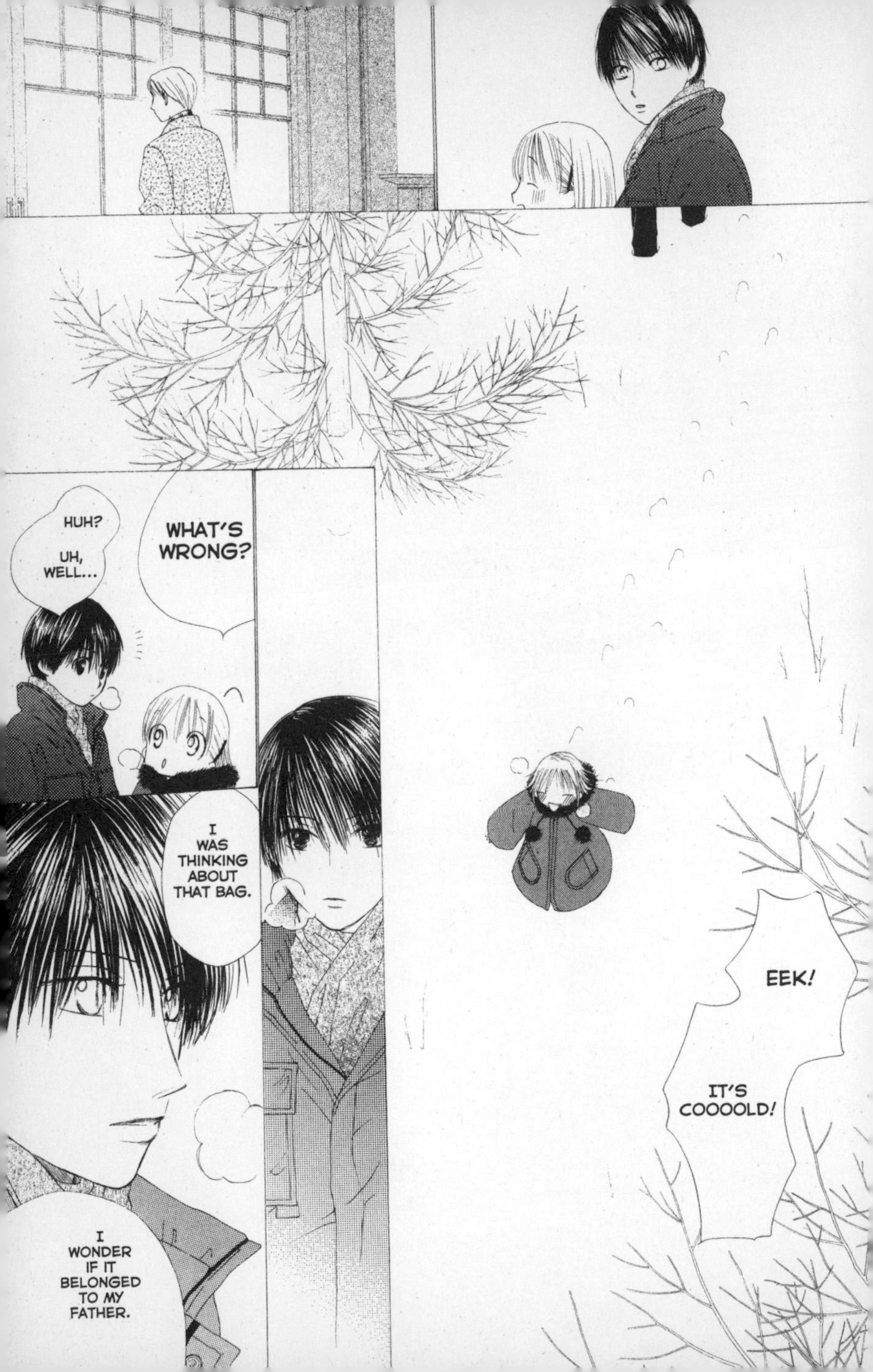
EEK!
IT'S COOOOLD!
WHAT'S WRONG?
HUH? UH, WELL...
I WAS THINKING ABOUT THAT BAG.
I WONDER IF IT BELONGED TO MY FATHER.

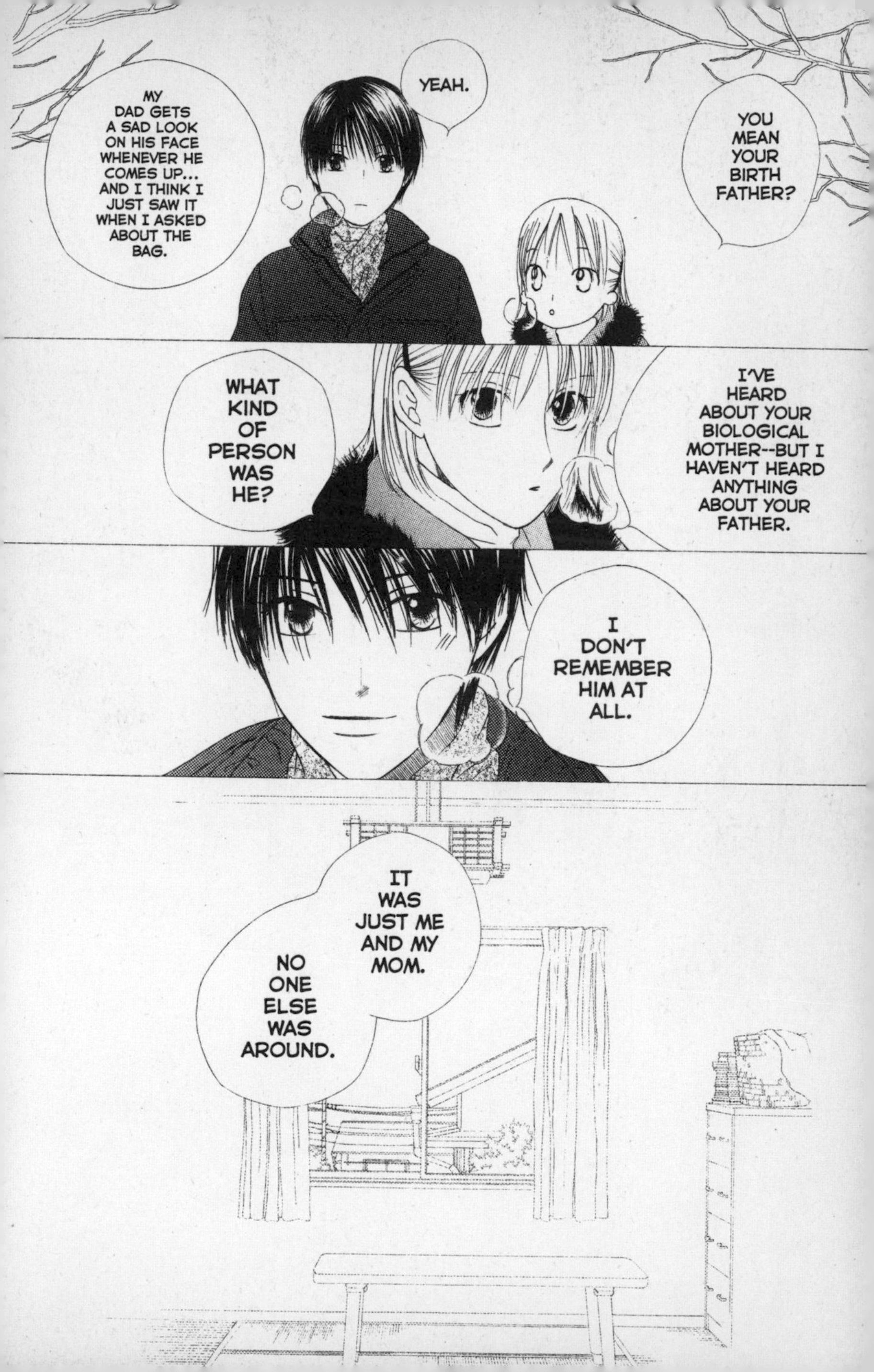
YOU MEAN YOUR BIRTH FATHER?
YEAH.
MY DAD GETS A SAD LOOK ON HIS FACE WHENEVER HE COMES UP... AND I THINK I JUST SAW IT WHEN I ASKED ABOUT THE BAG.
I'VE HEARD ABOUT YOUR BIOLOGICAL MOTHER--BUT I HAVEN'T HEARD ANYTHING ABOUT YOUR FATHER.
WHAT KIND OF PERSON WAS HE?
I DON'T REMEMBER HIM AT ALL.
IT WAS JUST ME AND MY MOM.
NO ONE ELSE WAS AROUND.

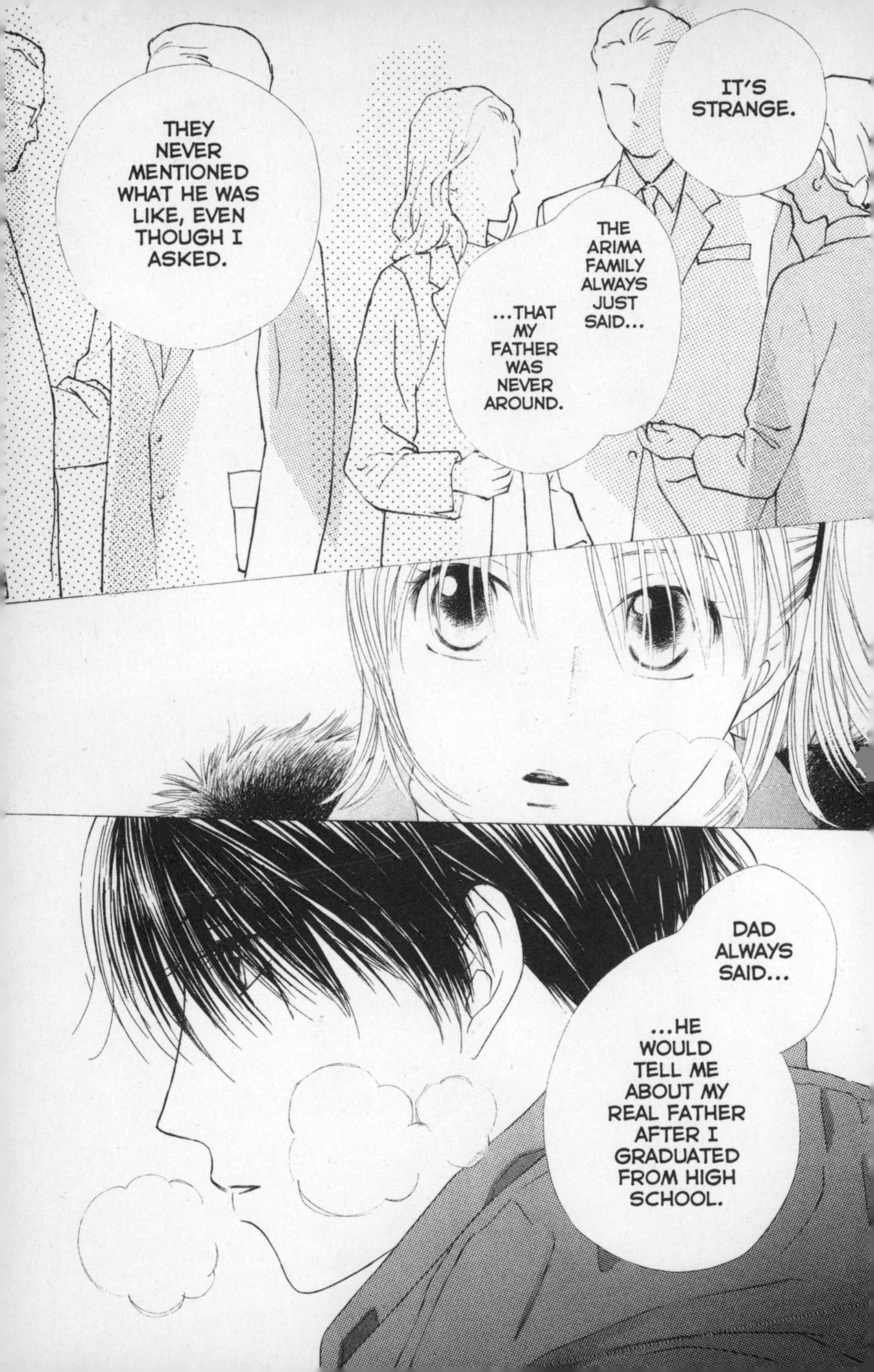
IT'S STRANGE.
THE ARIMA FAMILY ALWAYS JUST SAID...
...THAT MY FATHER WAS NEVER AROUND.
THEY NEVER MENTIONED WHAT HE WAS LIKE, EVEN THOUGH I ASKED.
DAD ALWAYS SAID...
...HE WOULD TELL ME ABOUT MY REAL FATHER AFTER I GRADUATED FROM HIGH SCHOOL.

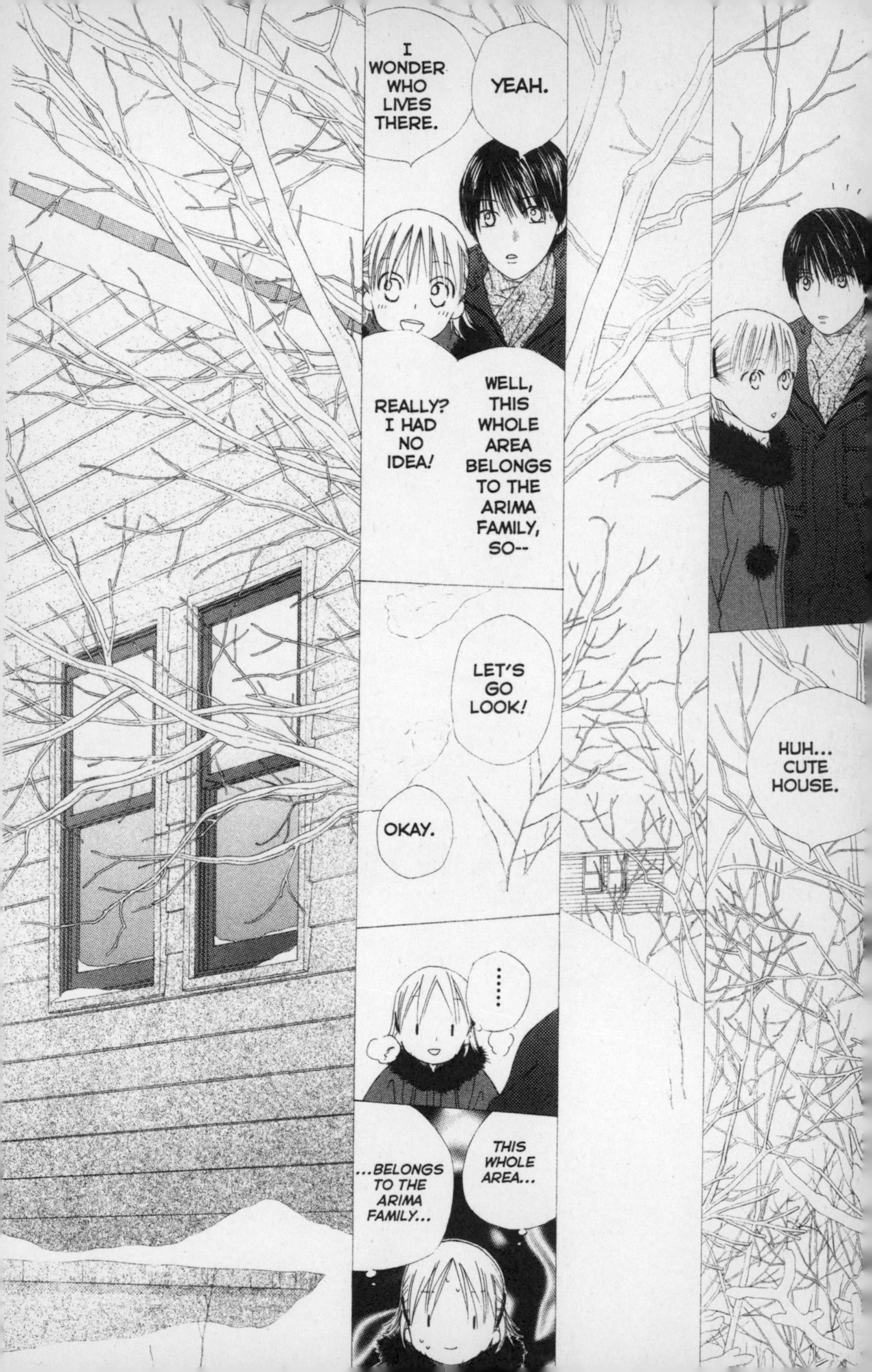
HUH... CUTE HOUSE.
I WONDER WHO LIVES THERE.
YEAH.
WELL, THIS WHOLE AREA BELONGS TO THE ARIMA FAMILY, SO--
REALLY? I HAD NO IDEA!
LET'S GO LOOK!
OKAY.
......
THIS WHOLE AREA...
...BELONGS TO THE ARIMA FAMILY...

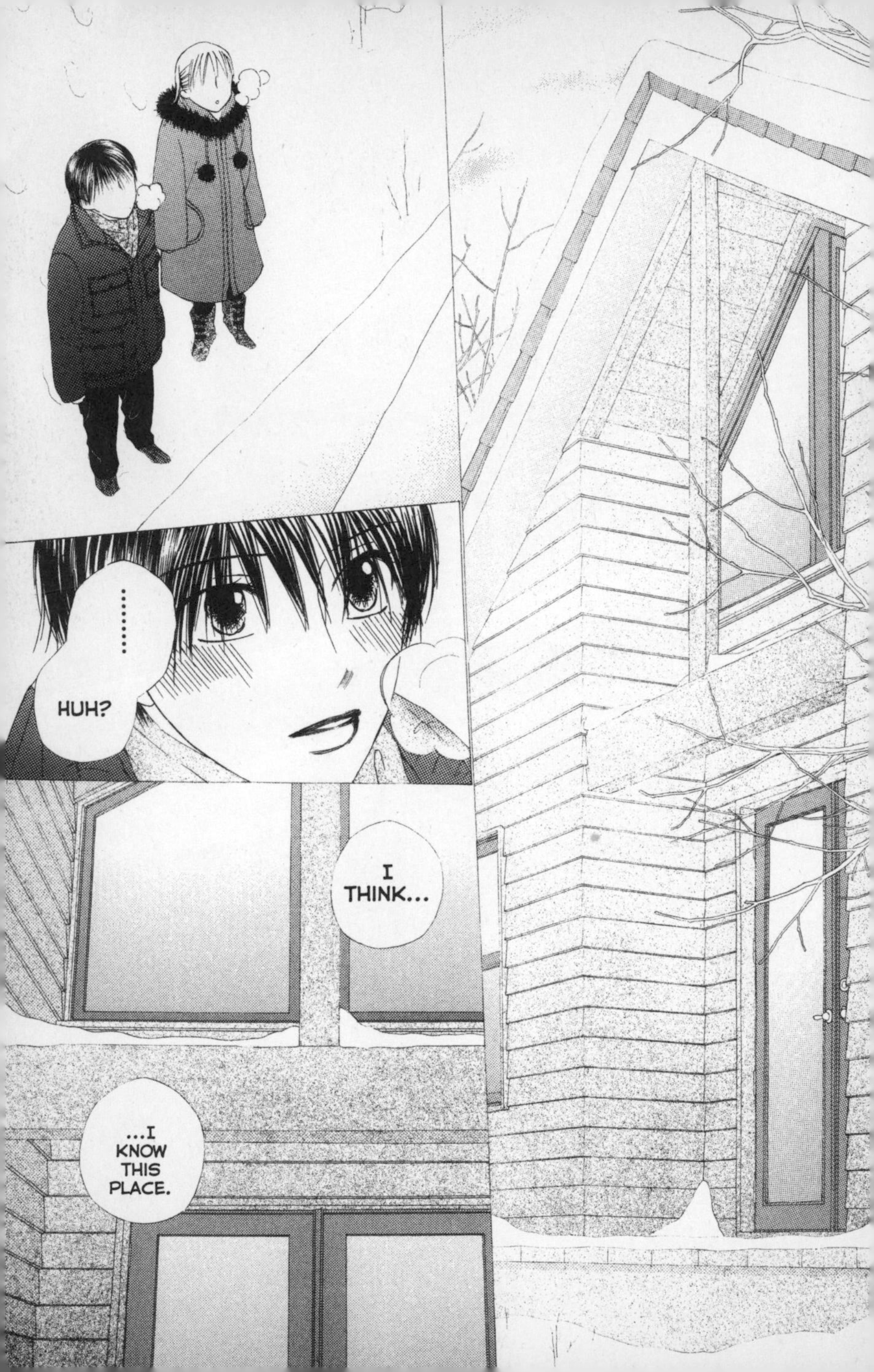
......
HUH?
I THINK...
...I KNOW THIS PLACE.

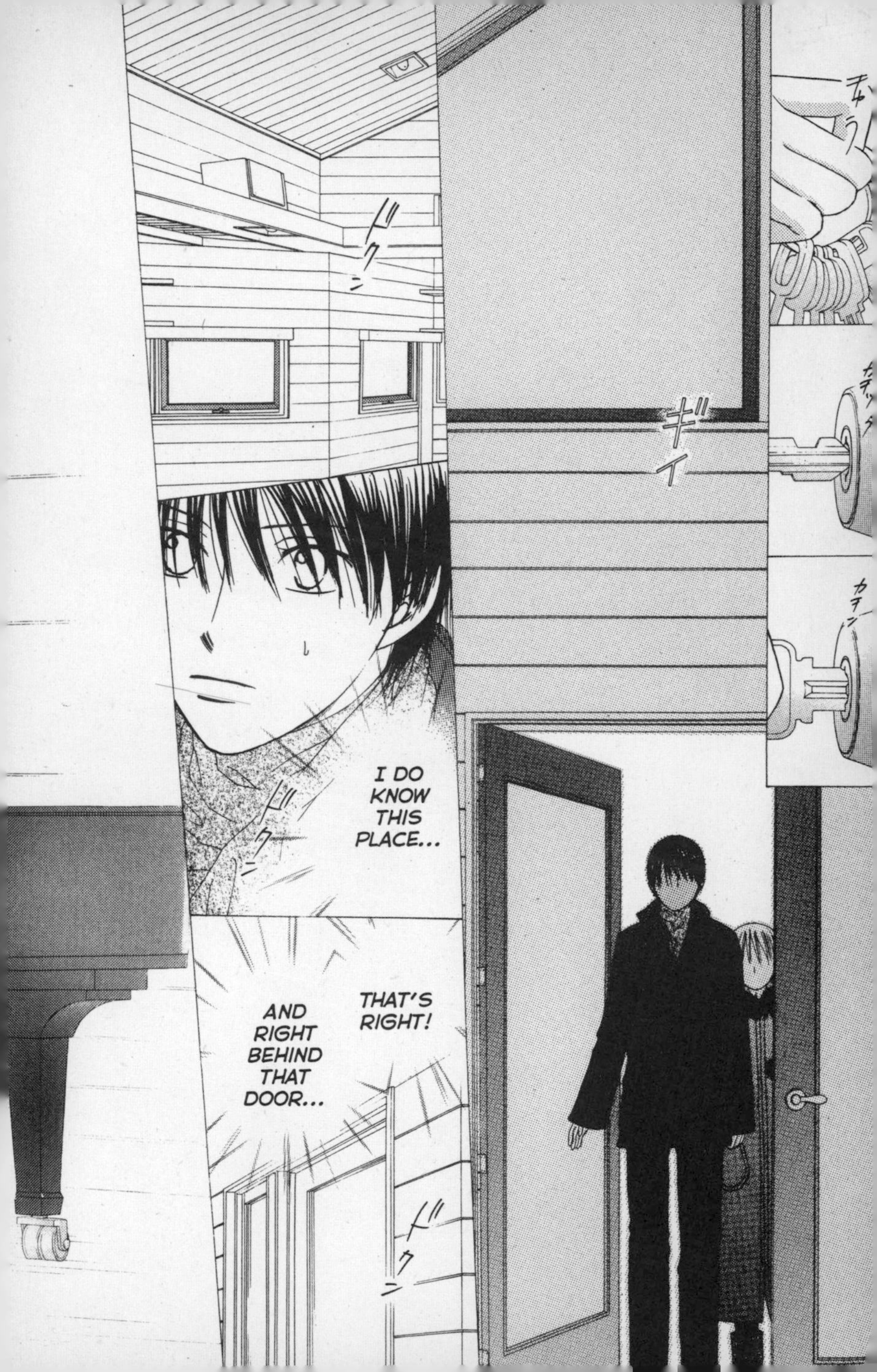
I DO KNOW THIS PLACE...
THAT'S RIGHT!
AND RIGHT BEHIND THAT DOOR...

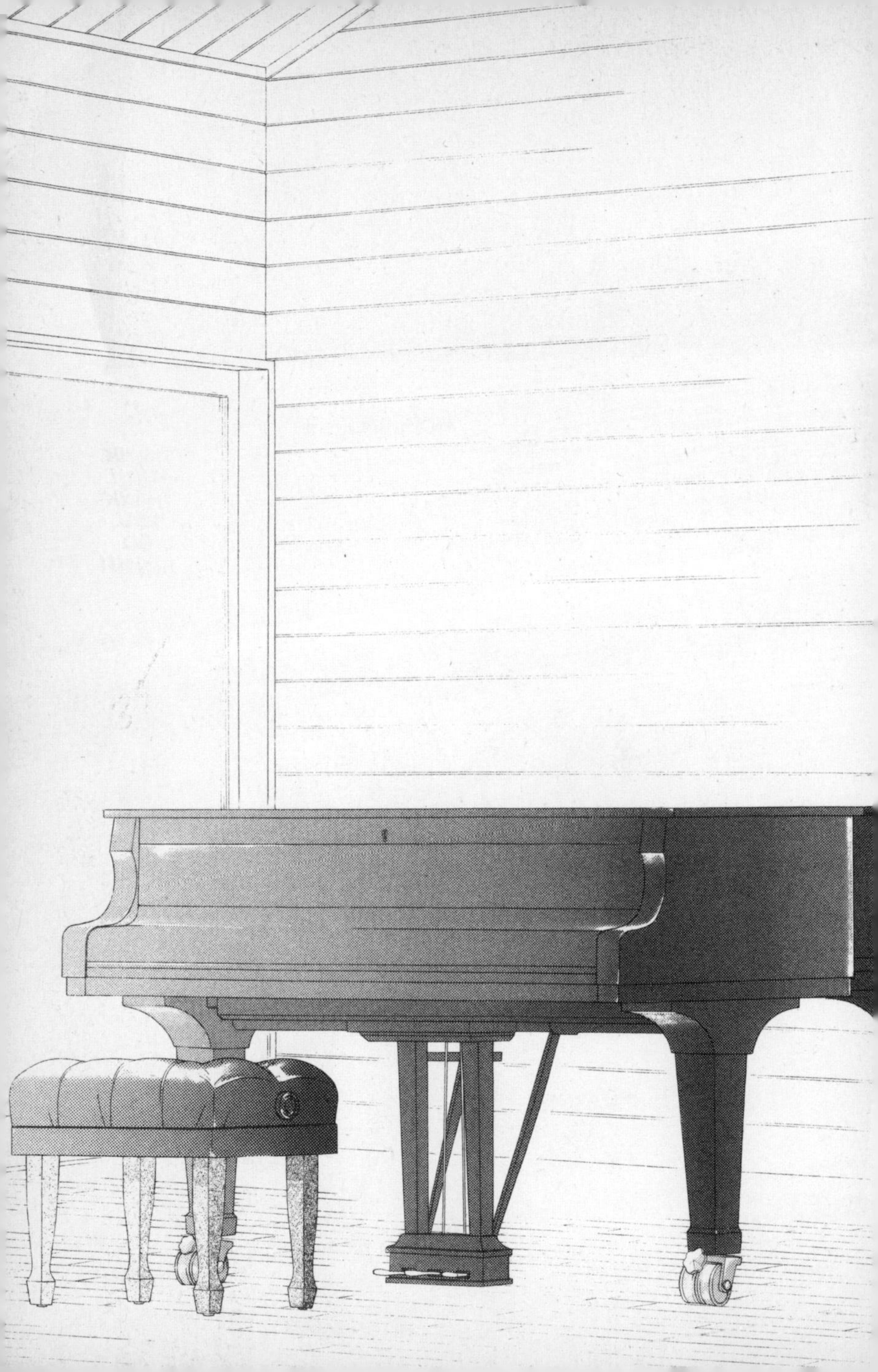

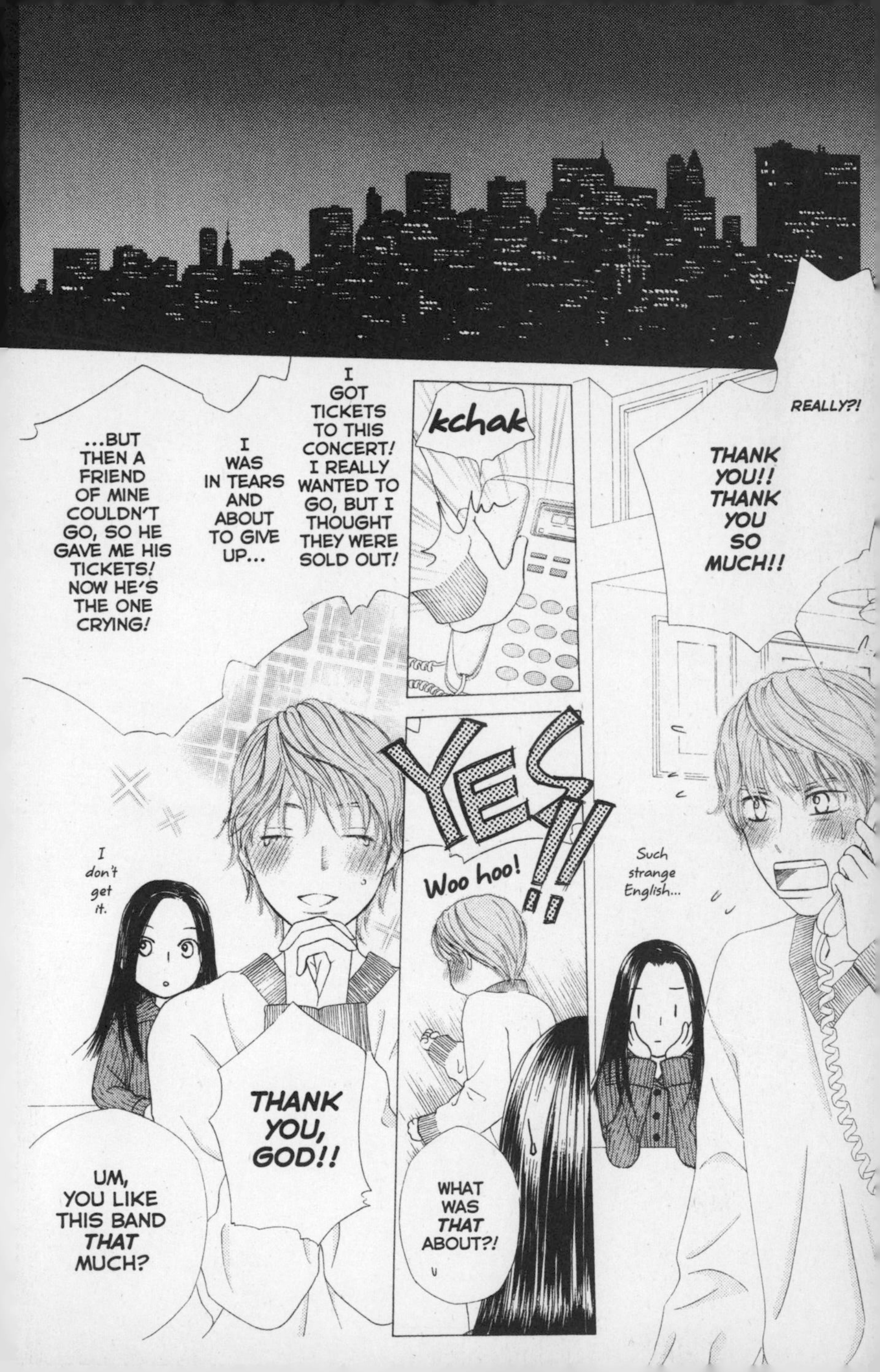
REALLY?!
THANK YOU!! THANK YOU SO MUCH!!
Such strange English...
kchak
YES!!
Woo hoo!
WHAT WAS THAT ABOUT?!
I GOT TICKETS TO THIS CONCERT! I REALLY WANTED TO GO, BUT I THOUGHT THEY WERE SOLD OUT!
I WAS IN TEARS AND ABOUT TO GIVE UP...
...BUT THEN A FRIEND OF MINE COULDN'T GO, SO HE GAVE ME HIS TICKETS! NOW HE'S THE ONE CRYING!
THANK YOU, GOD!!
I don't get it.
UM, YOU LIKE THIS BAND THAT MUCH?

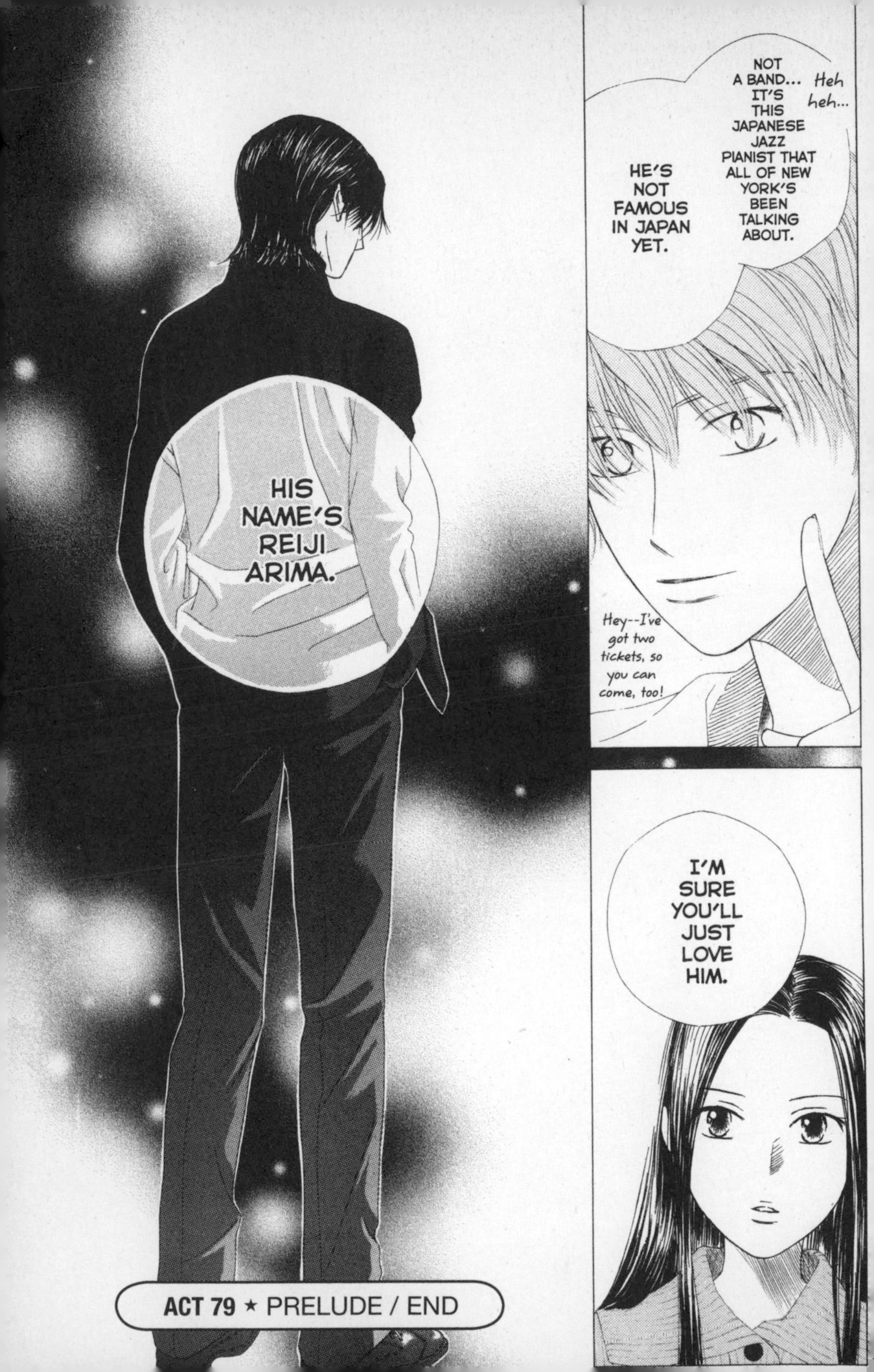
Heh heh...
NOT A BAND... IT'S THIS JAPANESE JAZZ PIANIST THAT ALL OF NEW YORK'S BEEN TALKING ABOUT.
HE'S NOT FAMOUS IN JAPAN YET.
Hey--I've got two tickets, so you can come, too!
I'M SURE YOU'LL JUST LOVE HIM.
HIS NAME'S REIJI ARIMA.
ACT 79 ★ PRELUDE / END

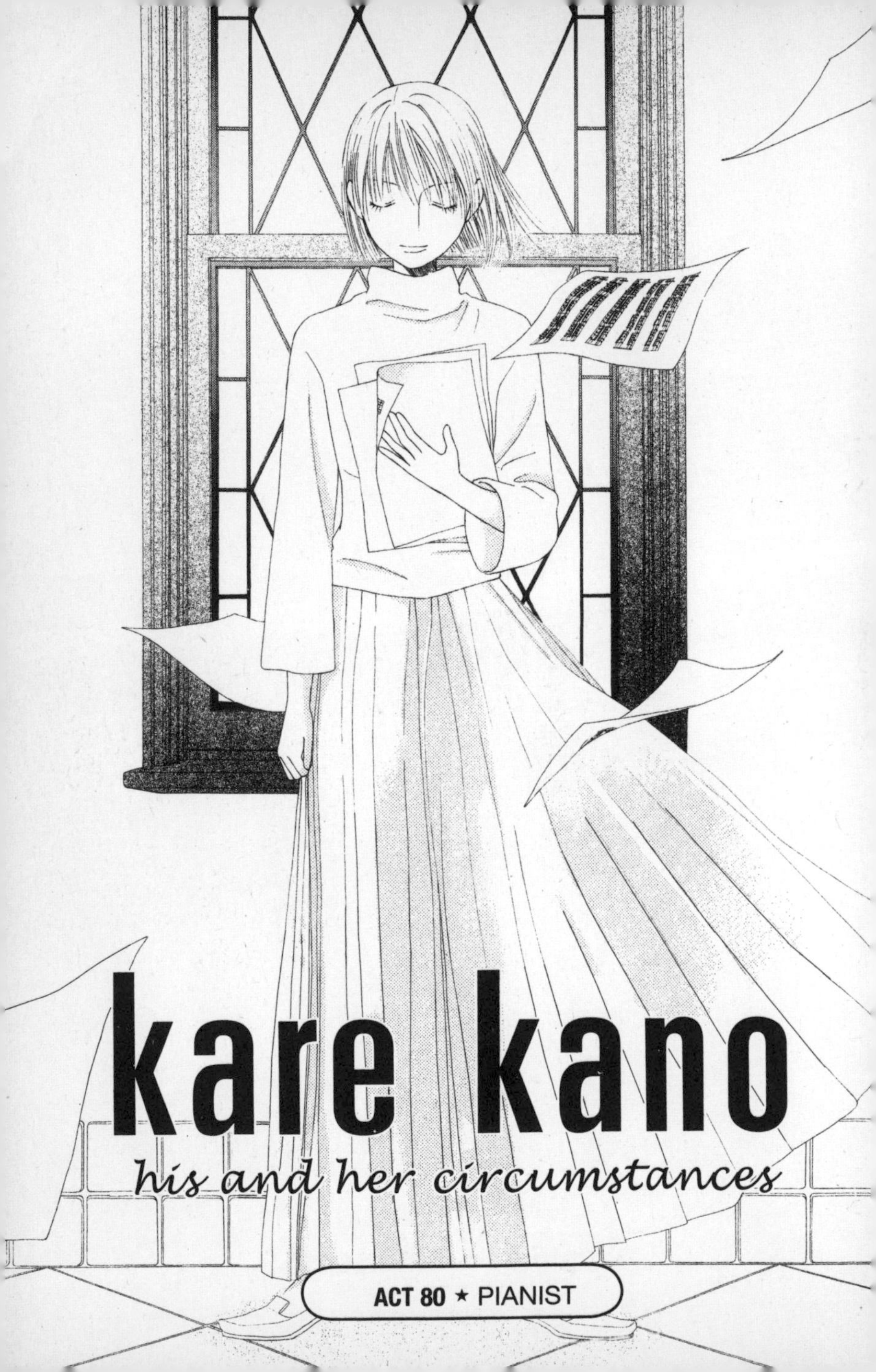
kare kano
his and her circumstances
ACT 80 ★ PIANIST

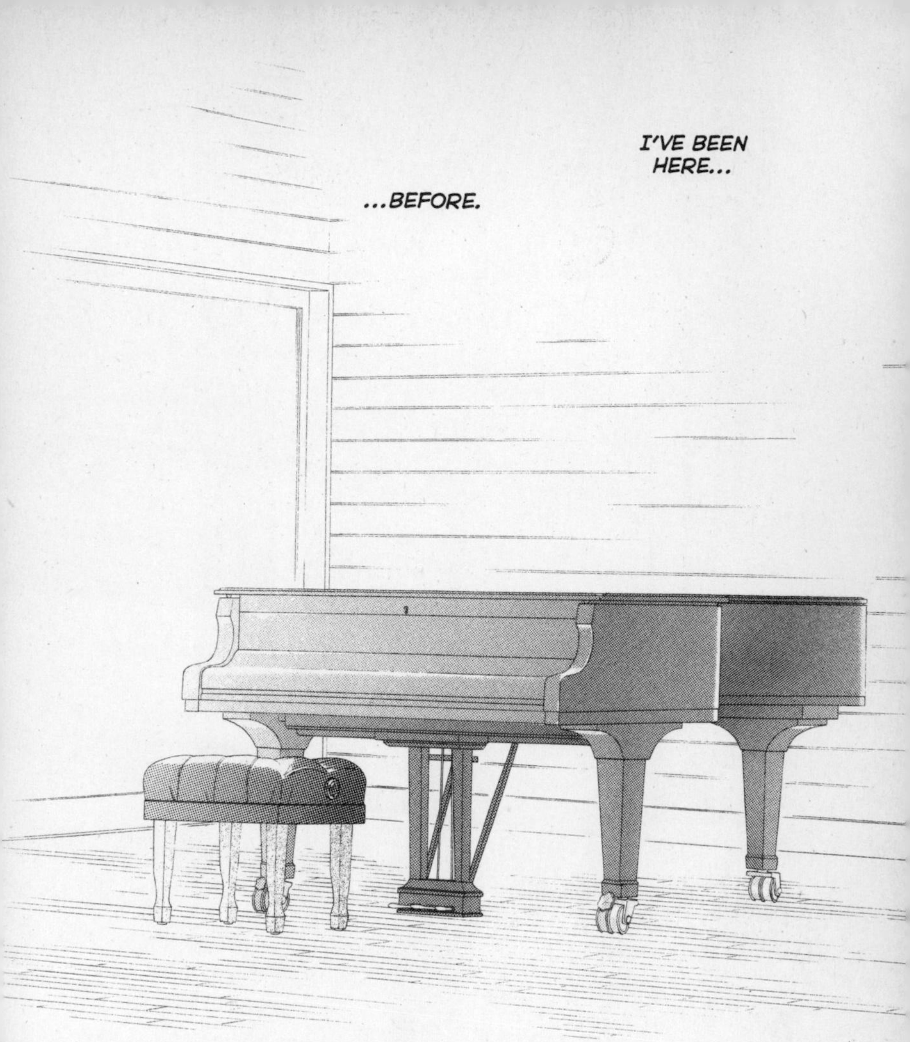
I'VE BEEN HERE...
...BEFORE.

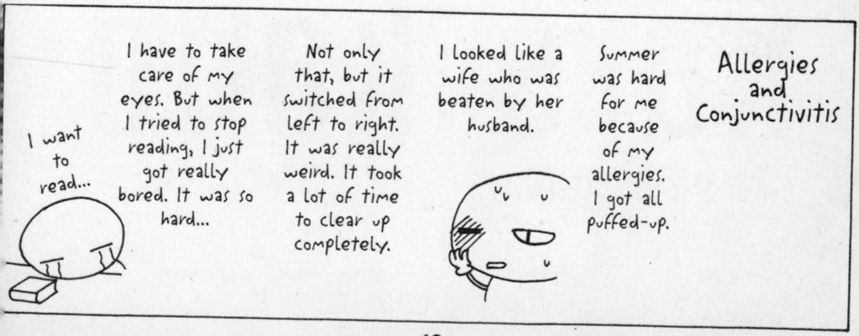
Allergies and Conjunctivitis
Summer was hard for me because of my allergies. I got all puffed-up.
I looked like a wife who was beaten by her husband.
Not only that, but it switched from left to right. It was really weird. It took a lot of time to clear up completely.
I have to take care of my eyes. But when I tried to stop reading, I just got really bored. It was so hard...
I want to read...

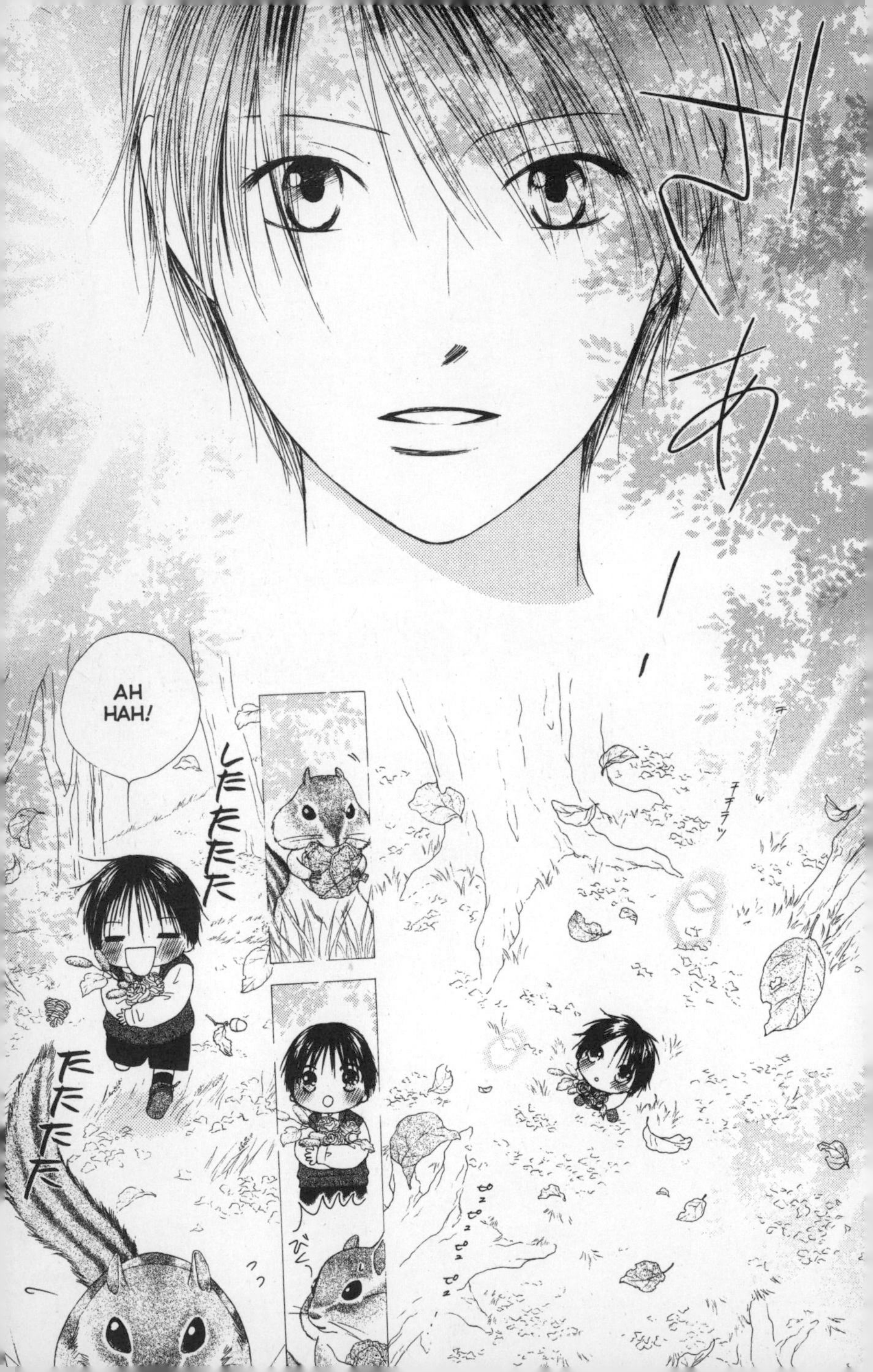
AH HAH!
したたたた
たたたた

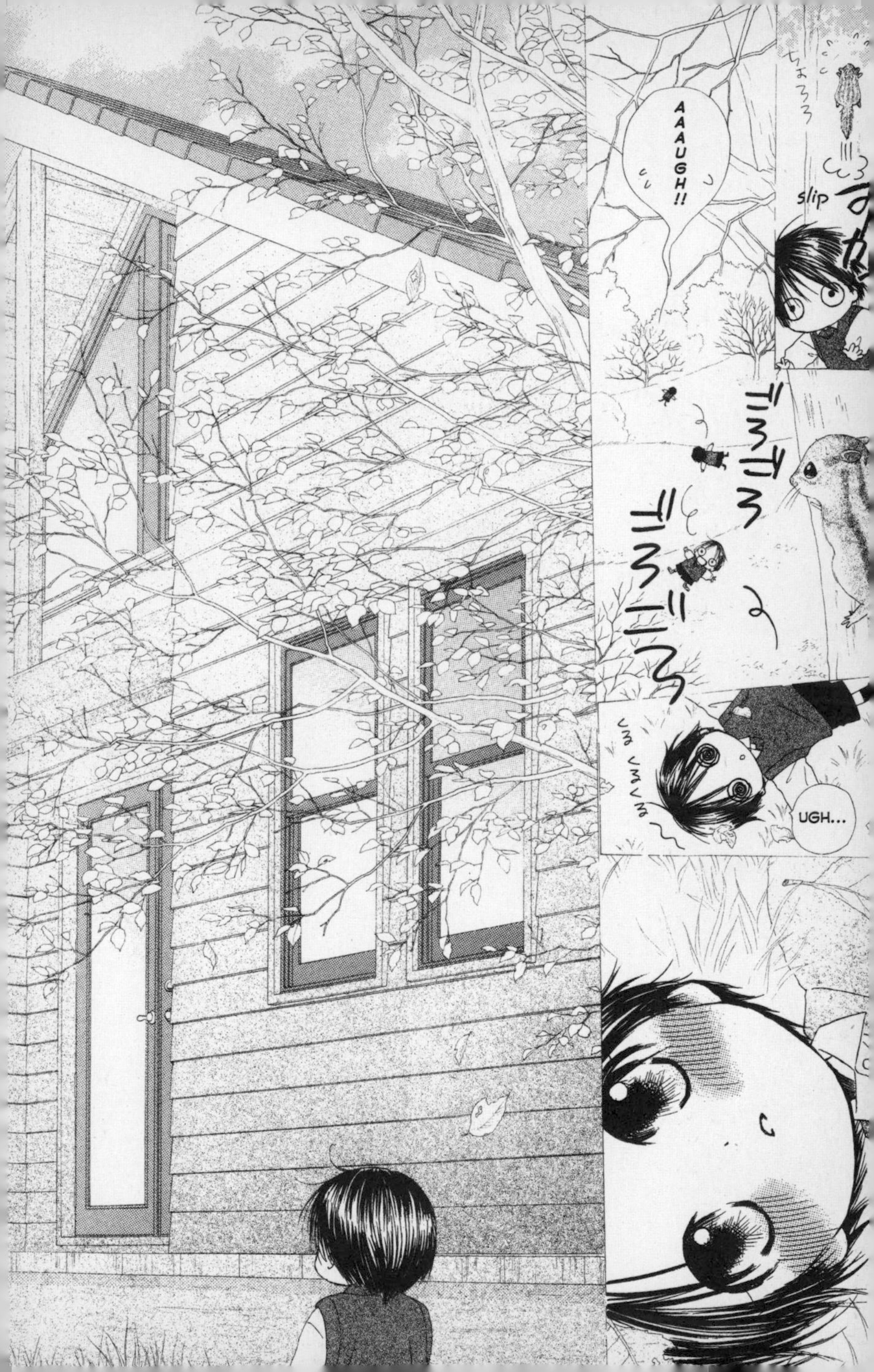
ちょろろろ
slip
AAAAUGH!!
ごろごろ
ごろごろ
UGH...

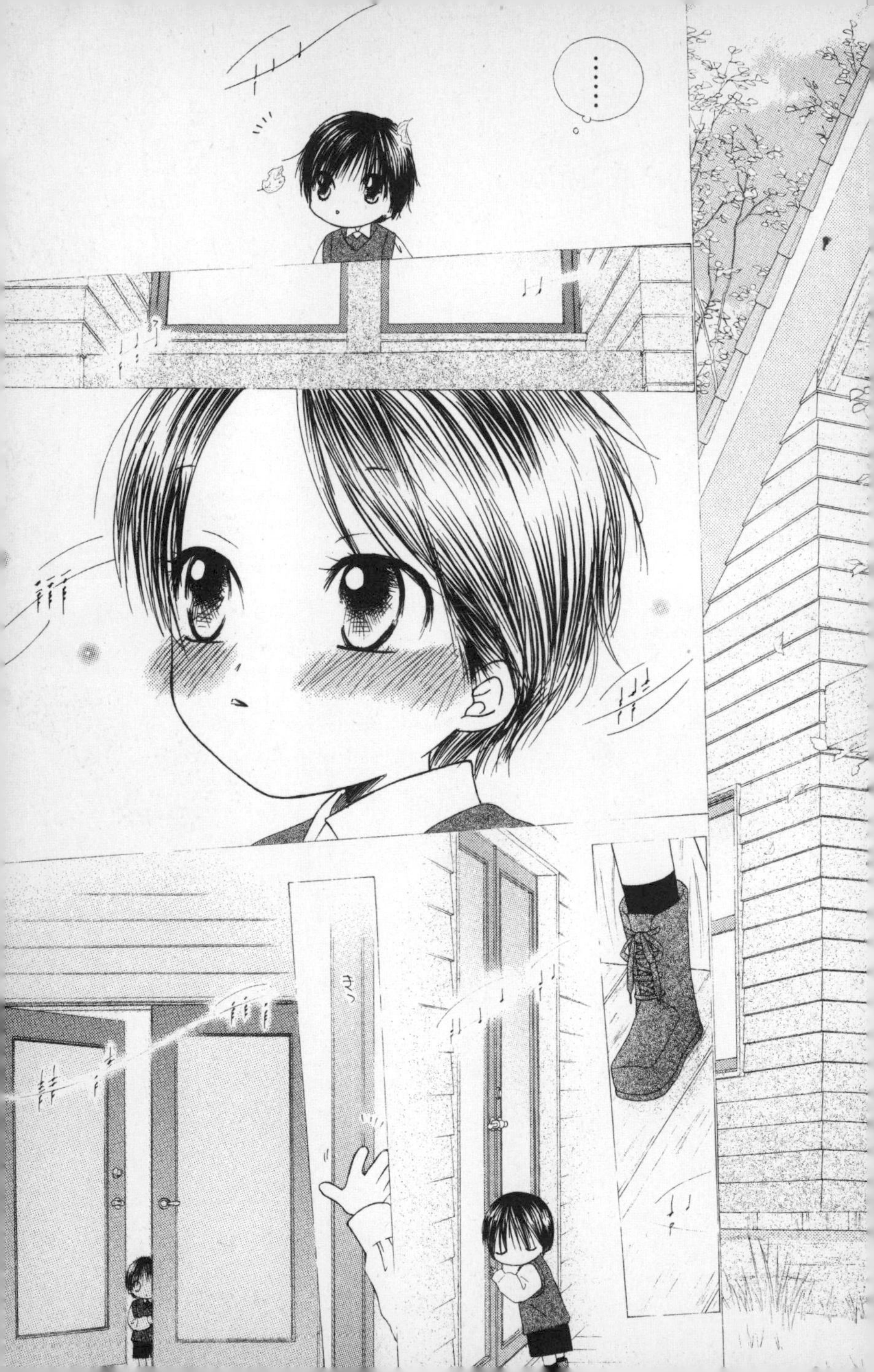
……

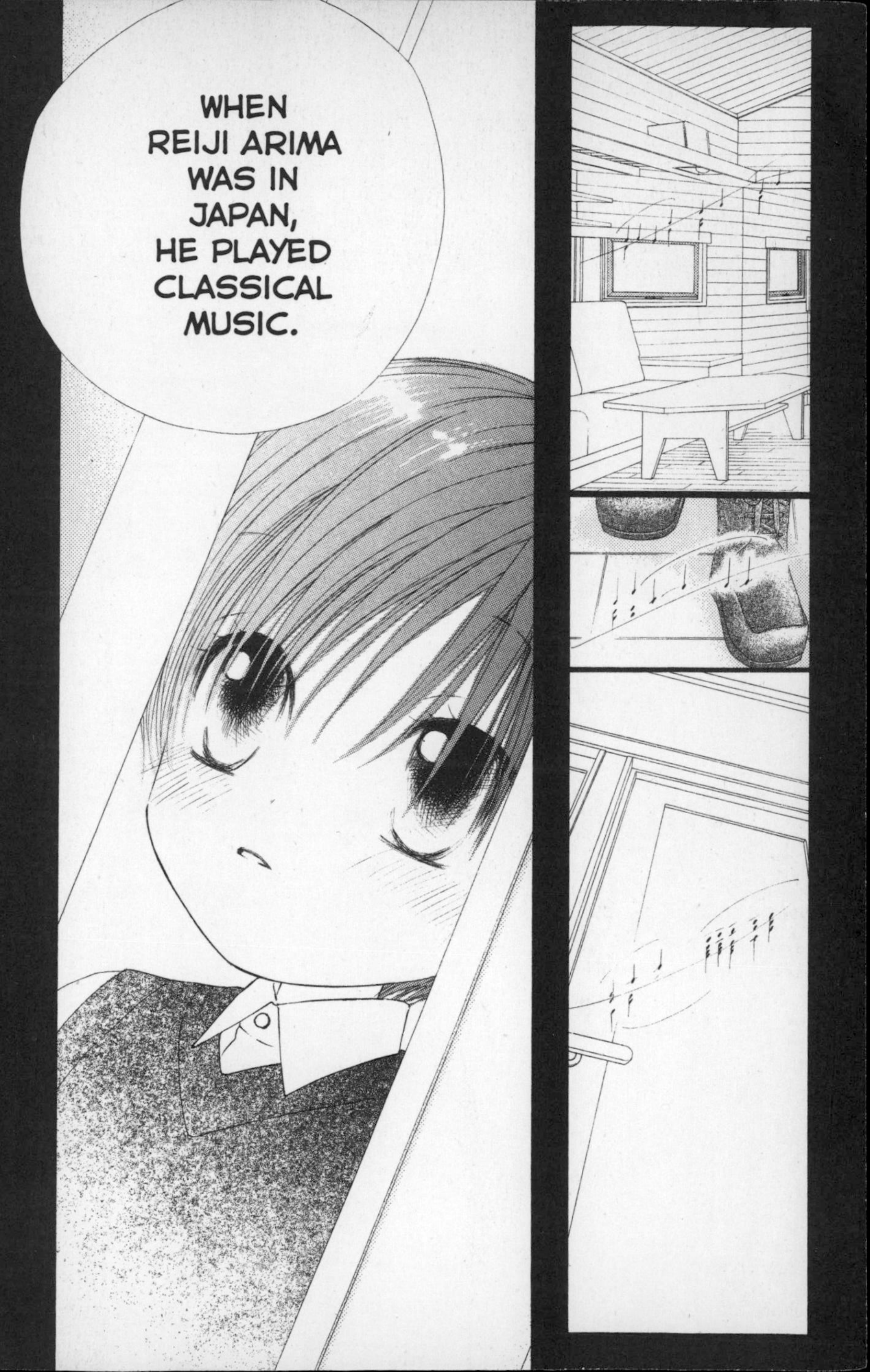
WHEN REIJI ARIMA WAS IN JAPAN, HE PLAYED CLASSICAL MUSIC.

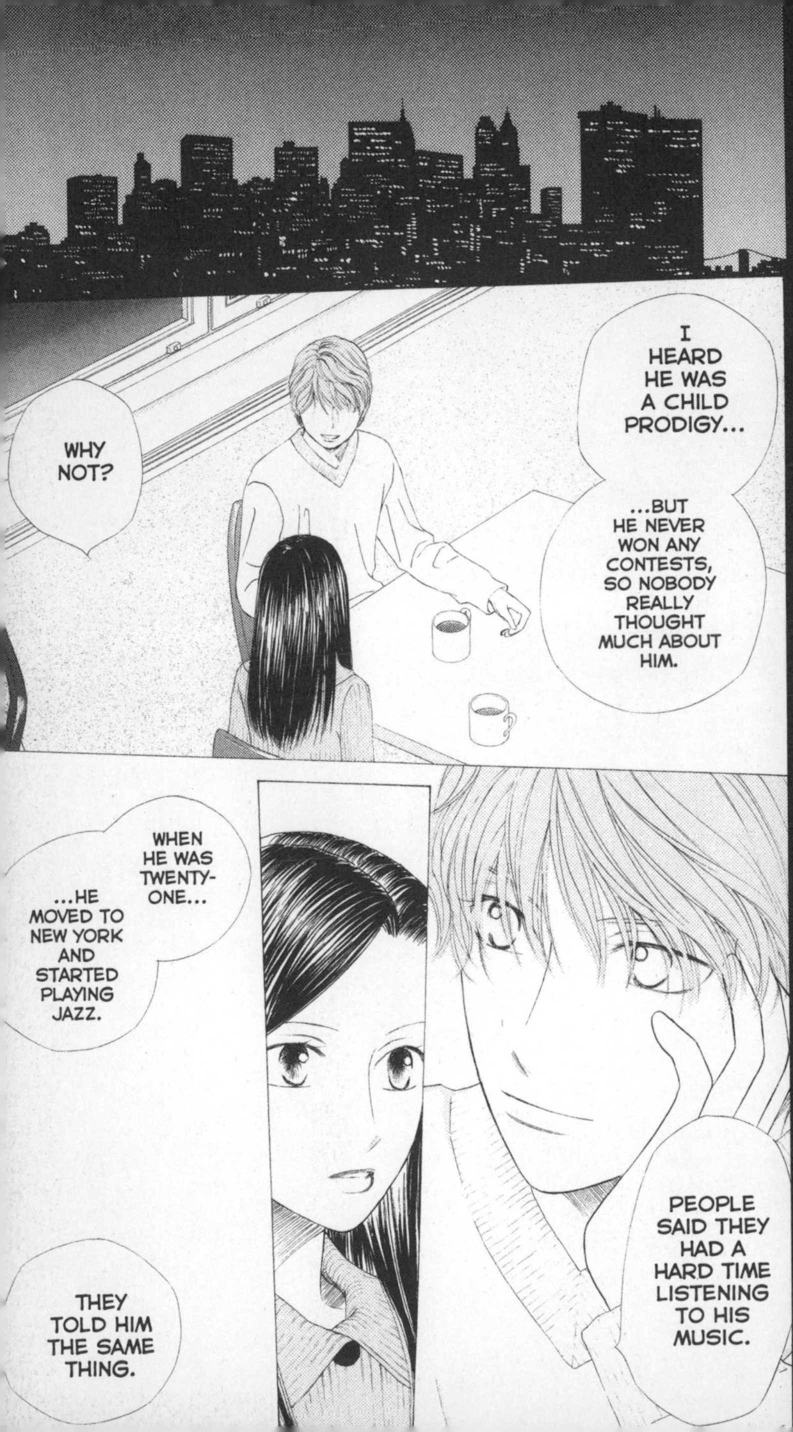
I HEARD HE WAS A CHILD PRODIGY...
...BUT HE NEVER WON ANY CONTESTS, SO NOBODY REALLY THOUGHT MUCH ABOUT HIM.
WHY NOT?
PEOPLE SAID THEY HAD A HARD TIME LISTENING TO HIS MUSIC.
WHEN HE WAS TWENTY-ONE...
...HE MOVED TO NEW YORK AND STARTED PLAYING JAZZ.
THEY TOLD HIM THE SAME THING.

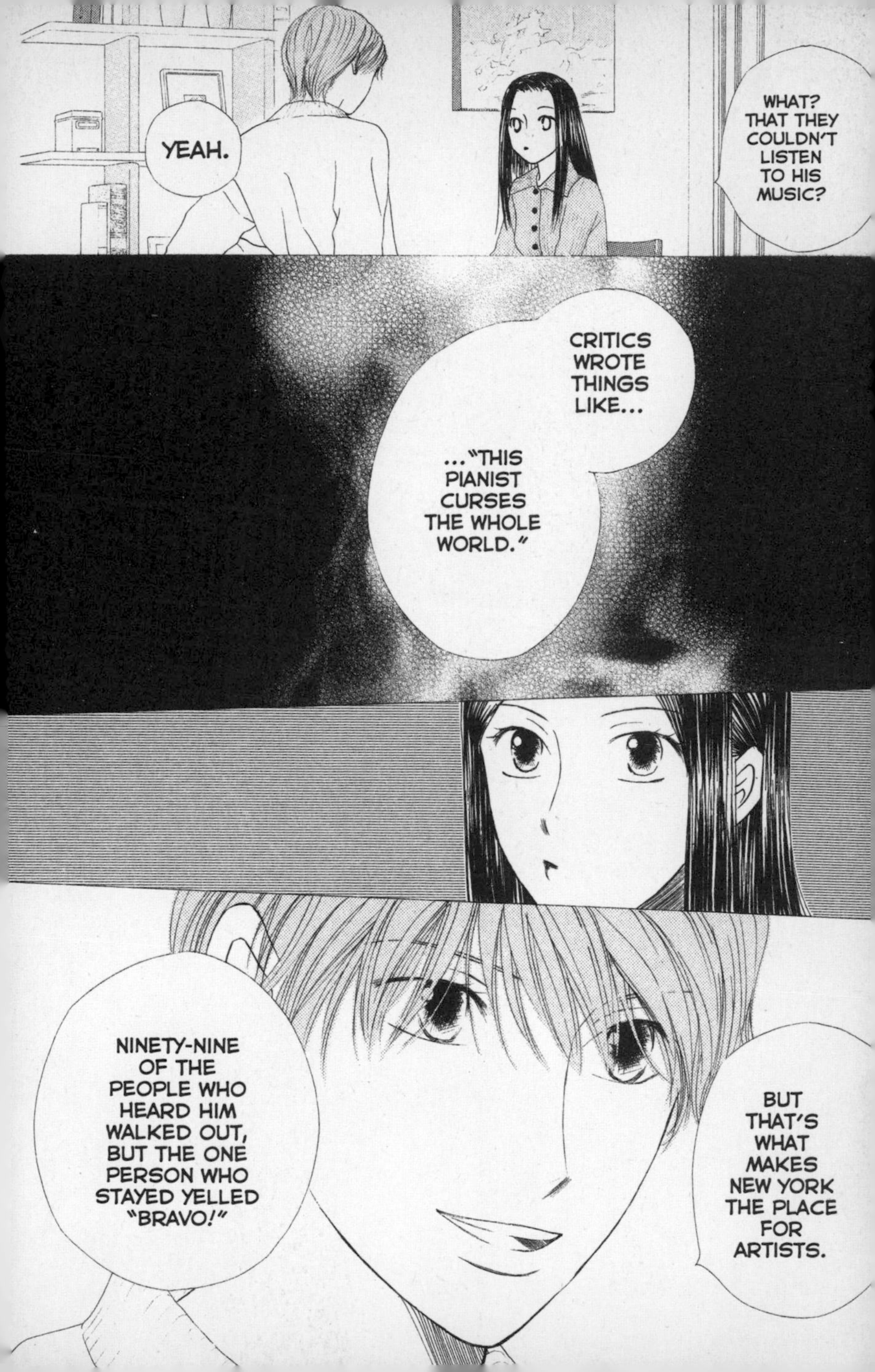
WHAT? THAT THEY COULDN'T LISTEN TO HIS MUSIC?
YEAH.
CRITICS WROTE THINGS LIKE...
..."THIS PIANIST CURSES THE WHOLE WORLD."
BUT THAT'S WHAT MAKES NEW YORK THE PLACE FOR ARTISTS.
NINETY-NINE OF THE PEOPLE WHO HEARD HIM WALKED OUT, BUT THE ONE PERSON WHO STAYED YELLED "BRAVO!"

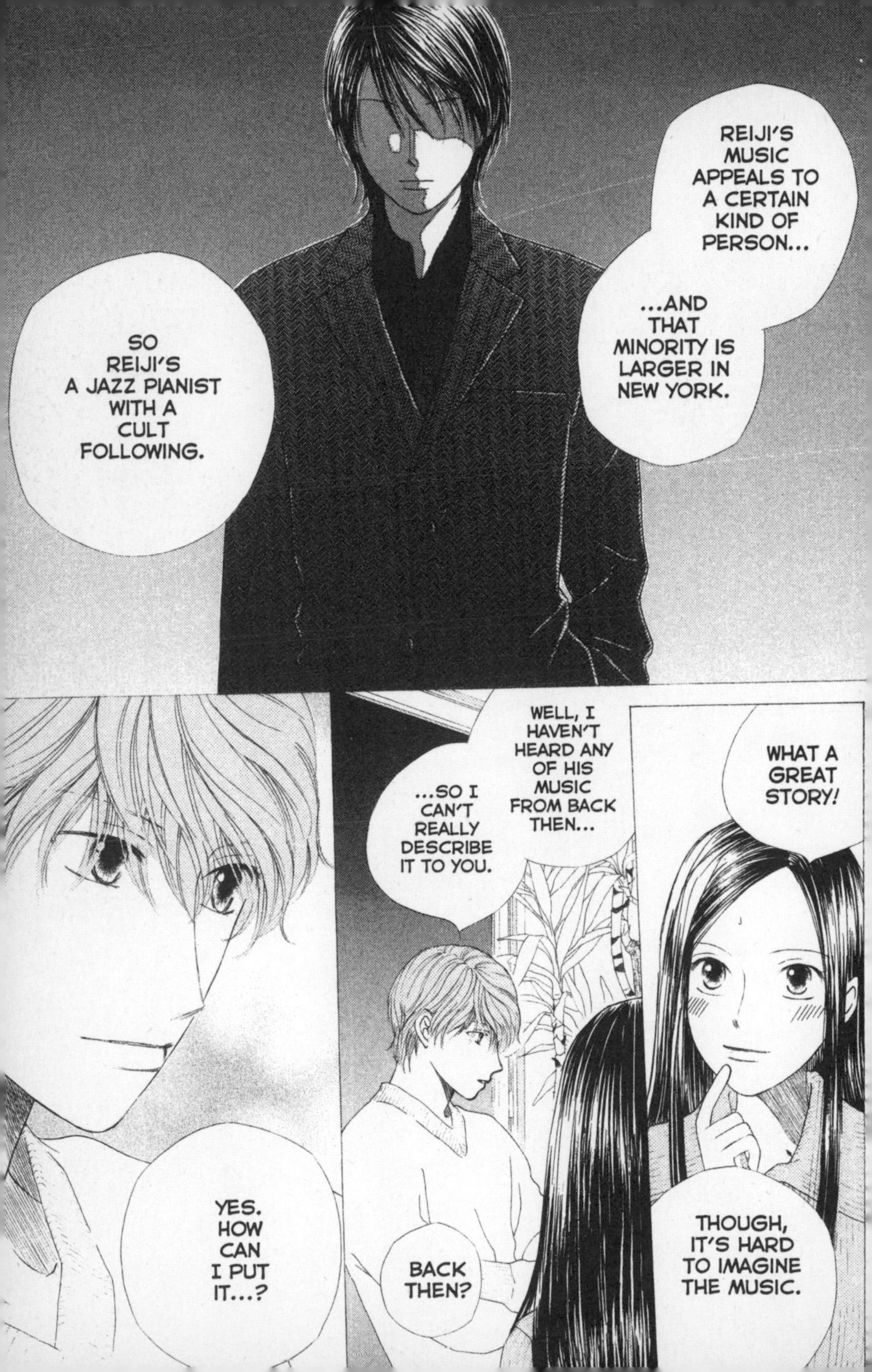
REIJI'S MUSIC APPEALS TO A CERTAIN KIND OF PERSON...
...AND THAT MINORITY IS LARGER IN NEW YORK.
SO REIJI'S A JAZZ PIANIST WITH A CULT FOLLOWING.
WHAT A GREAT STORY!
THOUGH, IT'S HARD TO IMAGINE THE MUSIC.
WELL, I HAVEN'T HEARD ANY OF HIS MUSIC FROM BACK THEN...
...SO I CAN'T REALLY DESCRIBE IT TO YOU.
BACK THEN?
YES. HOW CAN I PUT IT...?

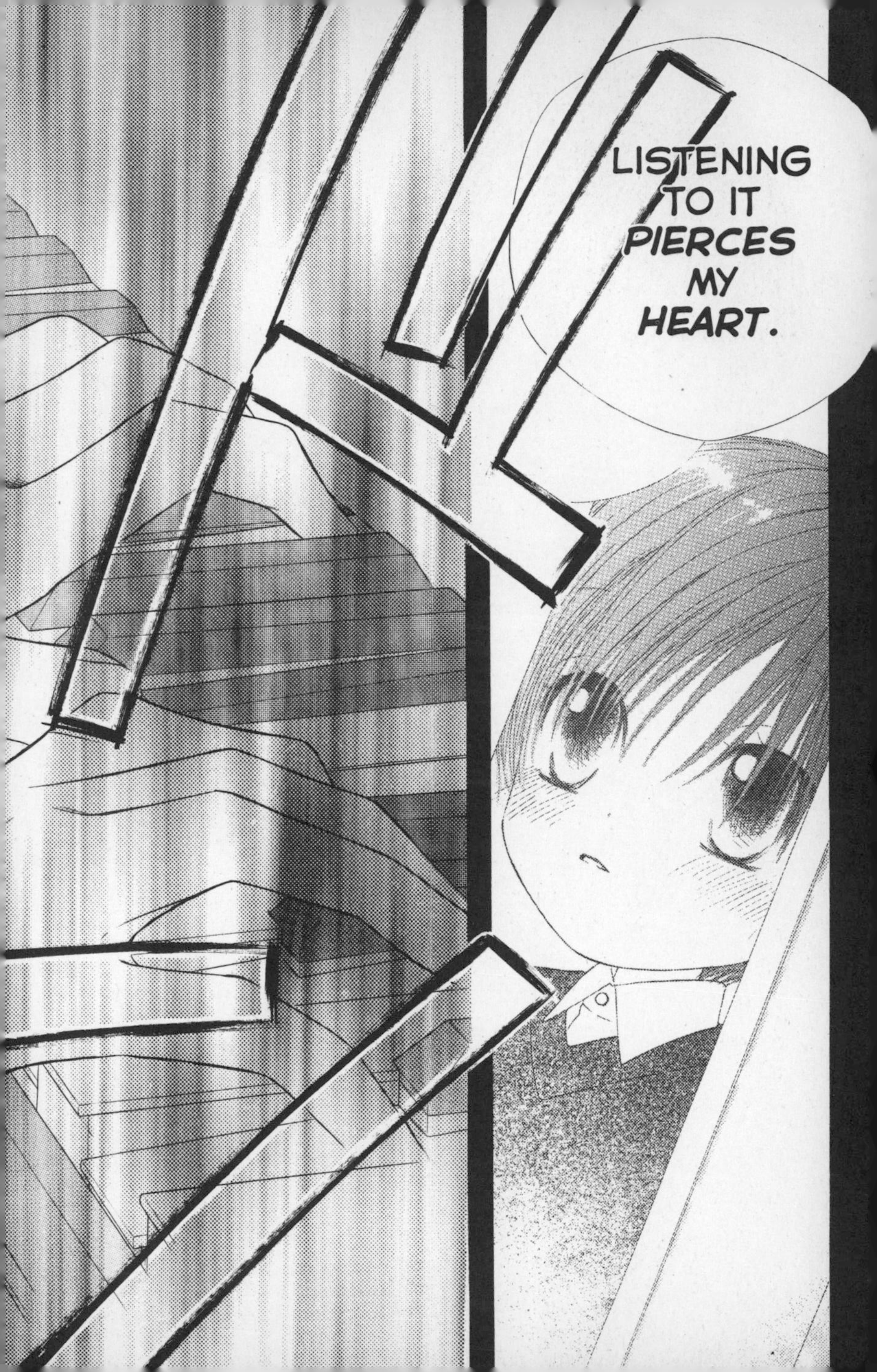
LISTENING TO IT PIERCES MY HEART.

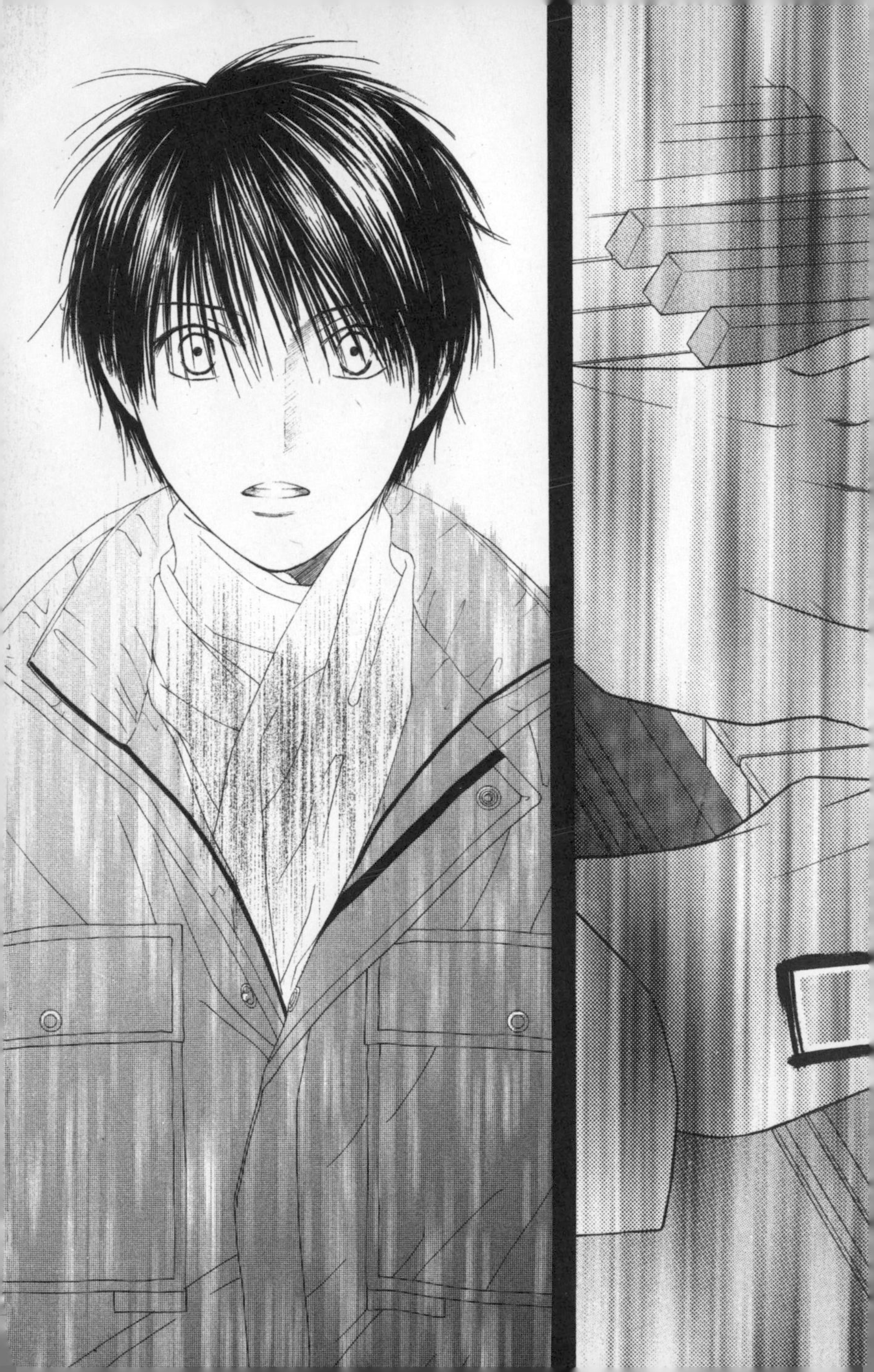

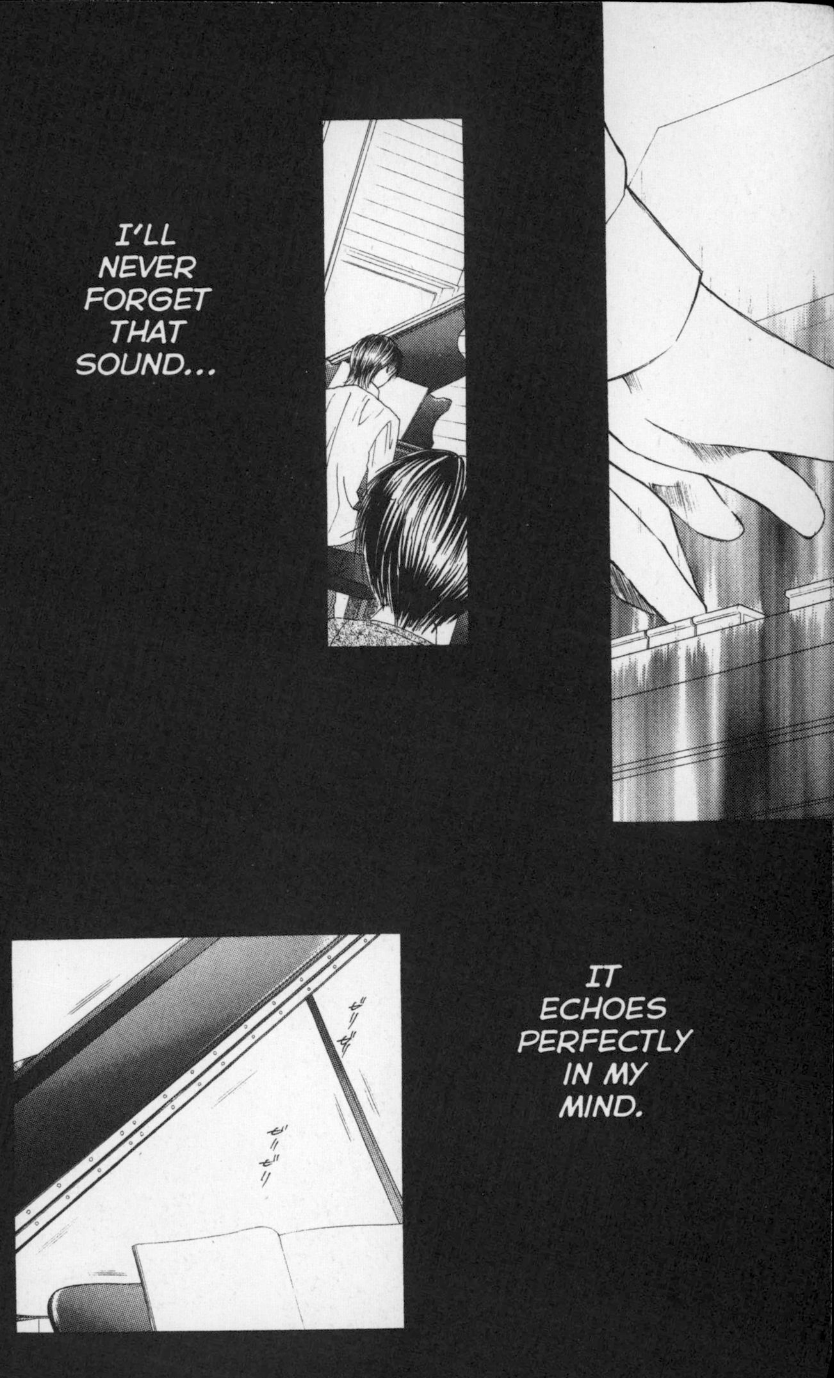
I'LL NEVER FORGET THAT SOUND...
IT ECHOES PERFECTLY IN MY MIND.

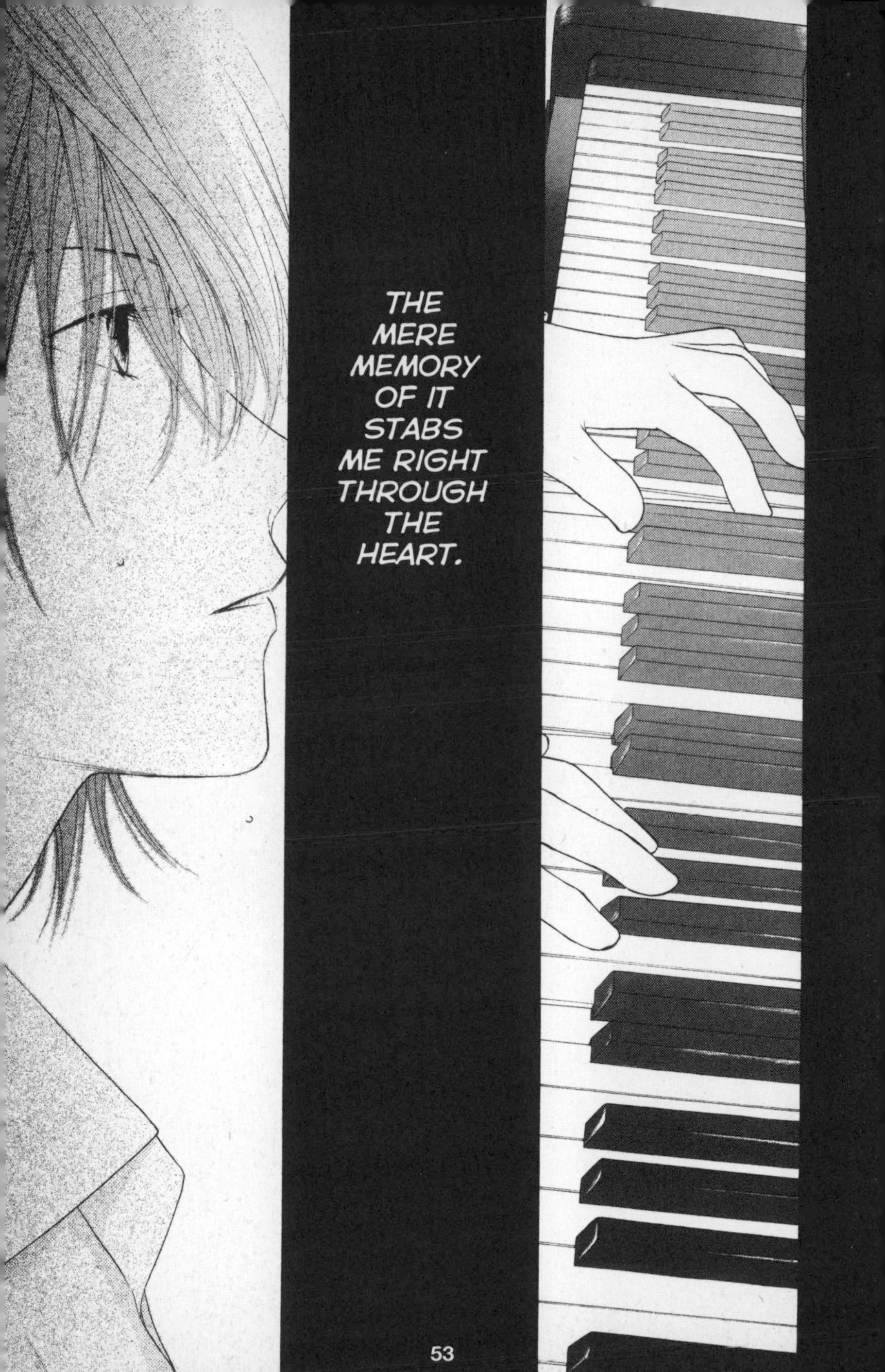
THE MERE MEMORY OF IT STABS ME RIGHT THROUGH THE HEART.

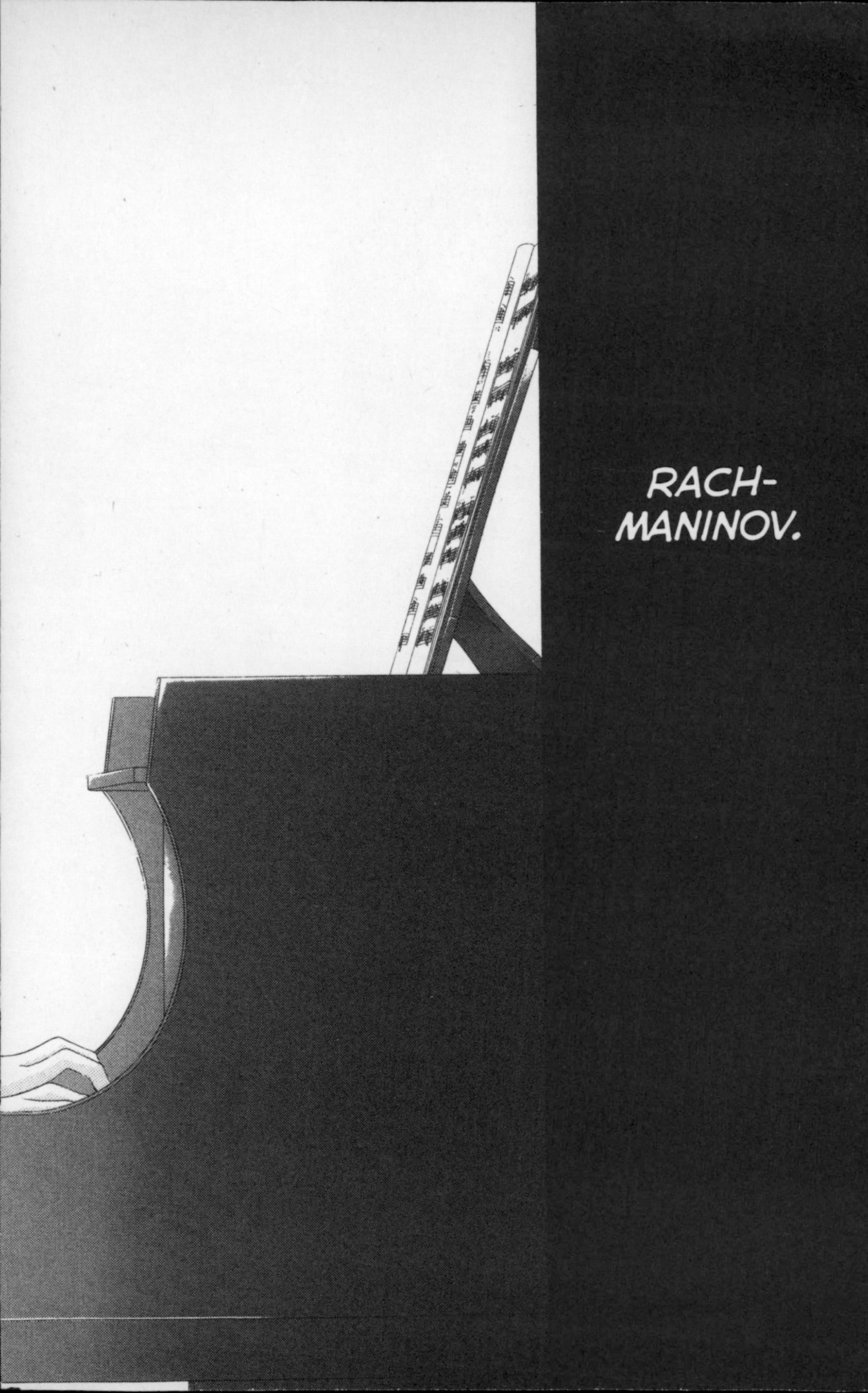
RACH-
MANINOV.

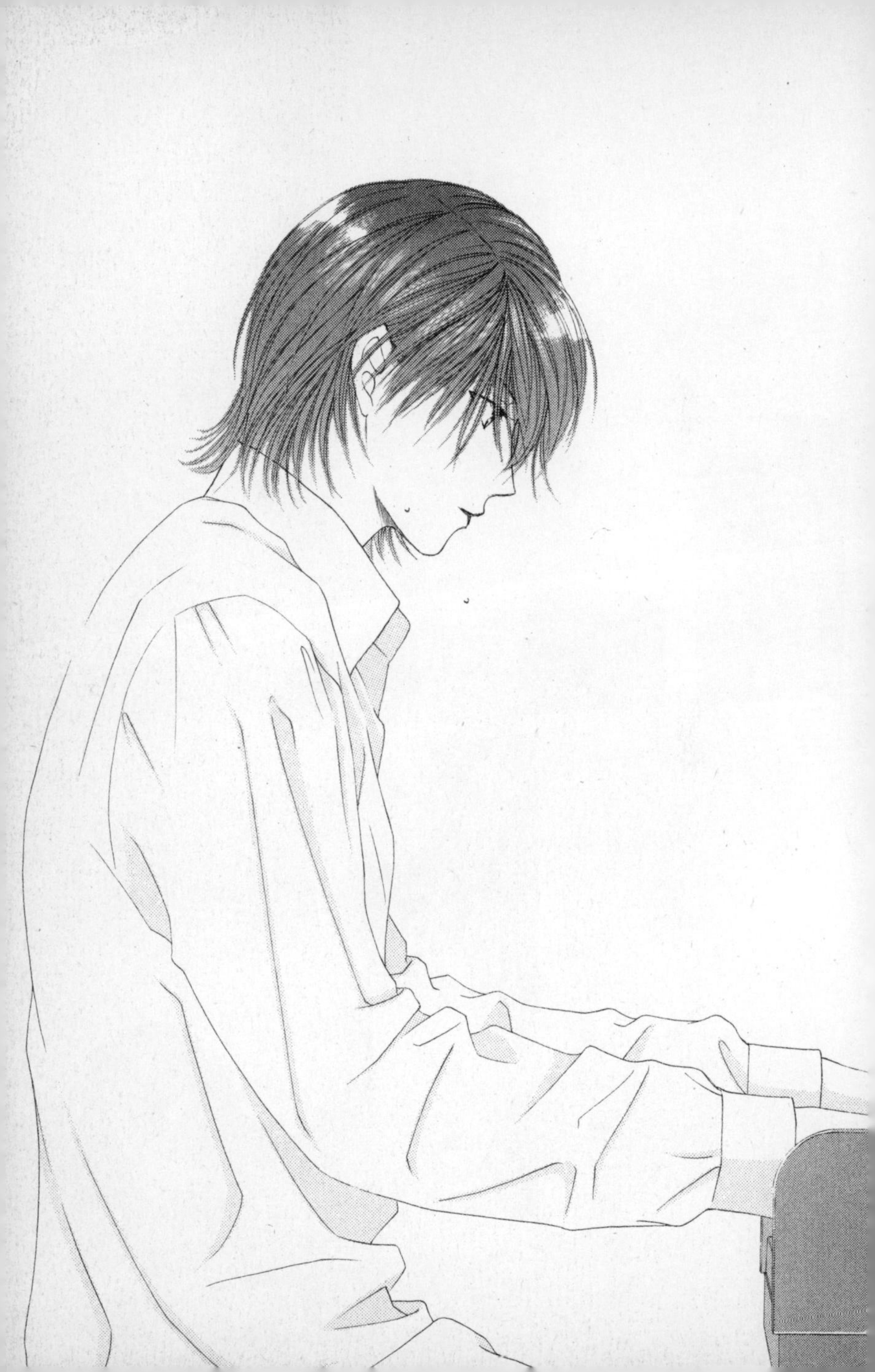

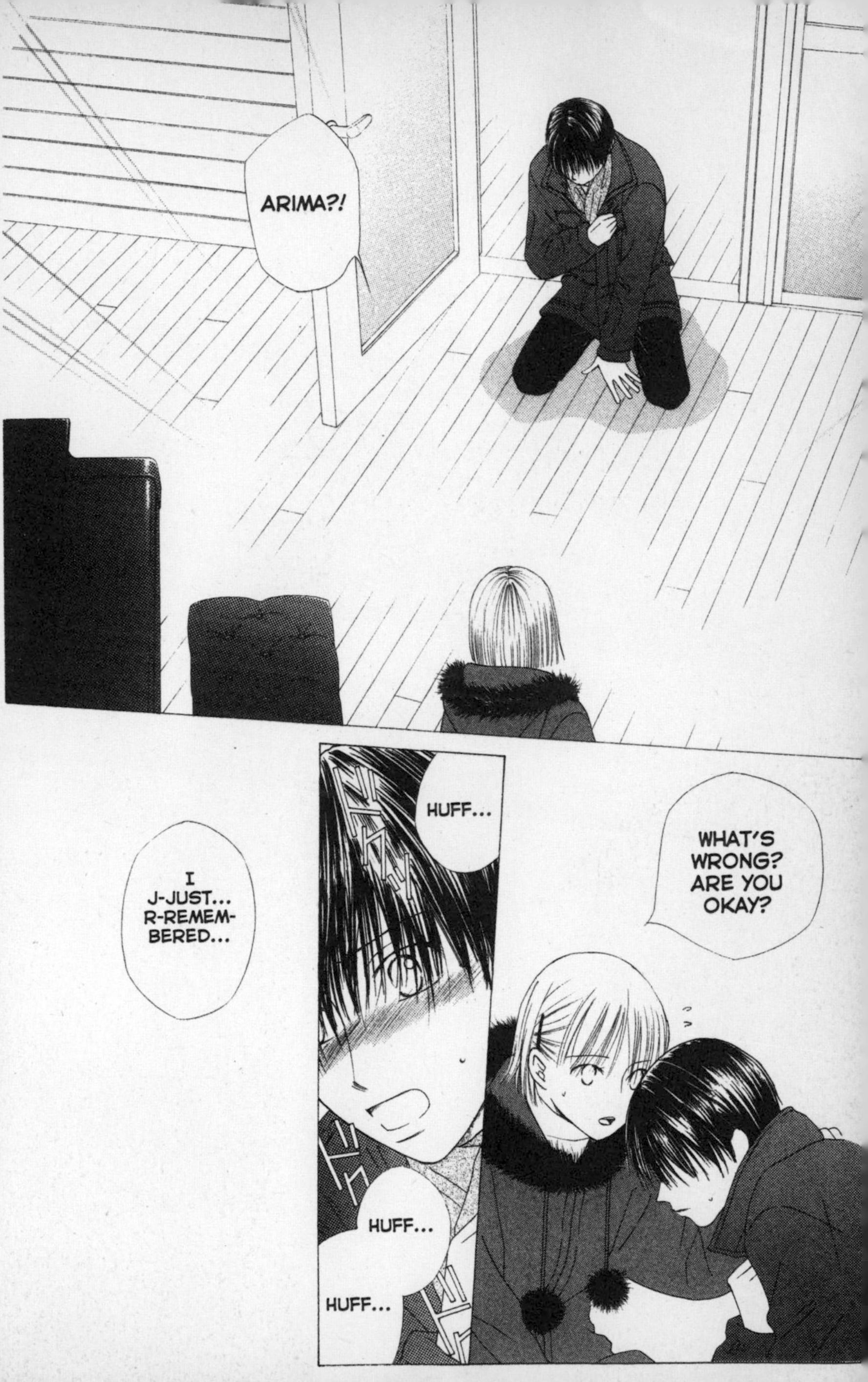
ARIMA?!
WHAT'S WRONG? ARE YOU OKAY?
HUFF...
I J-JUST... R-REMEMBERED...
HUFF...
HUFF...

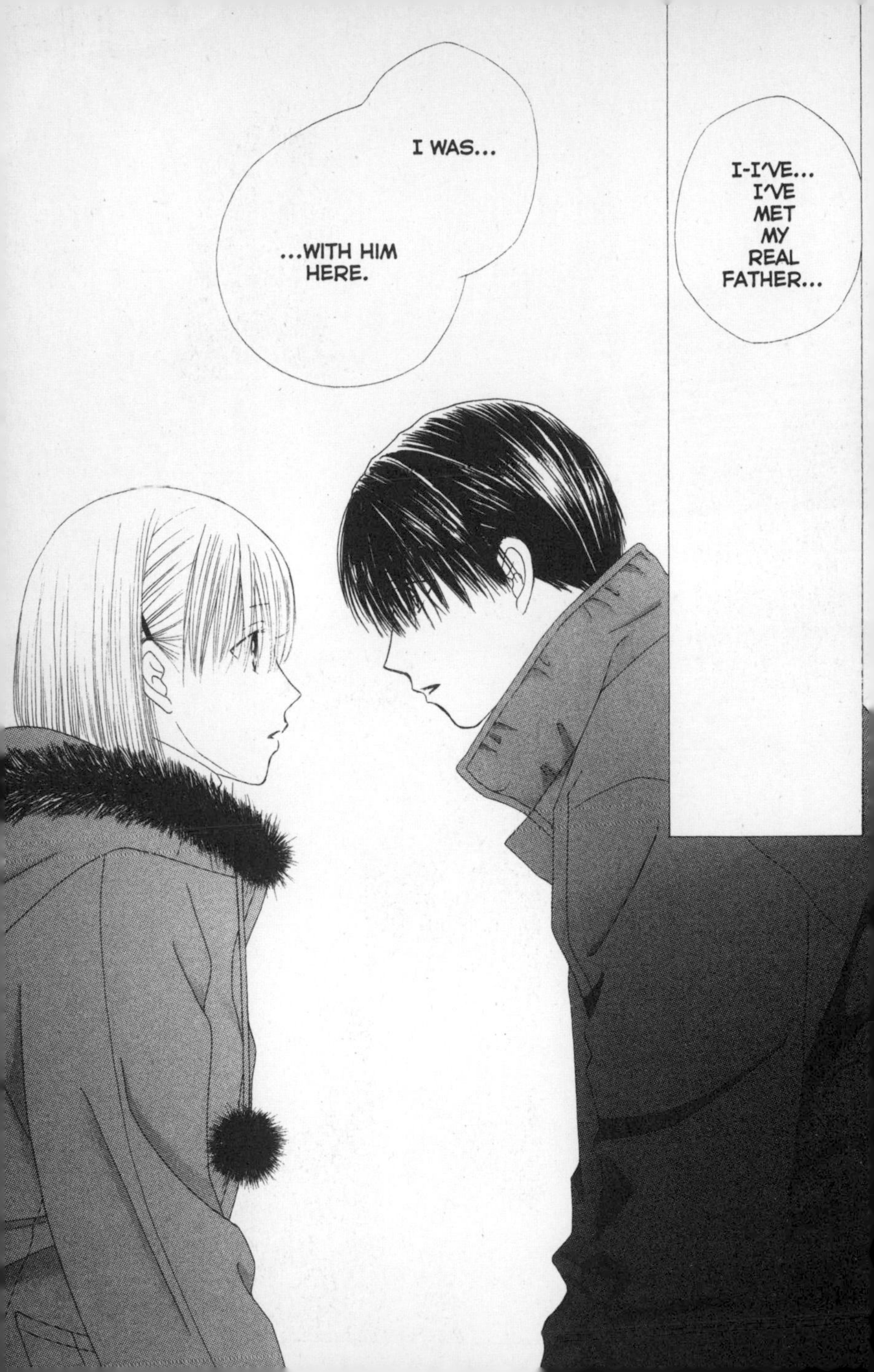
I-I'VE... I'VE MET MY REAL FATHER...
I WAS...
...WITH HIM HERE.

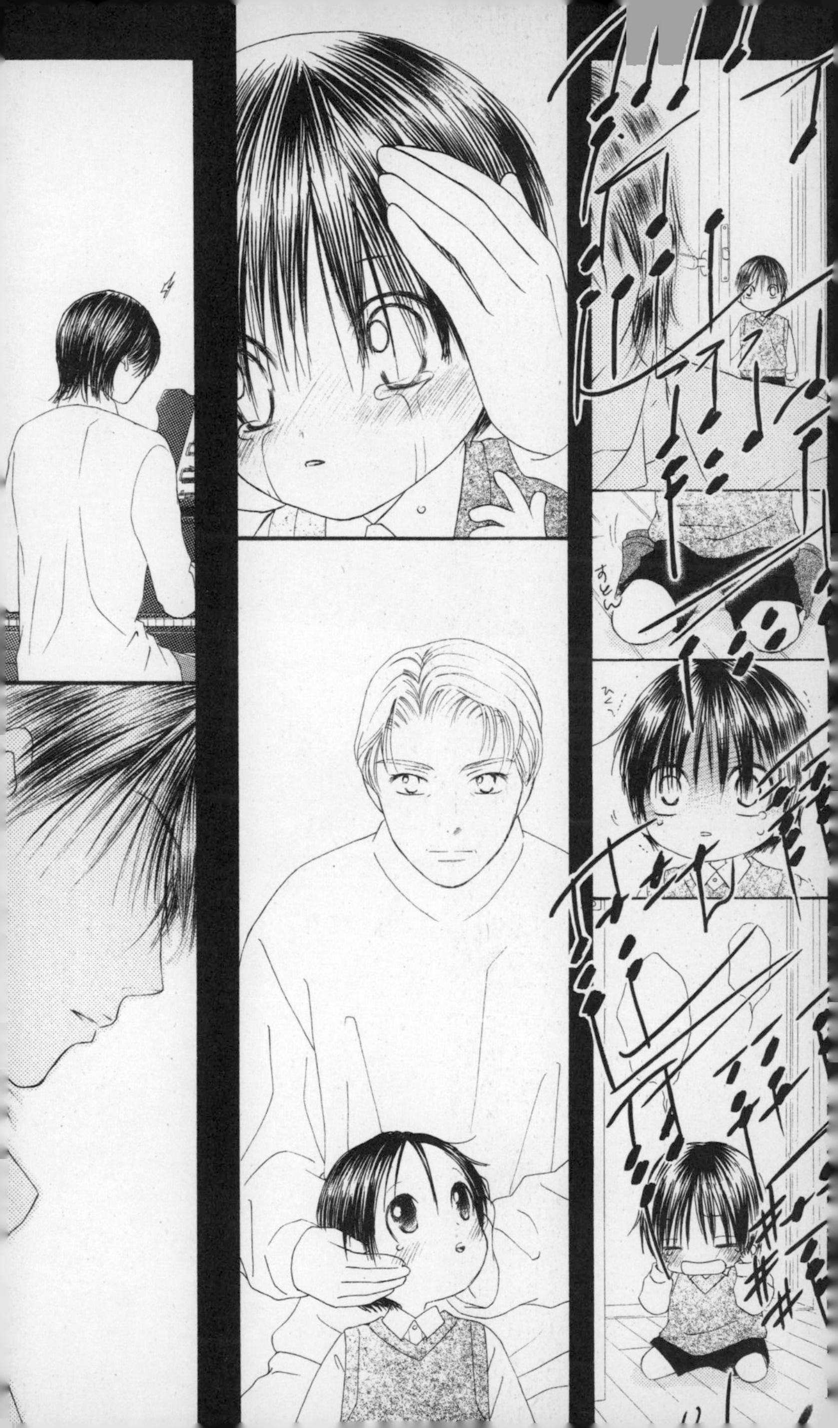
すとん
ひく…

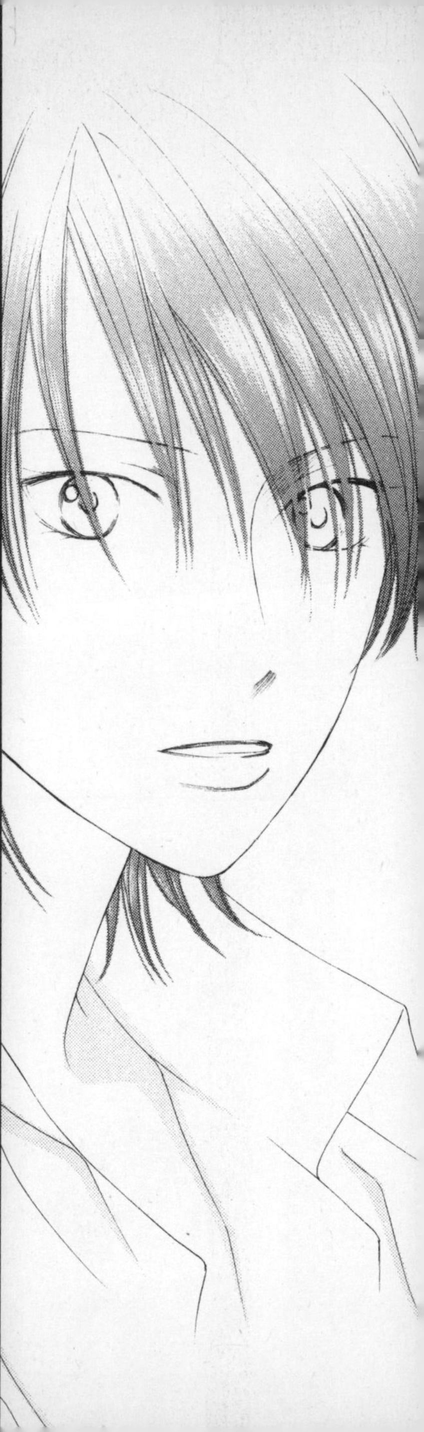

2

SLEEPWEAR

My skin is VERY sensitive (summer is HORRIBLE), so I've gotten really fussy about the materials my clothes are made of. I've even gotten pajamas like this!

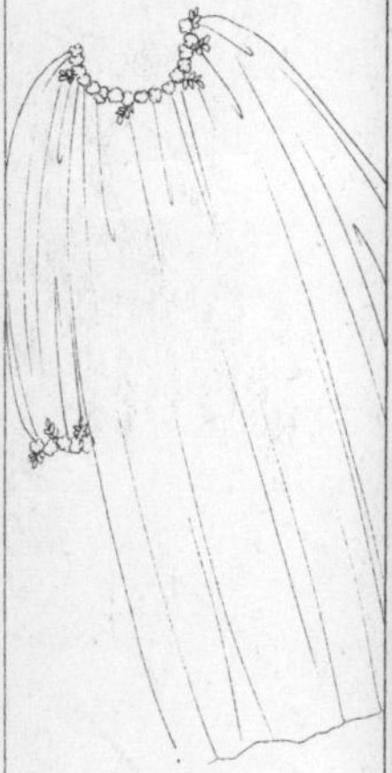

This was made in Germany. It looks like something that would show up in a foreign movie. It's made of a soft cotton blend. It's great for people with eczema or sensitive skin.

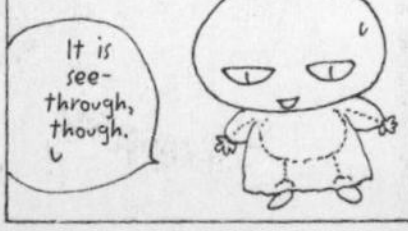
It is see-through, though.

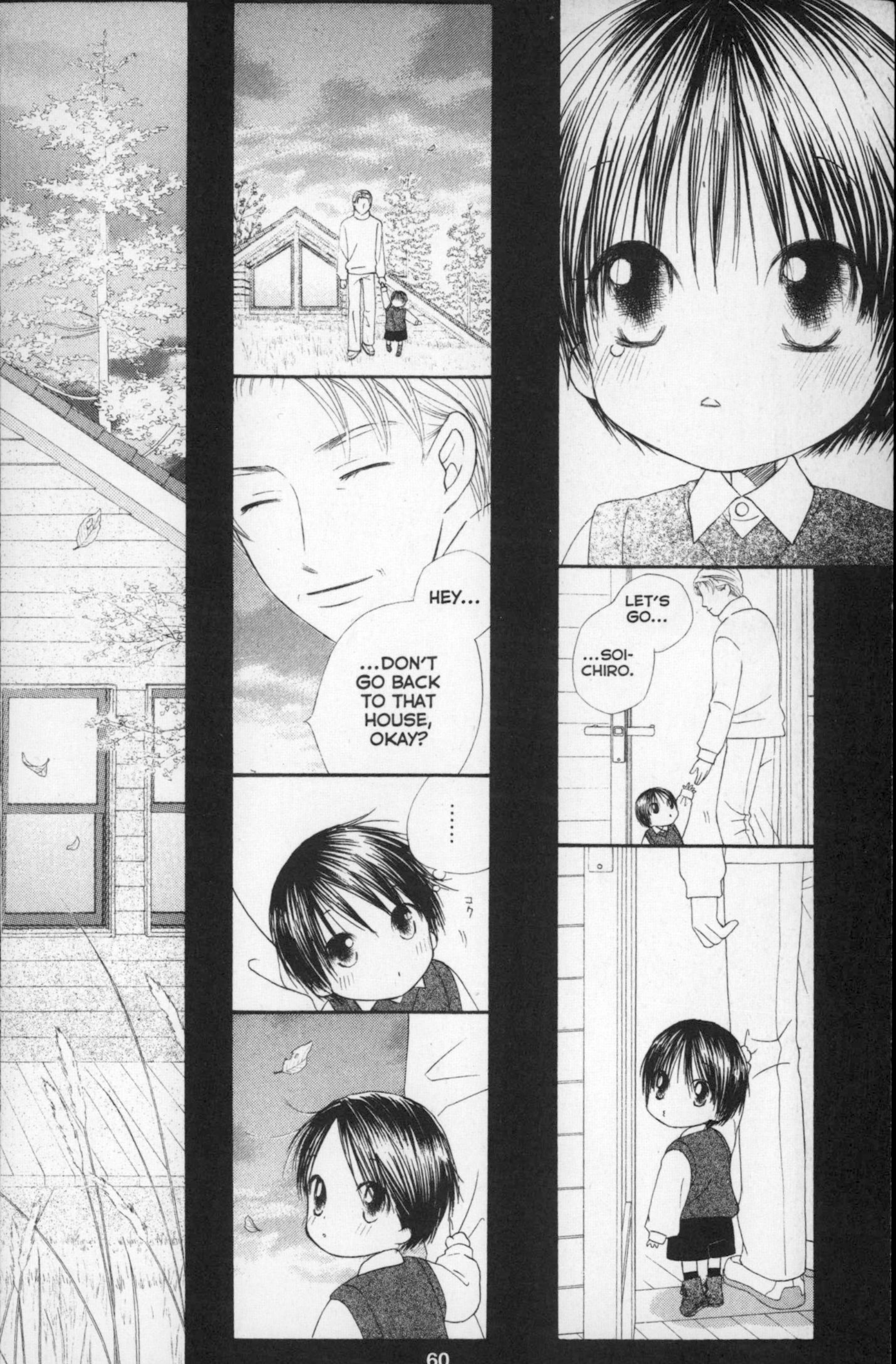
LET'S GO...
...SOI-CHIRO.
HEY...
...DON'T GO BACK TO THAT HOUSE, OKAY?
......
コク

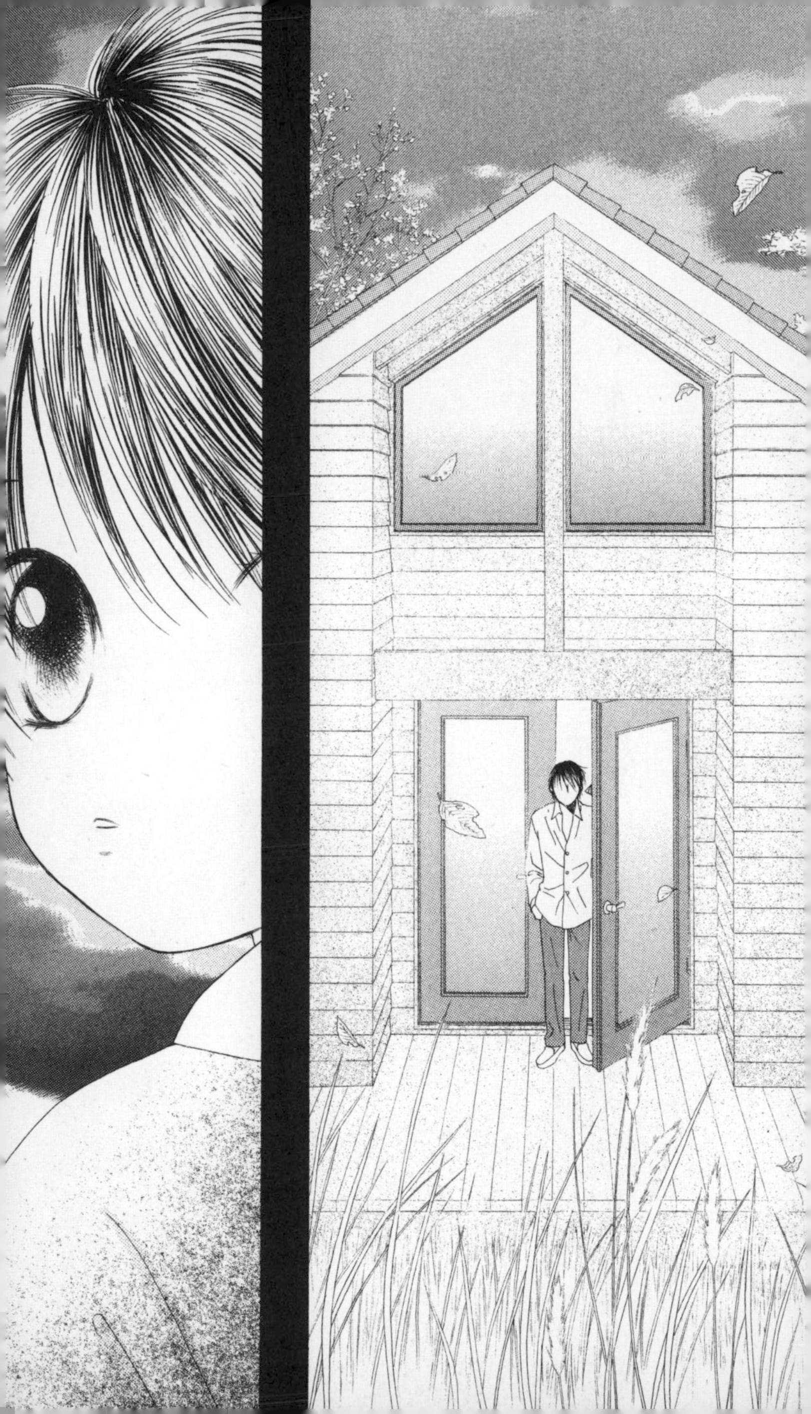

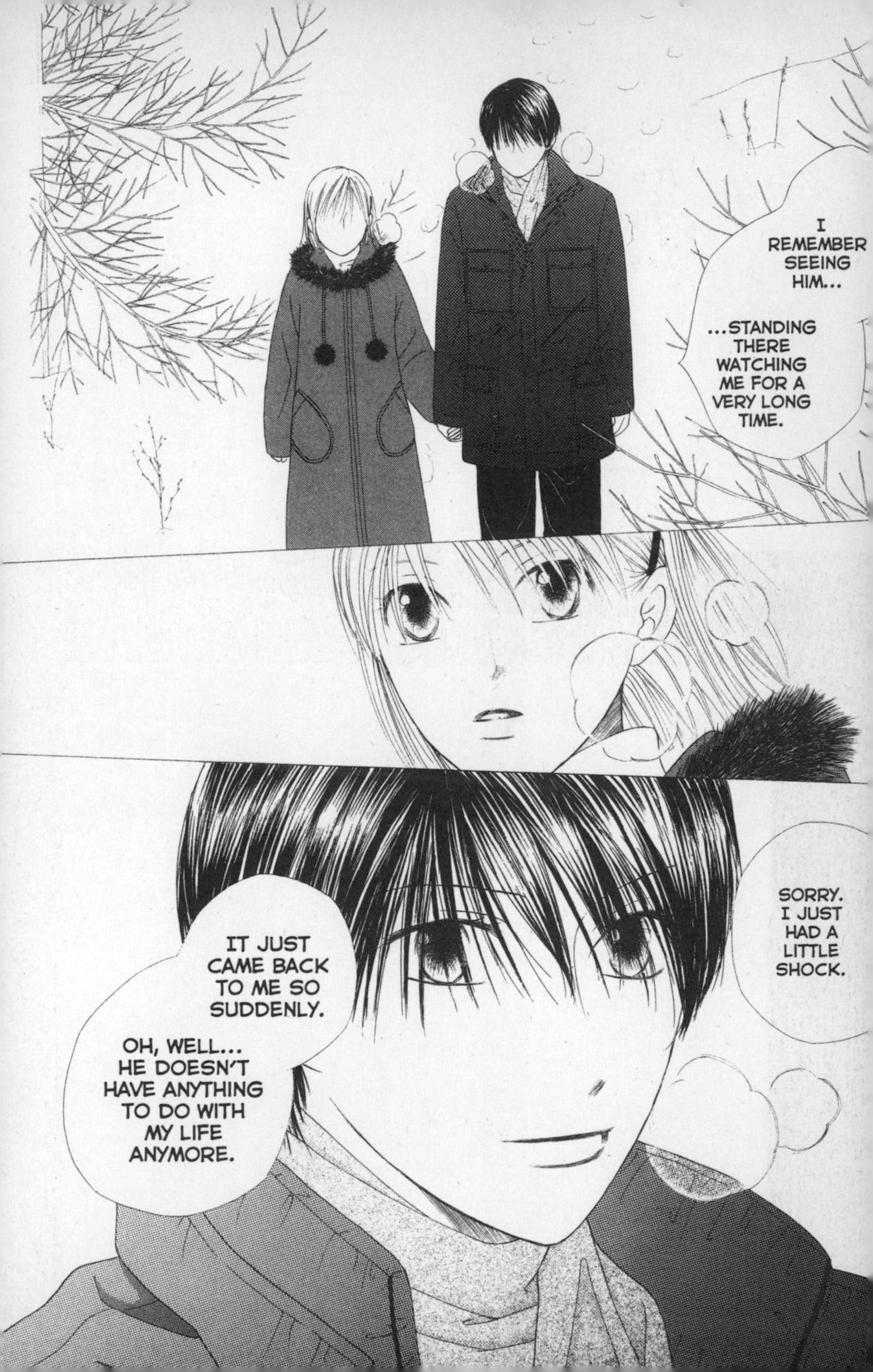
I REMEMBER SEEING HIM...
...STANDING THERE WATCHING ME FOR A VERY LONG TIME.
SORRY. I JUST HAD A LITTLE SHOCK.
IT JUST CAME BACK TO ME SO SUDDENLY.
OH, WELL... HE DOESN'T HAVE ANYTHING TO DO WITH MY LIFE ANYMORE.

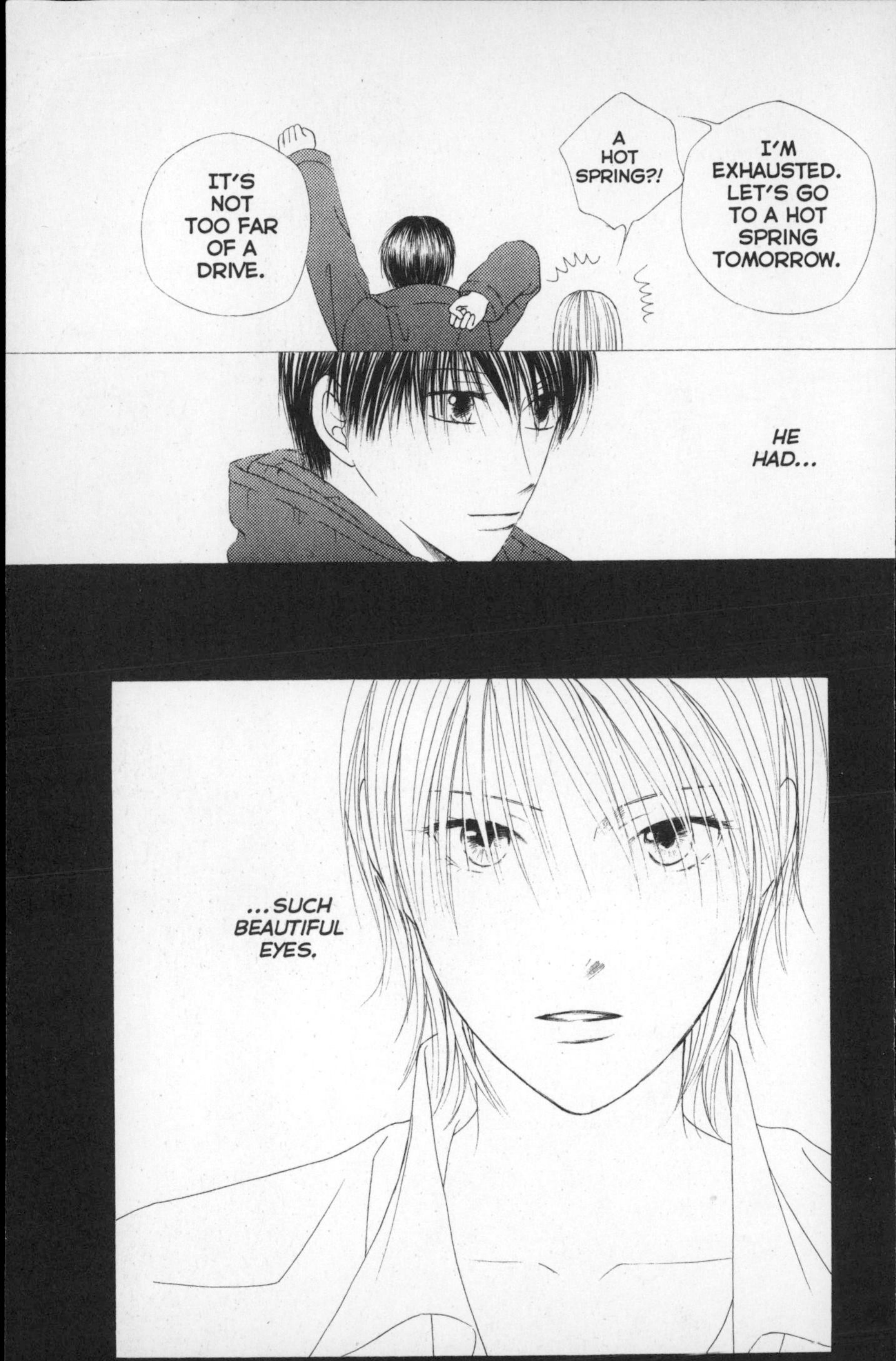
I'M EXHAUSTED. LET'S GO TO A HOT SPRING TOMORROW.
A HOT SPRING?!
IT'S NOT TOO FAR OF A DRIVE.
HE HAD...
...SUCH BEAUTIFUL EYES.

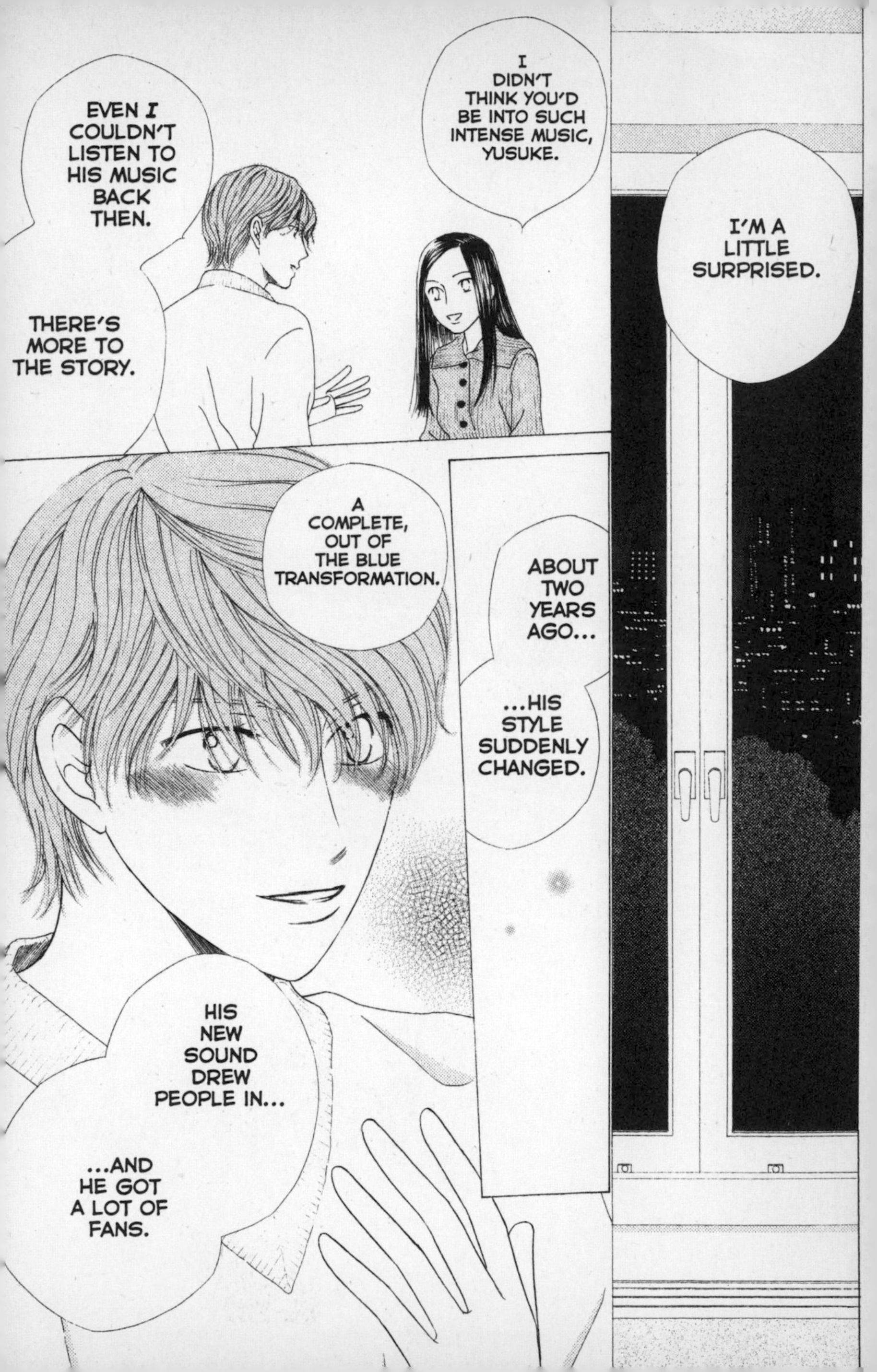
I'M A LITTLE SURPRISED.
I DIDN'T THINK YOU'D BE INTO SUCH INTENSE MUSIC, YUSUKE.
EVEN I COULDN'T LISTEN TO HIS MUSIC BACK THEN.
THERE'S MORE TO THE STORY.
ABOUT TWO YEARS AGO...
...HIS STYLE SUDDENLY CHANGED.
A COMPLETE, OUT OF THE BLUE TRANSFORMATION.
HIS NEW SOUND DREW PEOPLE IN...
...AND HE GOT A LOT OF FANS.

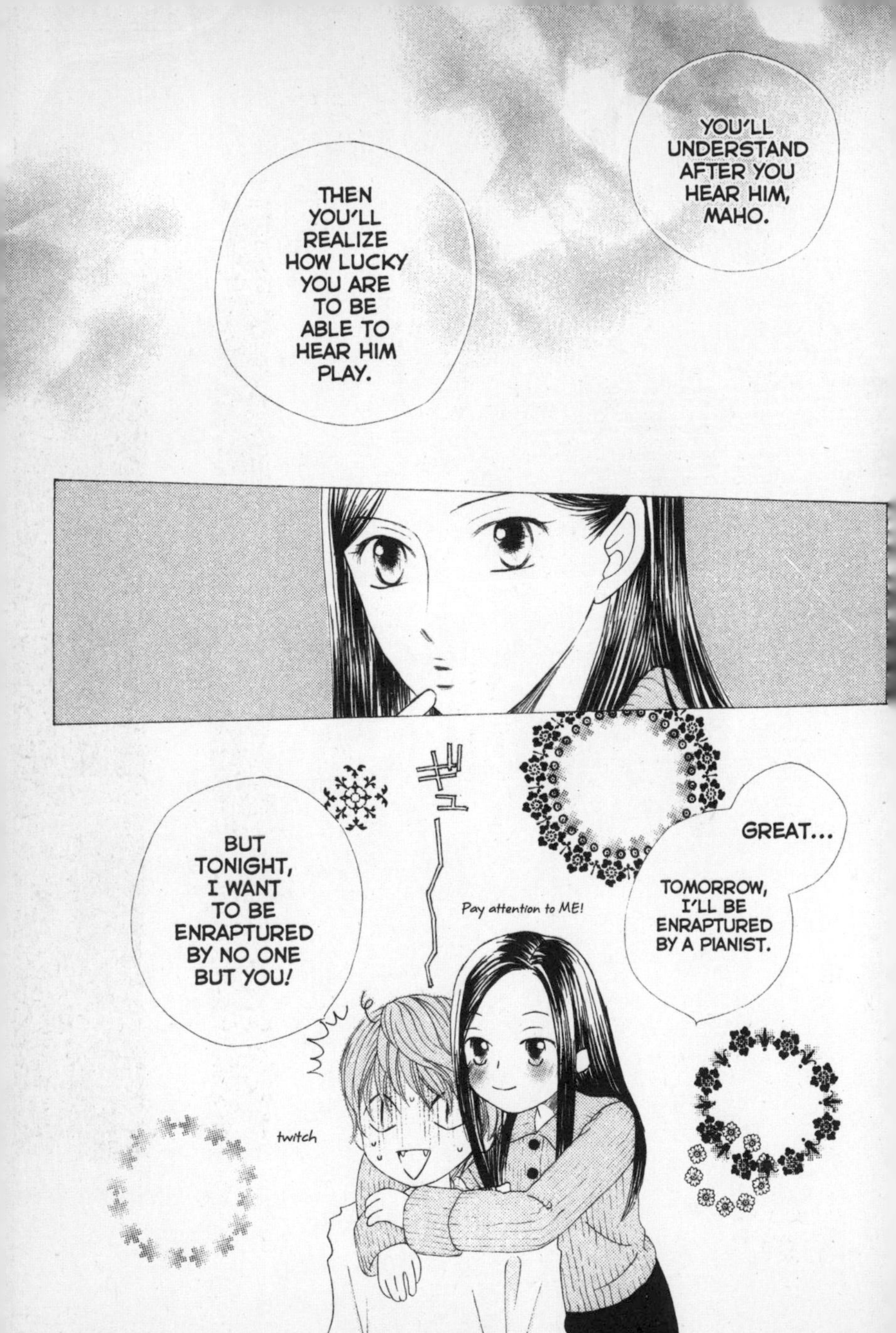
YOU'LL UNDERSTAND AFTER YOU HEAR HIM, MAHO.
THEN YOU'LL REALIZE HOW LUCKY YOU ARE TO BE ABLE TO HEAR HIM PLAY.
GREAT...
TOMORROW, I'LL BE ENRAPTURED BY A PIANIST.
Pay attention to ME!
ギュー
BUT TONIGHT, I WANT TO BE ENRAPTURED BY NO ONE BUT YOU!
twitch

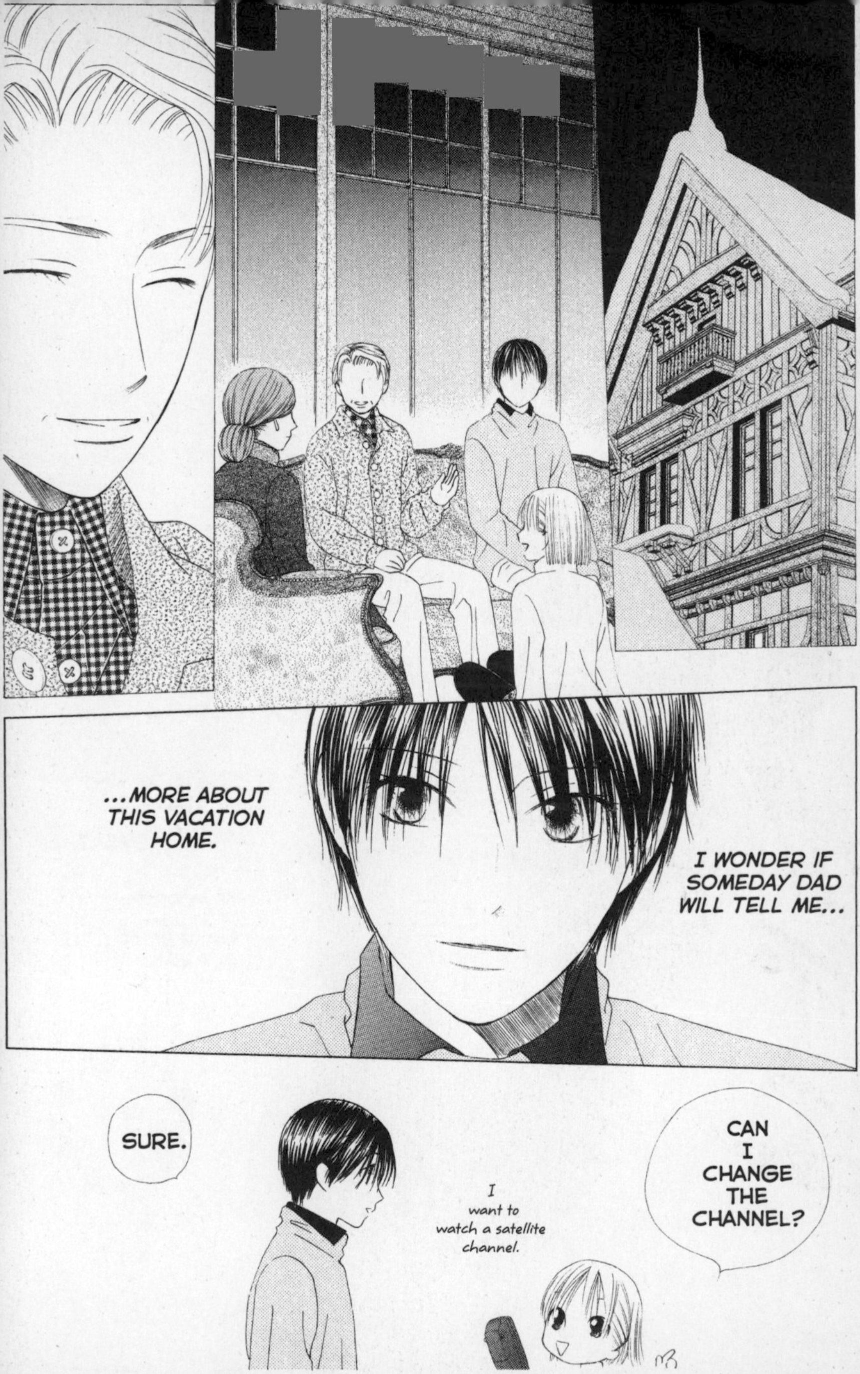
I WONDER IF SOMEDAY DAD WILL TELL ME...
...MORE ABOUT THIS VACATION HOME.
CAN I CHANGE THE CHANNEL?
I want to watch a satellite channel.
SURE.

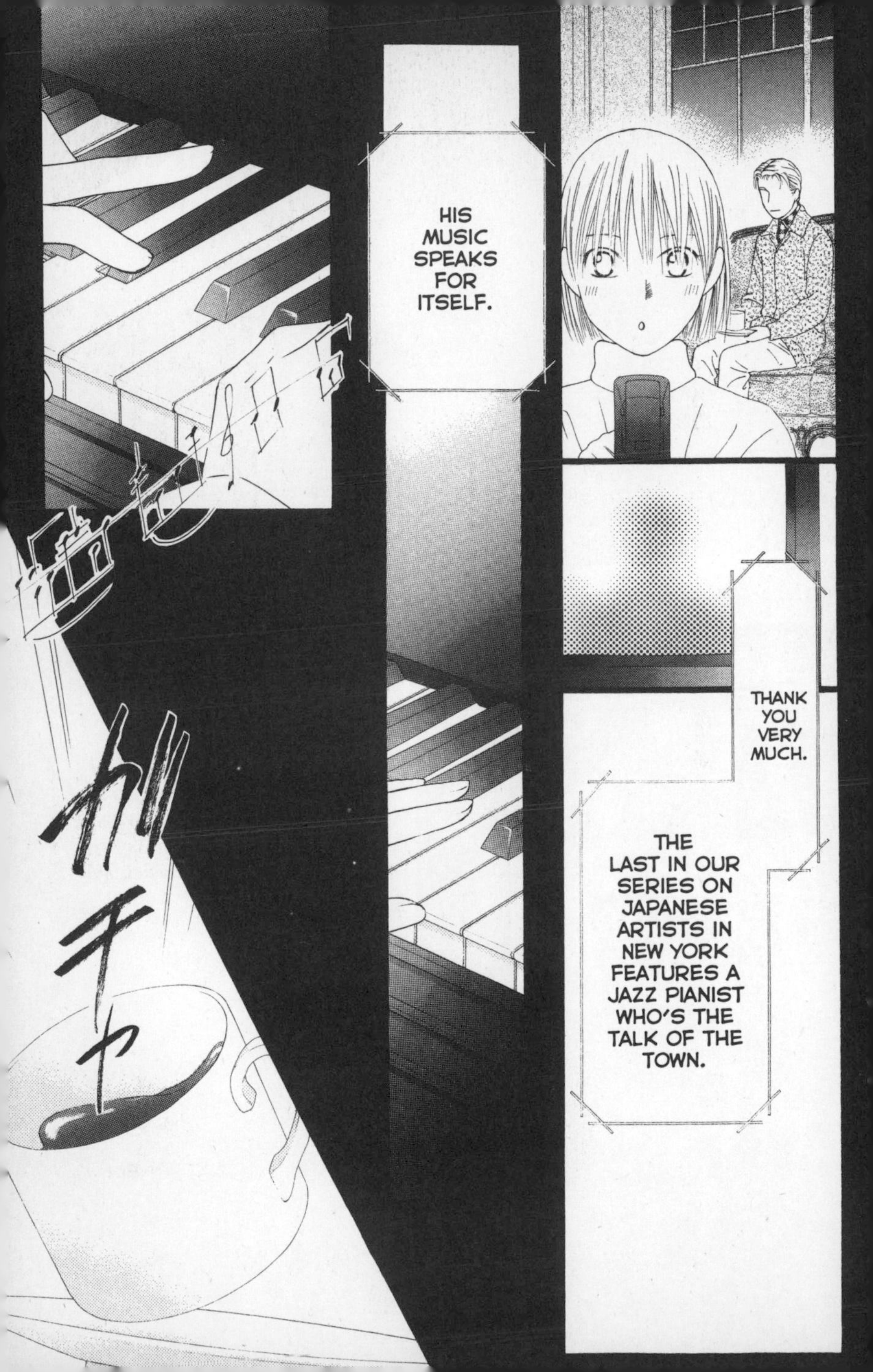
HIS MUSIC SPEAKS FOR ITSELF.
THANK YOU VERY MUCH.
THE LAST IN OUR SERIES ON JAPANESE ARTISTS IN NEW YORK FEATURES A JAZZ PIANIST WHO'S THE TALK OF THE TOWN.
カチャ

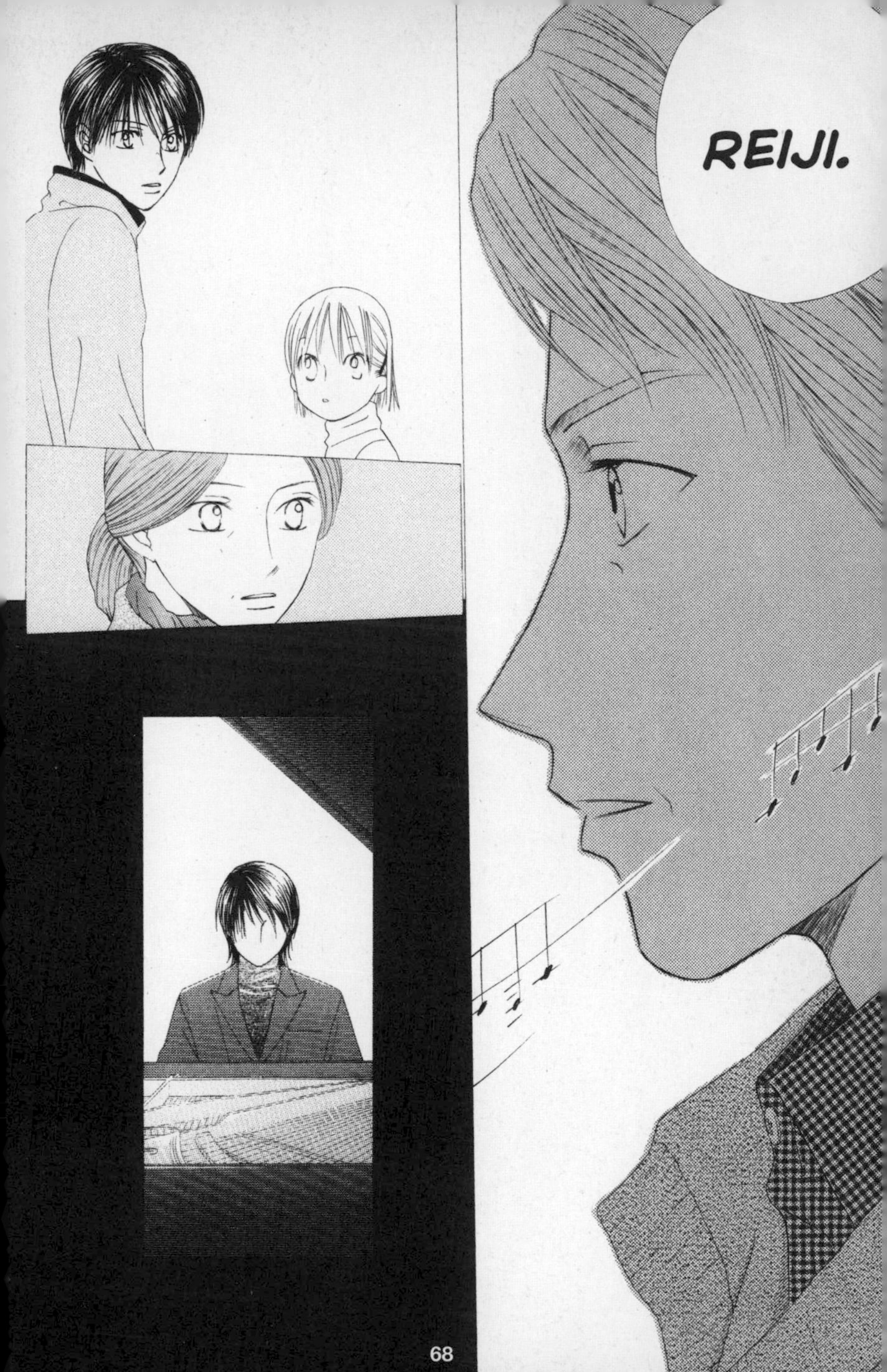
REIJI.

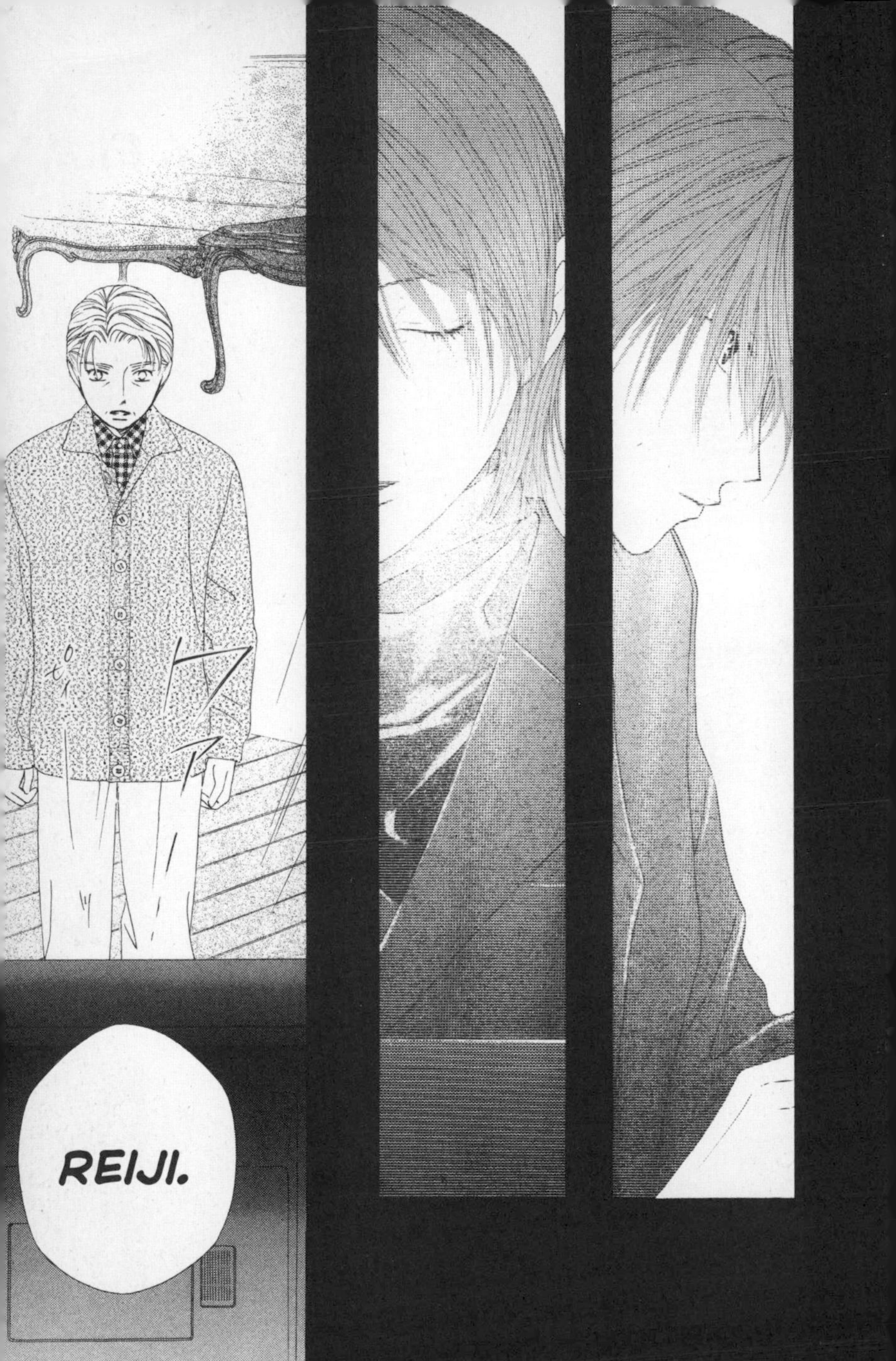
REIJI.

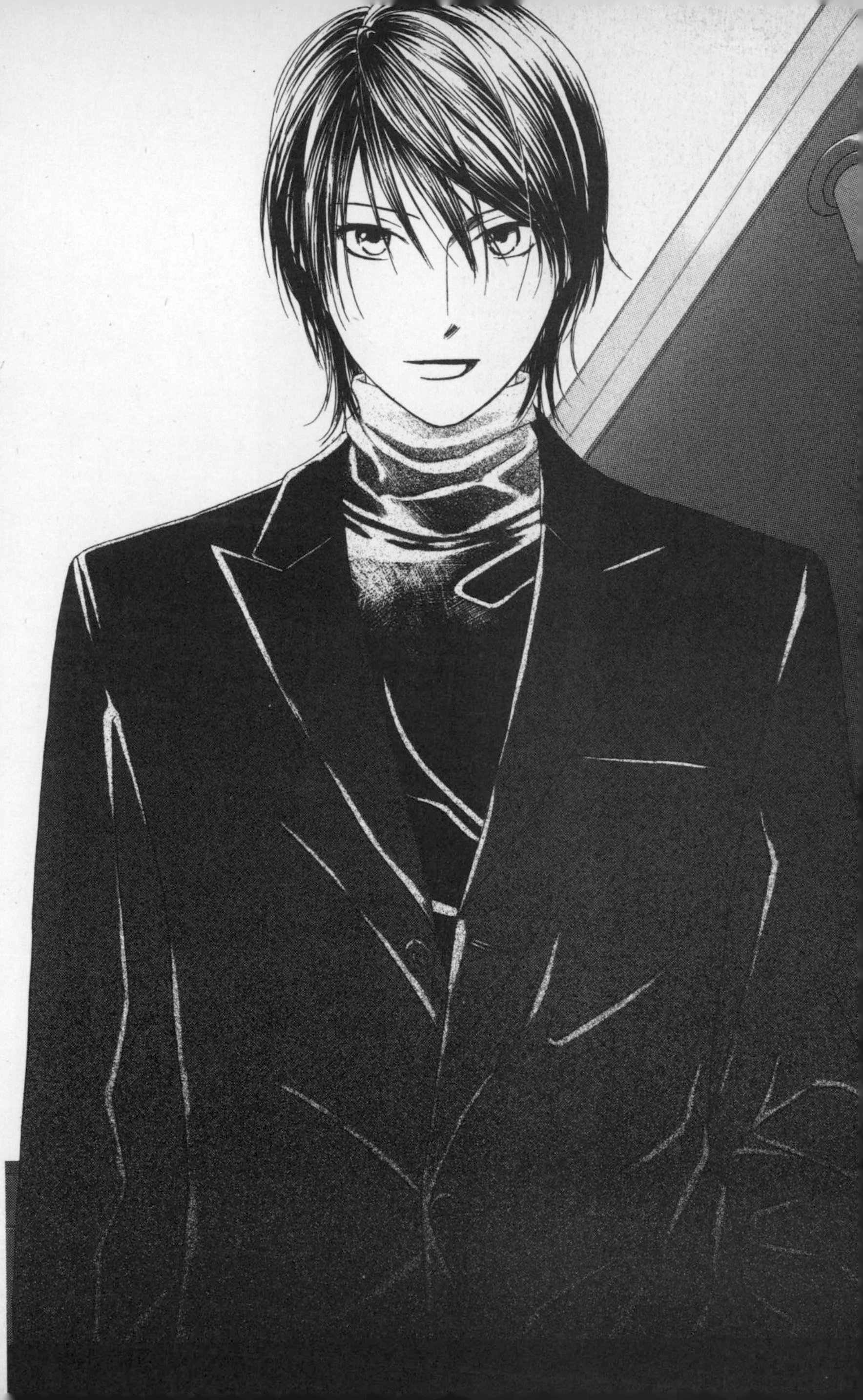

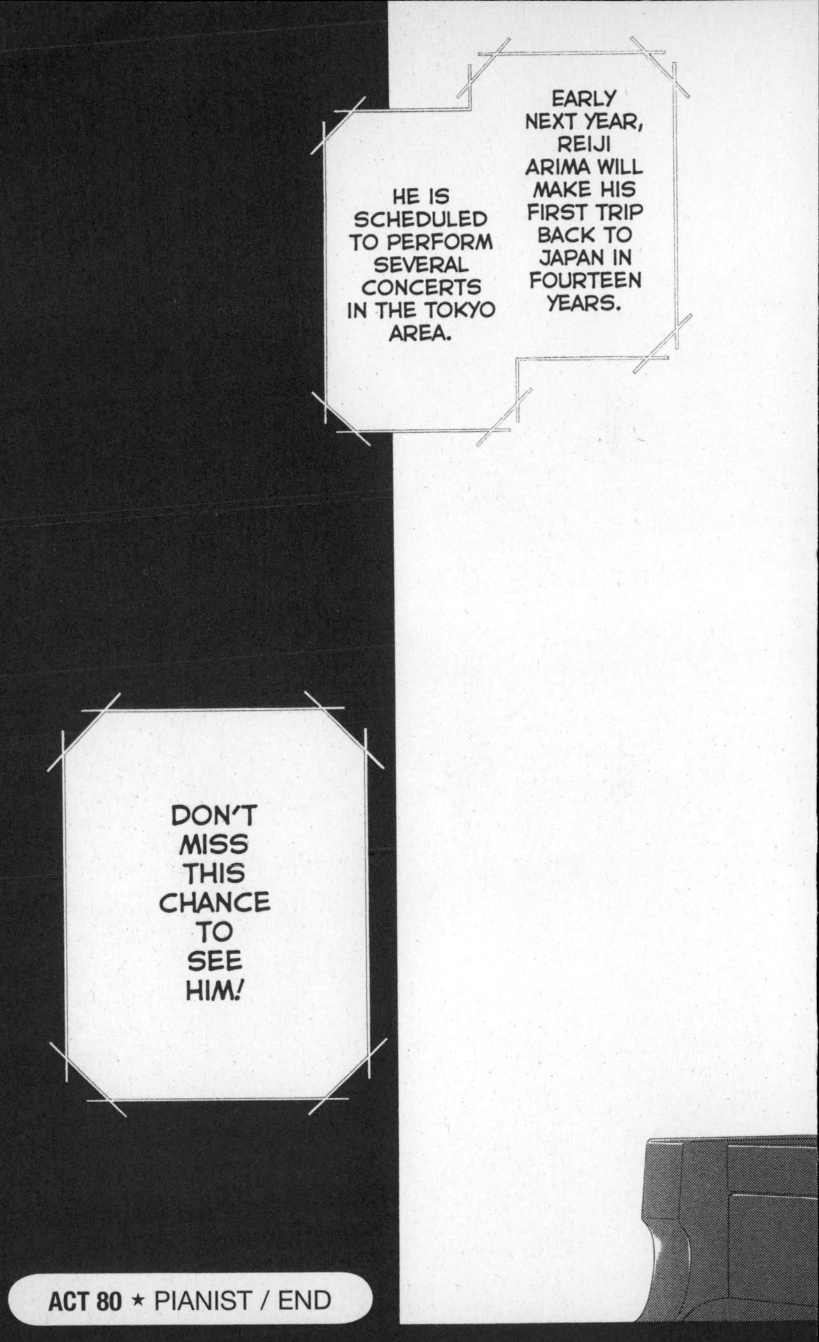
EARLY NEXT YEAR, REIJI ARIMA WILL MAKE HIS FIRST TRIP BACK TO JAPAN IN FOURTEEN YEARS.
HE IS SCHEDULED TO PERFORM SEVERAL CONCERTS IN THE TOKYO AREA.
DON'T MISS THIS CHANCE TO SEE HIM!
ACT 80 ★ PIANIST / END

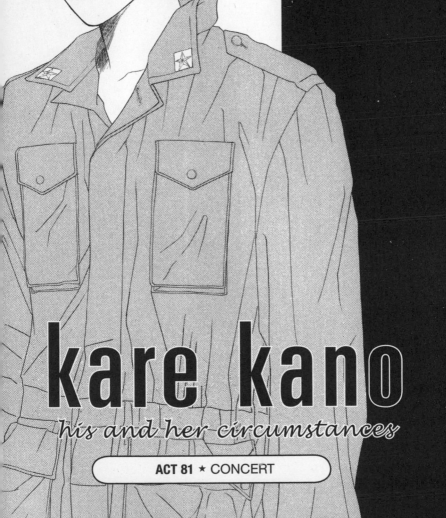

kare kano
his and her circumstances

ACT 81 ★ CONCERT

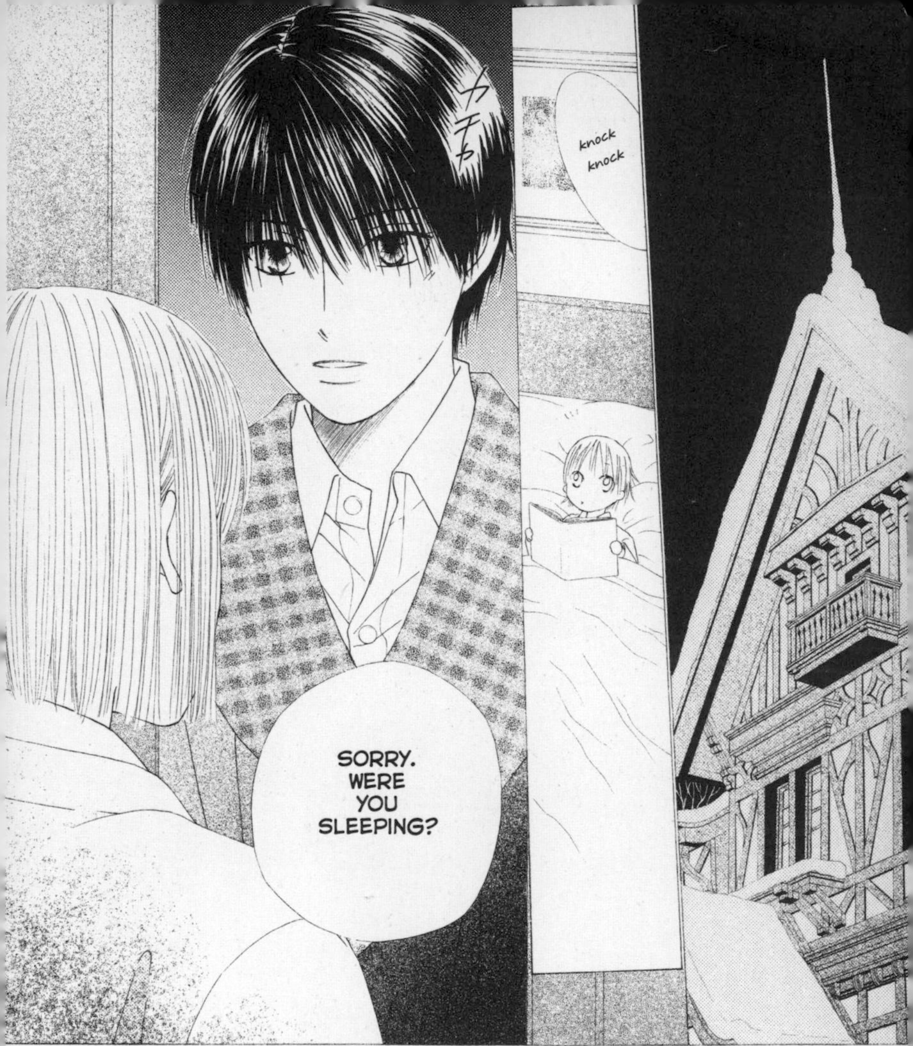
knock knock
カチャ
SORRY. WERE YOU SLEEPING?

WOWOW

I've subscribed to the WOWOW channel. There wasn't anything I wanted to watch on regular televison.

☆

And now I've realized how great foreign movie stars are! So I'm recording as many films as I can.

♡

Now if I could only find the time to watch them...

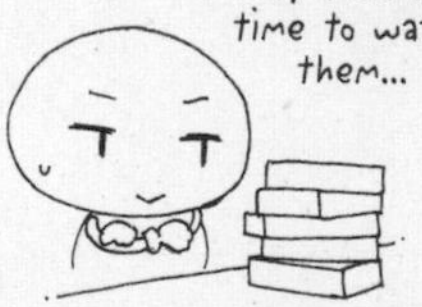

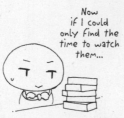

When I heard Johnny Depp was starring in Pirates of the Caribbean, I was SOOO happy! I'll probably watch it on WOWOW.

♡

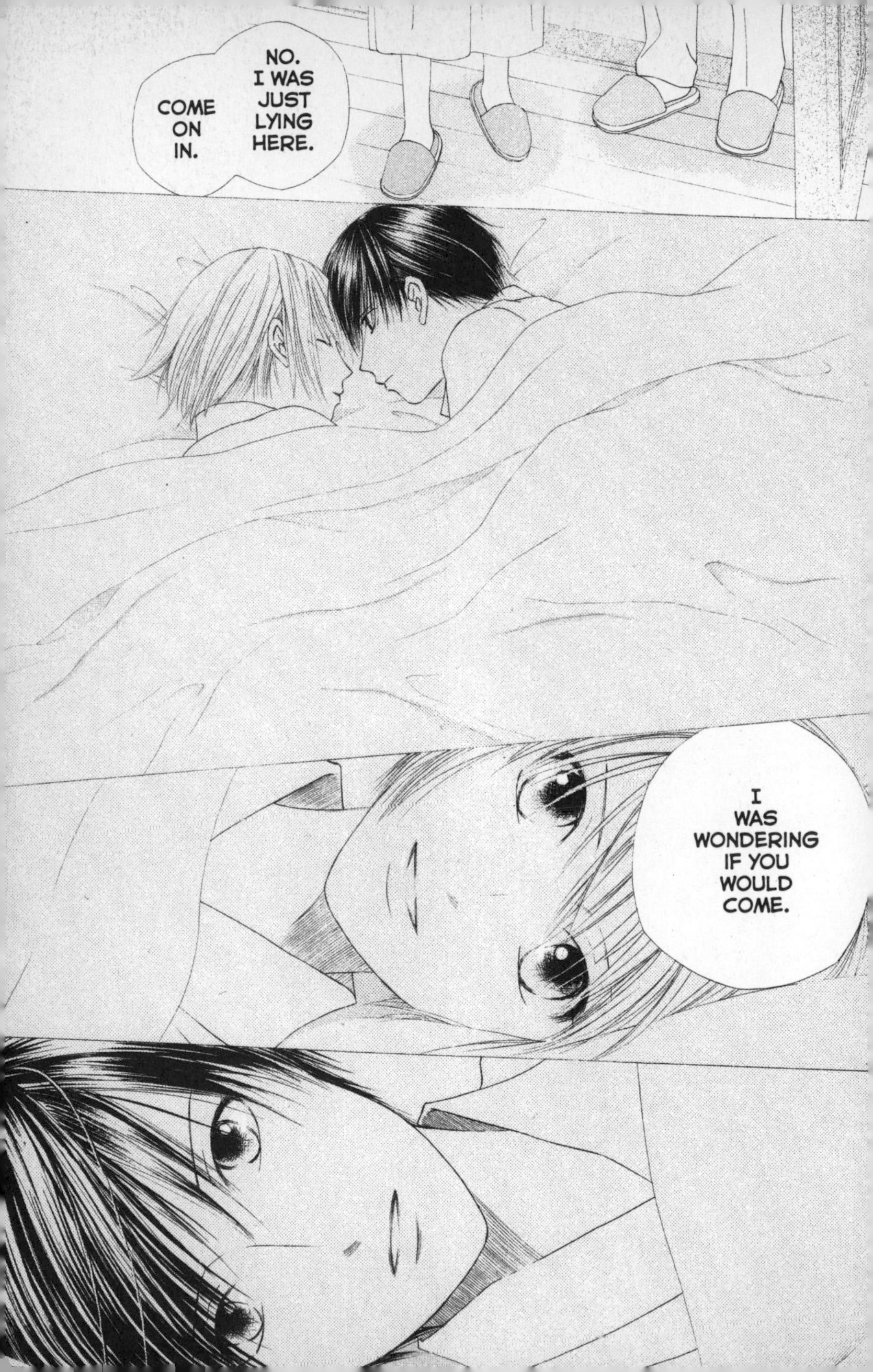
NO. I WAS JUST LYING HERE.
COME ON IN.
I WAS WONDERING IF YOU WOULD COME.

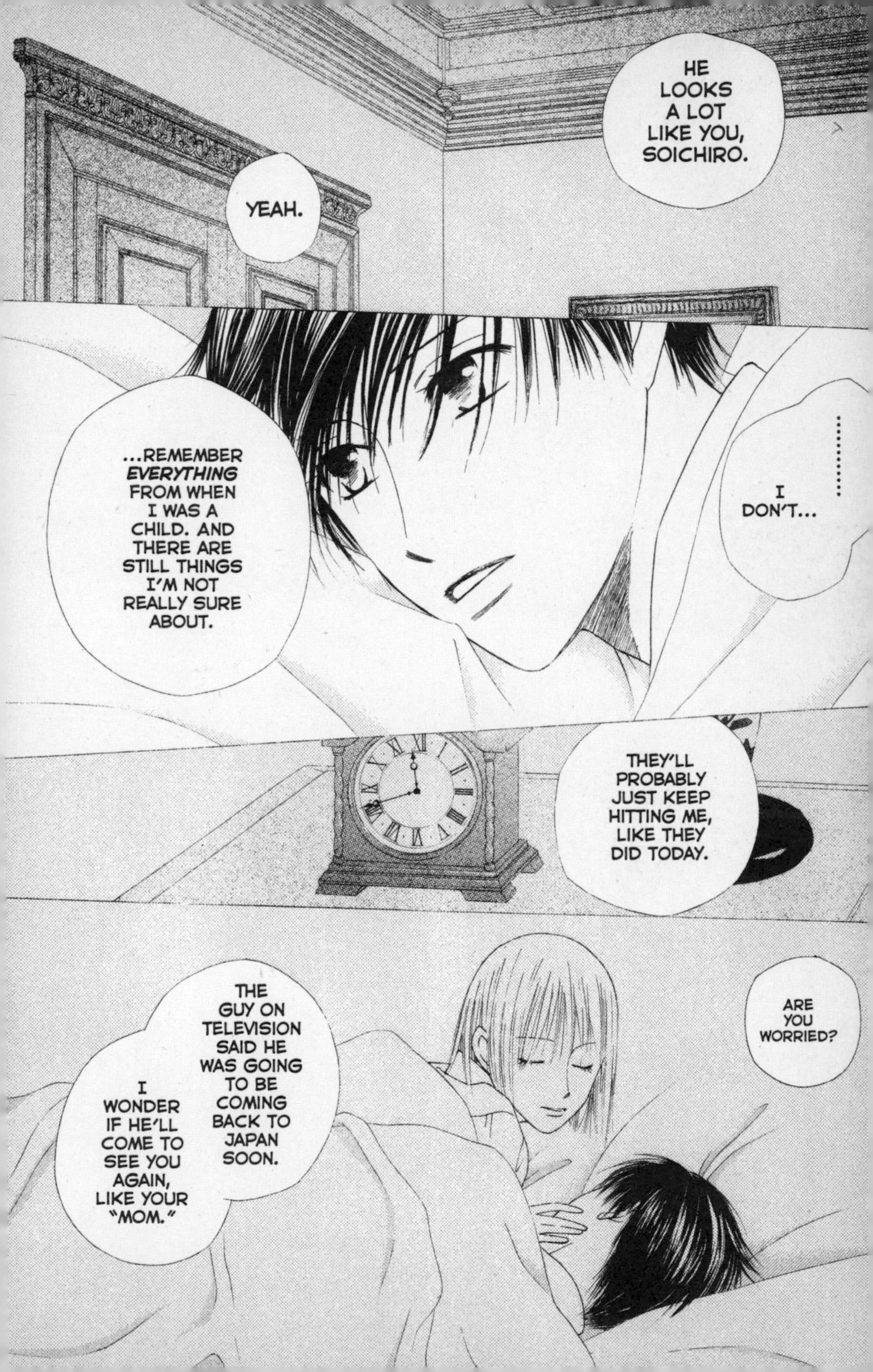

HE LOOKS A LOT LIKE YOU, SOICHIRO.
YEAH.
......
I DON'T...
...REMEMBER *EVERYTHING* FROM WHEN I WAS A CHILD. AND THERE ARE STILL THINGS I'M NOT REALLY SURE ABOUT.
THEY'LL PROBABLY JUST KEEP HITTING ME, LIKE THEY DID TODAY.
ARE YOU WORRIED?
THE GUY ON TELEVISION SAID HE WAS GOING TO BE COMING BACK TO JAPAN SOON.
I WONDER IF HE'LL COME TO SEE YOU AGAIN, LIKE YOUR "MOM."

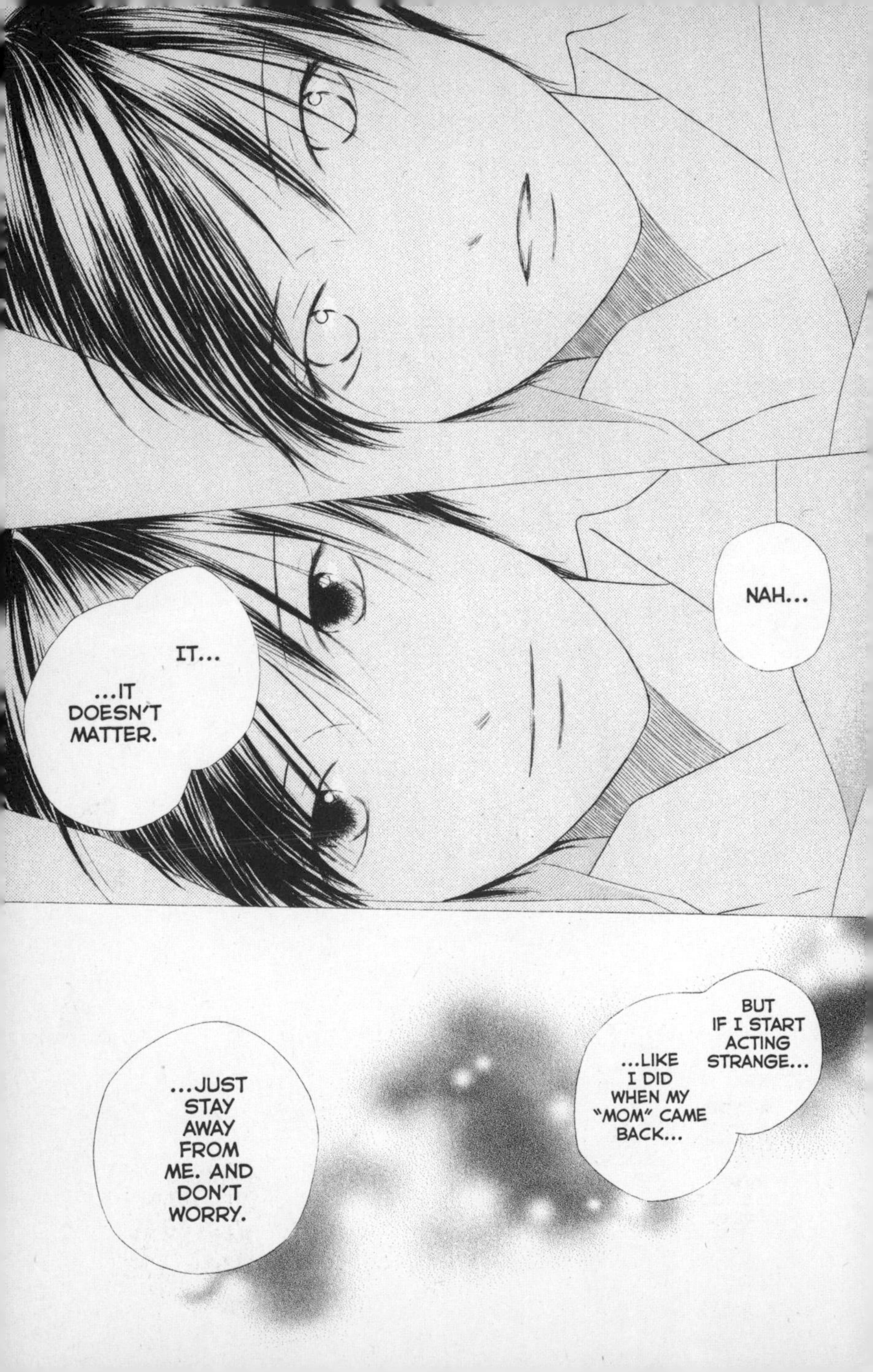
NAH...
IT... ...IT DOESN'T MATTER.
BUT IF I START ACTING STRANGE...
...LIKE I DID WHEN MY "MOM" CAME BACK...
...JUST STAY AWAY FROM ME. AND DON'T WORRY.

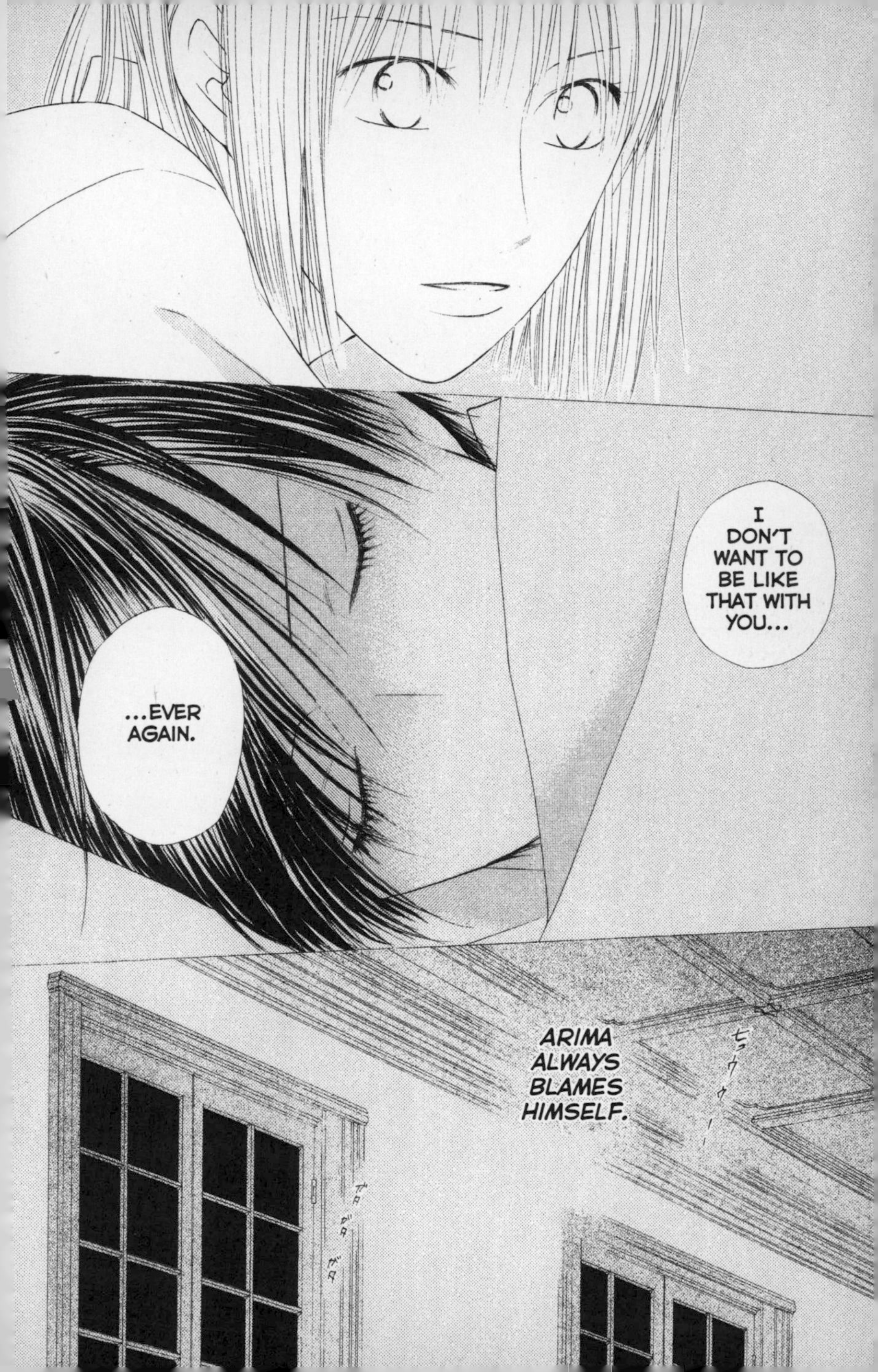
I DON'T WANT TO BE LIKE THAT WITH YOU...
...EVER AGAIN.
ARIMA ALWAYS BLAMES HIMSELF.

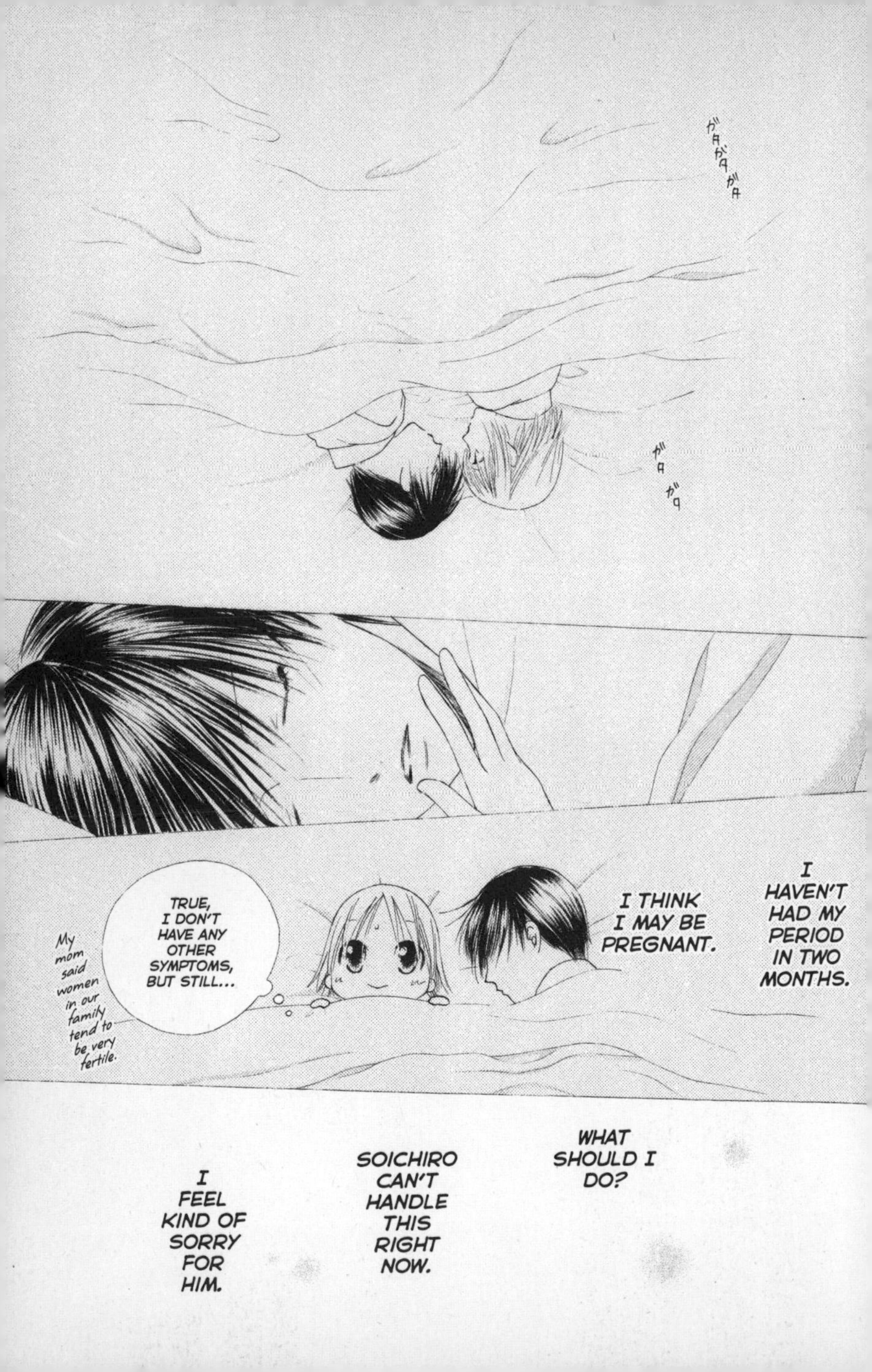
ガタガタガタ
ガタガタ
I HAVEN'T HAD MY PERIOD IN TWO MONTHS.
I THINK I MAY BE PREGNANT.
TRUE, I DON'T HAVE ANY OTHER SYMPTOMS, BUT STILL...
My mom said women in our family tend to be very fertile.
WHAT SHOULD I DO?
SOICHIRO CAN'T HANDLE THIS RIGHT NOW.
I FEEL KIND OF SORRY FOR HIM.

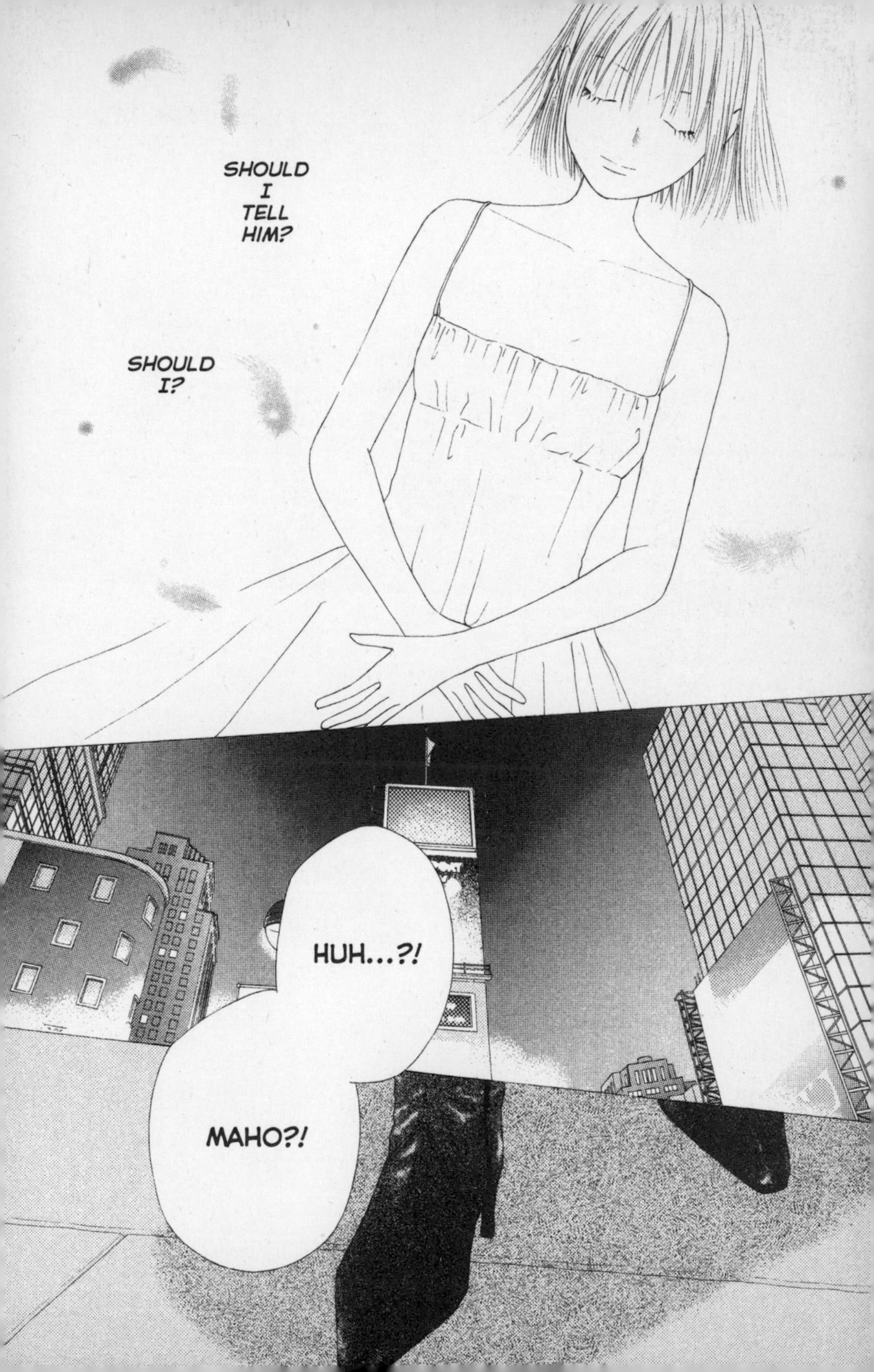
SHOULD I TELL HIM?
SHOULD I?
HUH...?!
MAHO?!

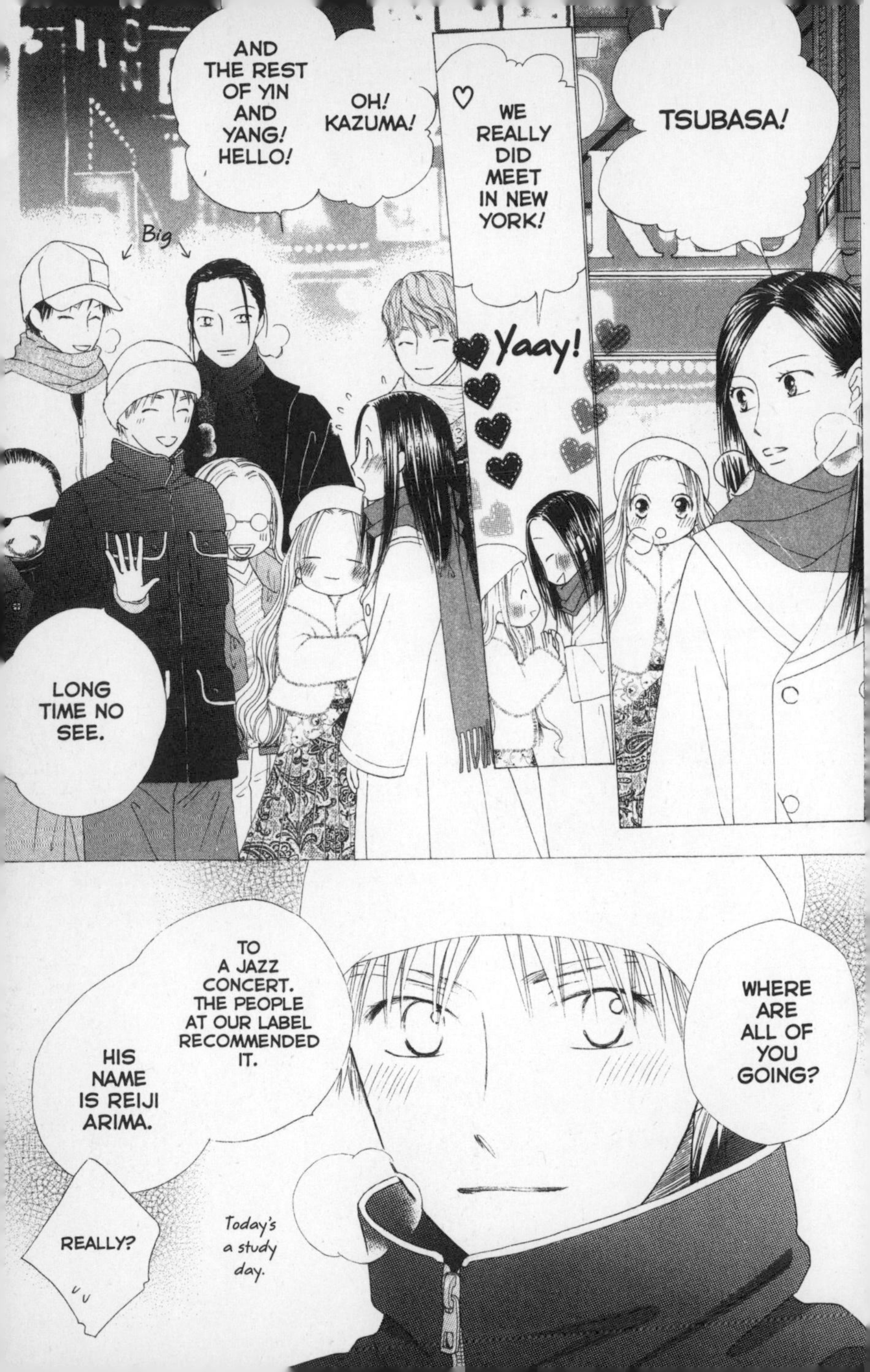
TSUBASA!
WE REALLY DID MEET IN NEW YORK!
Yaay!
OH! KAZUMA!
AND THE REST OF YIN AND YANG! HELLO!
Big
LONG TIME NO SEE.
WHERE ARE ALL OF YOU GOING?
TO A JAZZ CONCERT. THE PEOPLE AT OUR LABEL RECOMMENDED IT.
HIS NAME IS REIJI ARIMA.
Today's a study day.
REALLY?

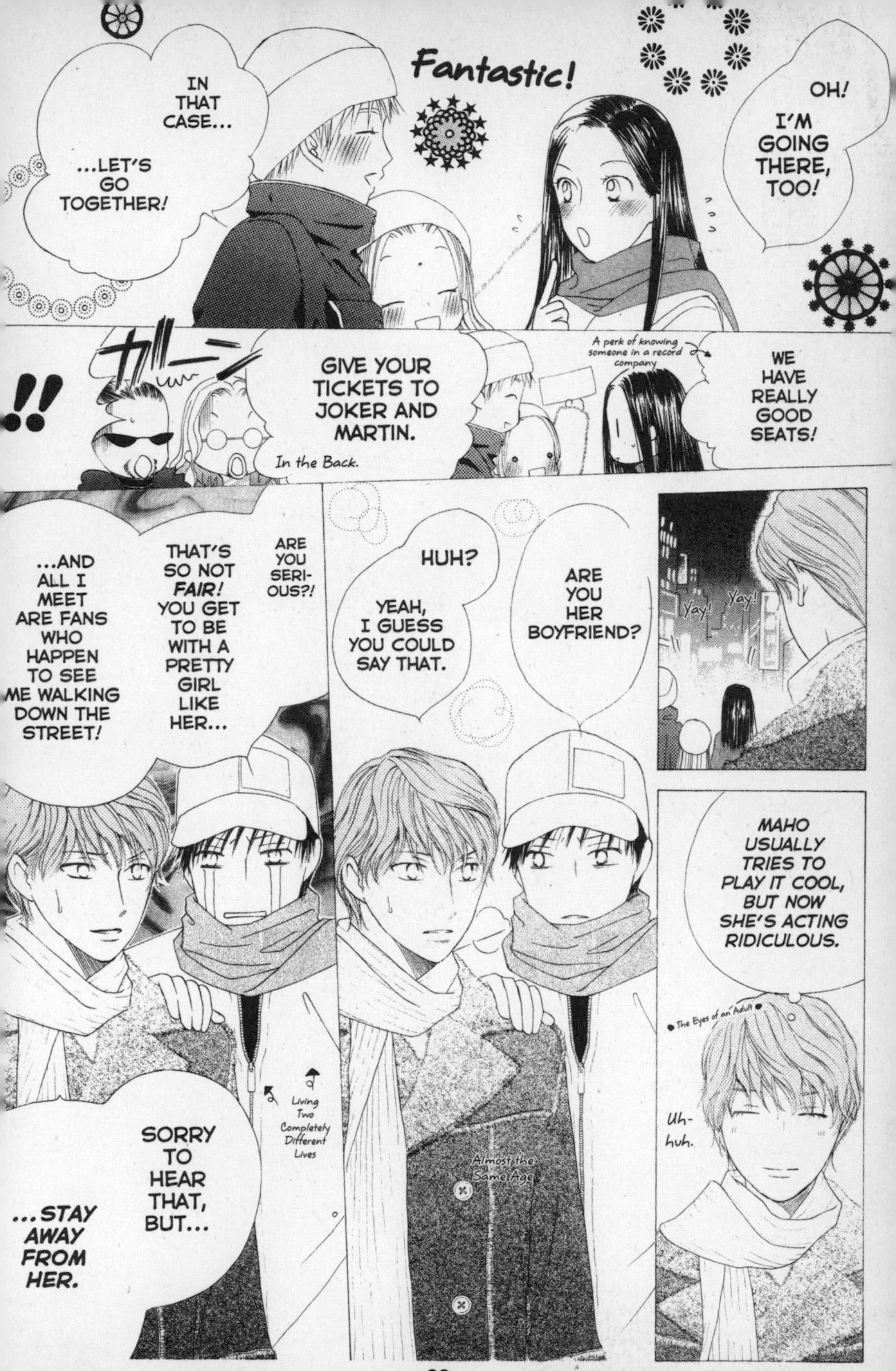
OH! I'M GOING THERE, TOO!
Fantastic!
IN THAT CASE...
...LET'S GO TOGETHER!
A perk of knowing someone in a record company
WE HAVE REALLY GOOD SEATS!
GIVE YOUR TICKETS TO JOKER AND MARTIN.
In the Back.
ガーン
!!
Yay!
Yay!
MAHO USUALLY TRIES TO PLAY IT COOL, BUT NOW SHE'S ACTING RIDICULOUS.
The Eyes of an Adult
Uh-huh.
ARE YOU HER BOYFRIEND?
HUH?
YEAH, I GUESS YOU COULD SAY THAT.
Almost the Same Age
ARE YOU SERIOUS?!
THAT'S SO NOT FAIR! YOU GET TO BE WITH A PRETTY GIRL LIKE HER...
...AND ALL I MEET ARE FANS WHO HAPPEN TO SEE ME WALKING DOWN THE STREET!
Living Two Completely Different Lives
SORRY TO HEAR THAT, BUT...
...STAY AWAY FROM HER.

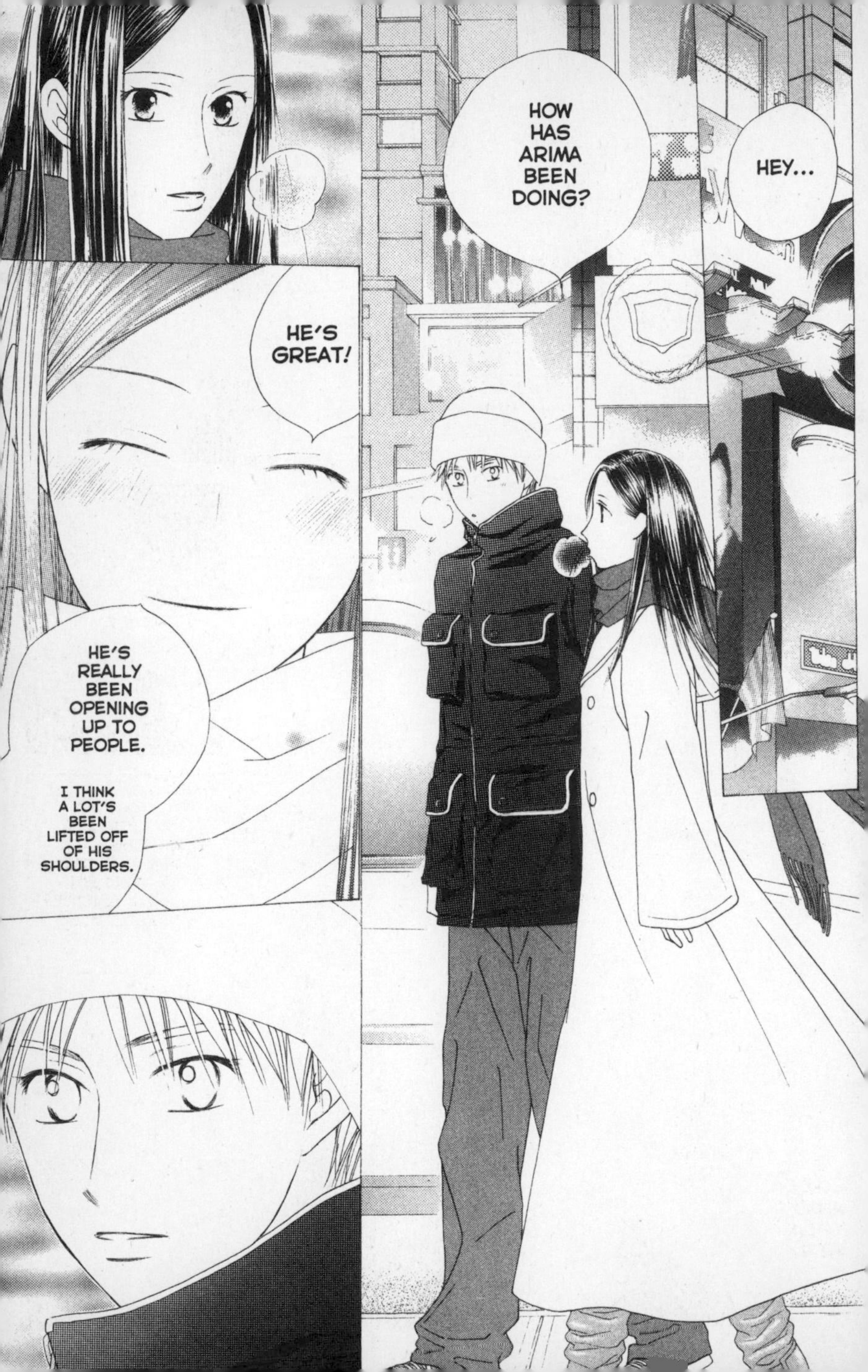
HEY...
HOW HAS ARIMA BEEN DOING?
HE'S GREAT!
HE'S REALLY BEEN OPENING UP TO PEOPLE.
I THINK A LOT'S BEEN LIFTED OFF OF HIS SHOULDERS.

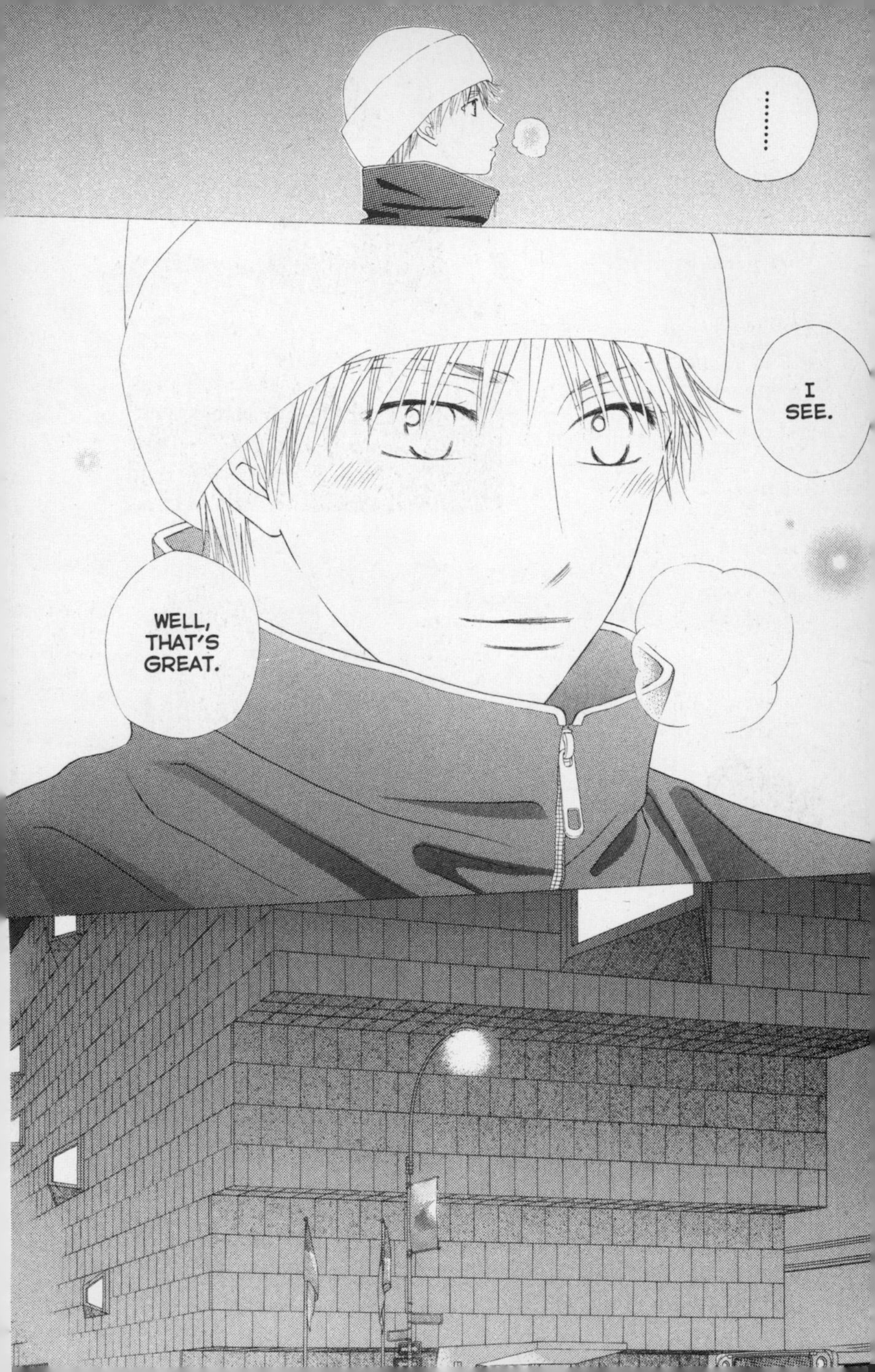
....
I SEE.
WELL, THAT'S GREAT.

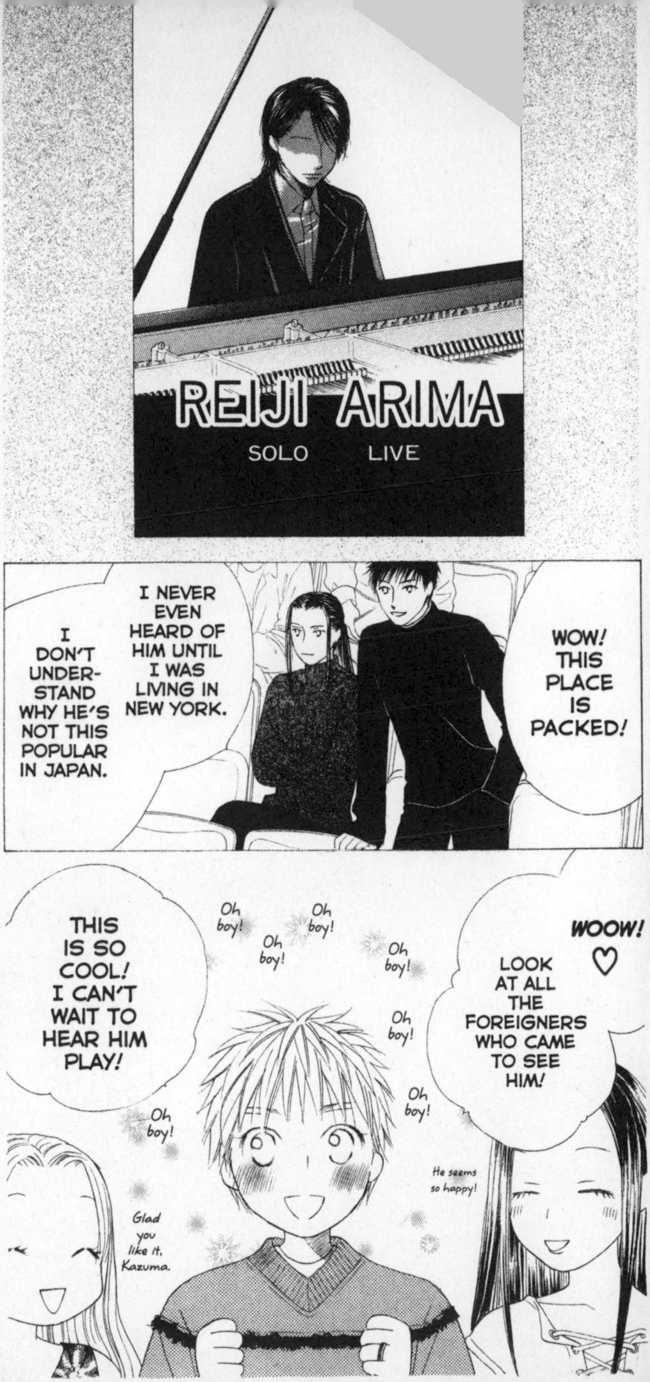
REIJI ARIMA
SOLO LIVE
WOW! THIS PLACE IS PACKED!
I NEVER EVEN HEARD OF HIM UNTIL I WAS LIVING IN NEW YORK.
I DON'T UNDERSTAND WHY HE'S NOT THIS POPULAR IN JAPAN.
WOOW! ♡
LOOK AT ALL THE FOREIGNERS WHO CAME TO SEE HIM!
Oh boy!
Oh boy!
Oh boy!
Oh boy!
Oh boy!
Oh boy!
Oh boy!
THIS IS SO COOL! I CAN'T WAIT TO HEAR HIM PLAY!
He seems so happy!
Glad you like it, Kazuma.

3

KIMONO

Traditional Japanese clothes are so great! When I go to a Kabuki performance, I notice a lot of guests dressed up in kimonos, so I'm always gazing at them in admiration. In fact, I've been buying a lot of books about kimonos lately. I think it's fun just looking at the beautiful colors. Even the names of the colors are pretty!

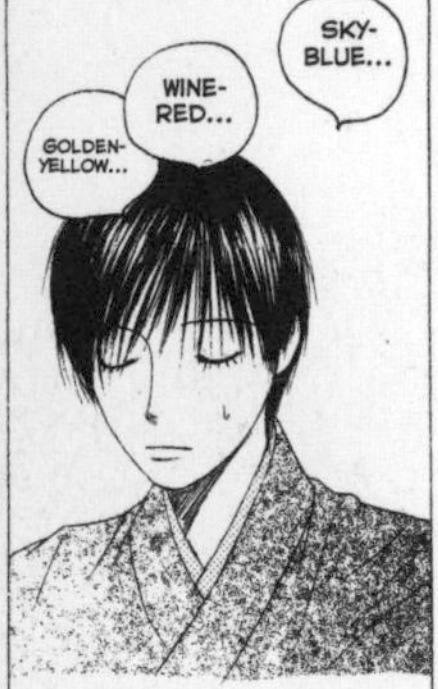
SKY-BLUE...
WINE-RED...
GOLDEN-YELLOW...

And now Arima can wear a kimono in color!

Little by little, I'm learning about Japanese clothes...

Aaaugh!

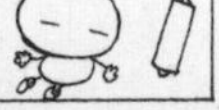

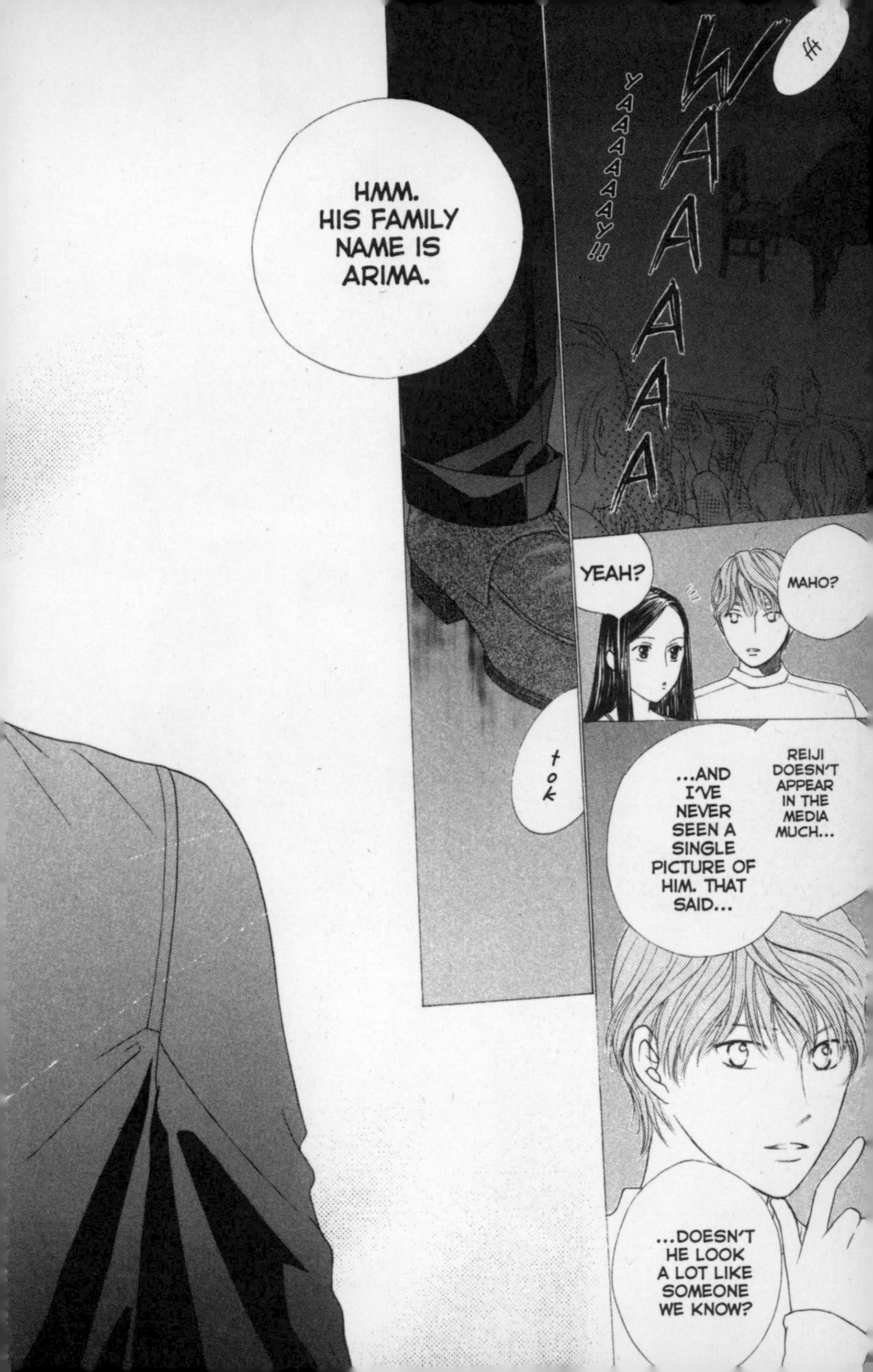
WAAAAAAA
YAAAAAAAY!!
MAHO?
YEAH?
REIJI DOESN'T APPEAR IN THE MEDIA MUCH...
...AND I'VE NEVER SEEN A SINGLE PICTURE OF HIM. THAT SAID...
...DOESN'T HE LOOK A LOT LIKE SOMEONE WE KNOW?
tok
HMM. HIS FAMILY NAME IS ARIMA.

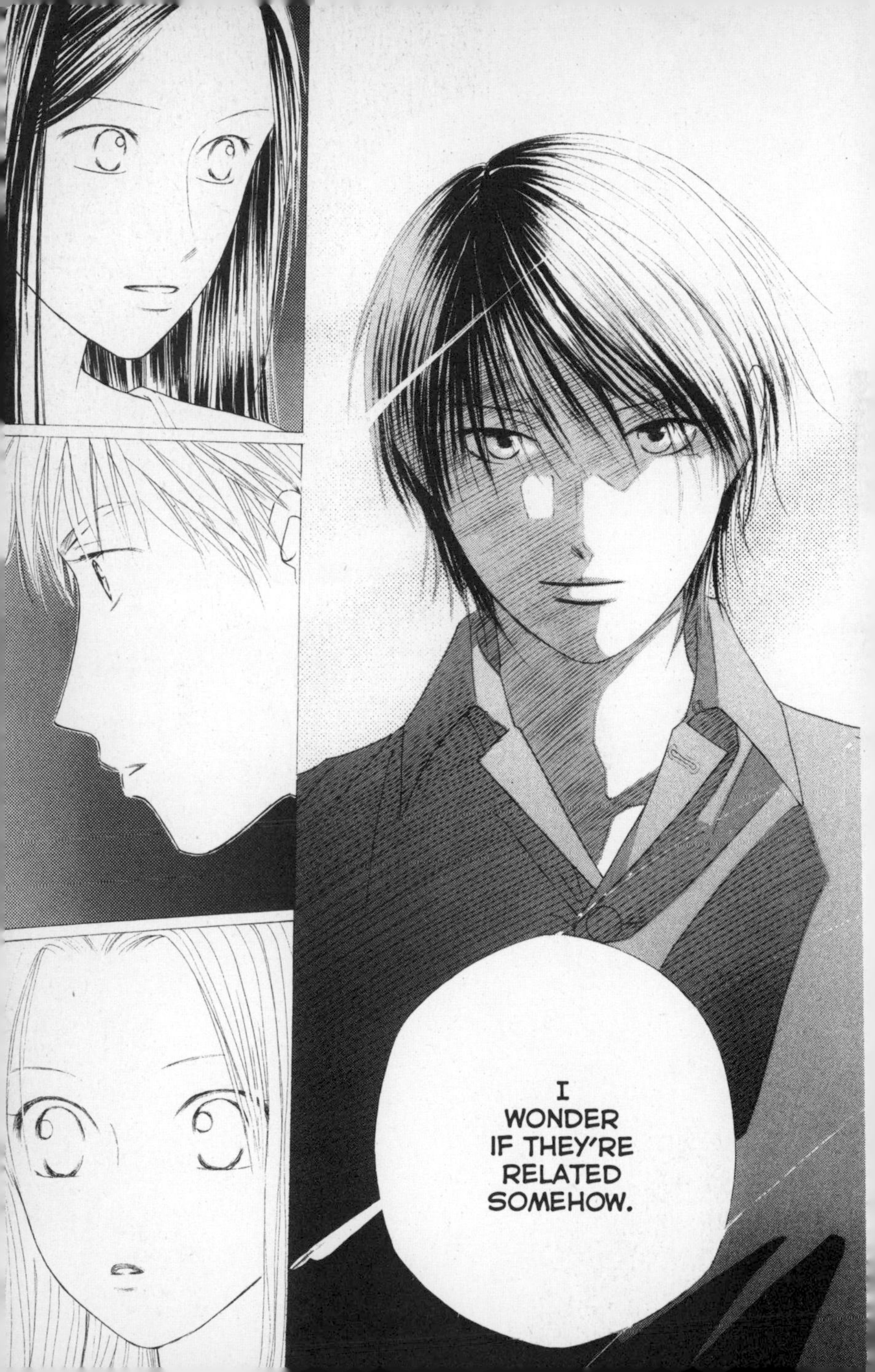
I WONDER IF THEY'RE RELATED SOMEHOW.

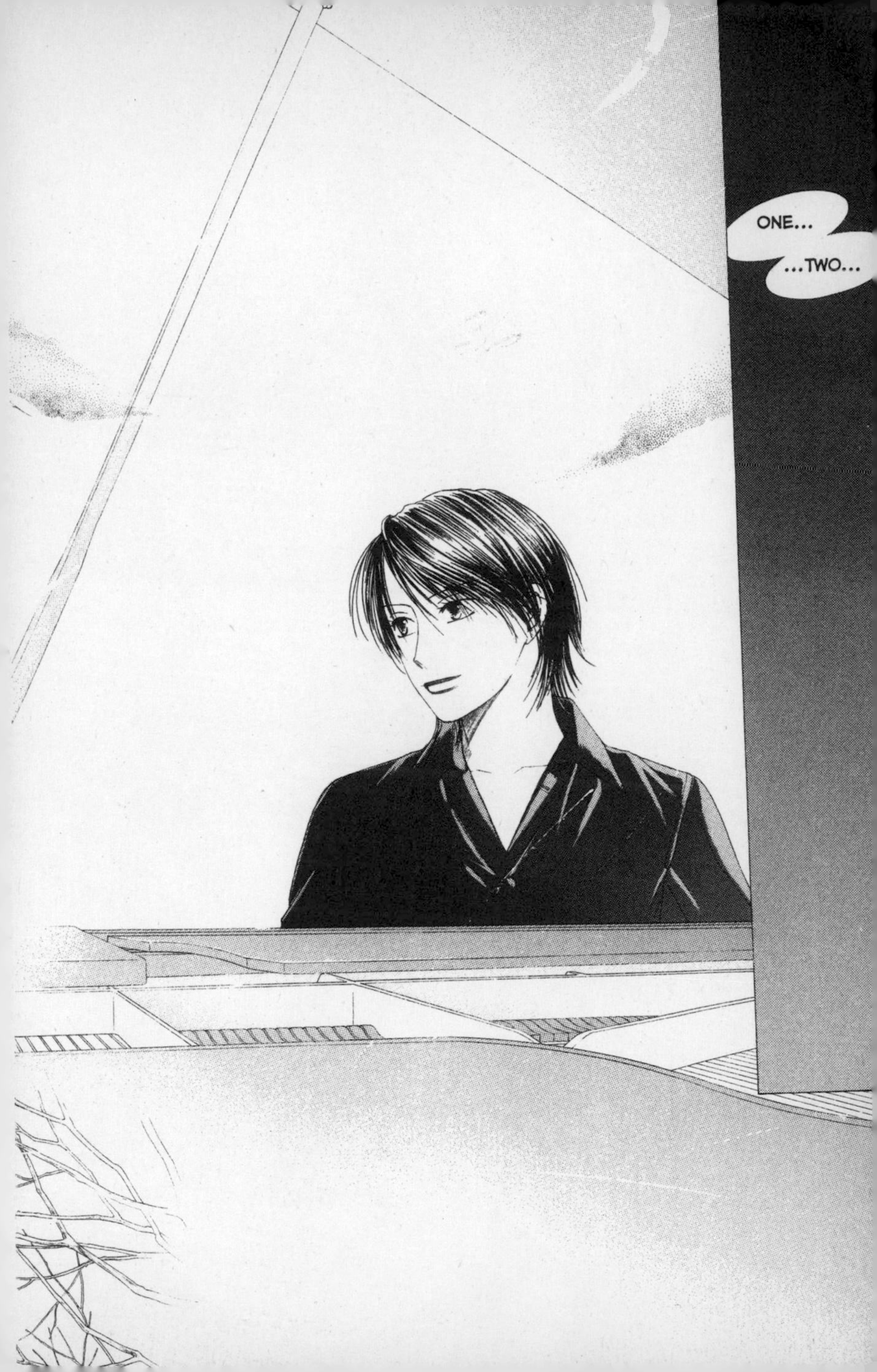
ONE...
...TWO...

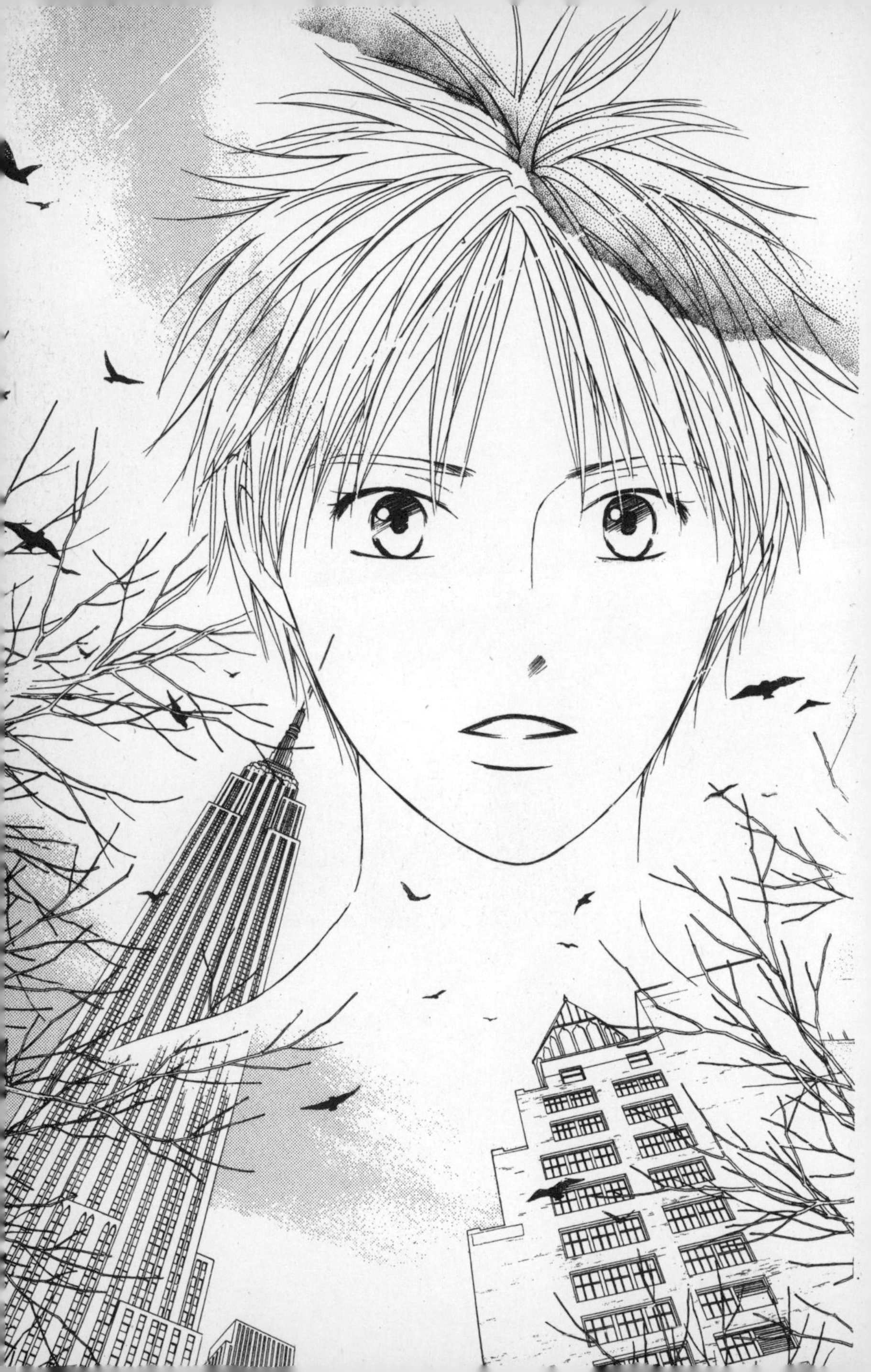

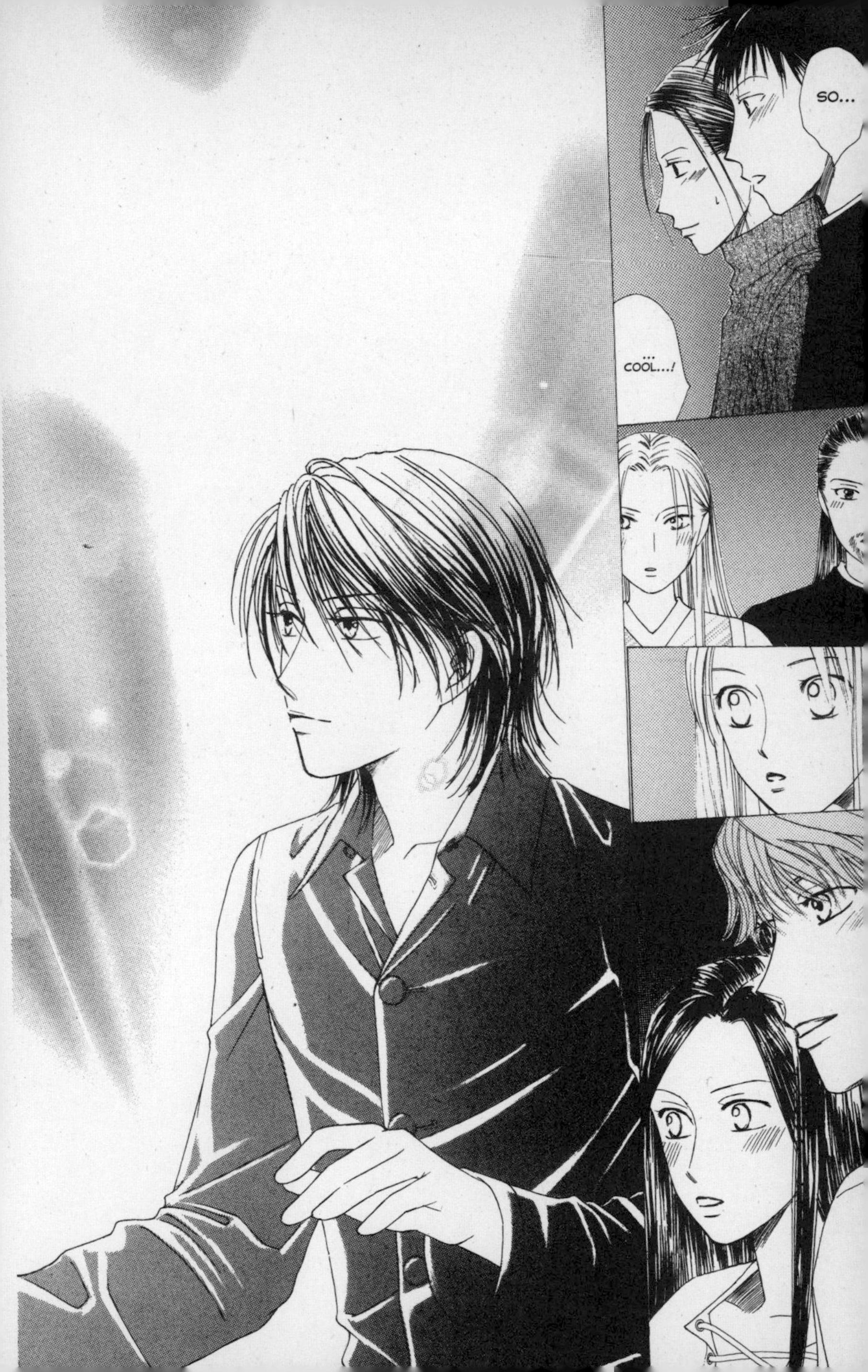
SO...
...COOL...!

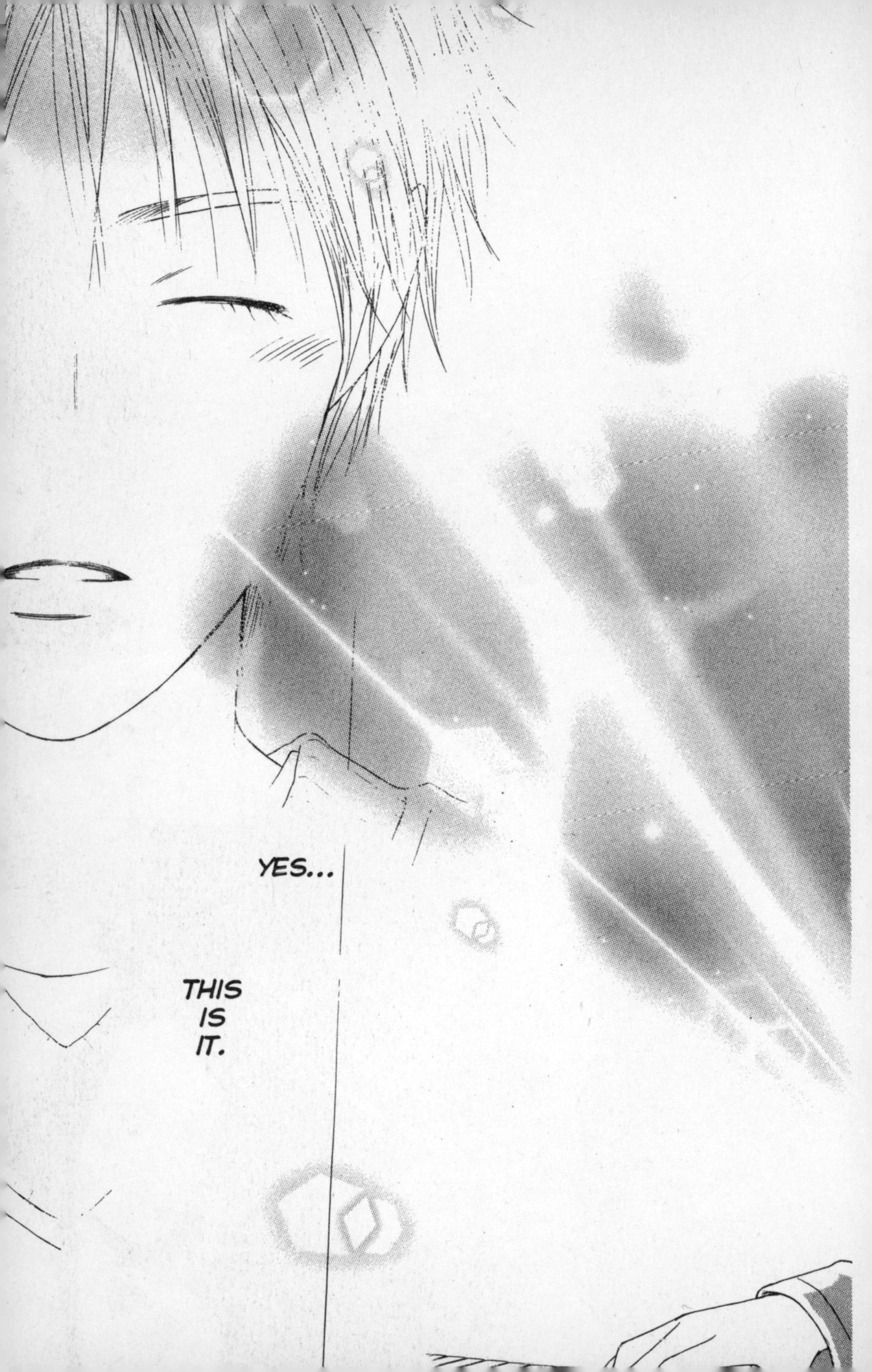
YES...
THIS IS IT.

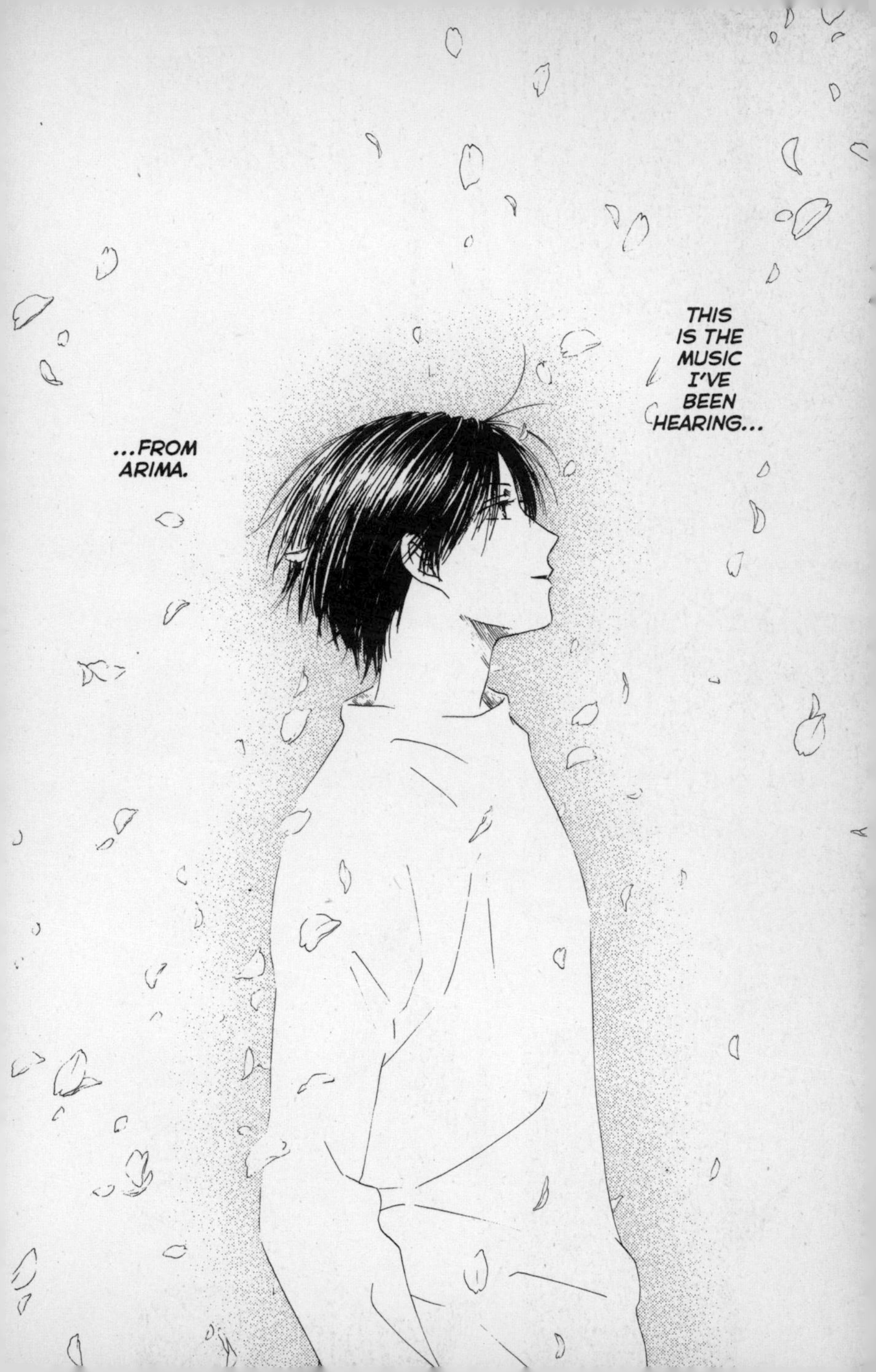
THIS IS THE MUSIC I'VE BEEN HEARING...
...FROM ARIMA.

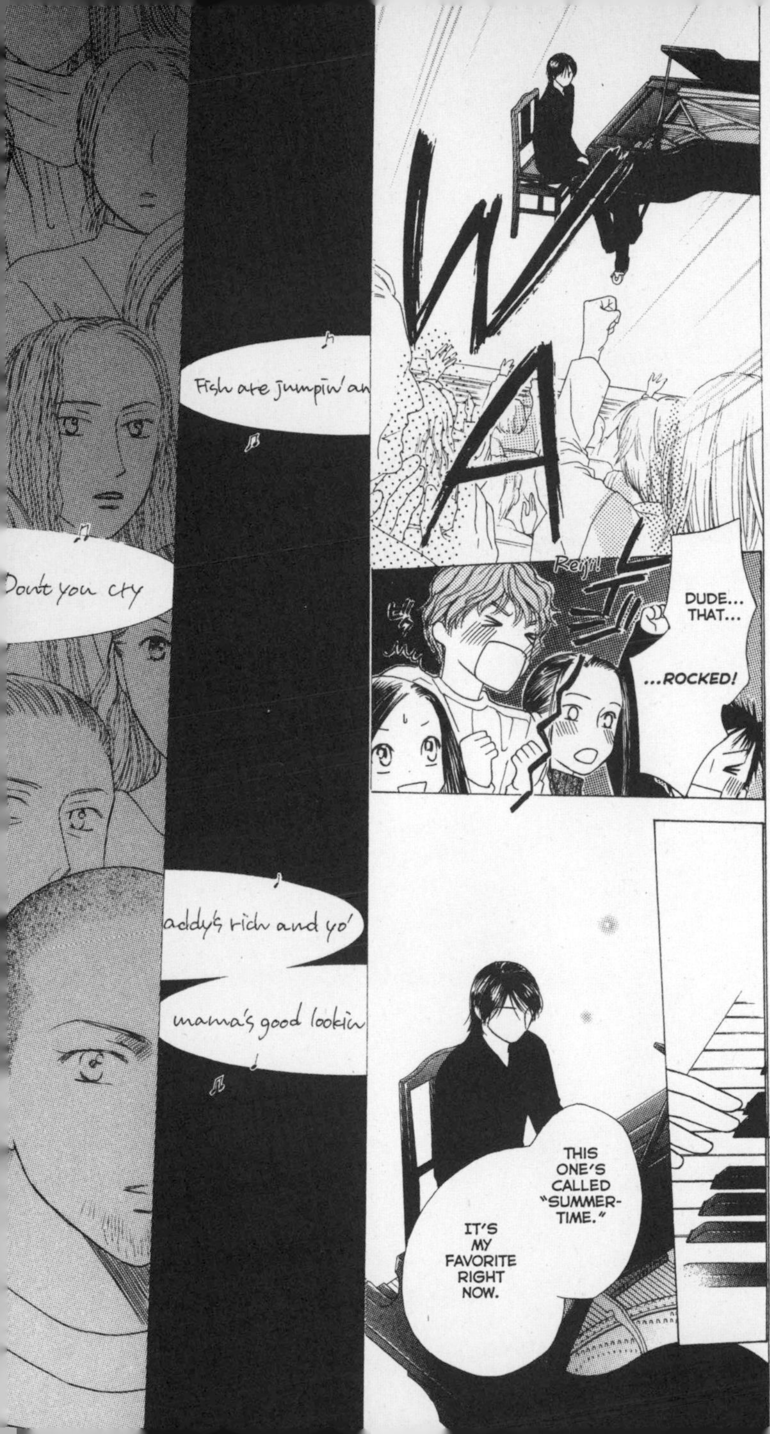
WA
Reiji!
DUDE... THAT...
...ROCKED!
THIS ONE'S CALLED "SUMMER-TIME."
IT'S MY FAVORITE RIGHT NOW.
Fish are jumpin' an
Dont you cry
addy's rich and yo'
mama's good lookin

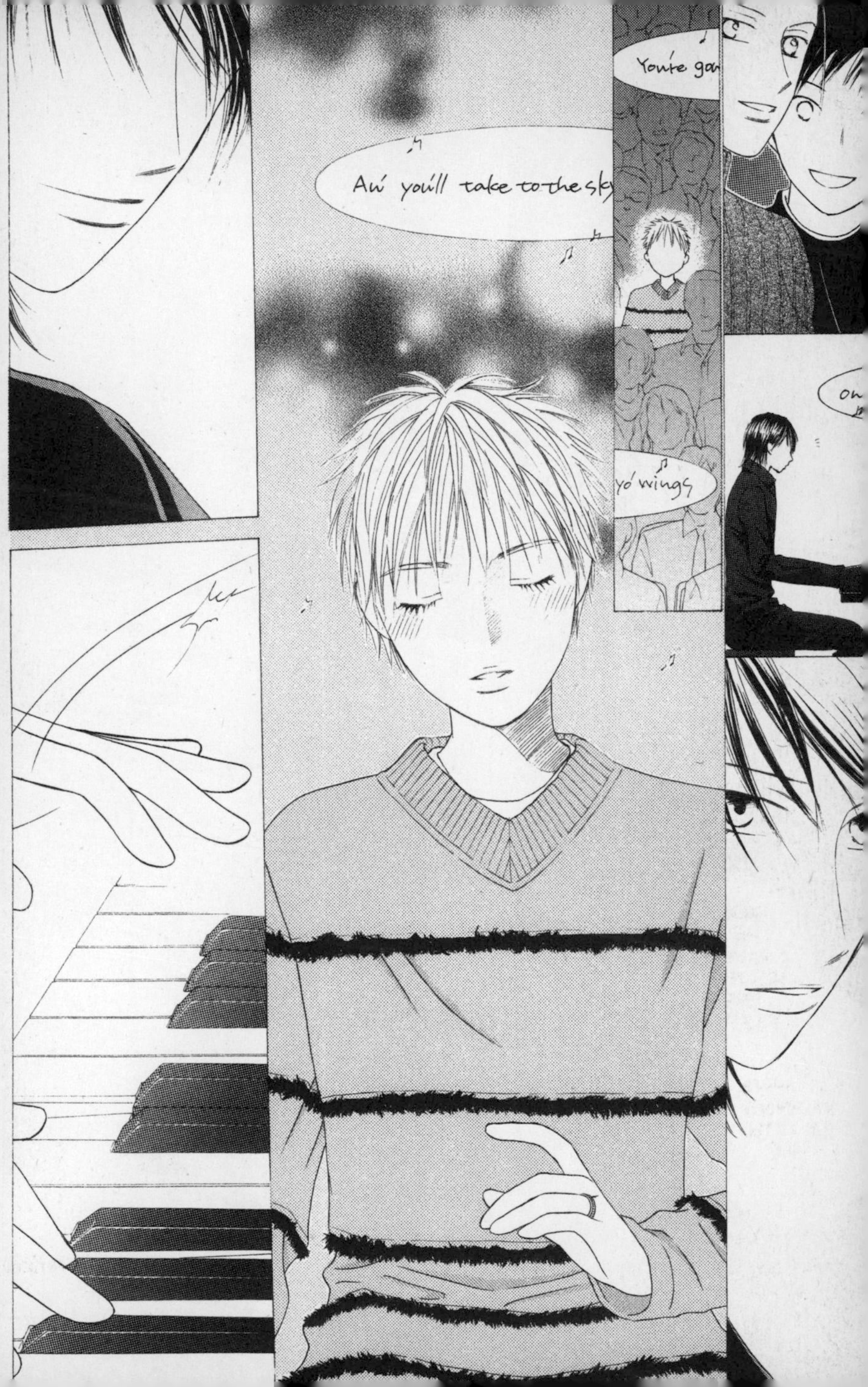
on
You're gon
yo' wings
Aw' you'll take to the sky

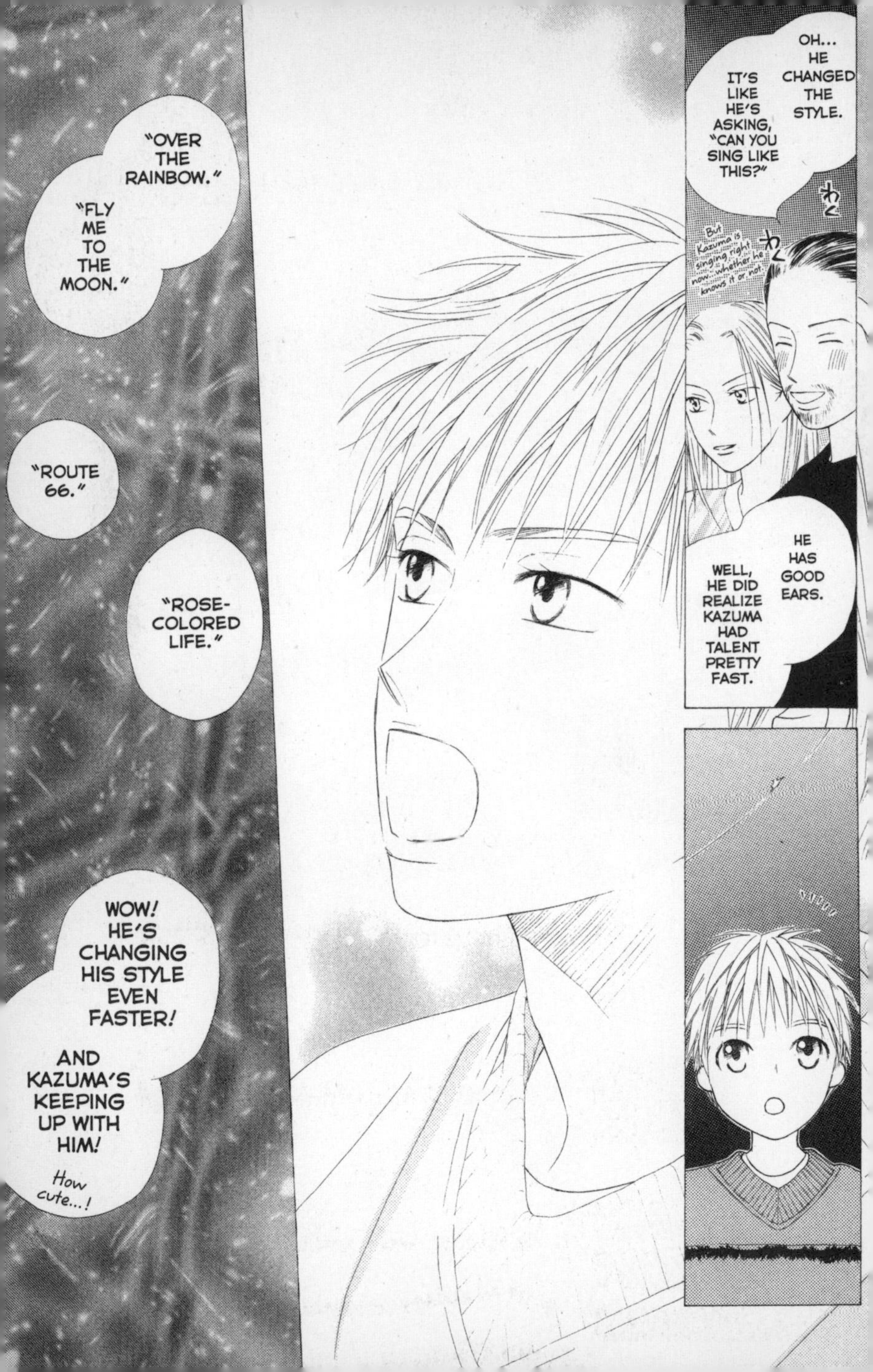
OH... HE CHANGED THE STYLE.
IT'S LIKE HE'S ASKING, "CAN YOU SING LIKE THIS?"
わく
わく
But Kazuma is singing right now... whether he knows it or not.
HE HAS GOOD EARS.
WELL, HE DID REALIZE KAZUMA HAD TALENT PRETTY FAST.
"OVER THE RAINBOW."
"FLY ME TO THE MOON."
"ROUTE 66."
"ROSE-COLORED LIFE."
WOW! HE'S CHANGING HIS STYLE EVEN FASTER!
AND KAZUMA'S KEEPING UP WITH HIM!
How cute...!

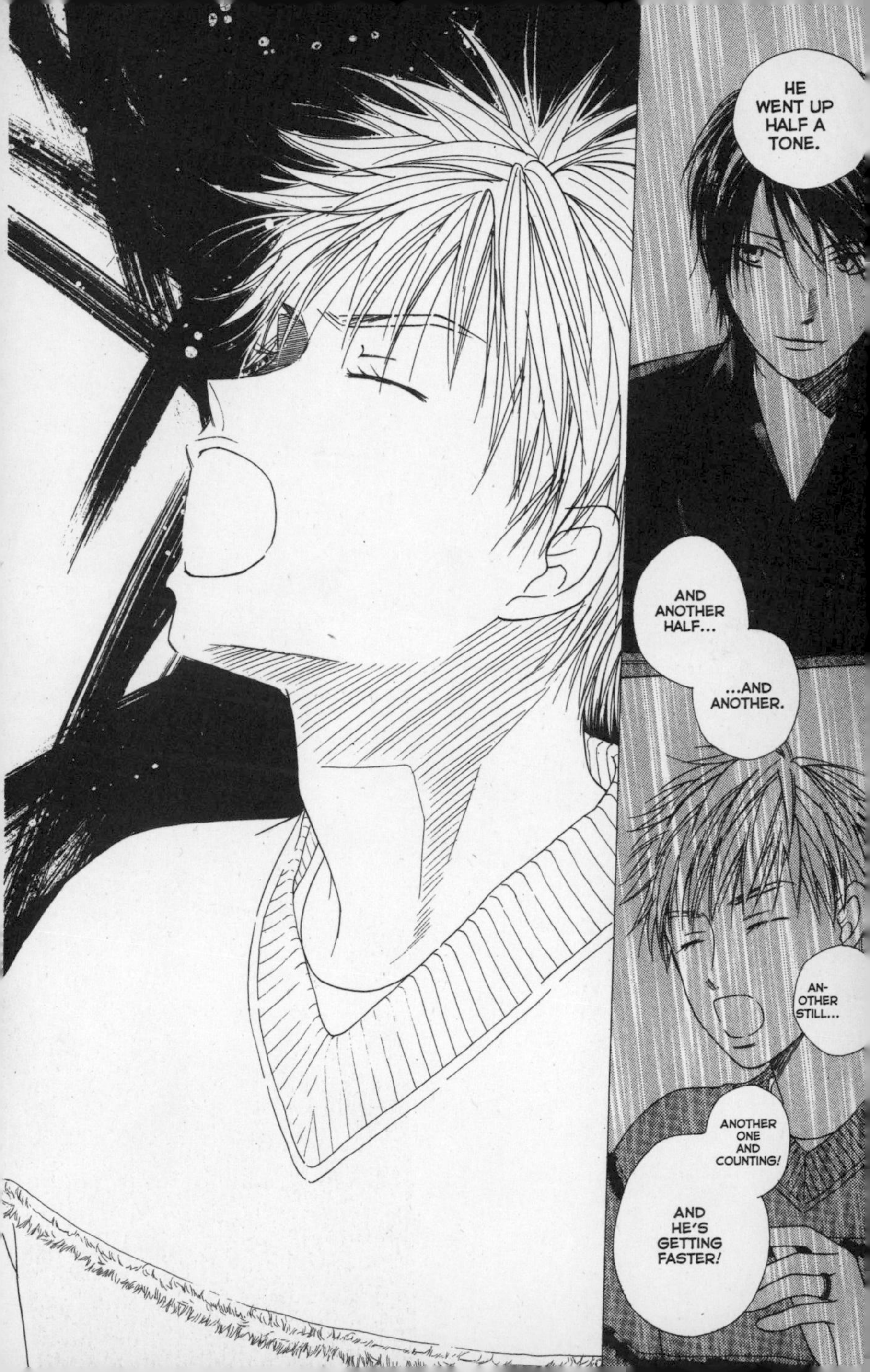
HE WENT UP HALF A TONE.
AND ANOTHER HALF...
...AND ANOTHER.
AN-OTHER STILL...
ANOTHER ONE AND COUNTING!
AND HE'S GETTING FASTER!

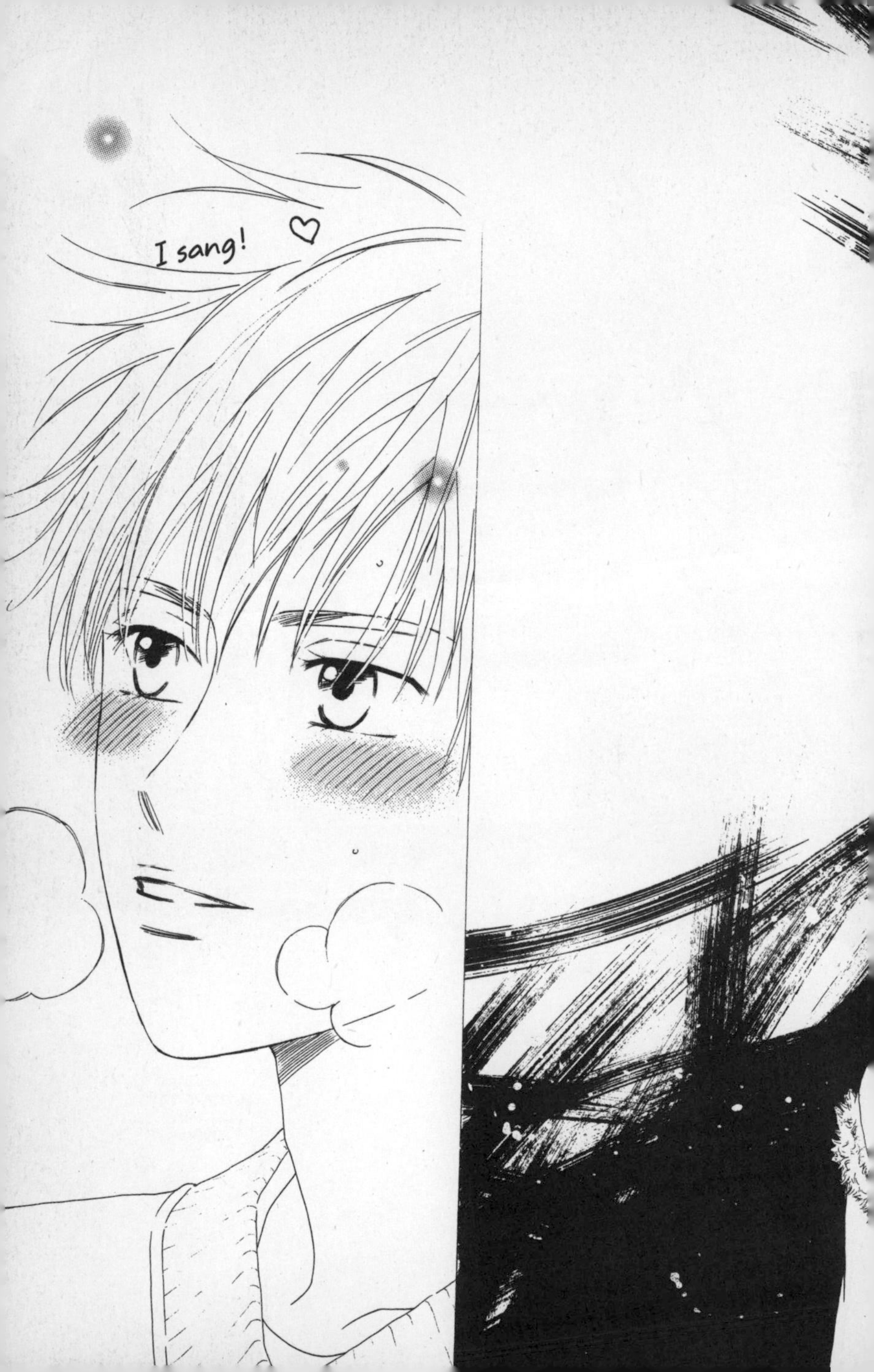
I sang!

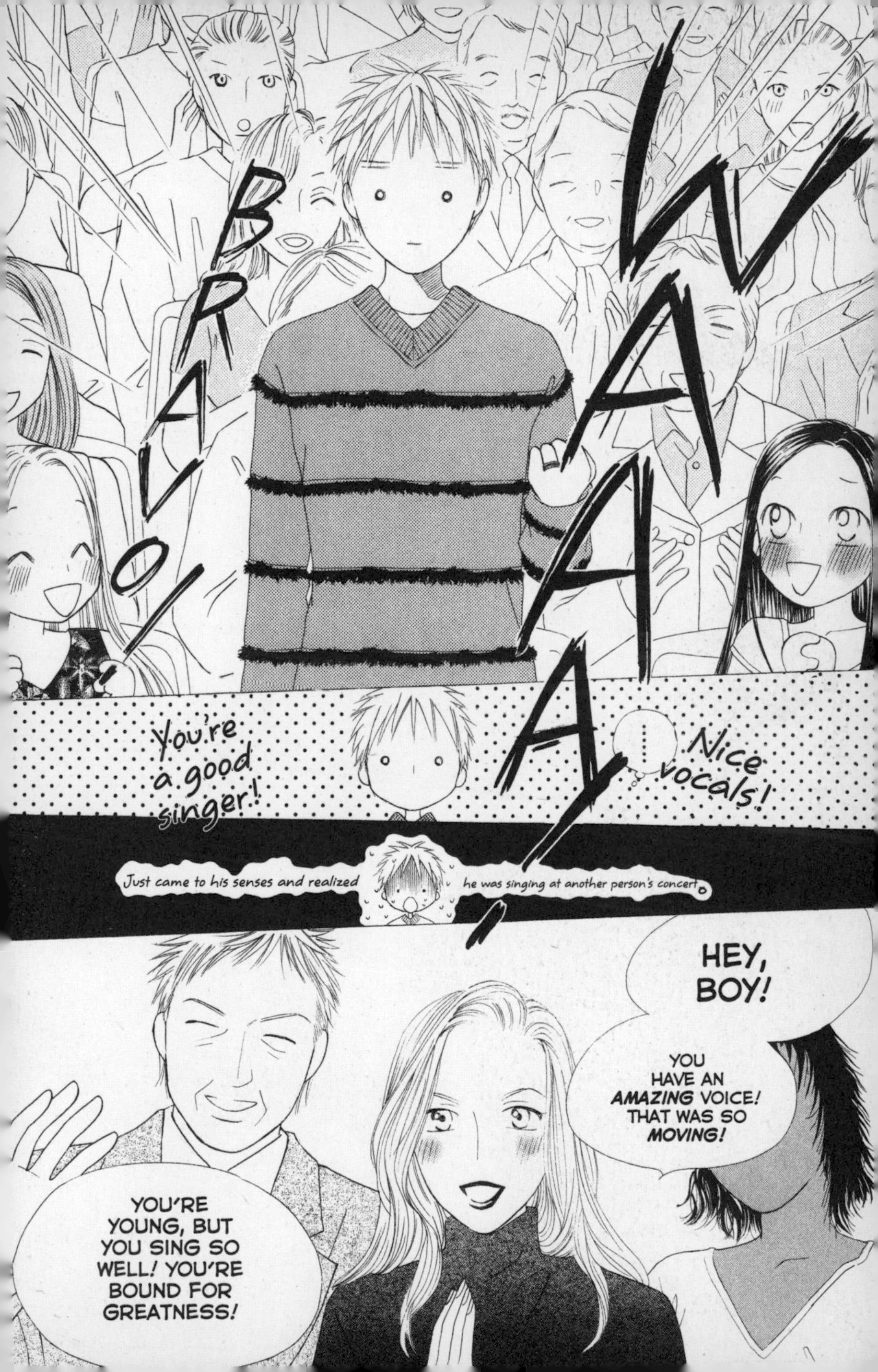
WAAAAY!
BRAVO!
Nice vocals!
You're a good singer!
Just came to his senses and realized he was singing at another person's concert.
HEY, BOY!
YOU HAVE AN *AMAZING* VOICE! THAT WAS SO *MOVING!*
YOU'RE YOUNG, BUT YOU SING SO WELL! YOU'RE BOUND FOR GREATNESS!

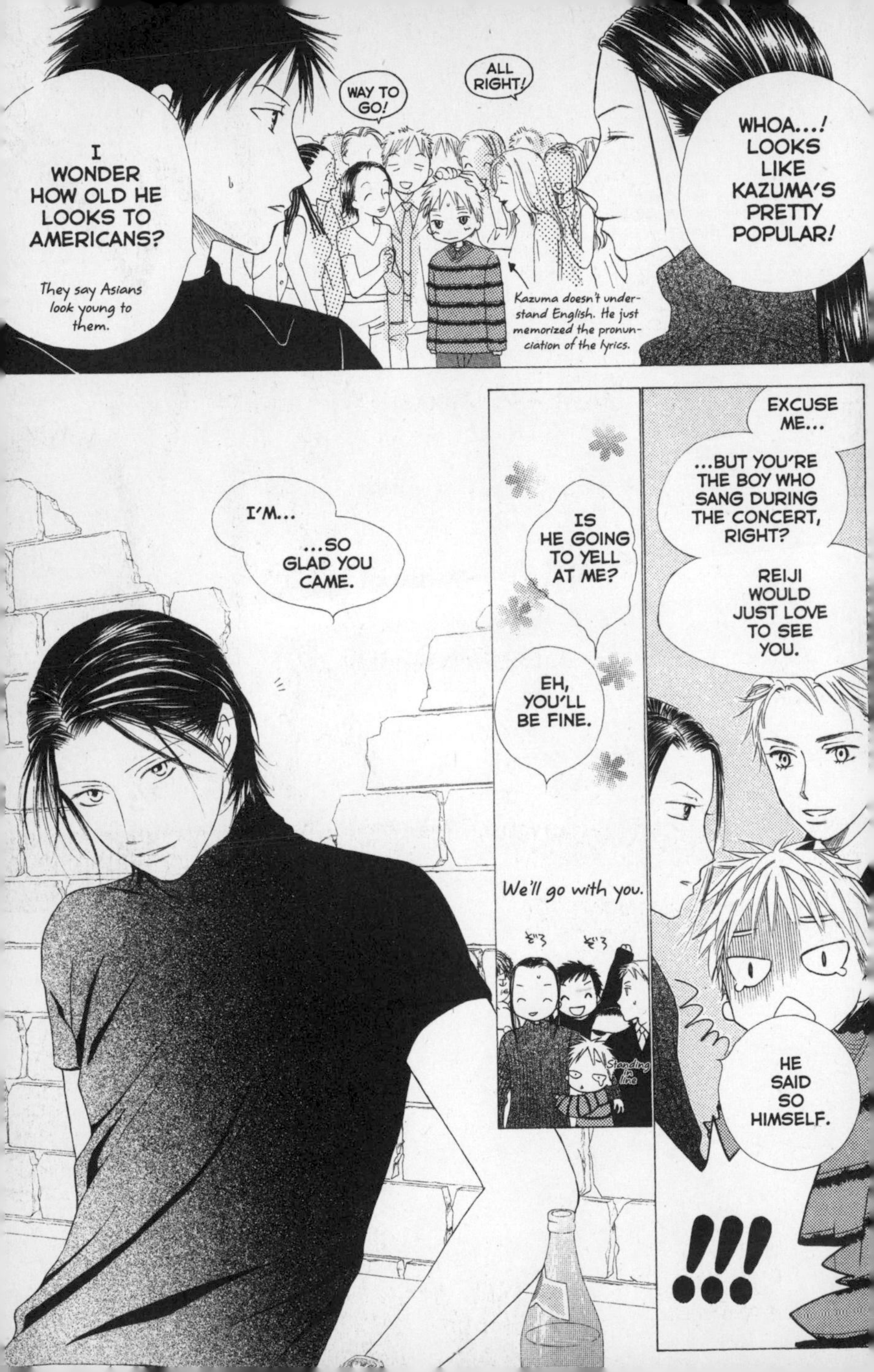
WHOA...! LOOKS LIKE KAZUMA'S PRETTY POPULAR!
ALL RIGHT!
WAY TO GO!
Kazuma doesn't understand English. He just memorized the pronunciation of the lyrics.
I WONDER HOW OLD HE LOOKS TO AMERICANS?
They say Asians look young to them.
EXCUSE ME...
...BUT YOU'RE THE BOY WHO SANG DURING THE CONCERT, RIGHT?
REIJI WOULD JUST LOVE TO SEE YOU.
HE SAID SO HIMSELF.
!!!
IS HE GOING TO YELL AT ME?
EH, YOU'LL BE FINE.
We'll go with you.
ぞろ
ぞろ
Standing in line
I'M...
...SO GLAD YOU CAME.

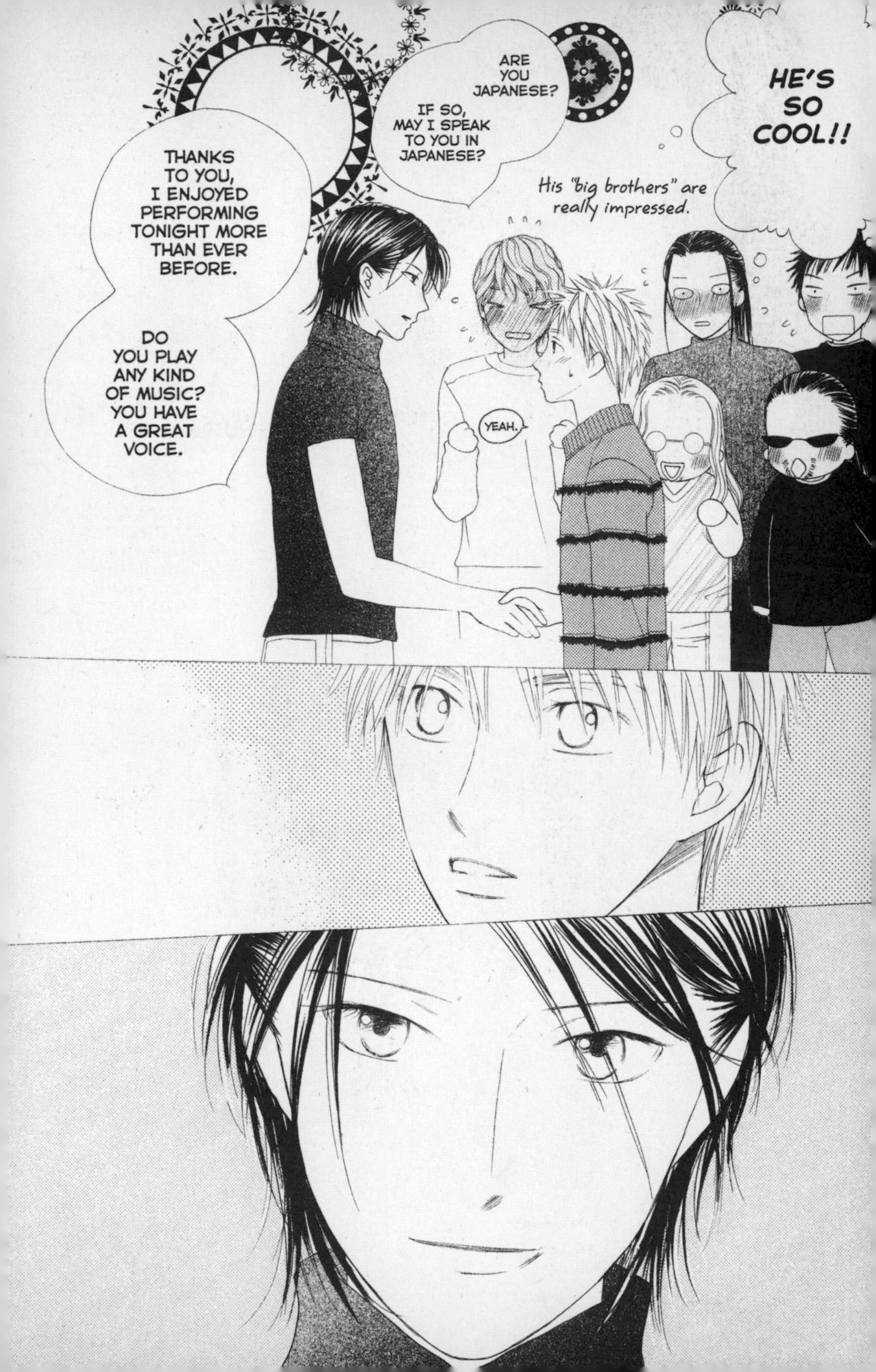
HE'S SO COOL!!
ARE YOU JAPANESE?
IF SO, MAY I SPEAK TO YOU IN JAPANESE?
His "big brothers" are really impressed.
THANKS TO YOU, I ENJOYED PERFORMING TONIGHT MORE THAN EVER BEFORE.
DO YOU PLAY ANY KIND OF MUSIC? YOU HAVE A GREAT VOICE.
YEAH.

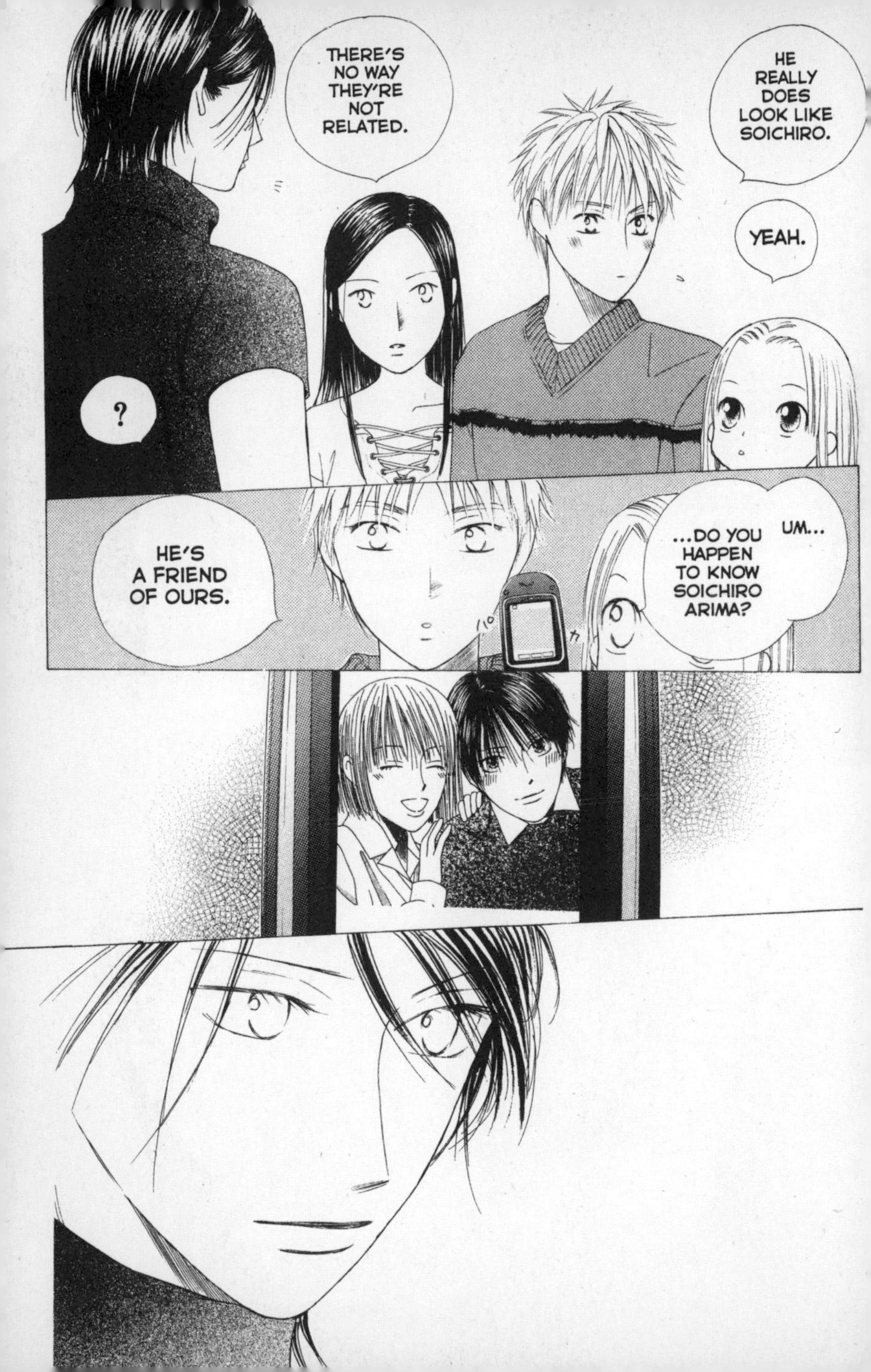
HE REALLY DOES LOOK LIKE SOICHIRO.
YEAH.
THERE'S NO WAY THEY'RE NOT RELATED.
?
UM...
...DO YOU HAPPEN TO KNOW SOICHIRO ARIMA?
HE'S A FRIEND OF OURS.

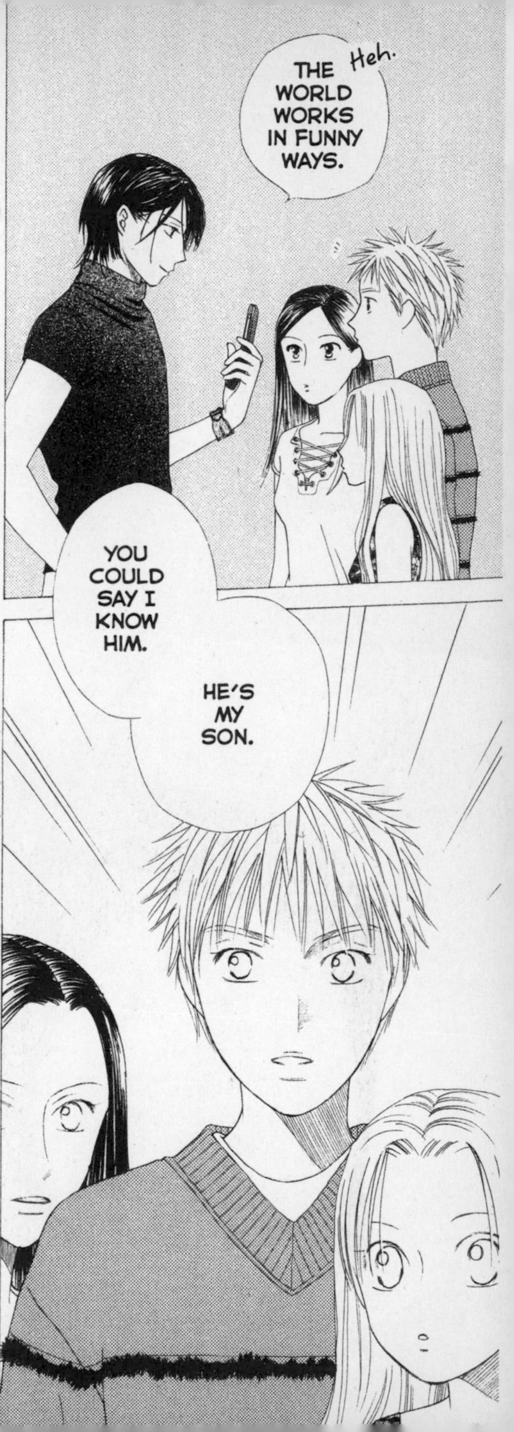
Heh.
THE WORLD WORKS IN FUNNY WAYS.
YOU COULD SAY I KNOW HIM.
HE'S MY SON.
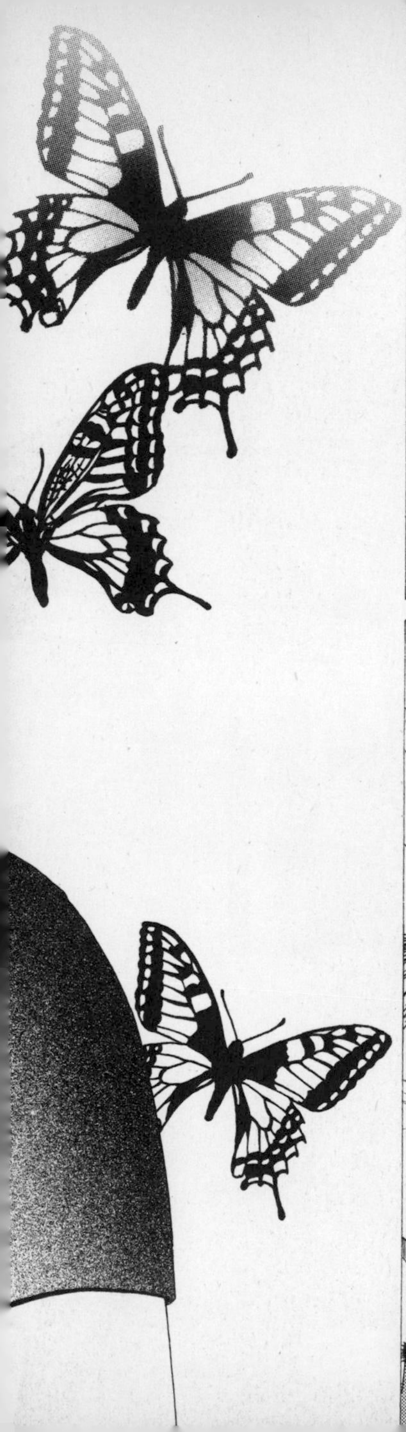

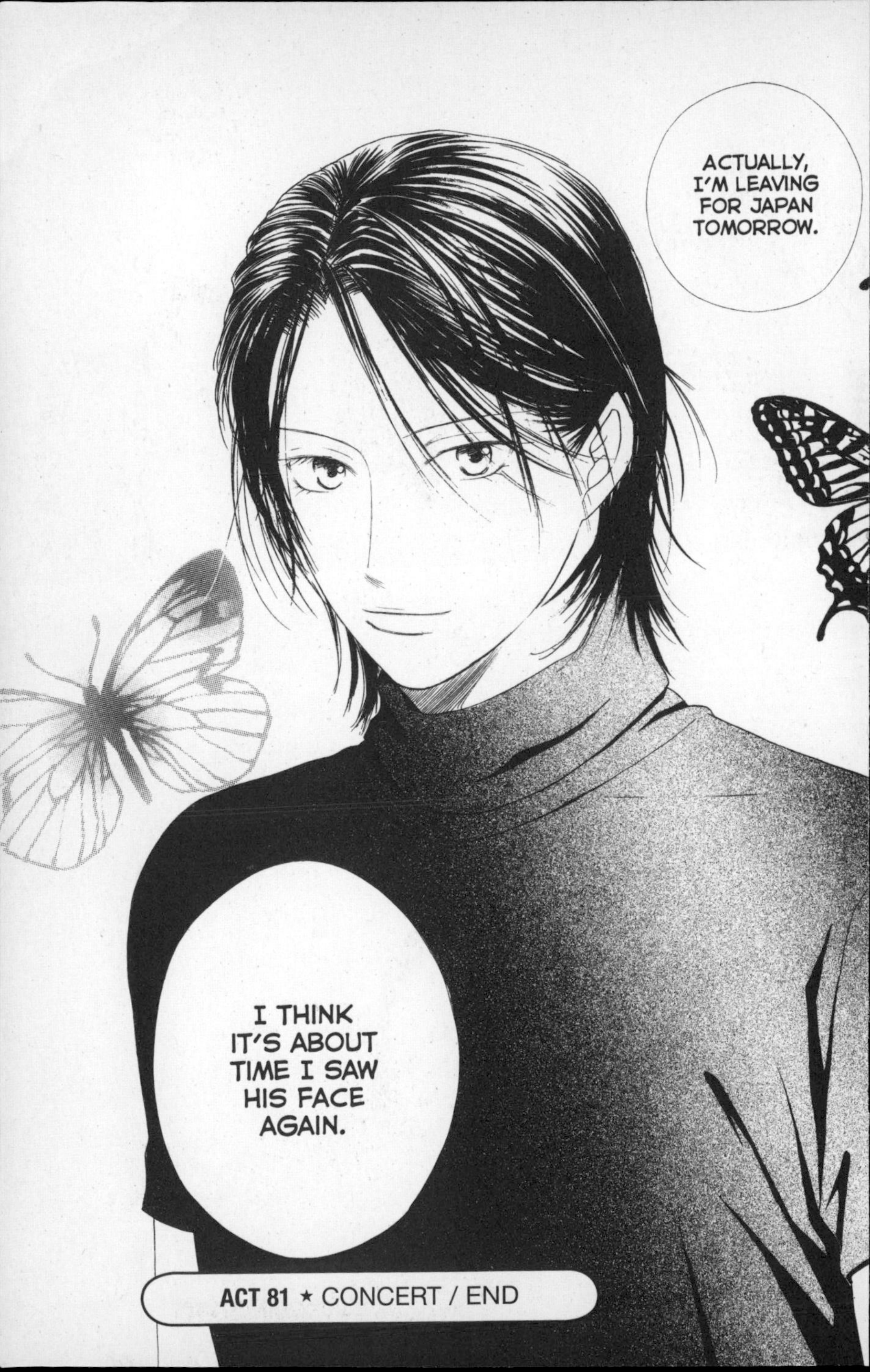
ACTUALLY, I'M LEAVING FOR JAPAN TOMORROW.
I THINK IT'S ABOUT TIME I SAW HIS FACE AGAIN.
ACT 81 ★ CONCERT / END

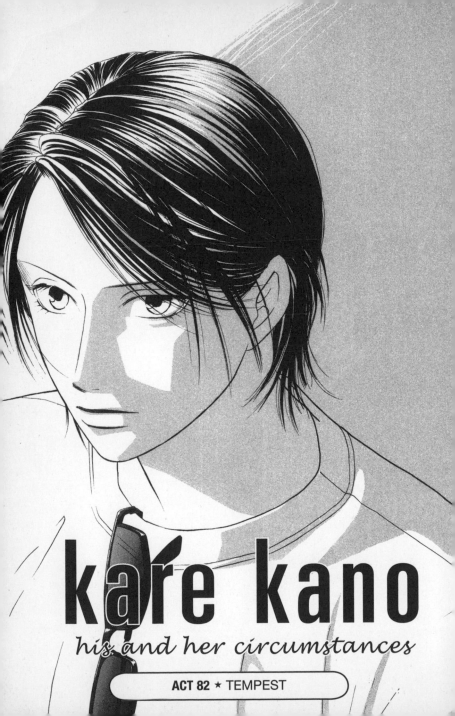

kare kano

his and her circumstances

ACT 82 ★ TEMPEST

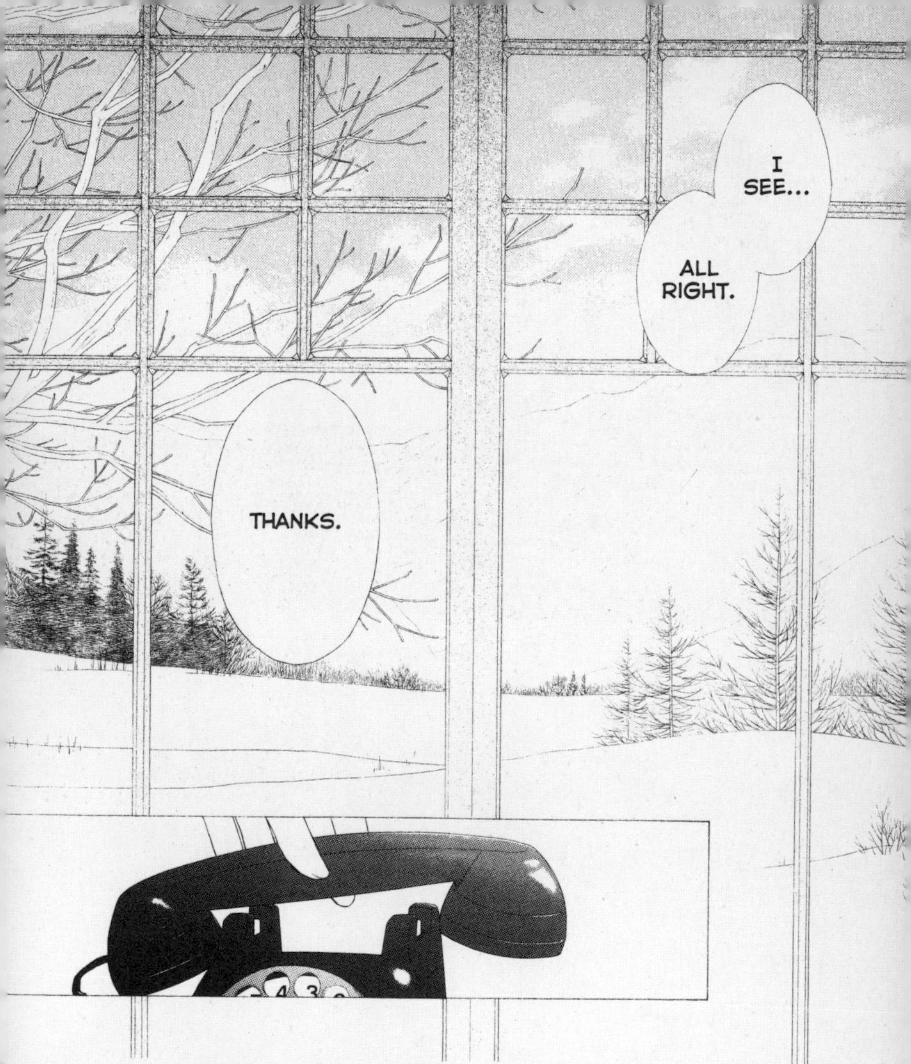
I SEE...
ALL RIGHT.
THANKS.

Chinese Food

I don't eat Chinese food much, but every time I DO eat it...

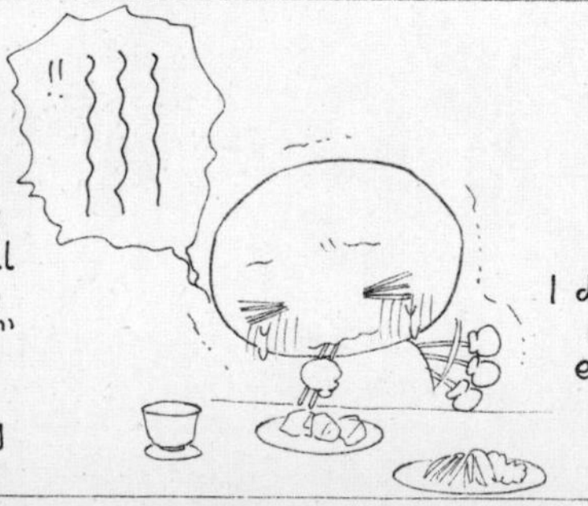
!!

...I get REALLY excited. So I guess that means I like it. Perhaps I'll make it the next "theme" for my next cooking experiment.

As for Chinese teas, I've been into buigancha lately.

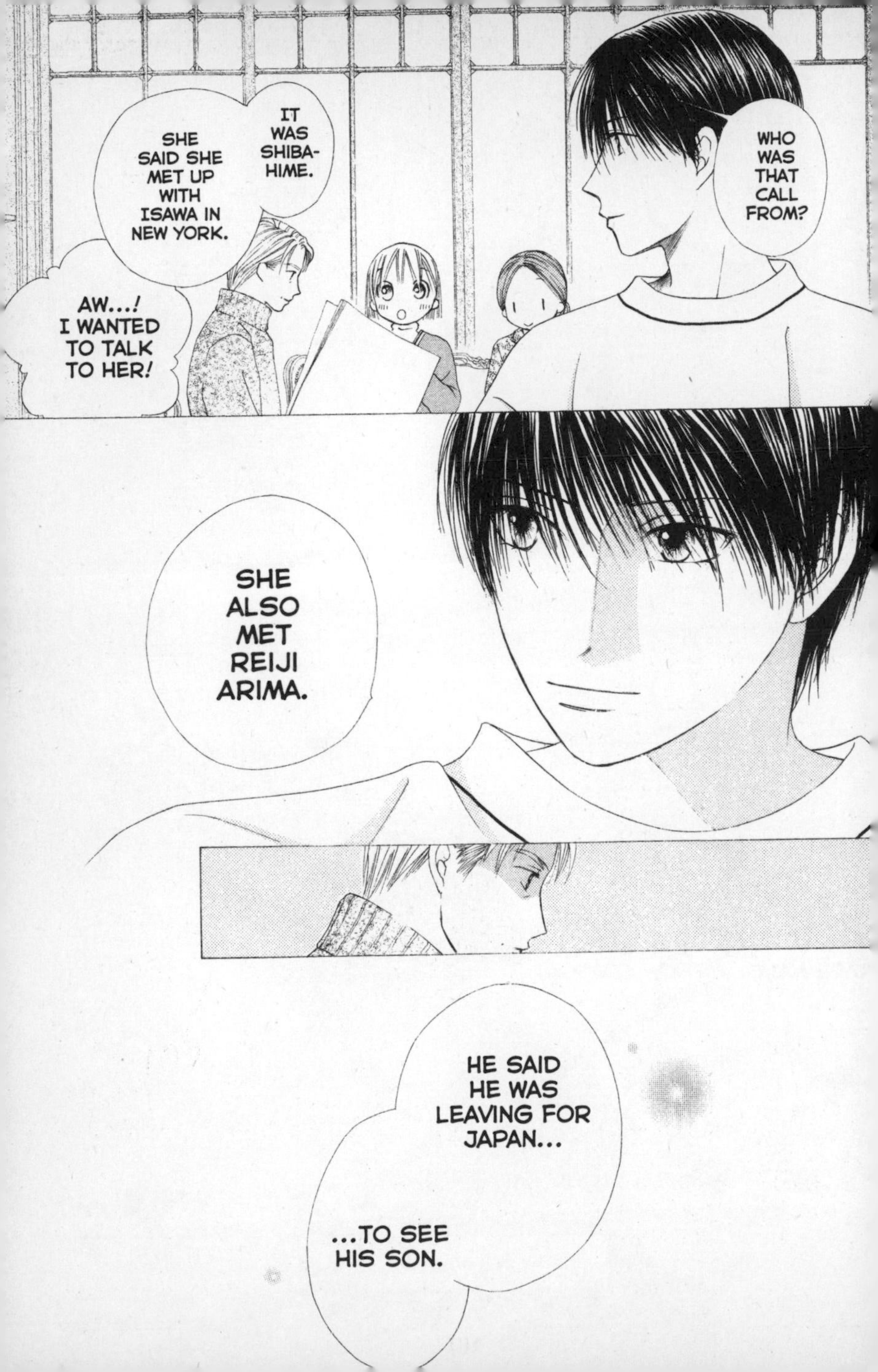
WHO WAS THAT CALL FROM?
IT WAS SHIBA-HIME.
SHE SAID SHE MET UP WITH ISAWA IN NEW YORK.
AW...! I WANTED TO TALK TO HER!
SHE ALSO MET REIJI ARIMA.
HE SAID HE WAS LEAVING FOR JAPAN...
...TO SEE HIS SON.

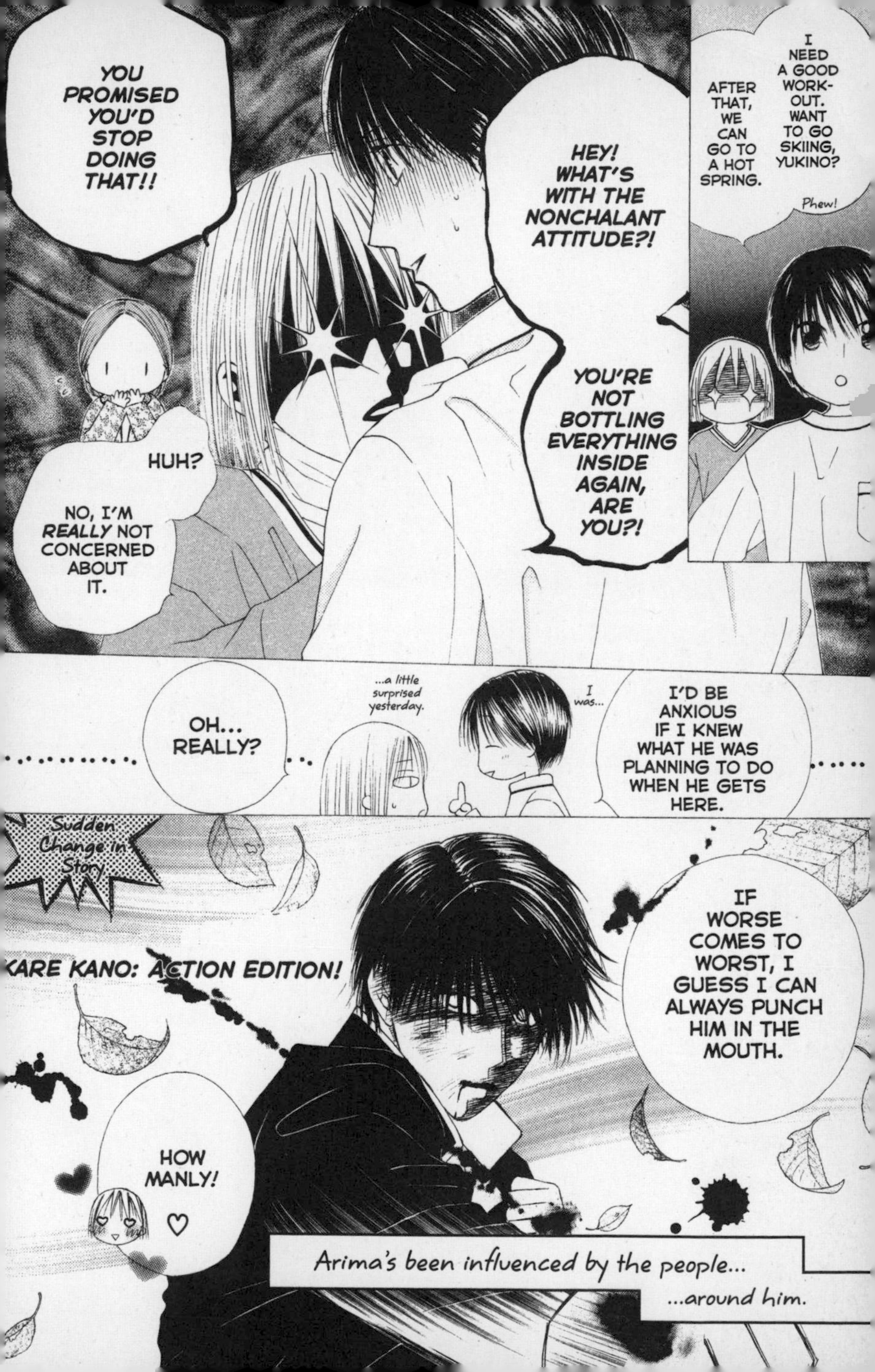
I NEED A GOOD WORK-OUT. WANT TO GO SKIING, YUKINO?
AFTER THAT, WE CAN GO TO A HOT SPRING.
Phew!
HEY! WHAT'S WITH THE NONCHALANT ATTITUDE?!
YOU'RE NOT BOTTLING EVERYTHING INSIDE AGAIN, ARE YOU?!
YOU PROMISED YOU'D STOP DOING THAT!!
HUH?
NO, I'M *REALLY* NOT CONCERNED ABOUT IT.
I'D BE ANXIOUS IF I KNEW WHAT HE WAS PLANNING TO DO WHEN HE GETS HERE.
I was...
...a little surprised yesterday.
OH... REALLY?
IF WORSE COMES TO WORST, I GUESS I CAN ALWAYS PUNCH HIM IN THE MOUTH.
Sudden Change in Story
KARE KANO: ACTION EDITION!
HOW MANLY!
Arima's been influenced by the people...
...around him.

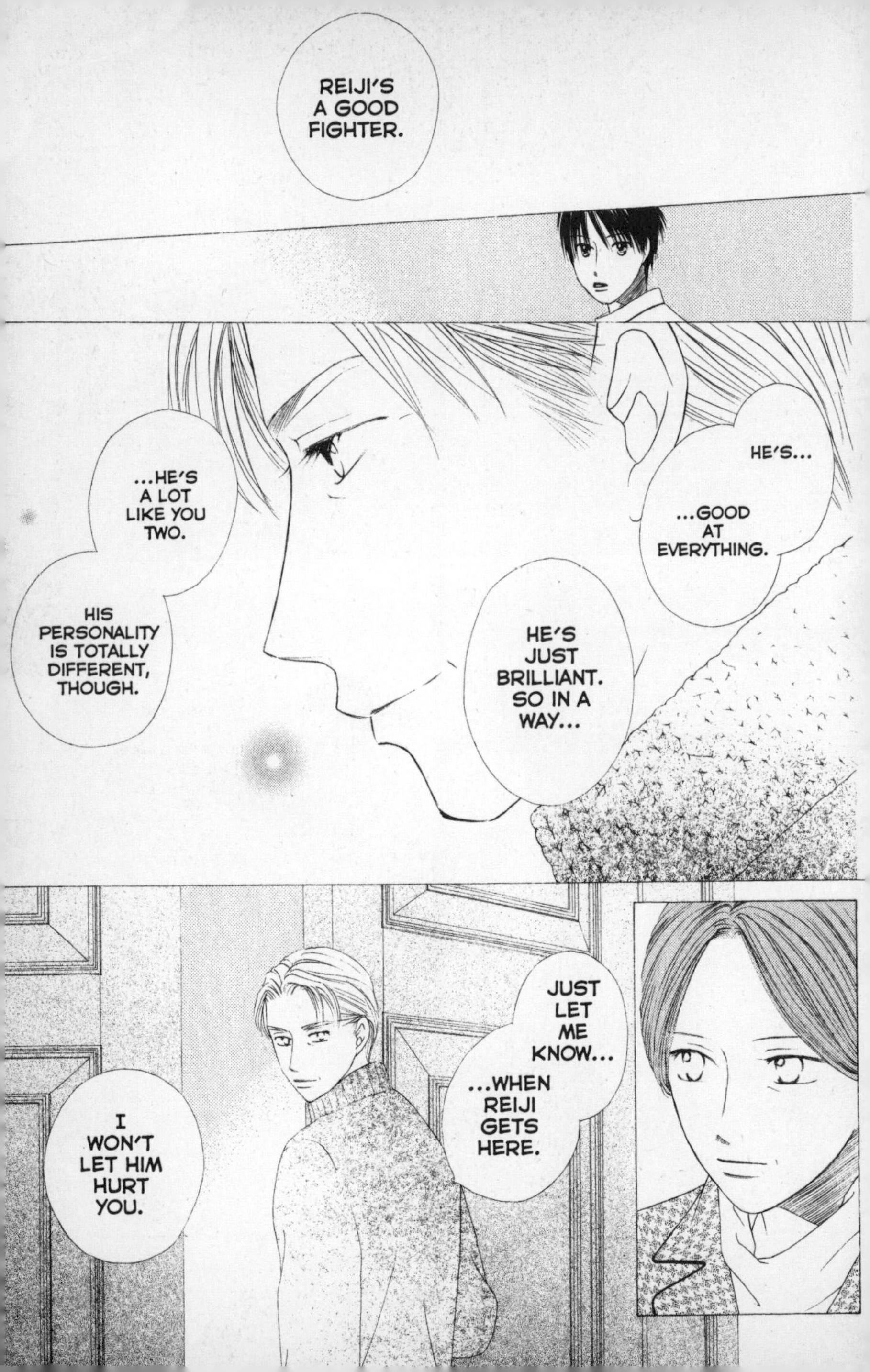
REIJI'S A GOOD FIGHTER.
HE'S...
...GOOD AT EVERYTHING.
HE'S JUST BRILLIANT. SO IN A WAY...
...HE'S A LOT LIKE YOU TWO.
HIS PERSONALITY IS TOTALLY DIFFERENT, THOUGH.
JUST LET ME KNOW...
...WHEN REIJI GETS HERE.
I WON'T LET HIM HURT YOU.

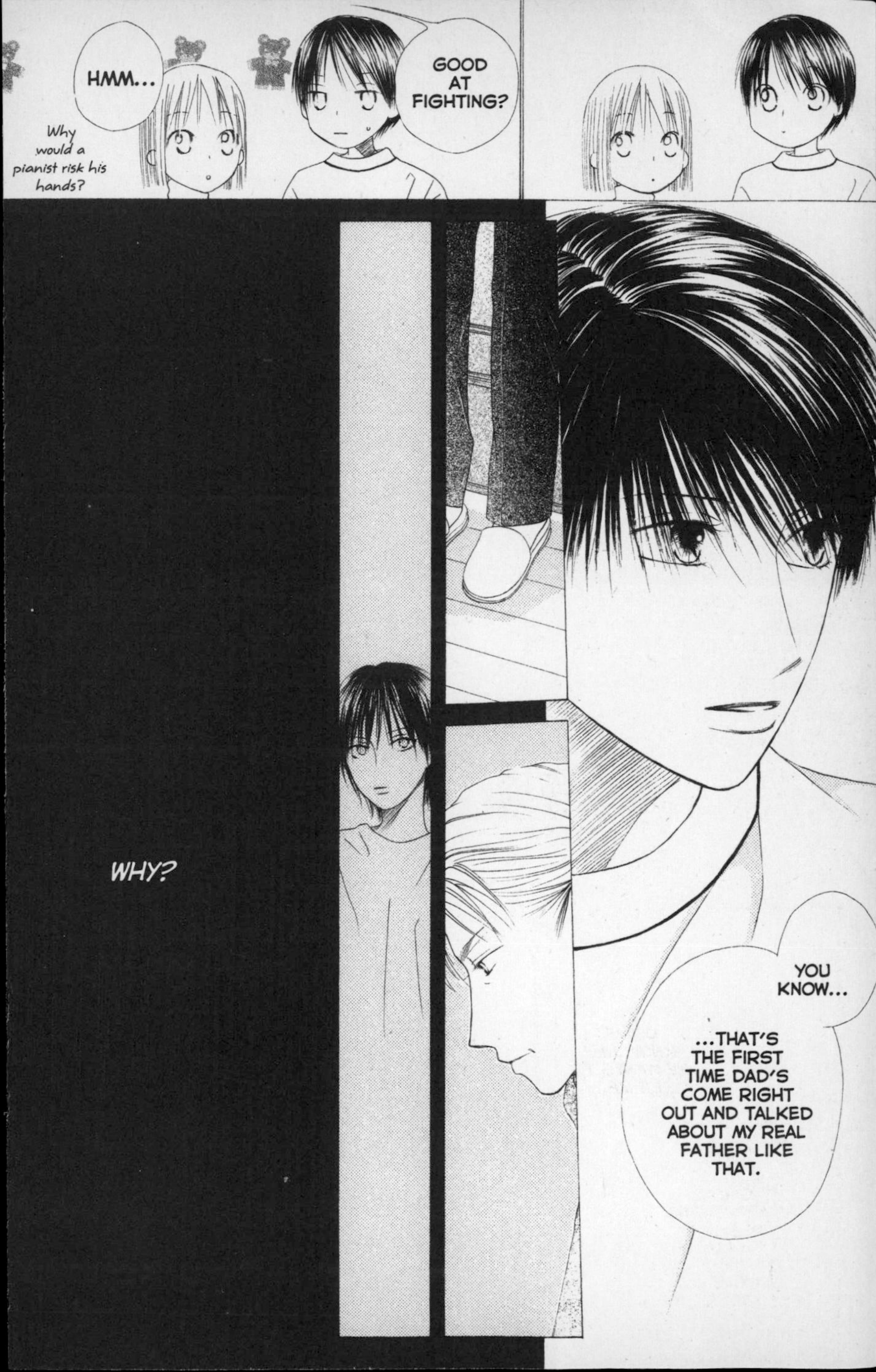
GOOD AT FIGHTING?
HMM...
Why would a pianist risk his hands?
YOU KNOW...
...THAT'S THE FIRST TIME DAD'S COME RIGHT OUT AND TALKED ABOUT MY REAL FATHER LIKE THAT.
WHY?

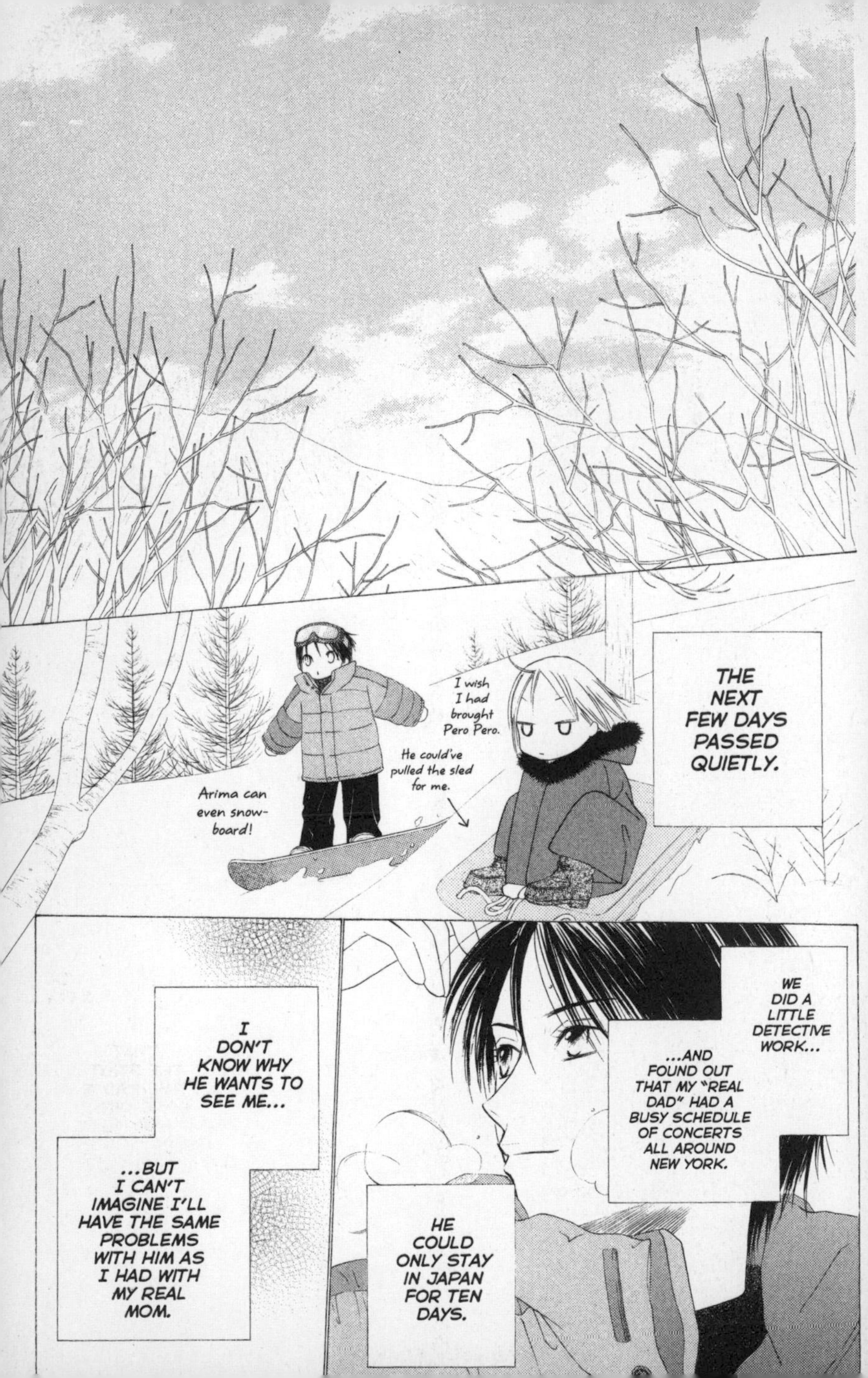
THE NEXT FEW DAYS PASSED QUIETLY.
I wish I had brought Pero Pero.
He could've pulled the sled for me.
Arima can even snow-board!
WE DID A LITTLE DETECTIVE WORK...
...AND FOUND OUT THAT MY "REAL DAD" HAD A BUSY SCHEDULE OF CONCERTS ALL AROUND NEW YORK.
HE COULD ONLY STAY IN JAPAN FOR TEN DAYS.
I DON'T KNOW WHY HE WANTS TO SEE ME...
...BUT I CAN'T IMAGINE I'LL HAVE THE SAME PROBLEMS WITH HIM AS I HAD WITH MY REAL MOM.

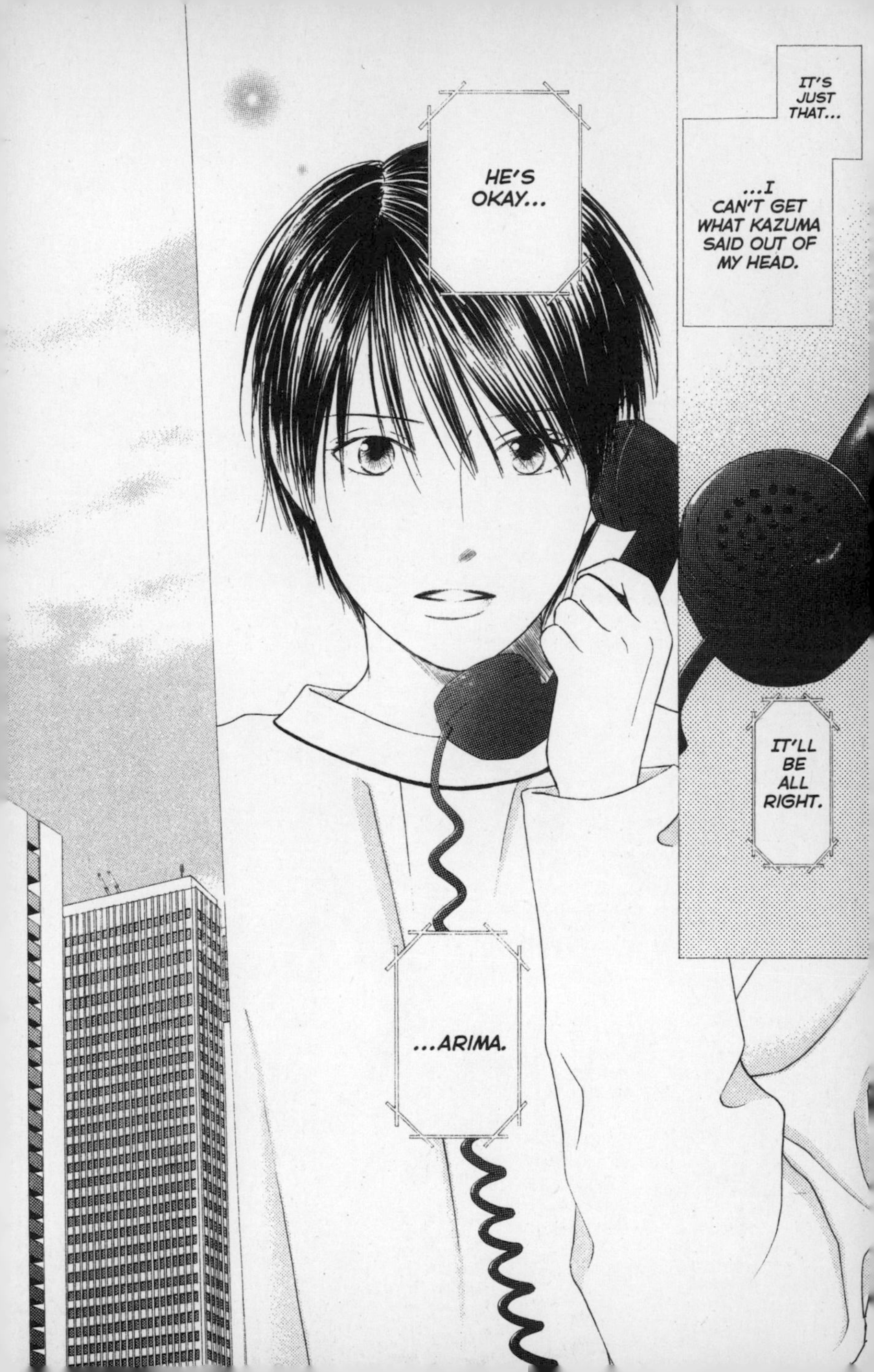
IT'S JUST THAT...
...I CAN'T GET WHAT KAZUMA SAID OUT OF MY HEAD.
IT'LL BE ALL RIGHT.
HE'S OKAY...
...ARIMA.

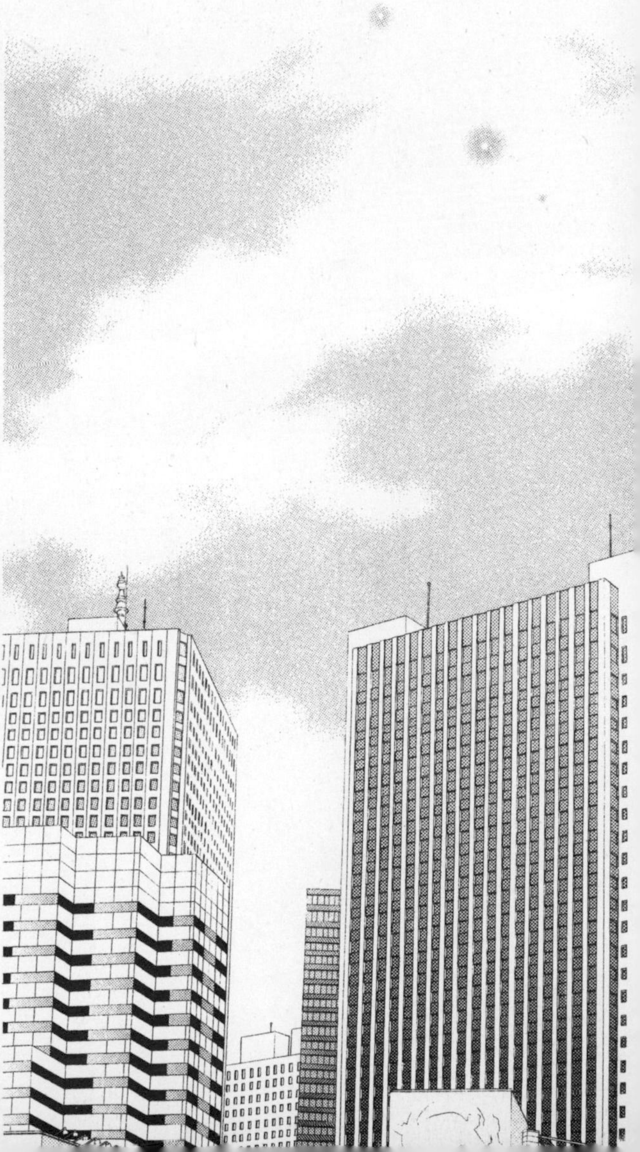

4

Tea Sets

When I'm working, I can guzzle down two or three liters of tea in a day. So I figure, why not be a little more discriminating?

Small luncheon set

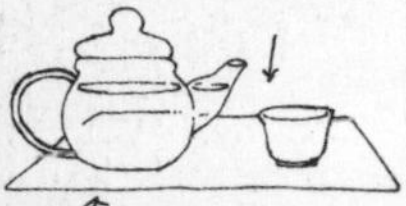

Once the tea is brewed, I put it into this pot.

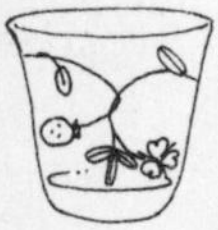

I saw this Wedgwood cup in a magazine, and went right out to buy it. There are wild straw-berries on it.

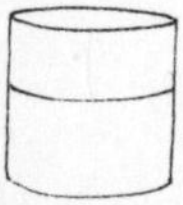

This is a silver tea can I bought at a tea shop. I put green tea in the bigger part and Chinese tea in the smaller part.

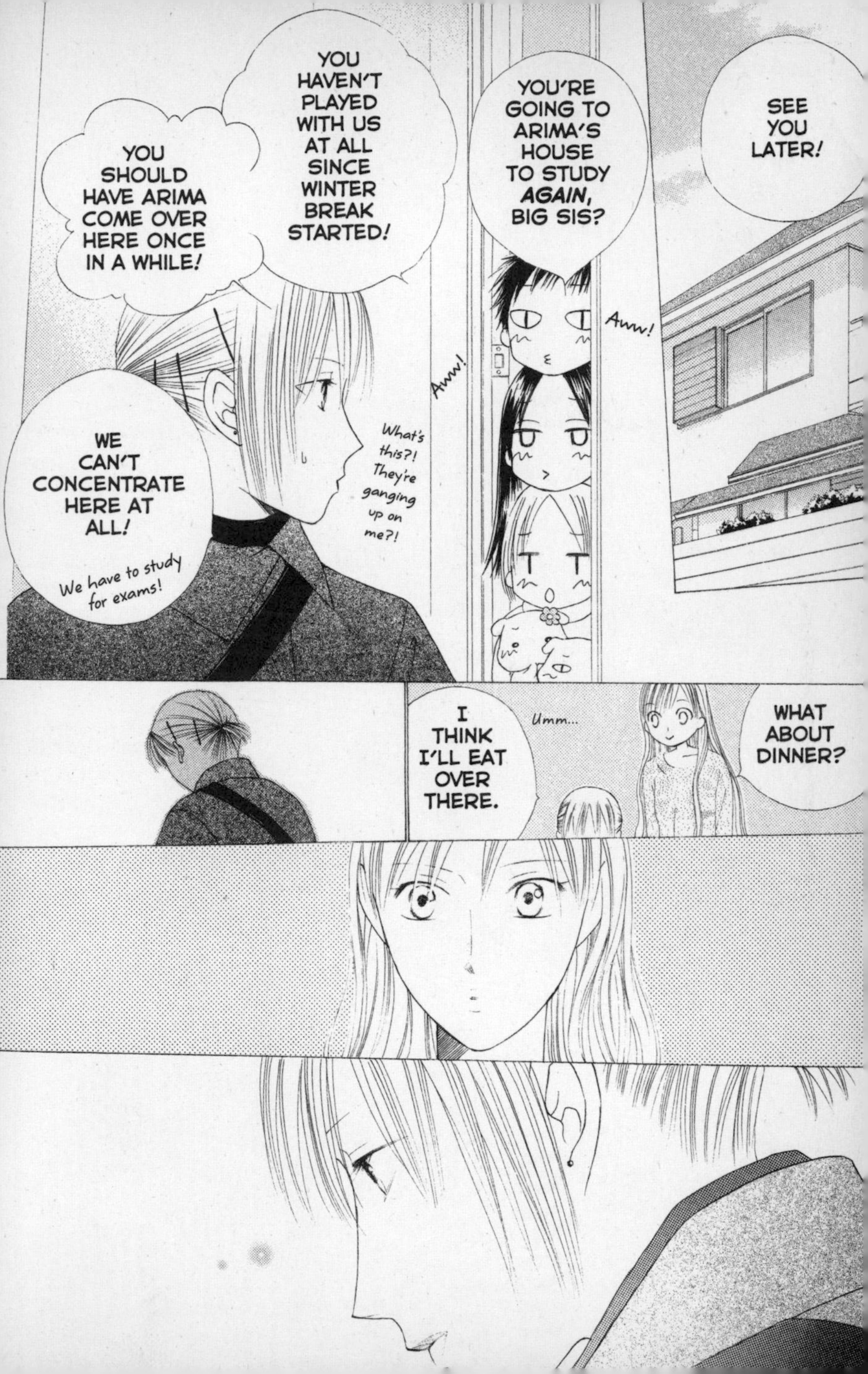
SEE YOU LATER!
YOU'RE GOING TO ARIMA'S HOUSE TO STUDY *AGAIN*, BIG SIS?
Aww!
Aww!
YOU HAVEN'T PLAYED WITH US AT ALL SINCE WINTER BREAK STARTED!
YOU SHOULD HAVE ARIMA COME OVER HERE ONCE IN A WHILE!
What's this?! They're ganging up on me?!
WE CAN'T CONCENTRATE HERE AT ALL!
We have to study for exams!
WHAT ABOUT DINNER?
Umm...
I THINK I'LL EAT OVER THERE.

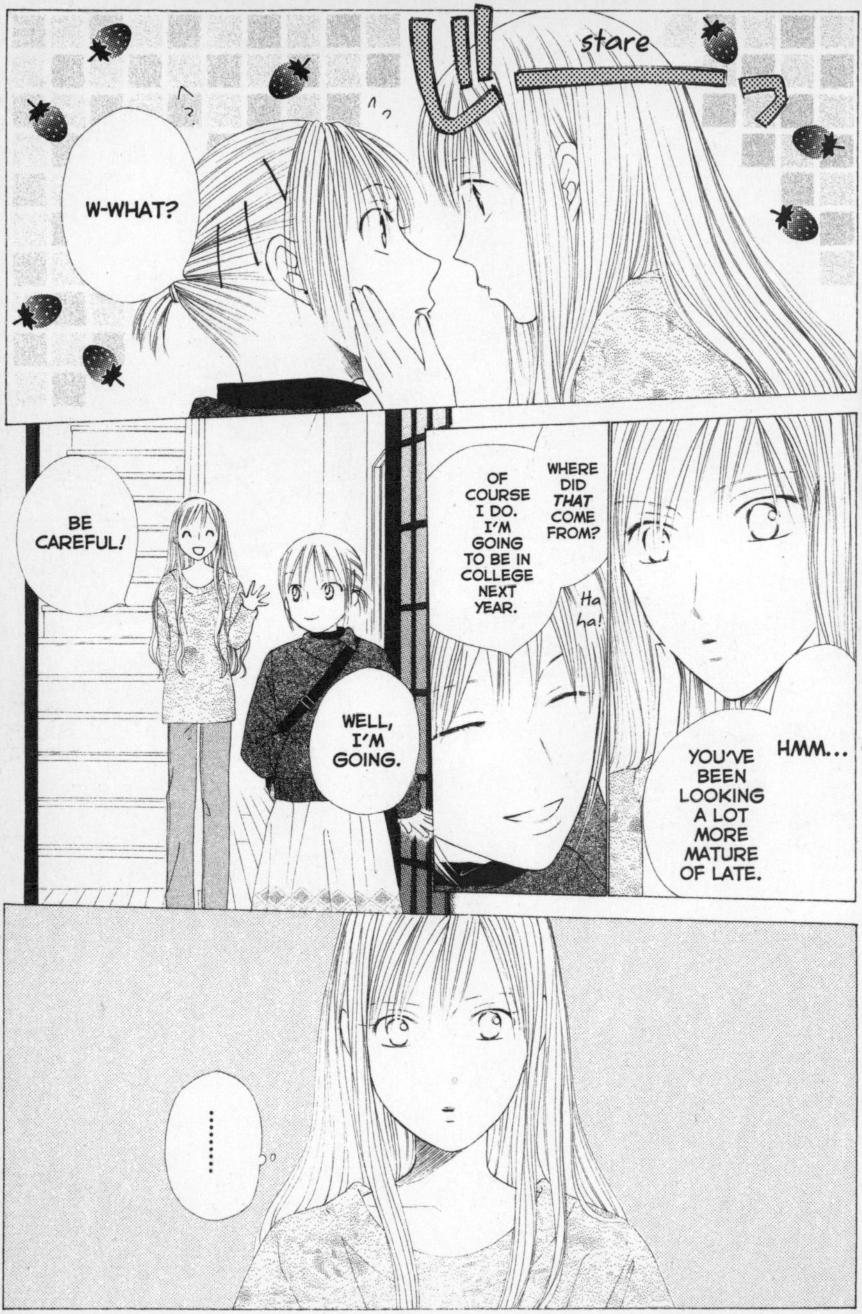
stare
W-WHAT?
HMM...
YOU'VE BEEN LOOKING A LOT MORE MATURE OF LATE.
WHERE DID *THAT* COME FROM?
Ha ha!
OF COURSE I DO. I'M GOING TO BE IN COLLEGE NEXT YEAR.
WELL, I'M GOING.
BE CAREFUL!
....

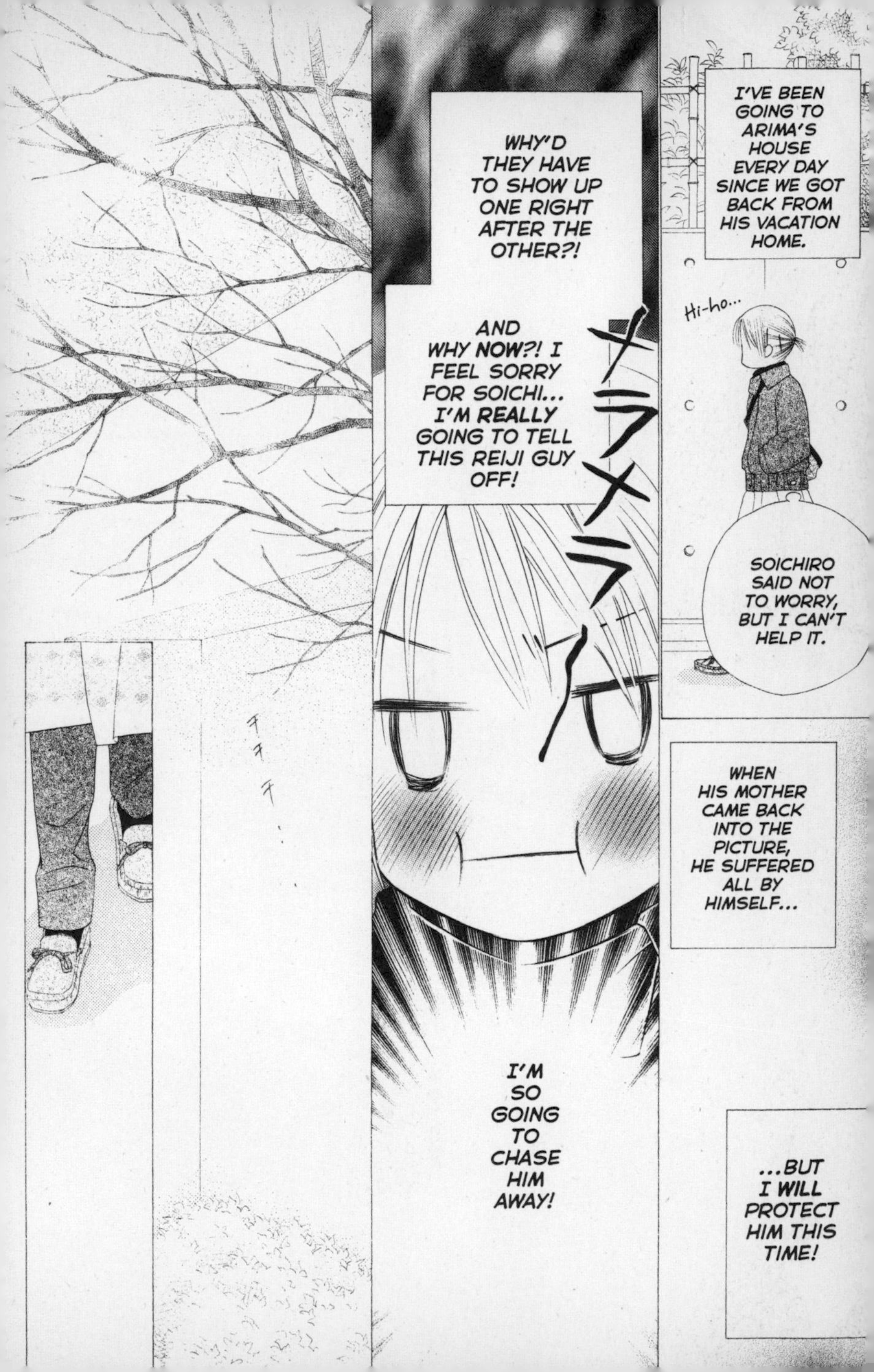
I'VE BEEN GOING TO ARIMA'S HOUSE EVERY DAY SINCE WE GOT BACK FROM HIS VACATION HOME.
Hi-ho...
SOICHIRO SAID NOT TO WORRY, BUT I CAN'T HELP IT.
WHEN HIS MOTHER CAME BACK INTO THE PICTURE, HE SUFFERED ALL BY HIMSELF...
...BUT I WILL PROTECT HIM THIS TIME!
WHY'D THEY HAVE TO SHOW UP ONE RIGHT AFTER THE OTHER?!
AND WHY NOW?! I FEEL SORRY FOR SOICHI... I'M REALLY GOING TO TELL THIS REIJI GUY OFF!
メラメラ
I'M SO GOING TO CHASE HIM AWAY!
チチチ

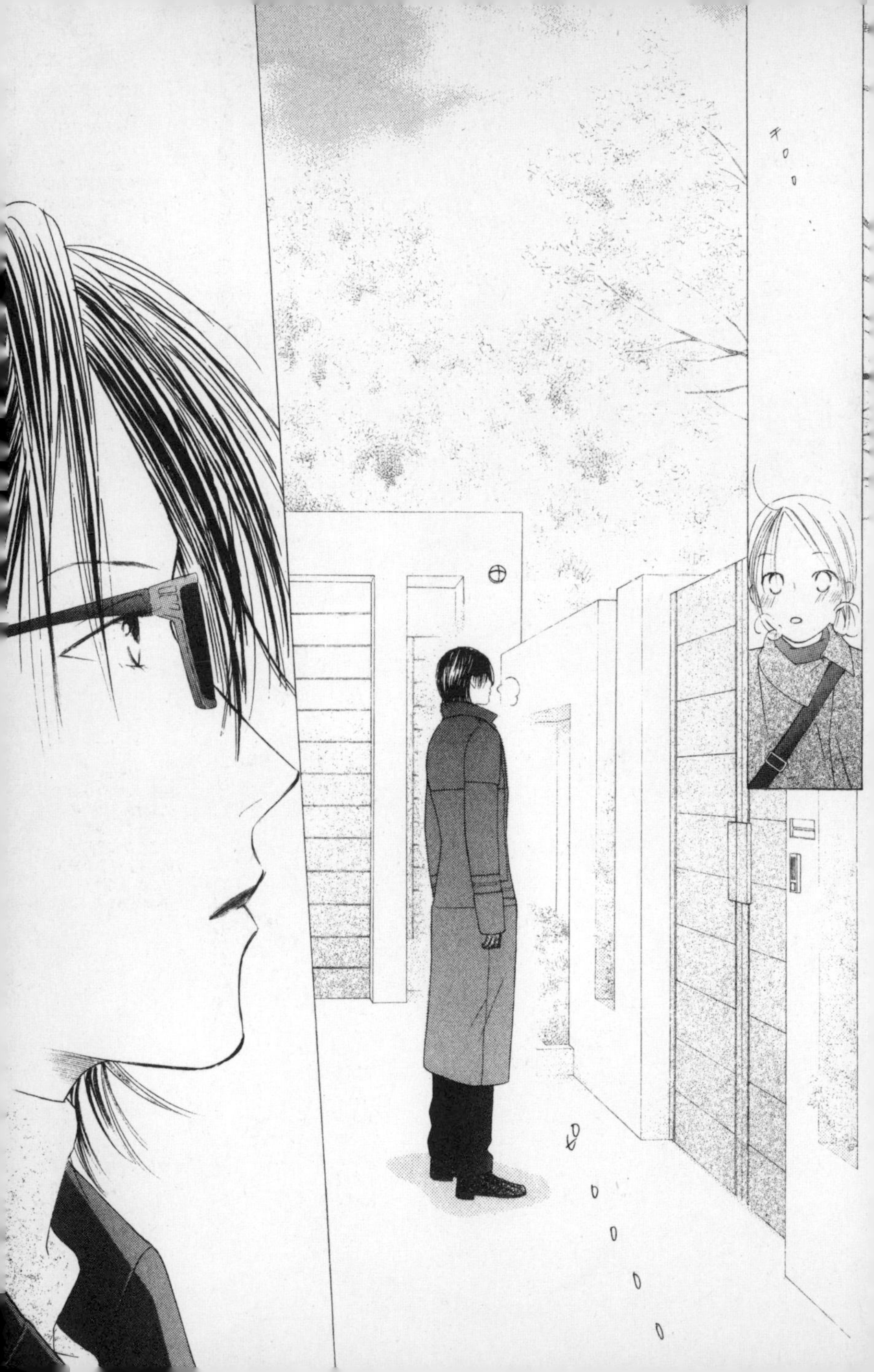

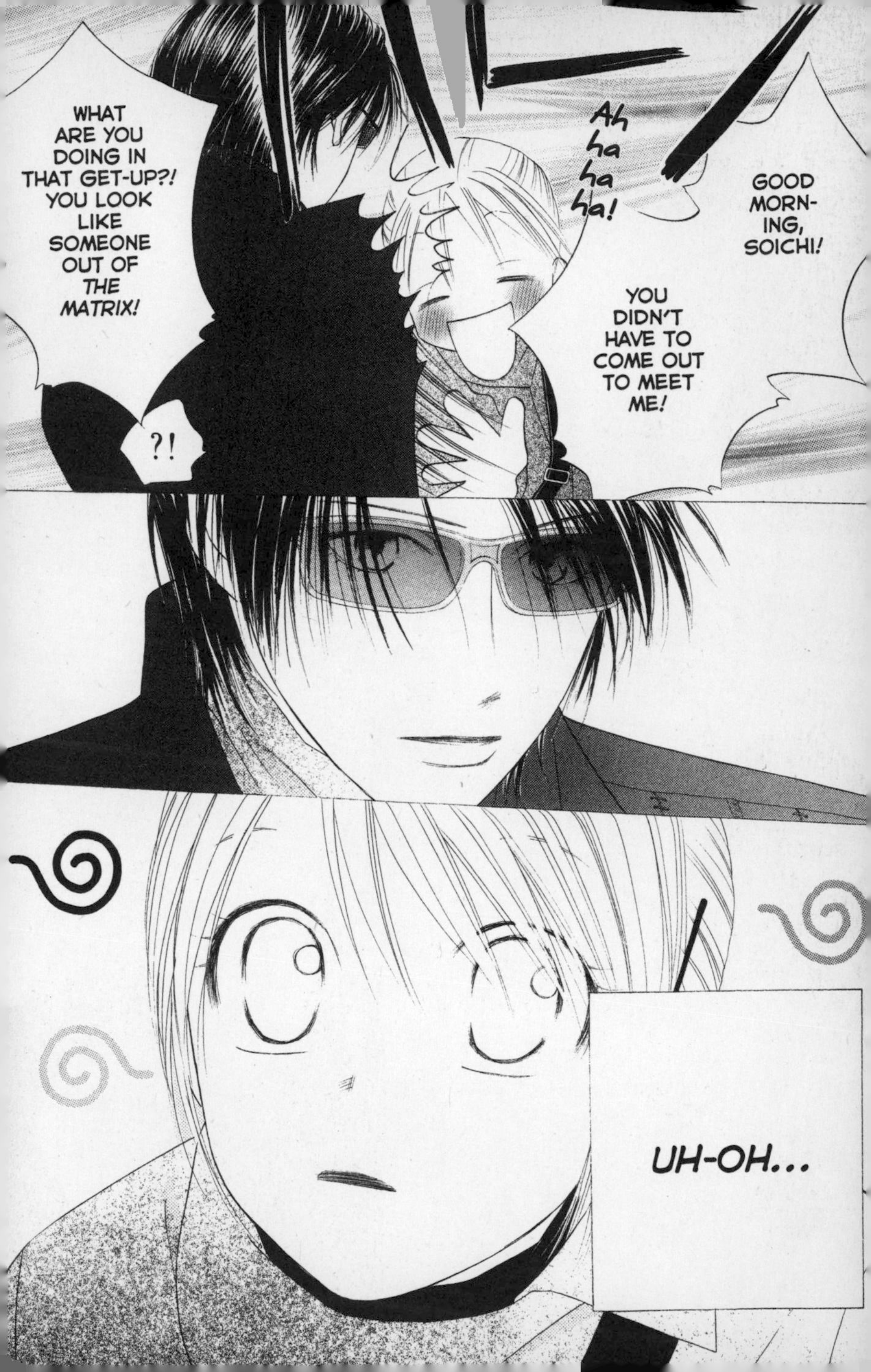
GOOD MORNING, SOICHI!
Ah ha ha ha!
YOU DIDN'T HAVE TO COME OUT TO MEET ME!
WHAT ARE YOU DOING IN THAT GET-UP?! YOU LOOK LIKE SOMEONE OUT OF THE MATRIX!
?!
UH-OH...

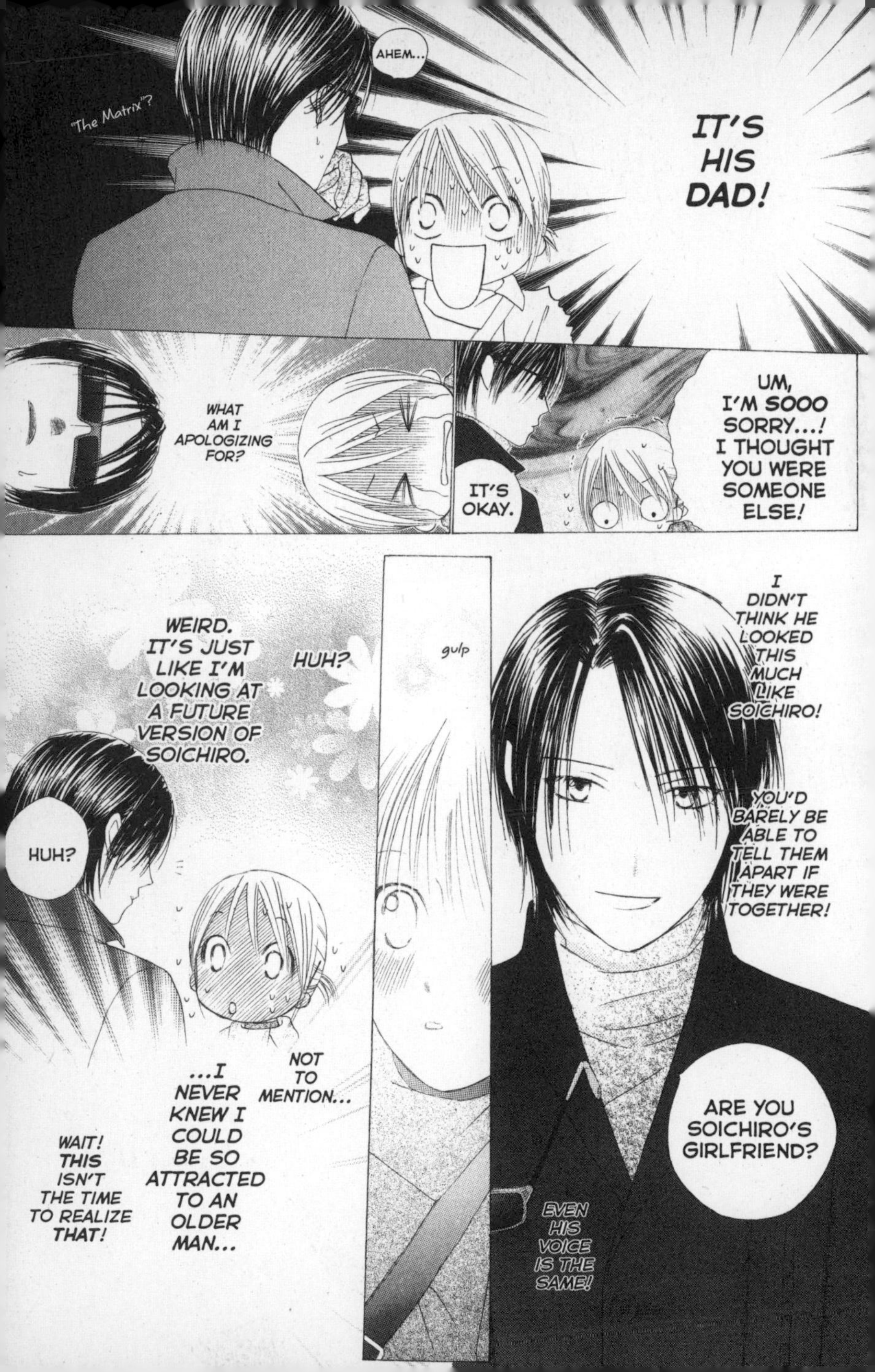
AHEM...
IT'S HIS DAD!
"The Matrix"?
UM, I'M SOOO SORRY...! I THOUGHT YOU WERE SOMEONE ELSE!
IT'S OKAY.
WHAT AM I APOLOGIZING FOR?
I DIDN'T THINK HE LOOKED THIS MUCH LIKE SOICHIRO!
YOU'D BARELY BE ABLE TO TELL THEM APART IF THEY WERE TOGETHER!
ARE YOU SOICHIRO'S GIRLFRIEND?
EVEN HIS VOICE IS THE SAME!
gulp
HUH?
WEIRD. IT'S JUST LIKE I'M LOOKING AT A FUTURE VERSION OF SOICHIRO.
HUH?
NOT TO MENTION...
...I NEVER KNEW I COULD BE SO ATTRACTED TO AN OLDER MAN...
WAIT! THIS ISN'T THE TIME TO REALIZE THAT!

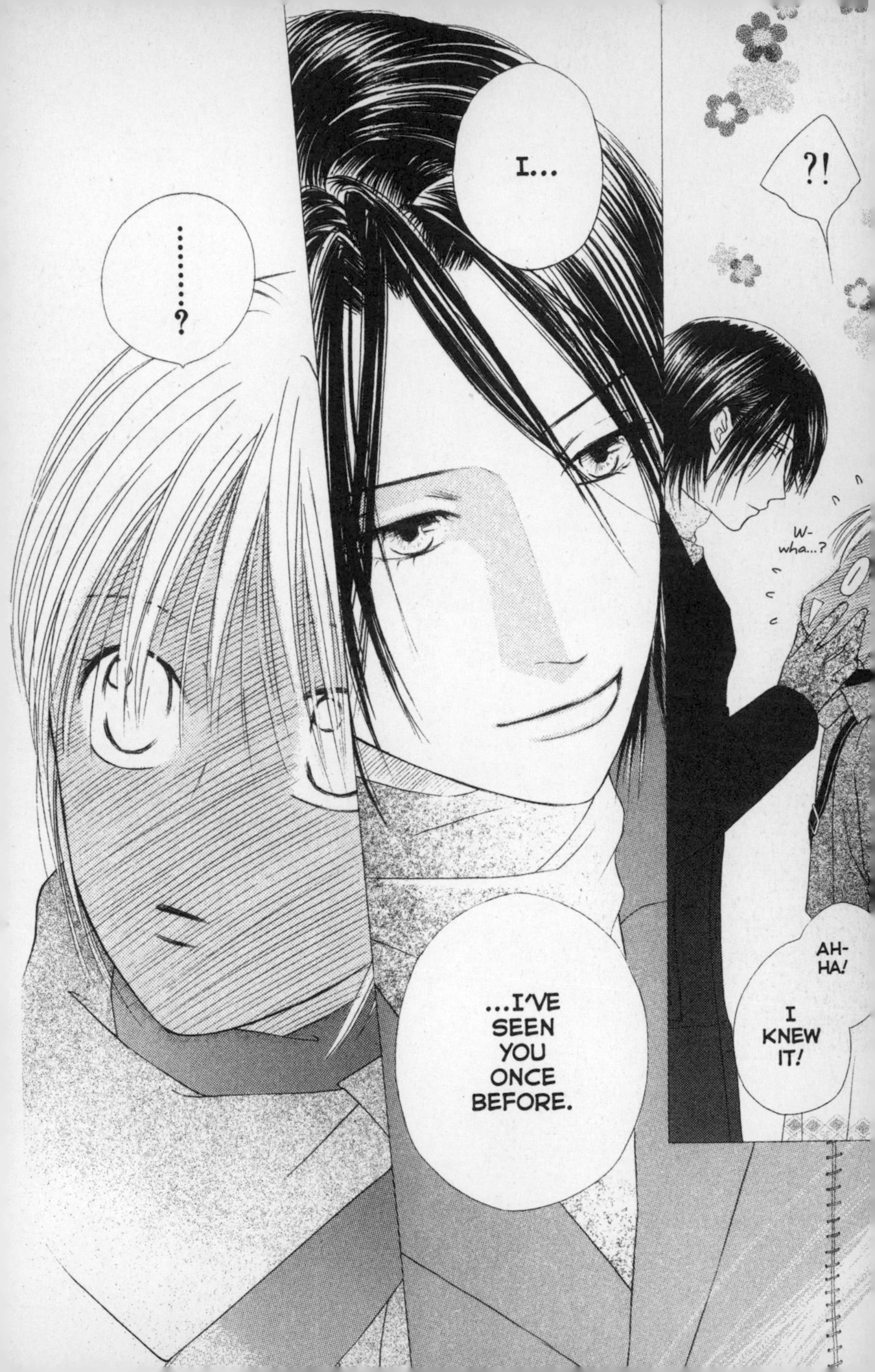
?!
W- wha...?
AH-HA! I KNEW IT!
I...
...I'VE SEEN YOU ONCE BEFORE.
......?

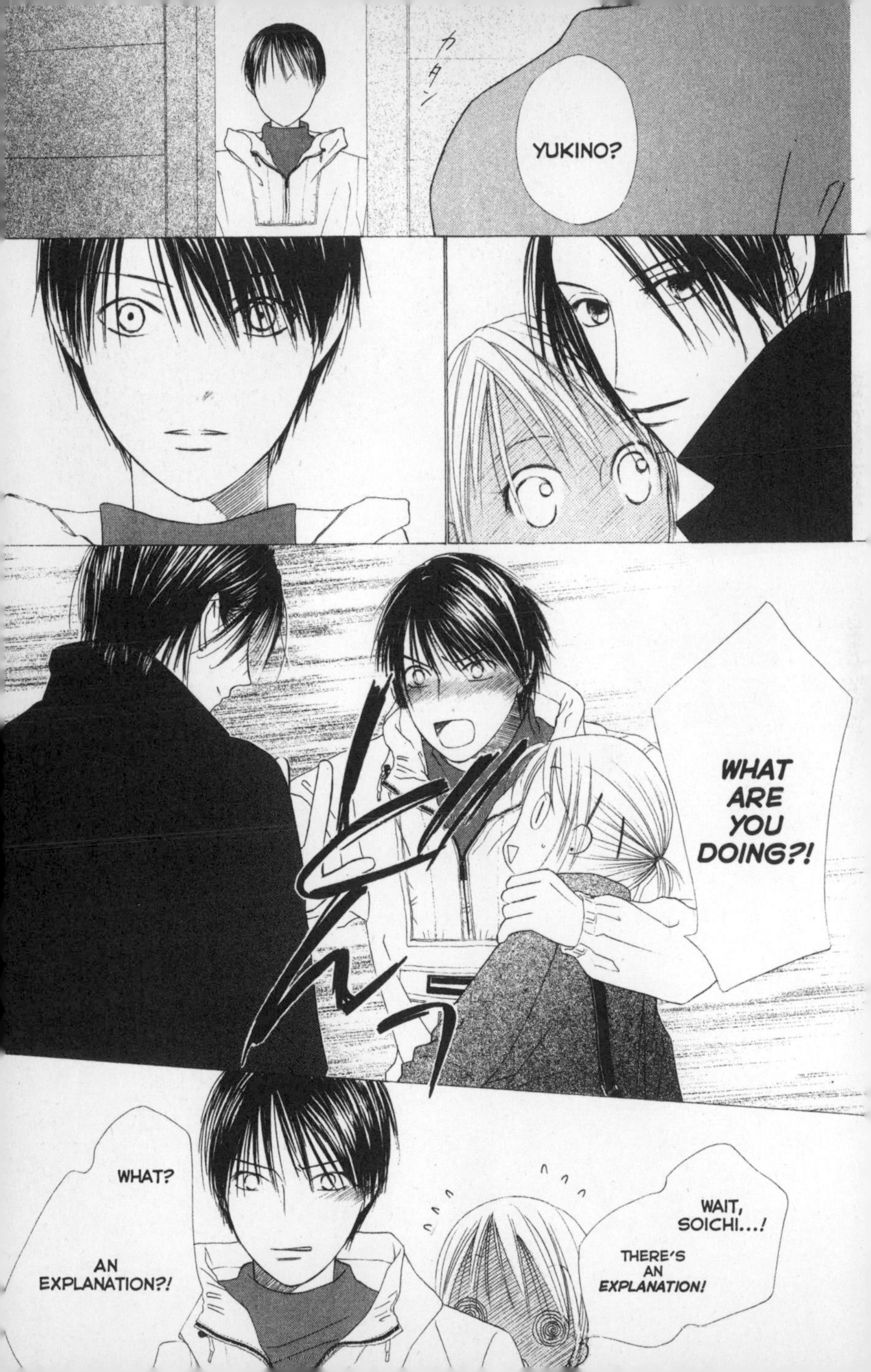
YUKINO?
カタン
WHAT ARE YOU DOING?!
WAIT, SOICHI...!
THERE'S AN EXPLANATION!
WHAT?
AN EXPLANATION?!

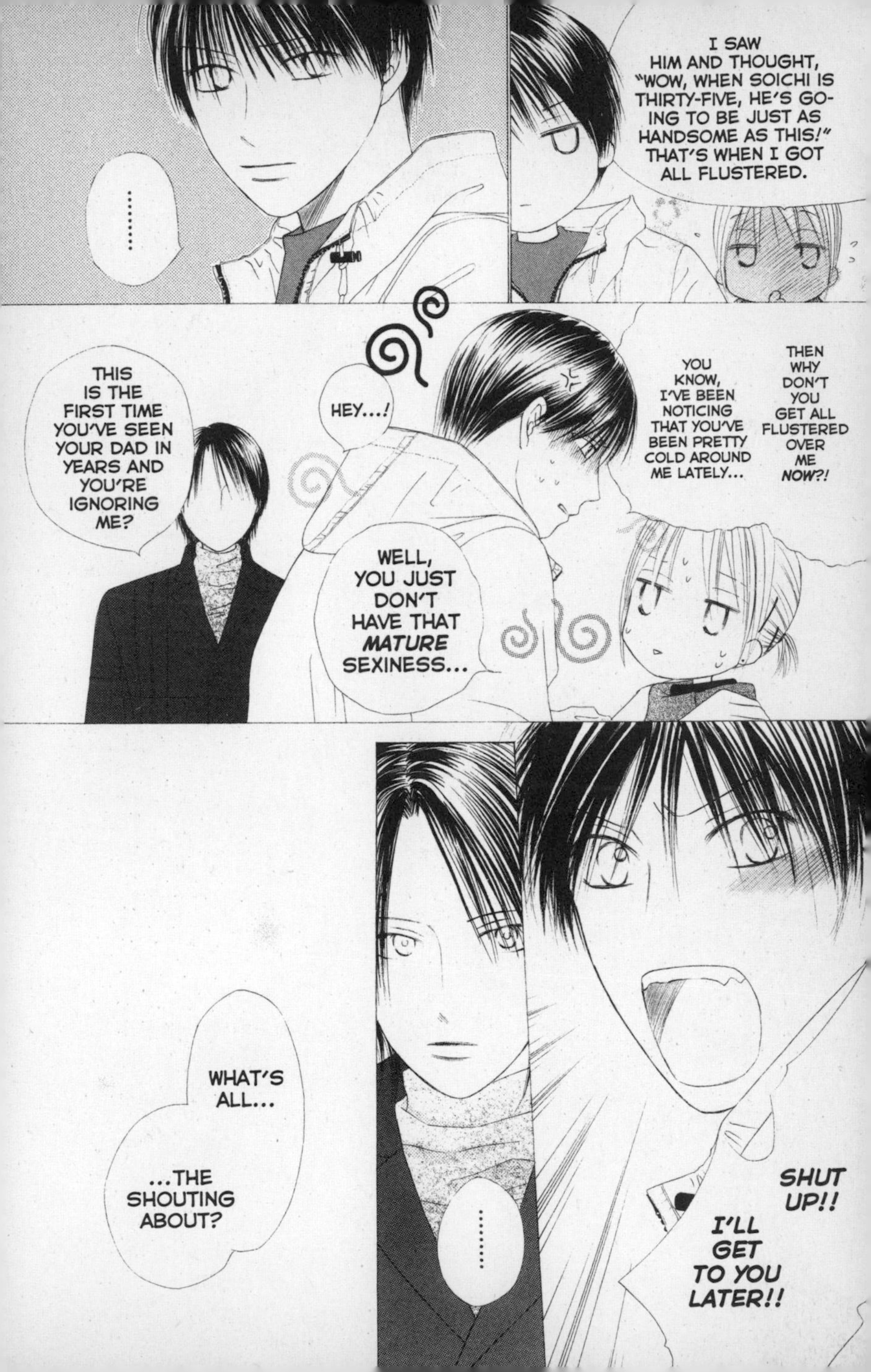
I SAW HIM AND THOUGHT, "WOW, WHEN SOICHI IS THIRTY-FIVE, HE'S GO-ING TO BE JUST AS HANDSOME AS THIS!" THAT'S WHEN I GOT ALL FLUSTERED.
......
THEN WHY DON'T YOU GET ALL FLUSTERED OVER ME *NOW?!*
YOU KNOW, I'VE BEEN NOTICING THAT YOU'VE BEEN PRETTY COLD AROUND ME LATELY...
WELL, YOU JUST DON'T HAVE THAT *MATURE* SEXINESS...
HEY...!
THIS IS THE FIRST TIME YOU'VE SEEN YOUR DAD IN YEARS AND YOU'RE IGNORING ME?
SHUT UP!!
I'LL GET TO YOU LATER!!
......
WHAT'S ALL...
...THE SHOUTING ABOUT?

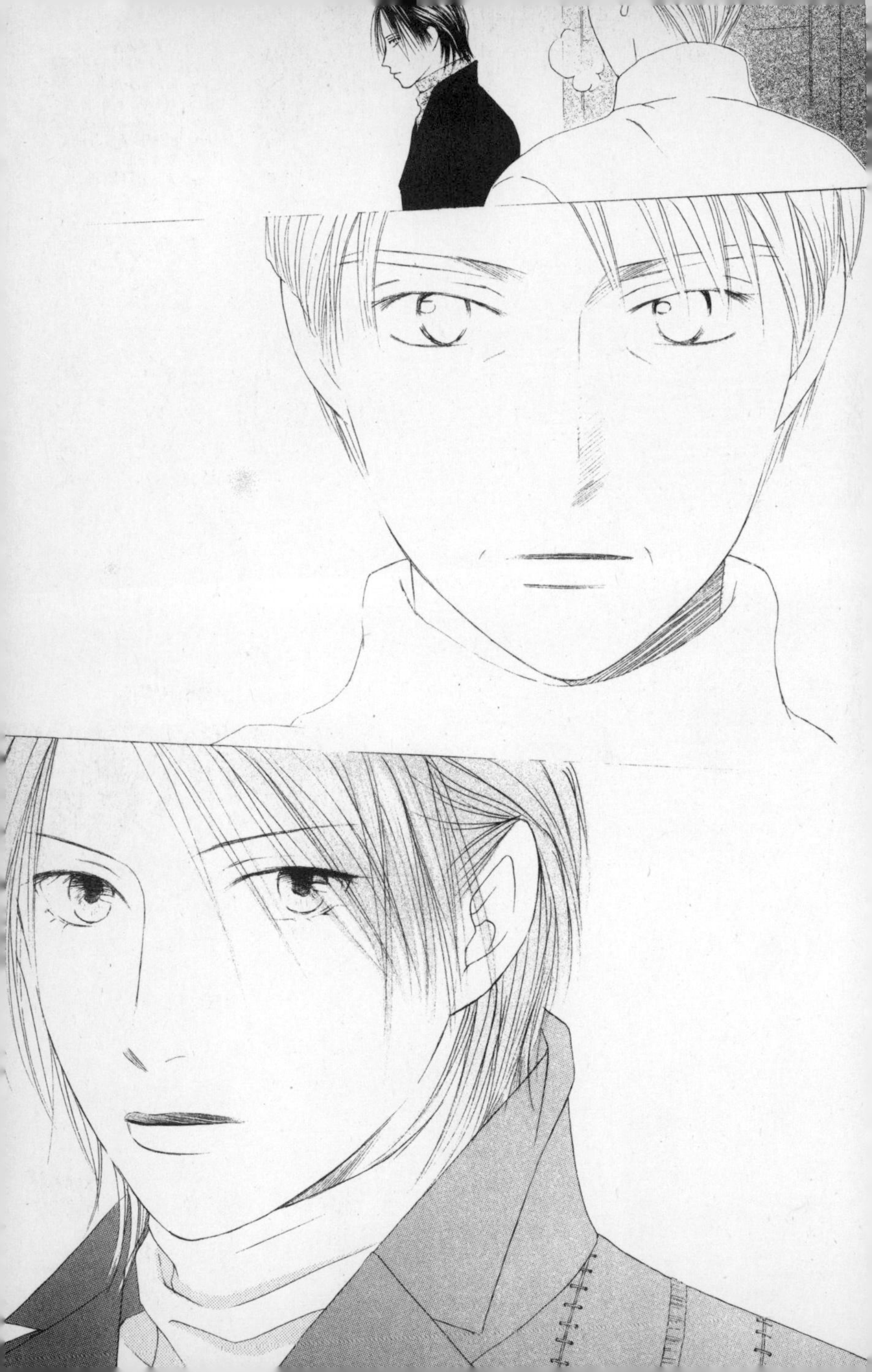

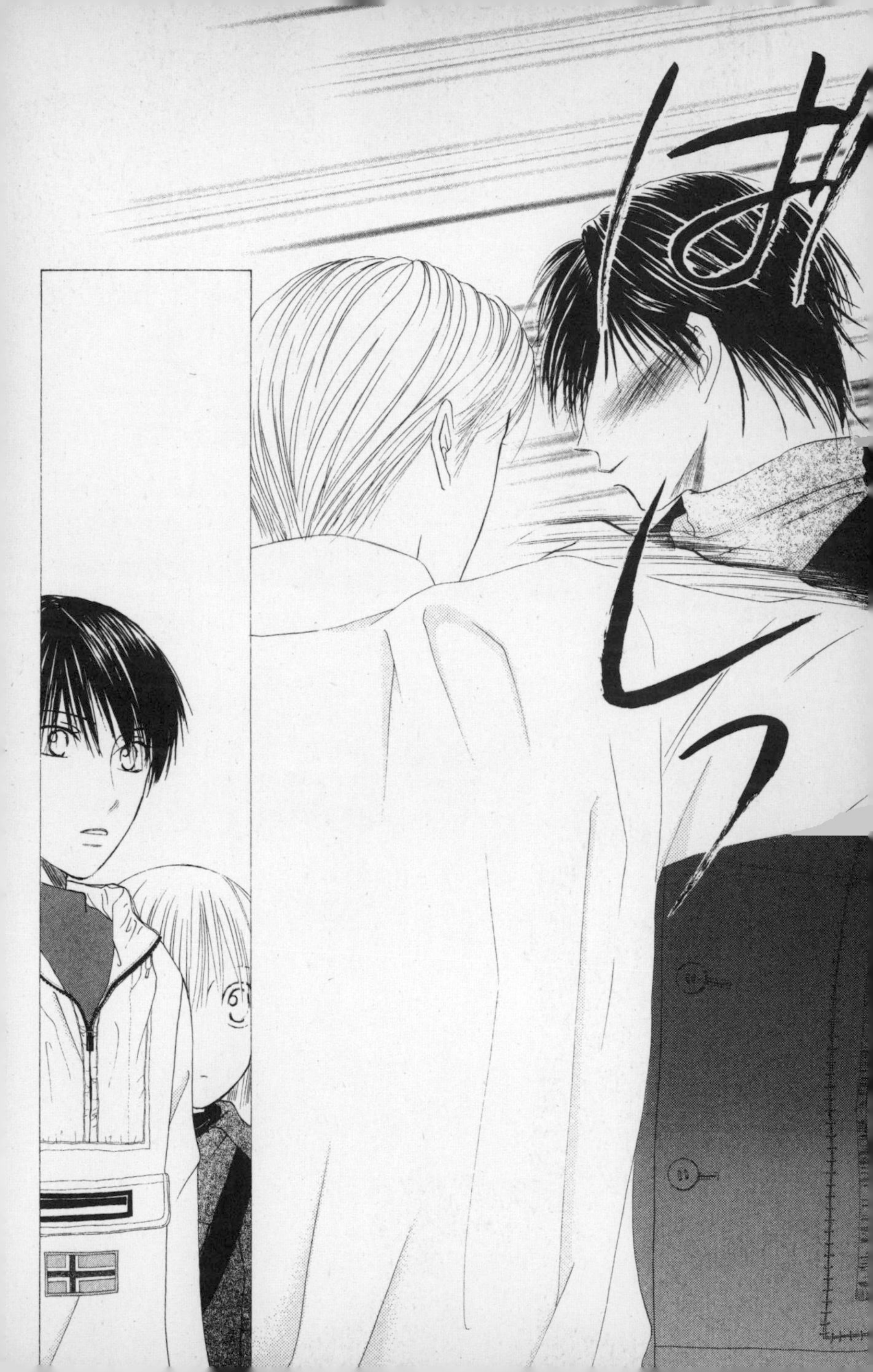
ばしっ

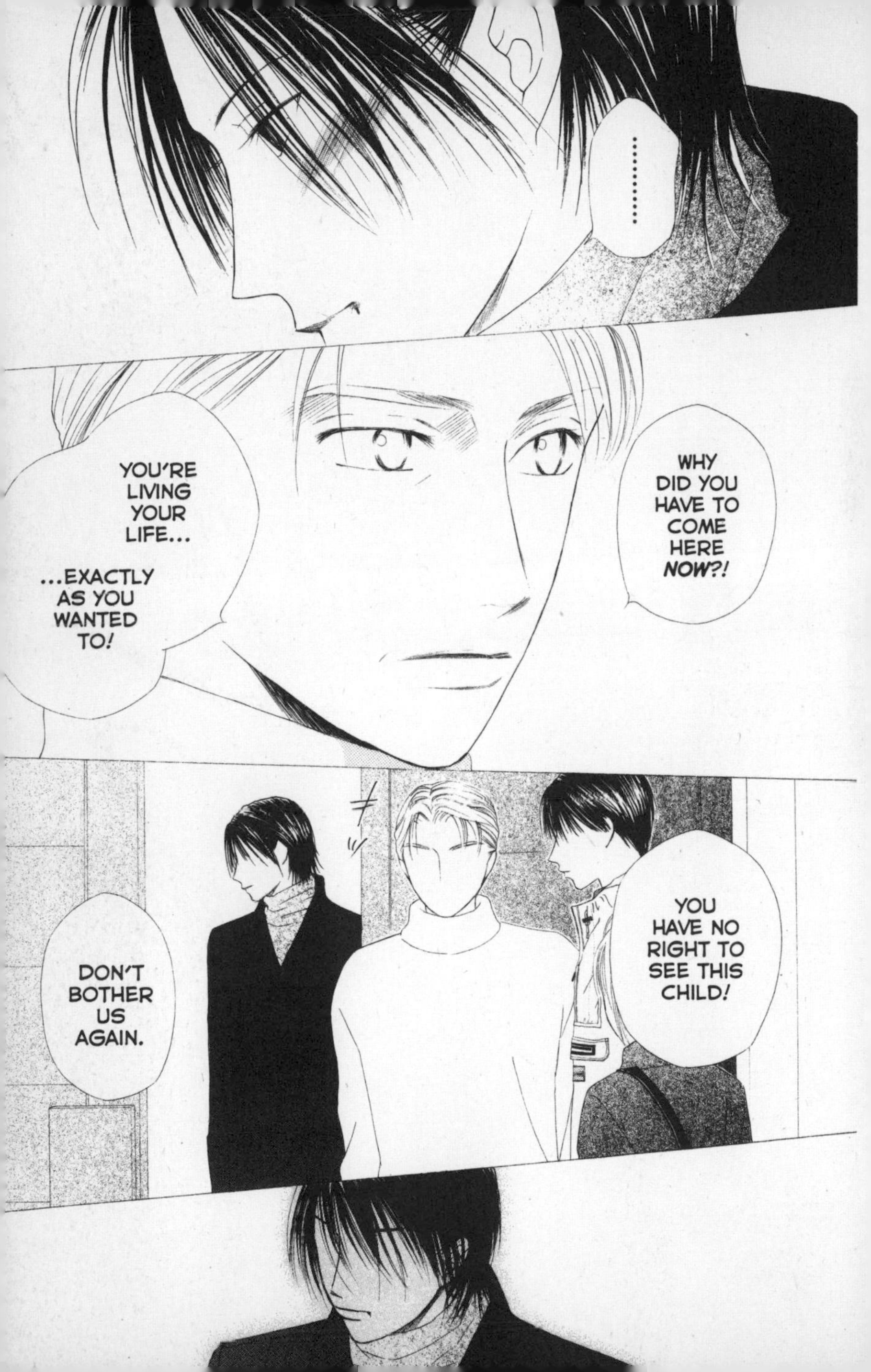
……
WHY DID YOU HAVE TO COME HERE *NOW?!*
YOU'RE LIVING YOUR LIFE...
...EXACTLY AS YOU WANTED TO!
YOU HAVE NO RIGHT TO SEE THIS CHILD!
DON'T BOTHER US AGAIN.

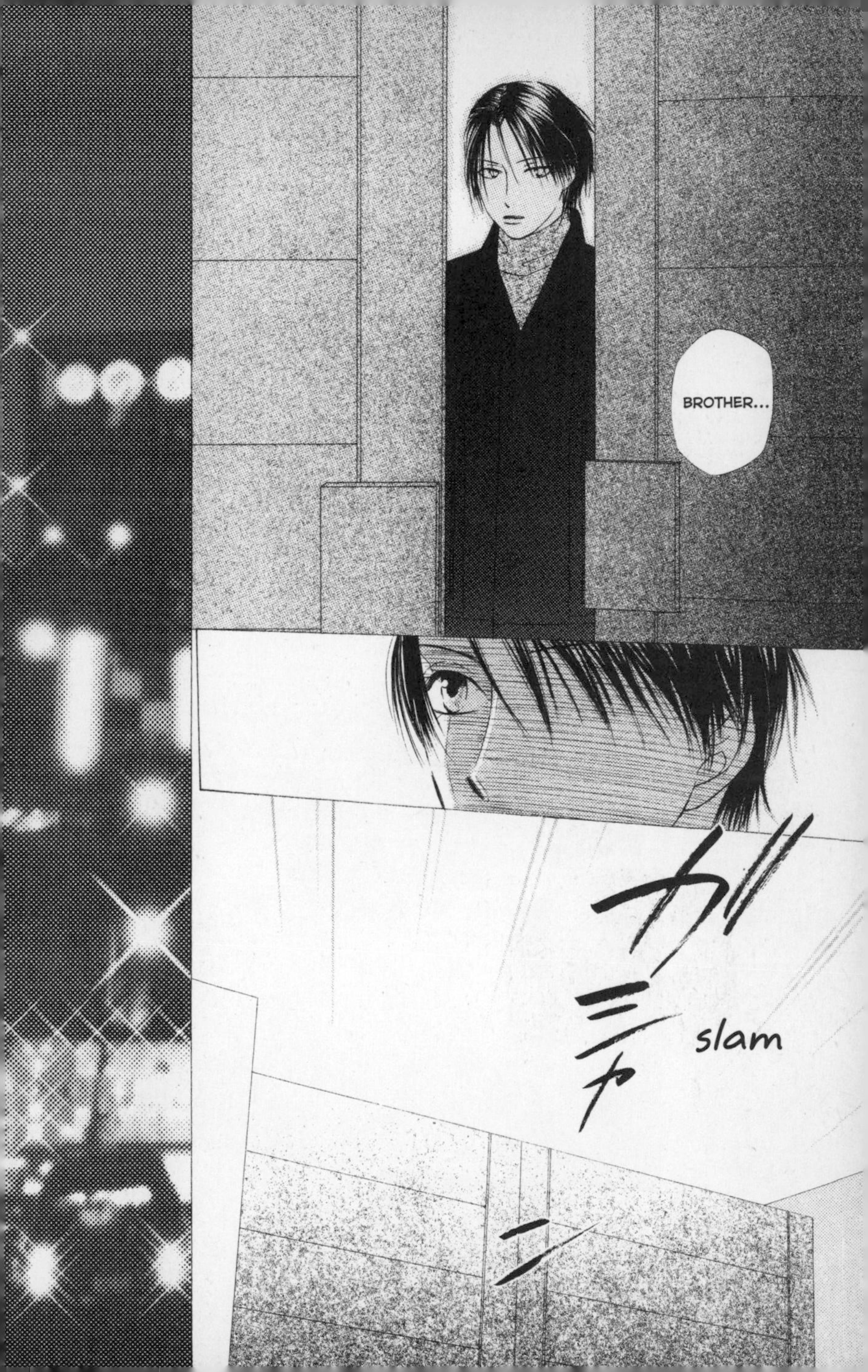
BROTHER...
slam

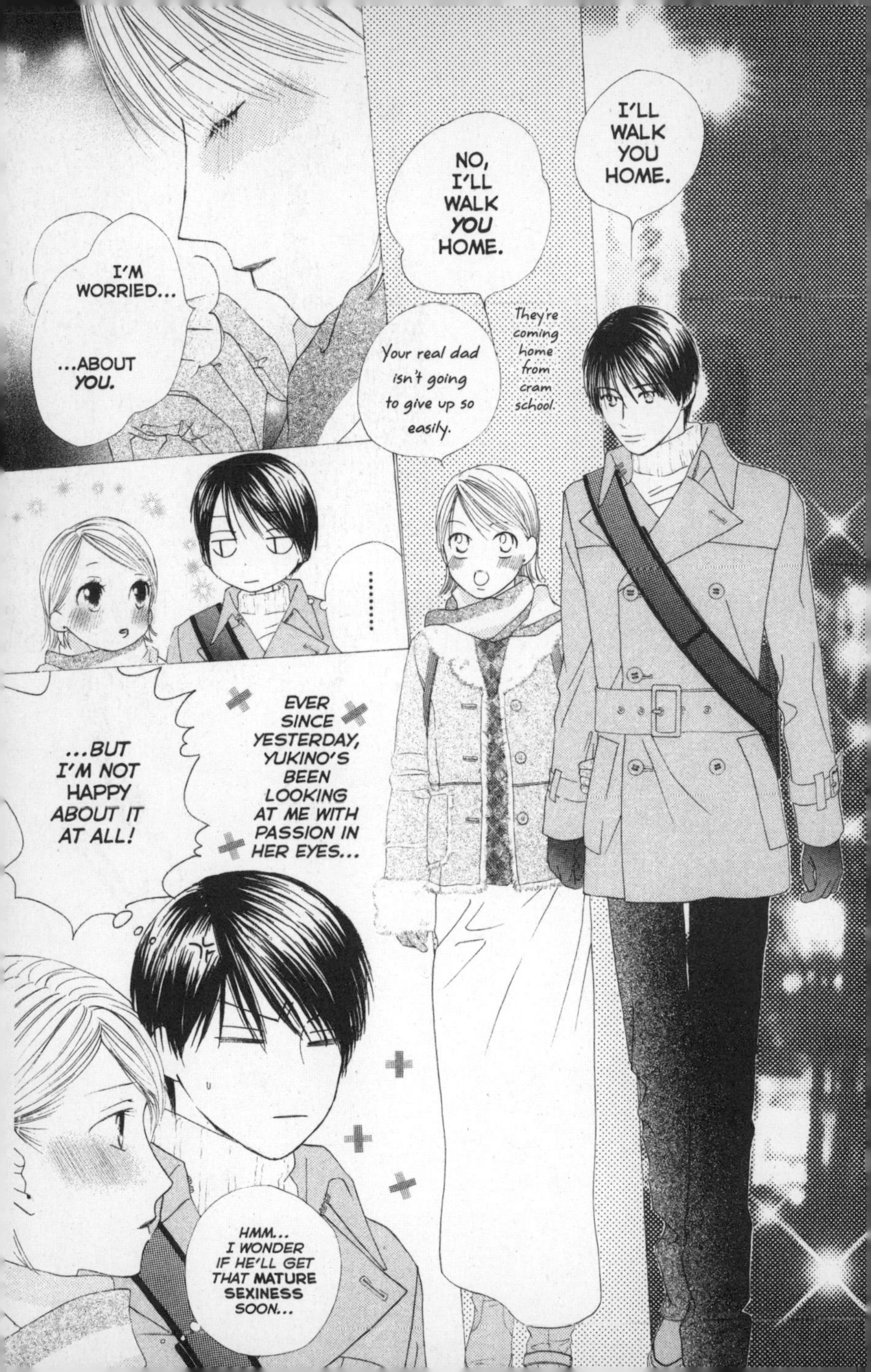
I'LL WALK YOU HOME.
NO, I'LL WALK YOU HOME.
They're coming home from cram school.
Your real dad isn't going to give up so easily.
I'M WORRIED...
...ABOUT YOU.
......
EVER SINCE YESTERDAY, YUKINO'S BEEN LOOKING AT ME WITH PASSION IN HER EYES...
...BUT I'M NOT HAPPY ABOUT IT AT ALL!
HMM... I WONDER IF HE'LL GET THAT MATURE SEXINESS SOON...

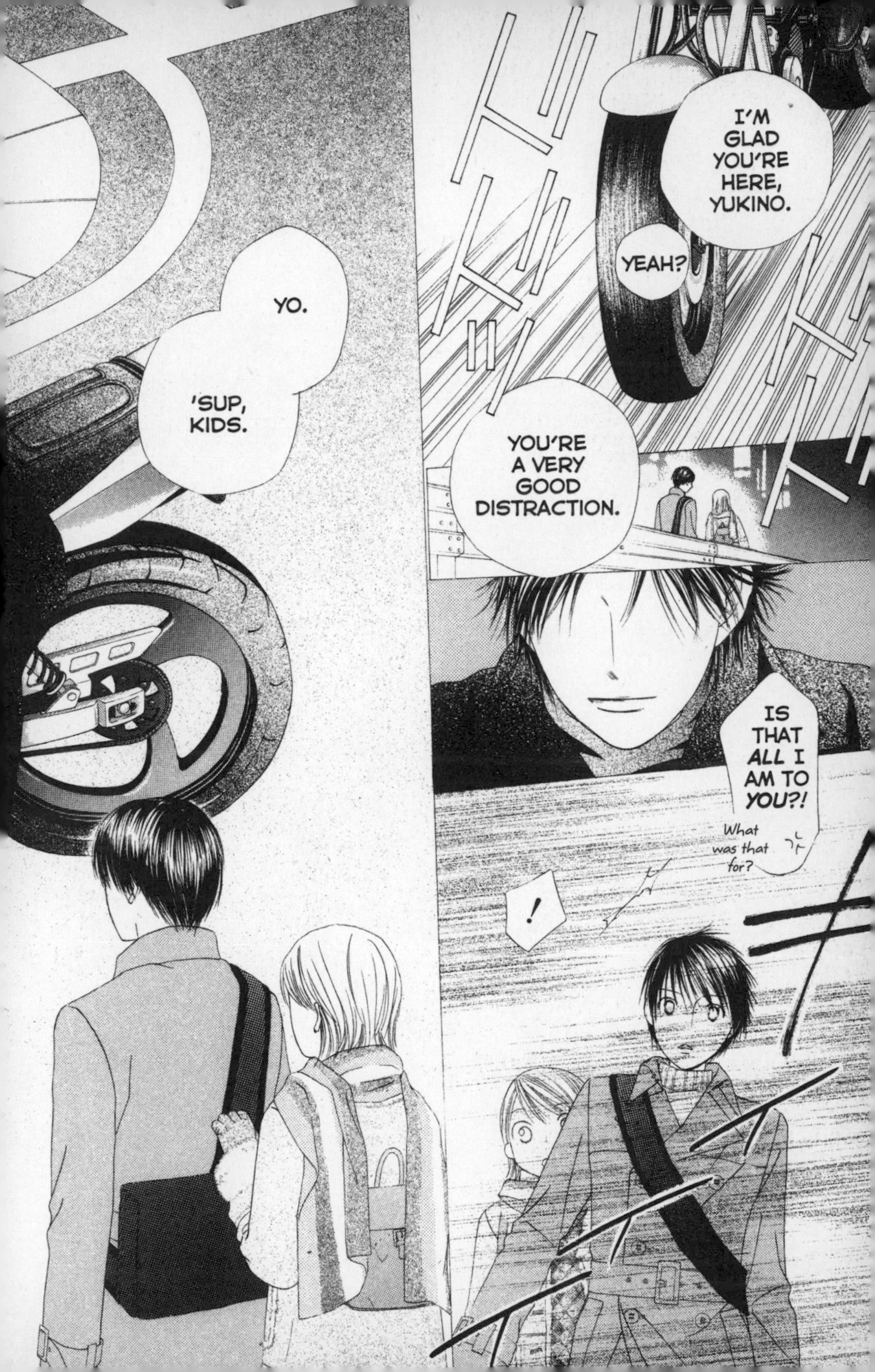
I'M GLAD YOU'RE HERE, YUKINO.
YEAH?
YOU'RE A VERY GOOD DISTRACTION.
IS THAT *ALL* I AM TO *YOU*?!
What was that for?
!
YO.
'SUP, KIDS.

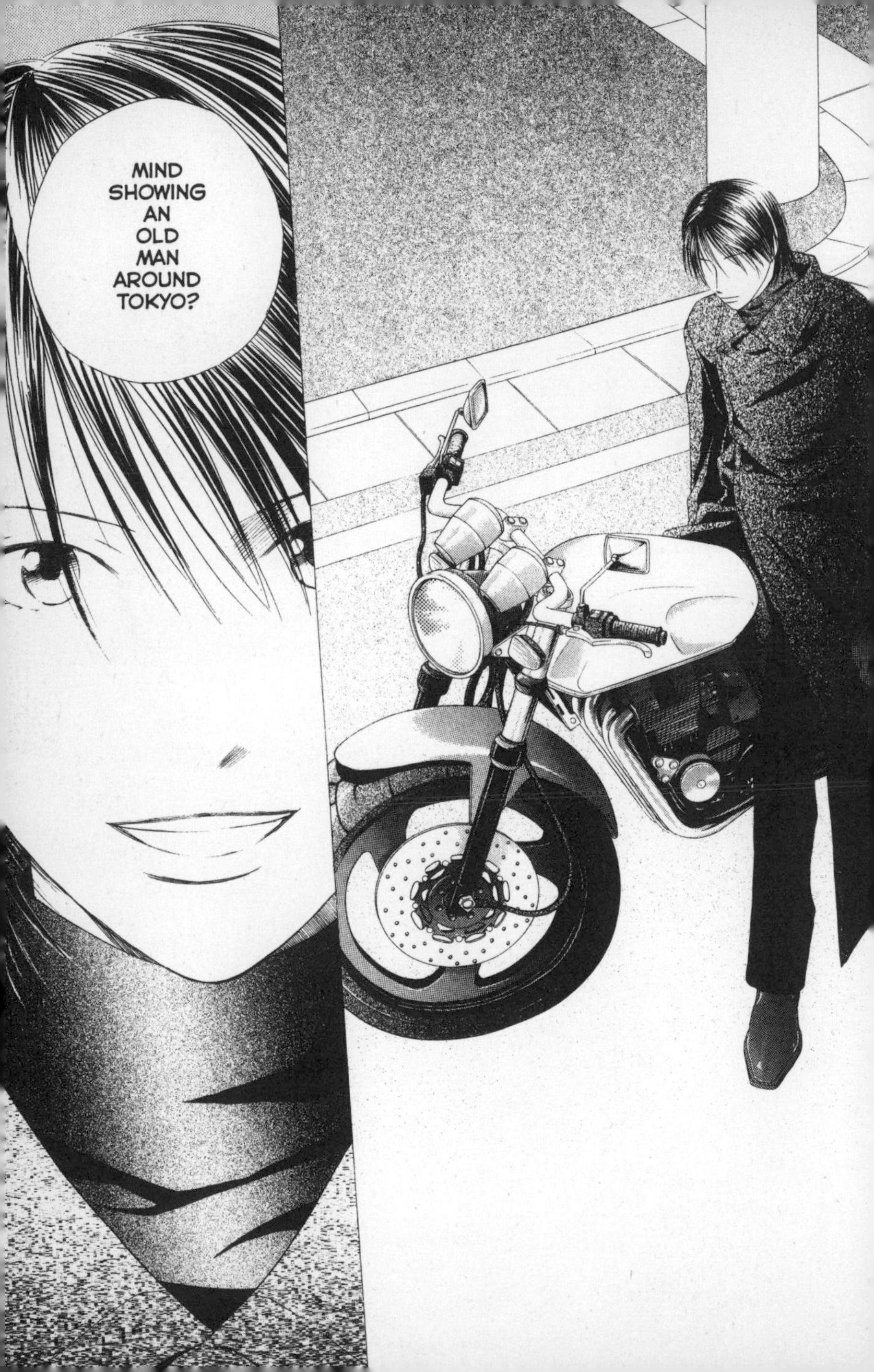
MIND SHOWING AN OLD MAN AROUND TOKYO?

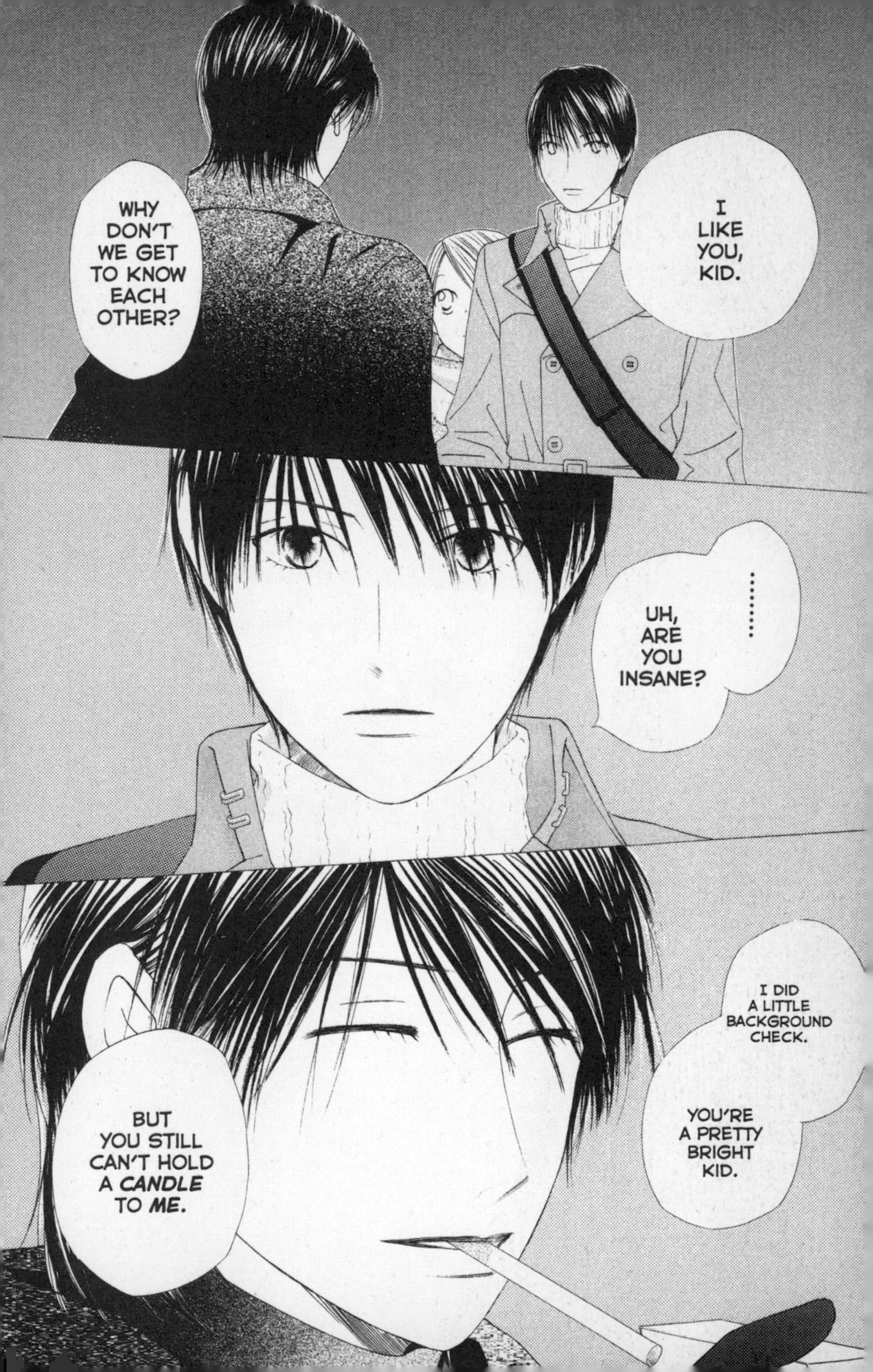
I LIKE YOU, KID.
WHY DON'T WE GET TO KNOW EACH OTHER?
......
UH, ARE YOU INSANE?
I DID A LITTLE BACKGROUND CHECK.
YOU'RE A PRETTY BRIGHT KID.
BUT YOU STILL CAN'T HOLD A *CANDLE* TO *ME*.

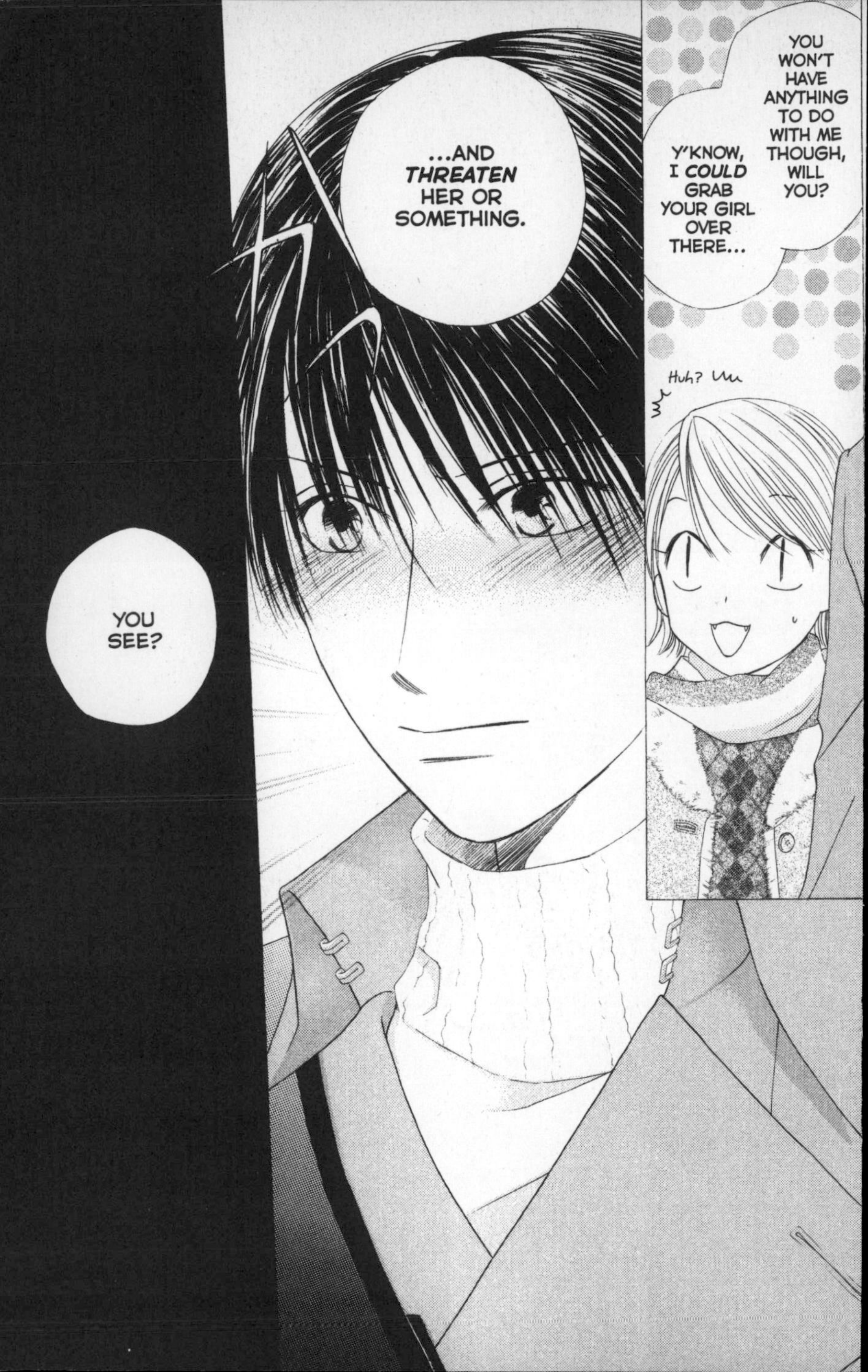
YOU WON'T HAVE ANYTHING TO DO WITH ME THOUGH, WILL YOU?
Y'KNOW, I *COULD* GRAB YOUR GIRL OVER THERE...
Huh? Uu
...AND *THREATEN* HER OR SOMETHING.
YOU SEE?

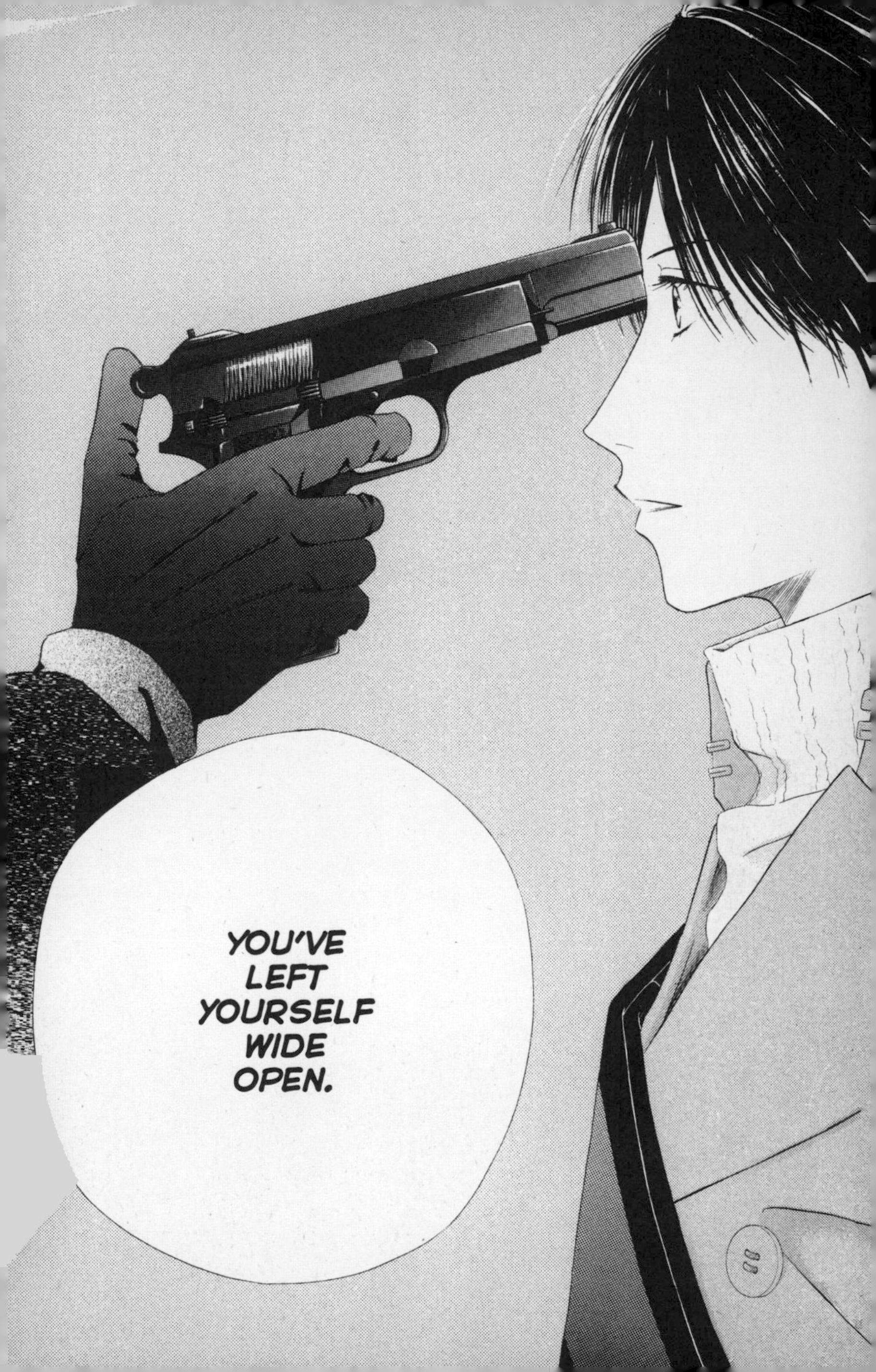
YOU'VE LEFT YOURSELF WIDE OPEN.

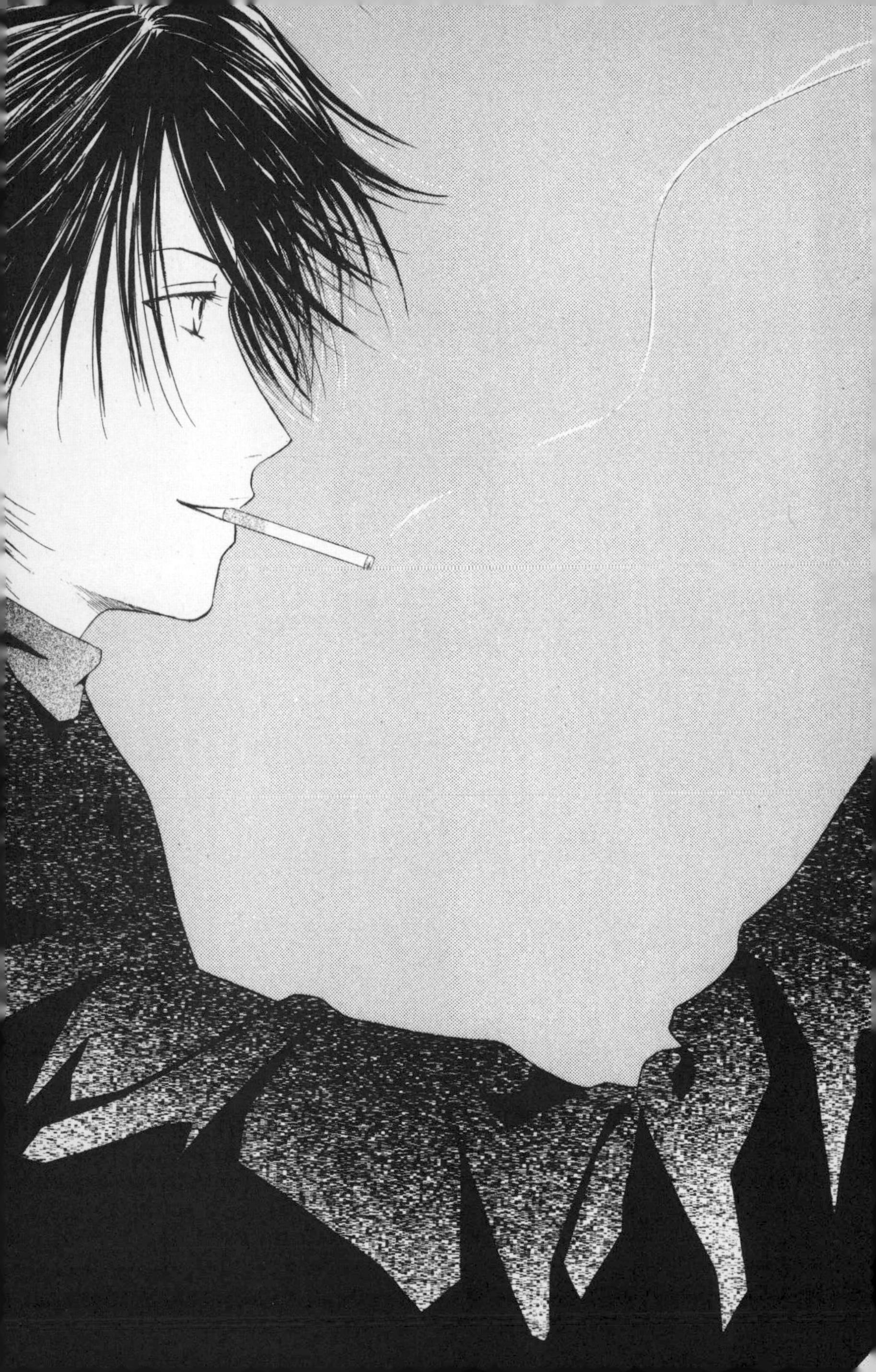

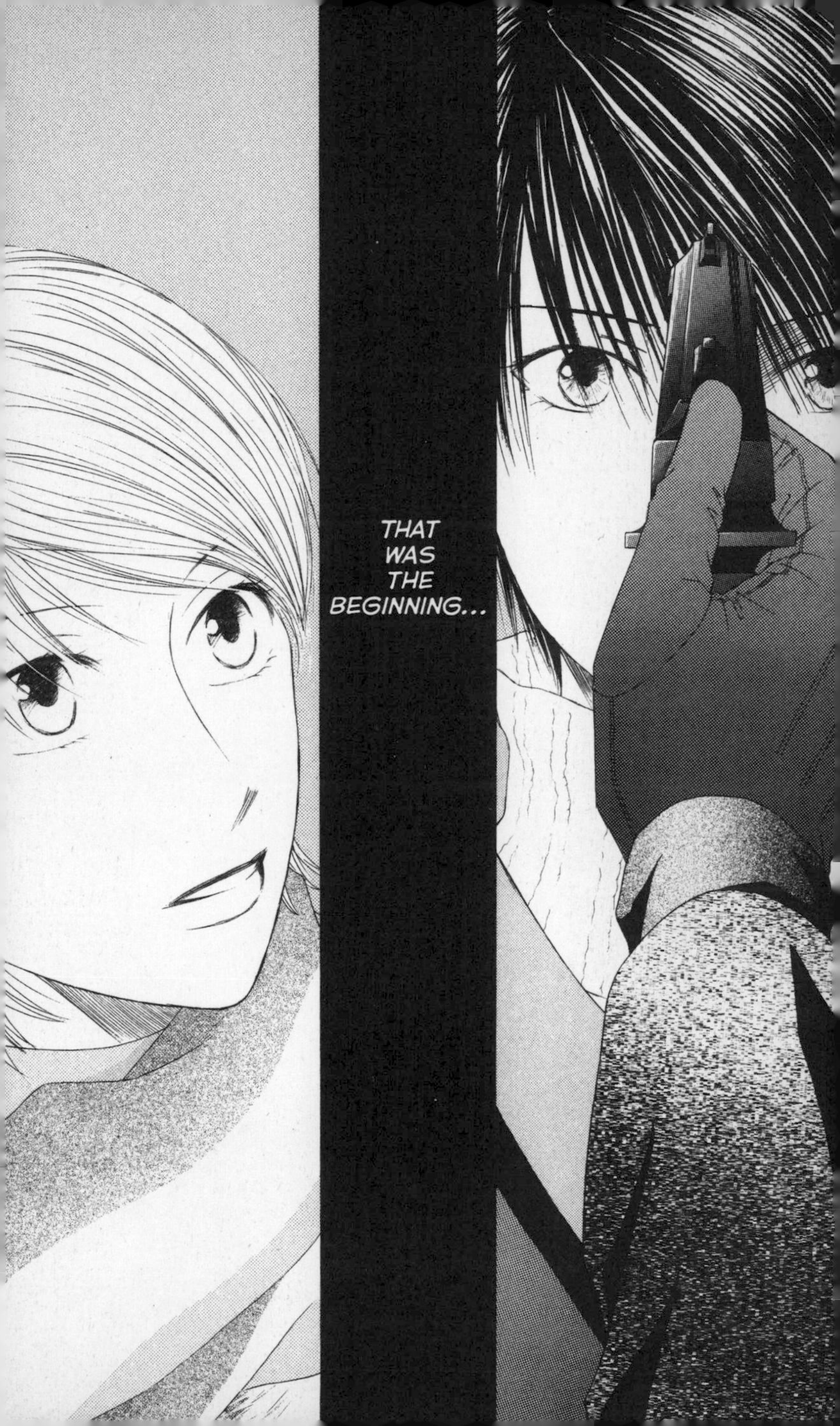
THAT WAS THE BEGINNING...

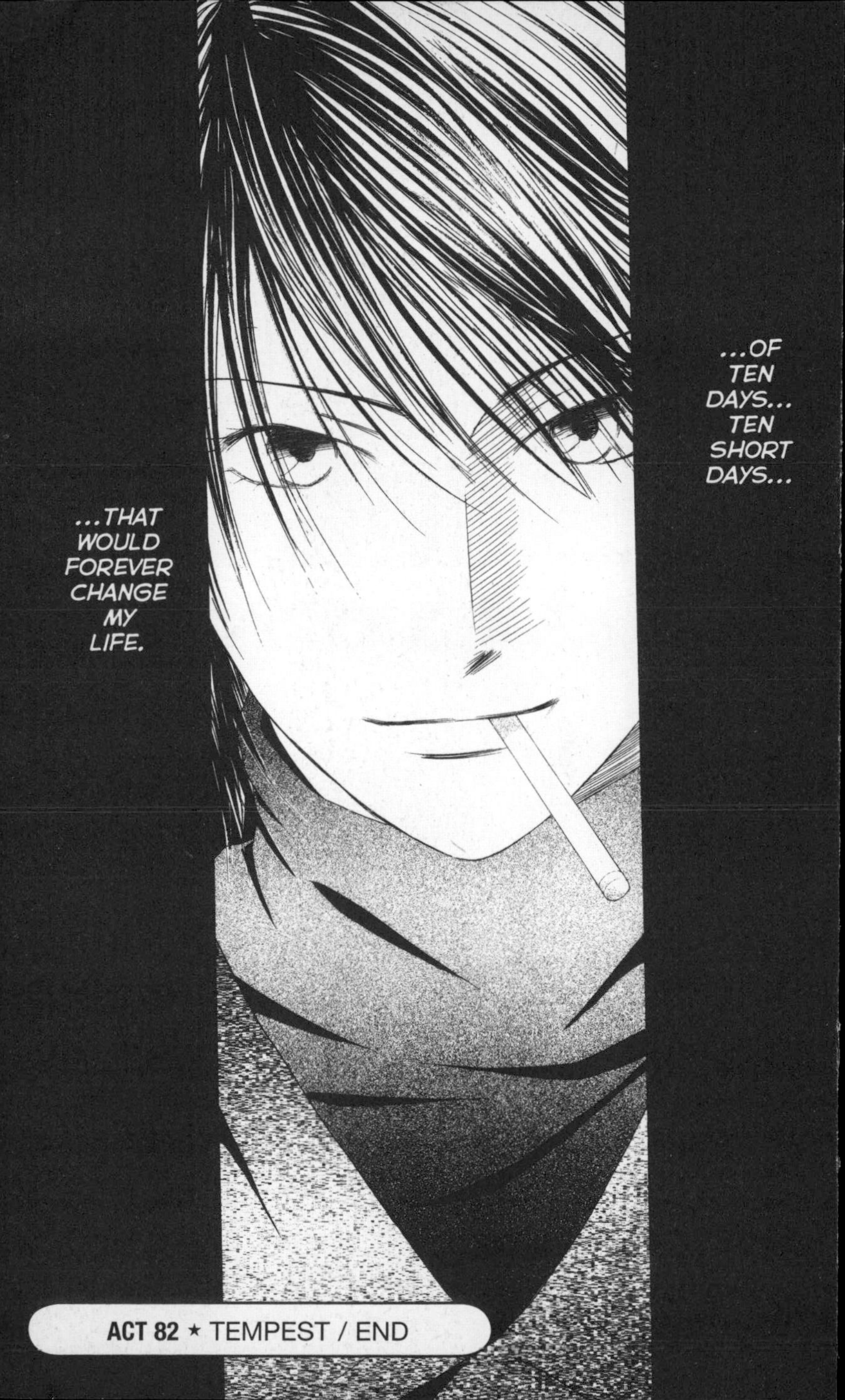
...OF TEN DAYS... TEN SHORT DAYS...
...THAT WOULD FOREVER CHANGE MY LIFE.
ACT 82 ★ TEMPEST / END

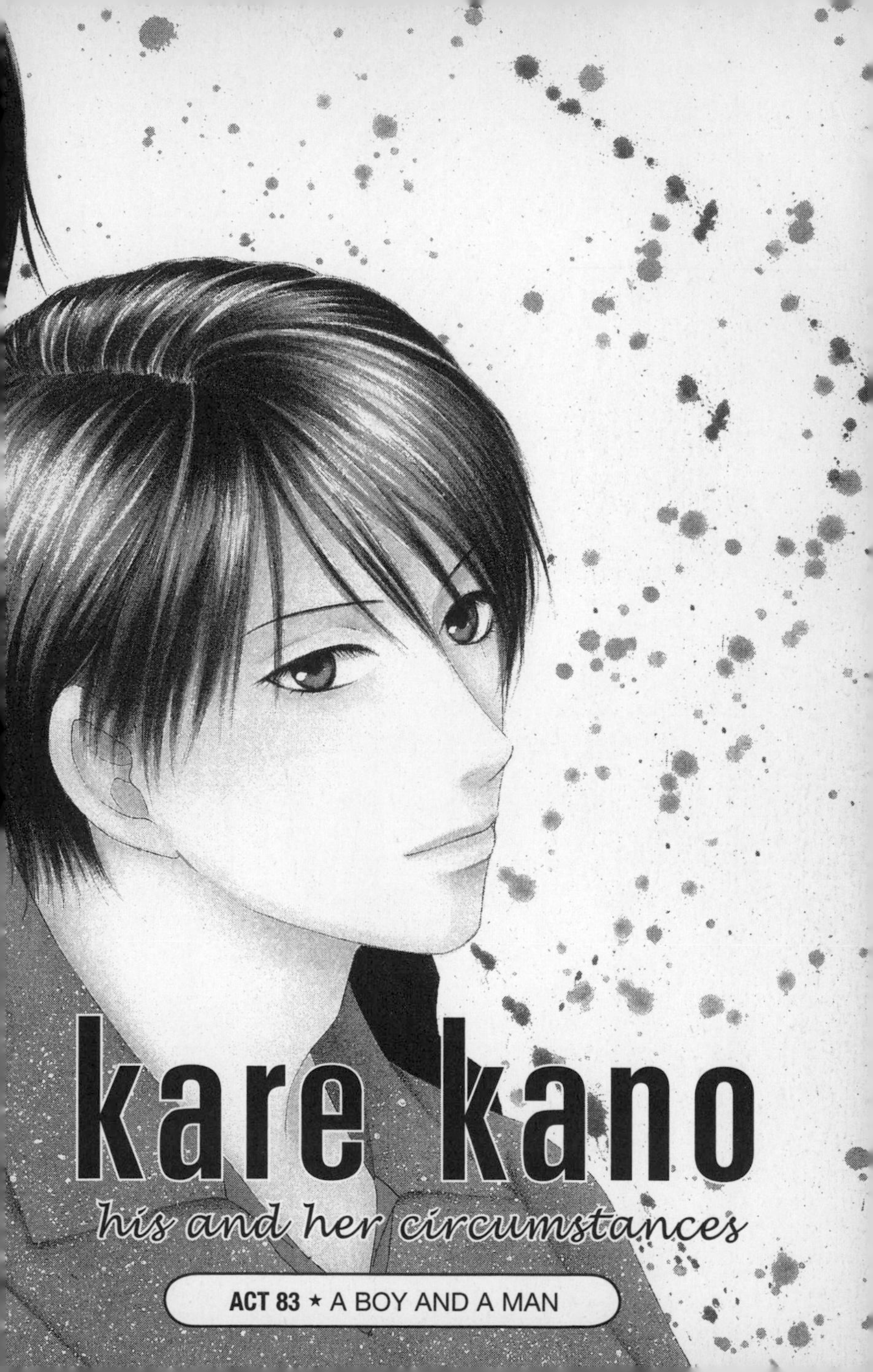
kare kano
his and her circumstances
ACT 83 ★ A BOY AND A MAN

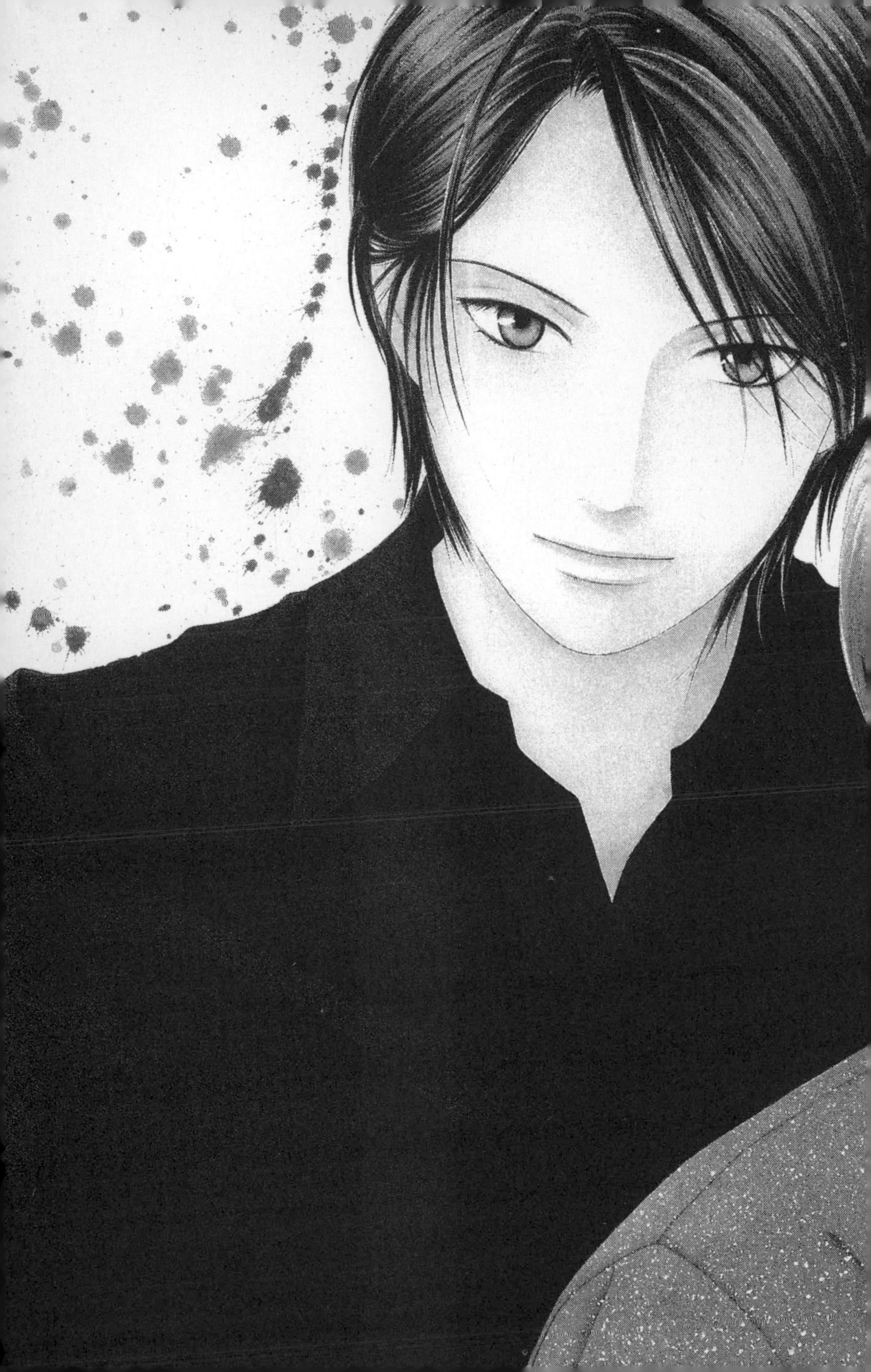

I DIDN'T WANT ANYONE TO UNDERSTAND MY PAIN.

WHEN YOUR DREAMS ARE UNATTAINABLE, THEY ONLY MAKE YOU MISERABLE.

IT'S JUST THE WAY I LIVE.

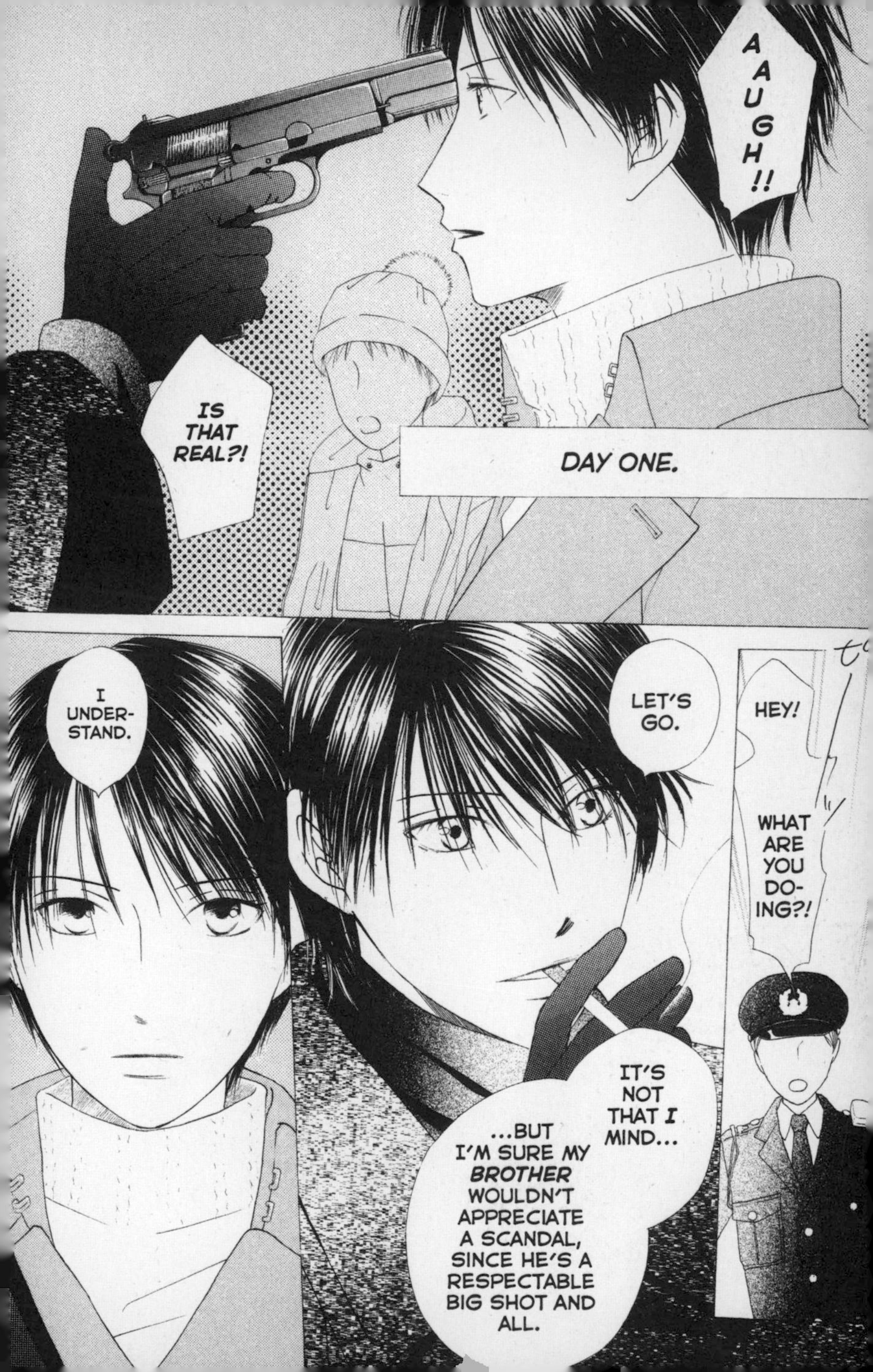
AAUGH!!
IS THAT REAL?!
DAY ONE.
HEY!
WHAT ARE YOU DO-ING?!
LET'S GO.
IT'S NOT THAT *I* MIND...
...BUT I'M SURE MY *BROTHER* WOULDN'T APPRECIATE A SCANDAL, SINCE HE'S A RESPECTABLE BIG SHOT AND ALL.
I UNDER-STAND.

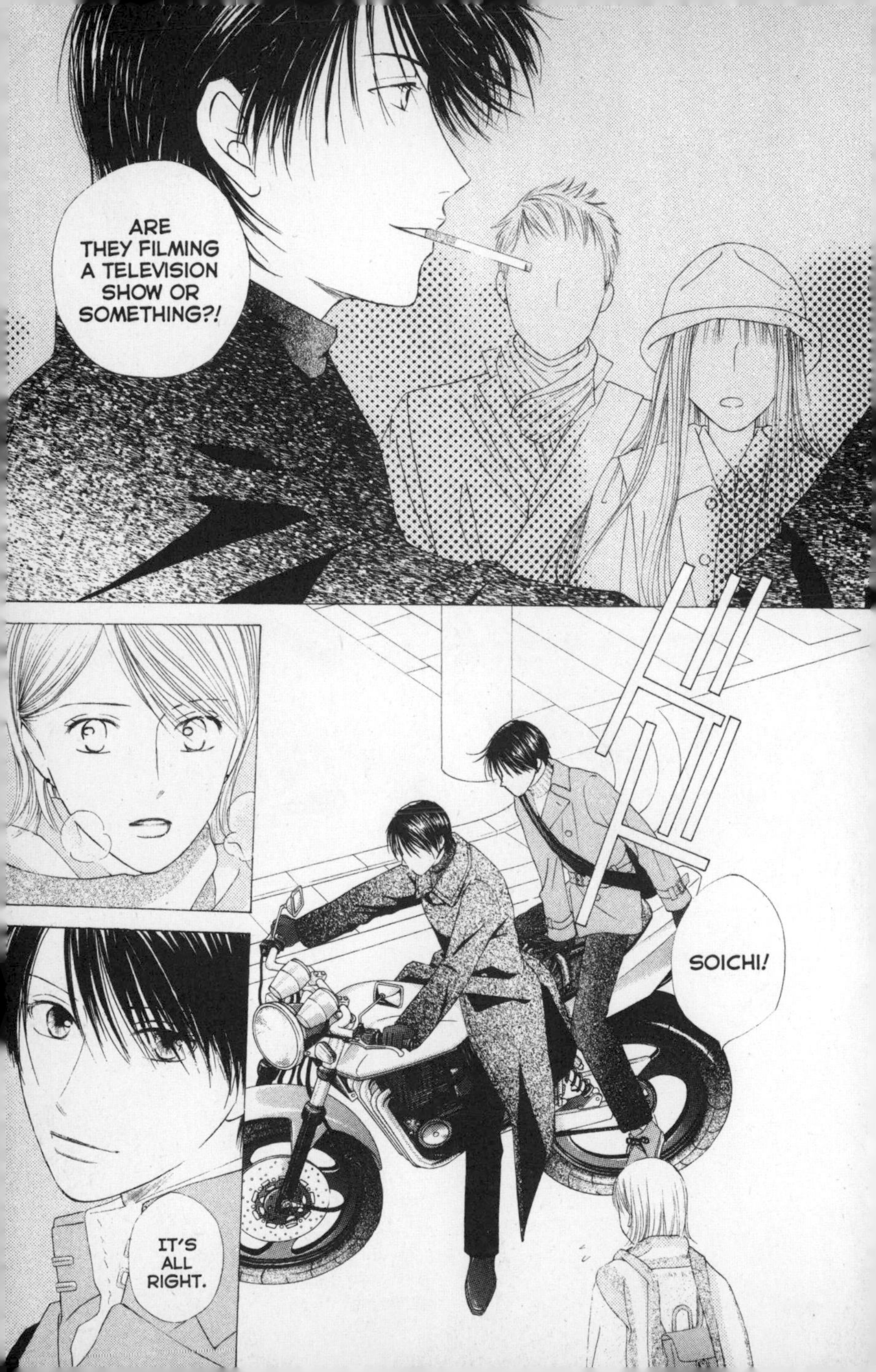
ARE THEY FILMING A TELEVISION SHOW OR SOMETHING?!
SOICHI!
IT'S ALL RIGHT.

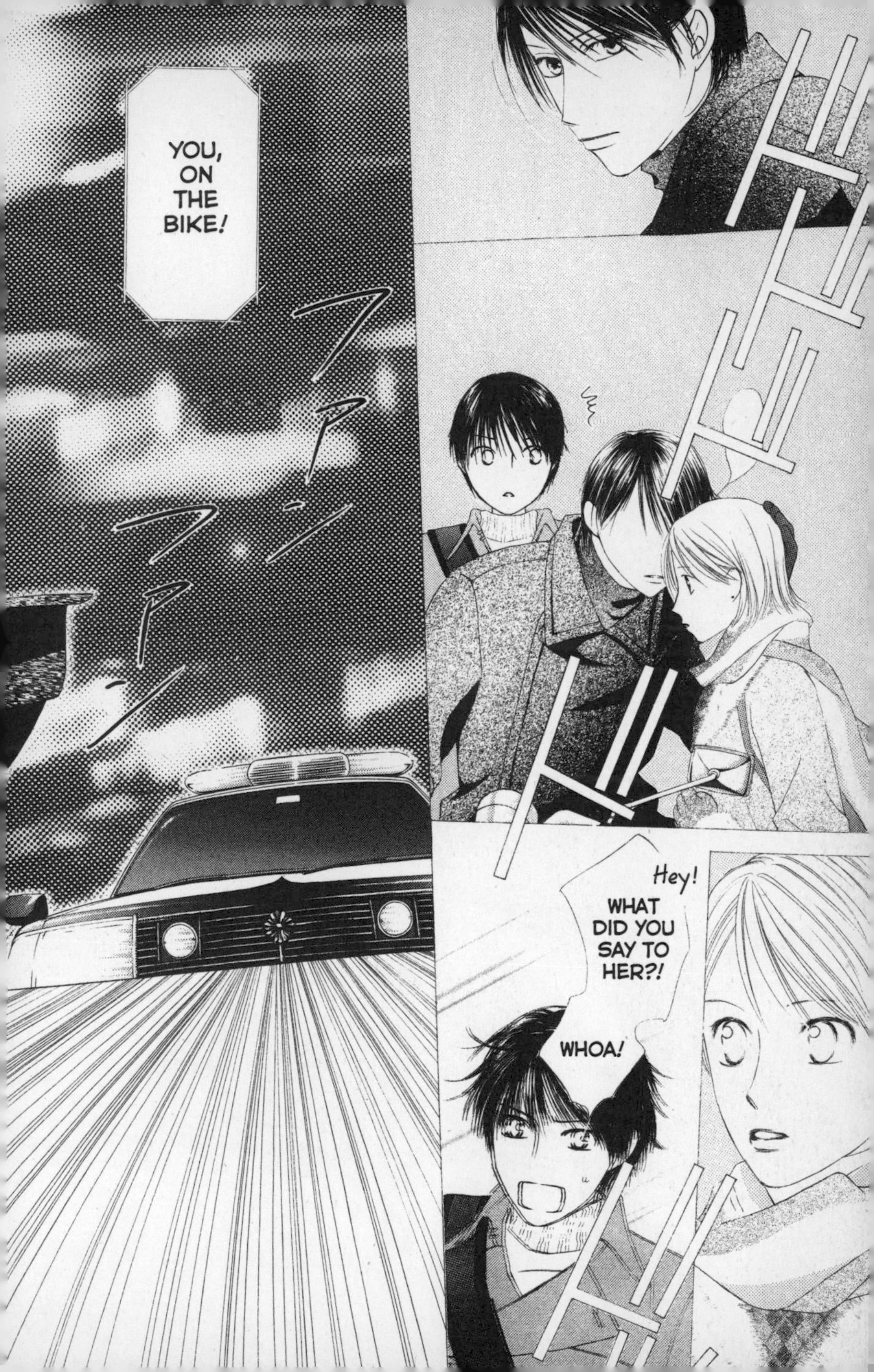
Hey!
WHAT DID YOU SAY TO HER?!
WHOA!
YOU, ON THE BIKE!

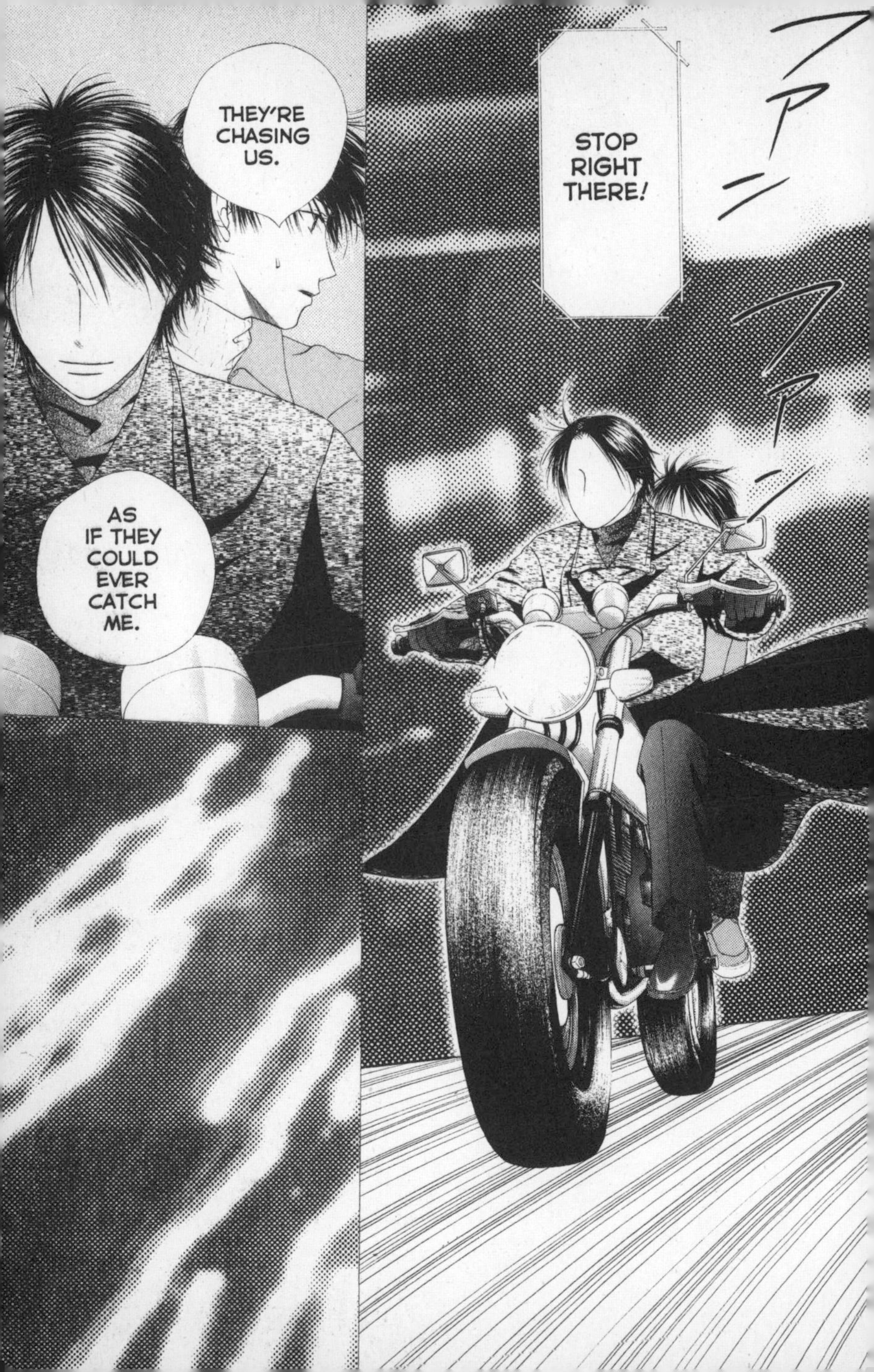
STOP RIGHT THERE!
THEY'RE CHASING US.
AS IF THEY COULD EVER CATCH ME.

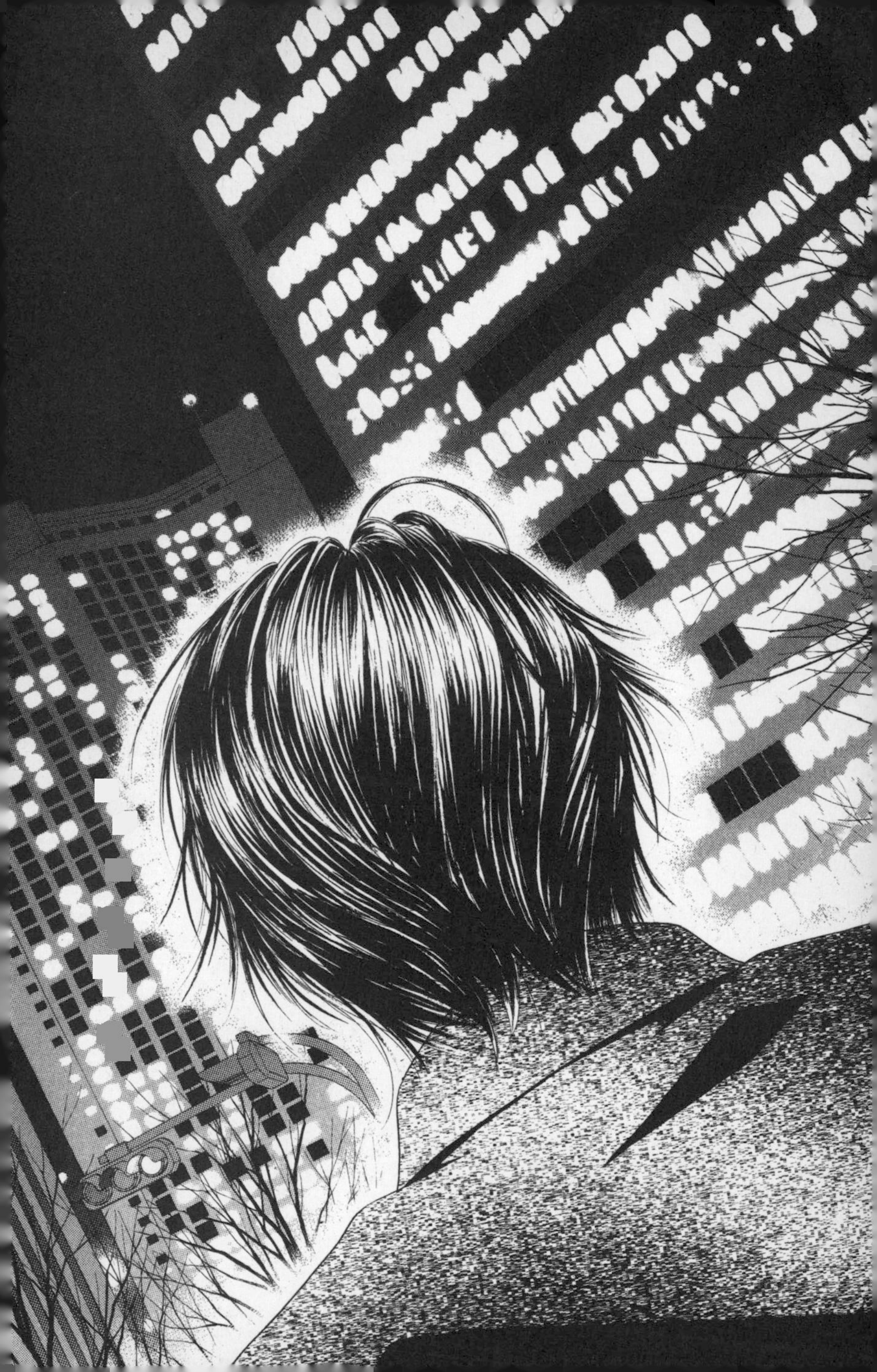

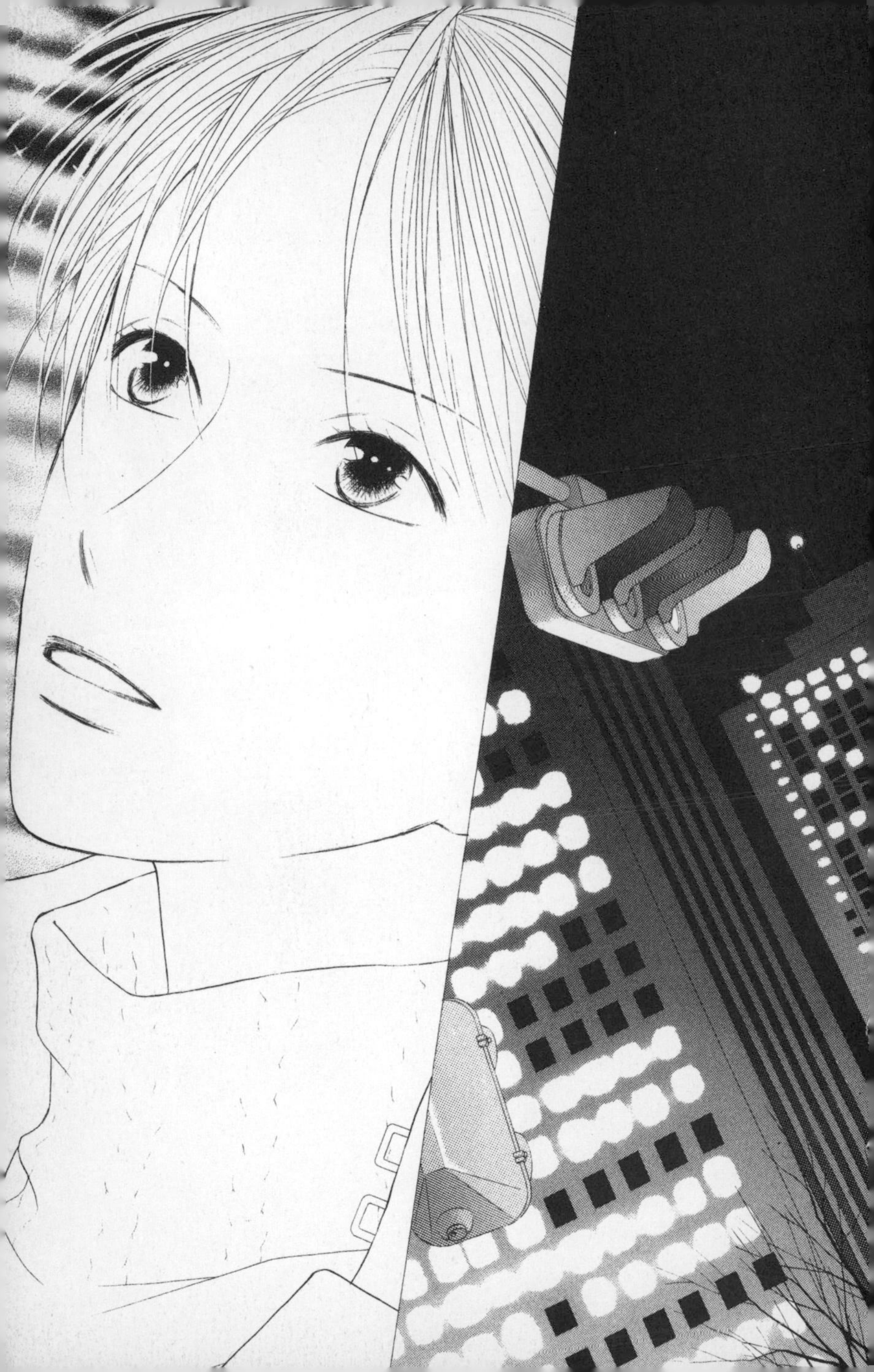

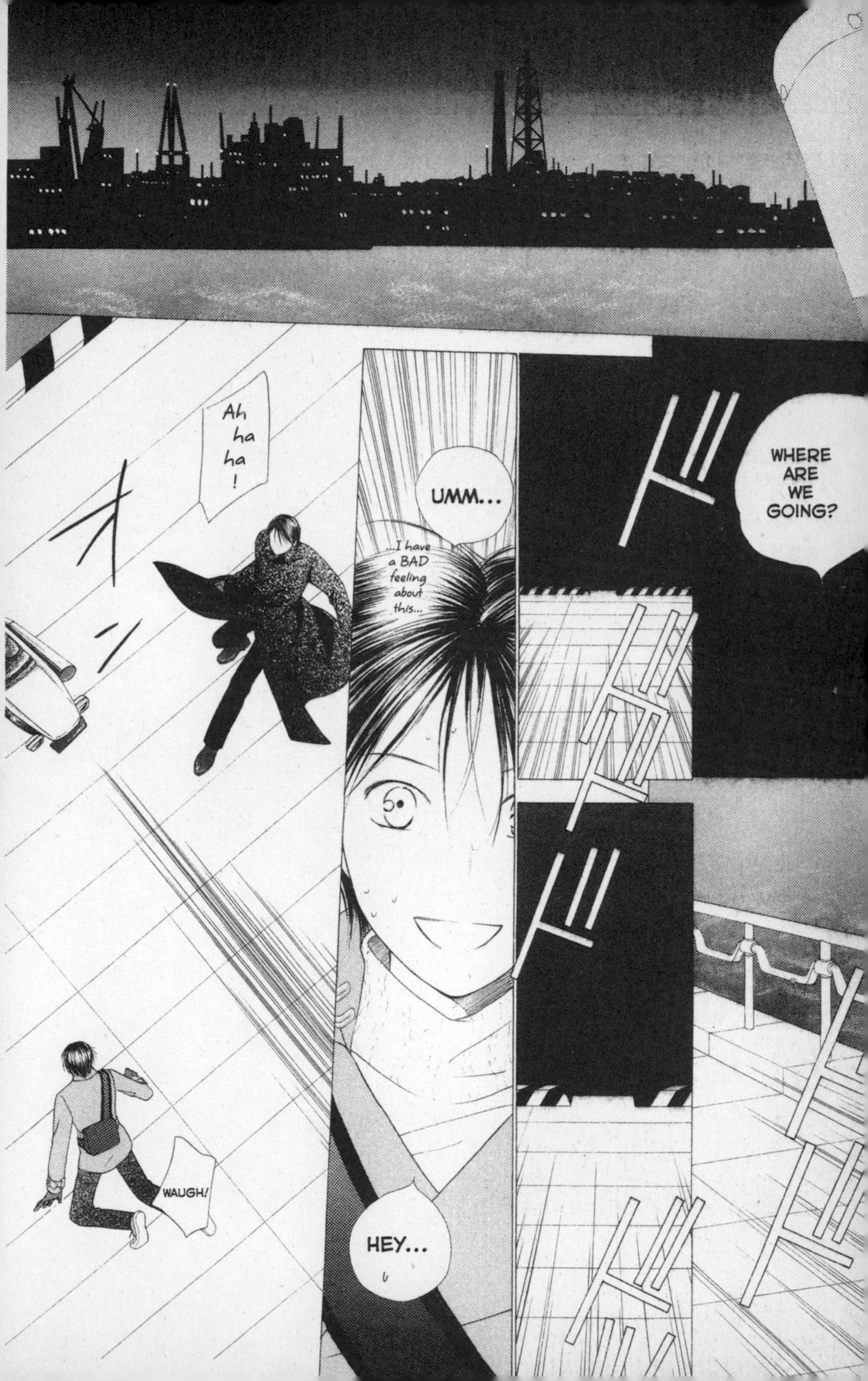
WHERE ARE WE GOING?
UMM...
...I have a BAD feeling about this...
HEY...
Ah ha ha!
WAUGH!

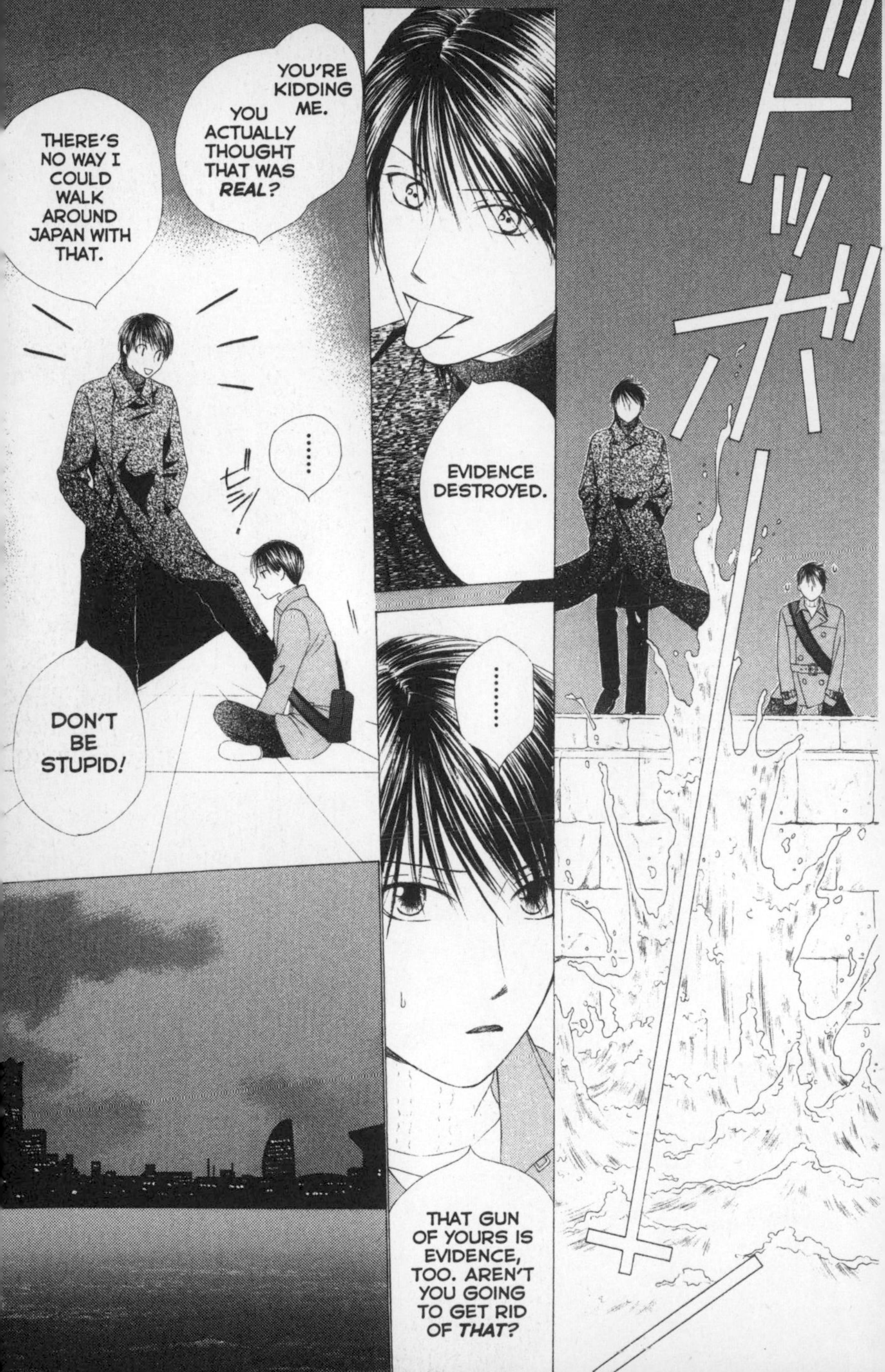
EVIDENCE DESTROYED.
......
THAT GUN OF YOURS IS EVIDENCE, TOO. AREN'T YOU GOING TO GET RID OF *THAT*?
YOU'RE KIDDING ME.
YOU ACTUALLY THOUGHT THAT WAS *REAL*?
THERE'S NO WAY I COULD WALK AROUND JAPAN WITH THAT.
......
DON'T BE STUPID!

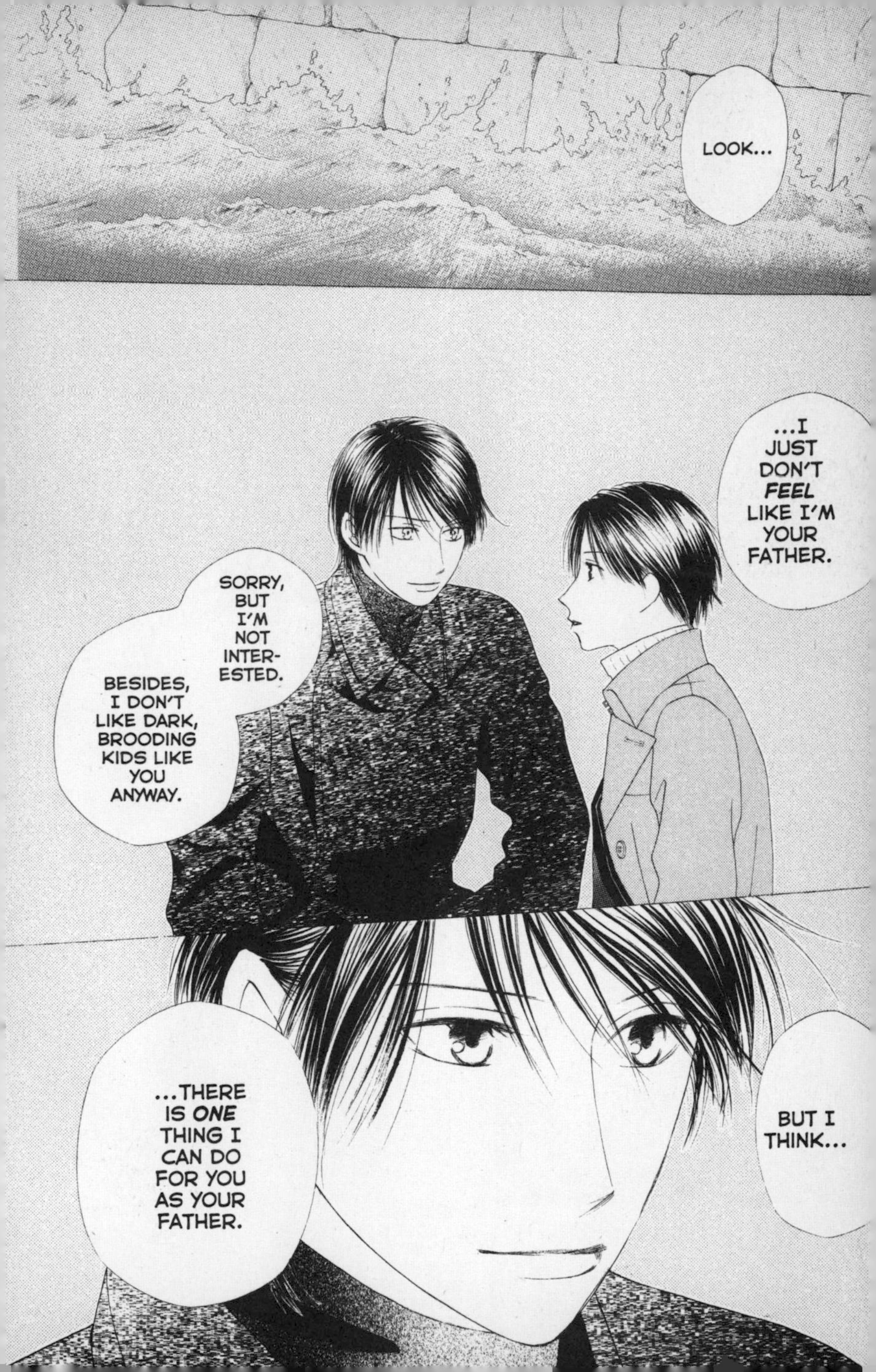
LOOK...
...I JUST DON'T *FEEL* LIKE I'M YOUR FATHER.
SORRY, BUT I'M NOT INTER-ESTED.
BESIDES, I DON'T LIKE DARK, BROODING KIDS LIKE YOU ANYWAY.
BUT I THINK...
...THERE IS *ONE* THING I CAN DO FOR YOU AS YOUR FATHER.

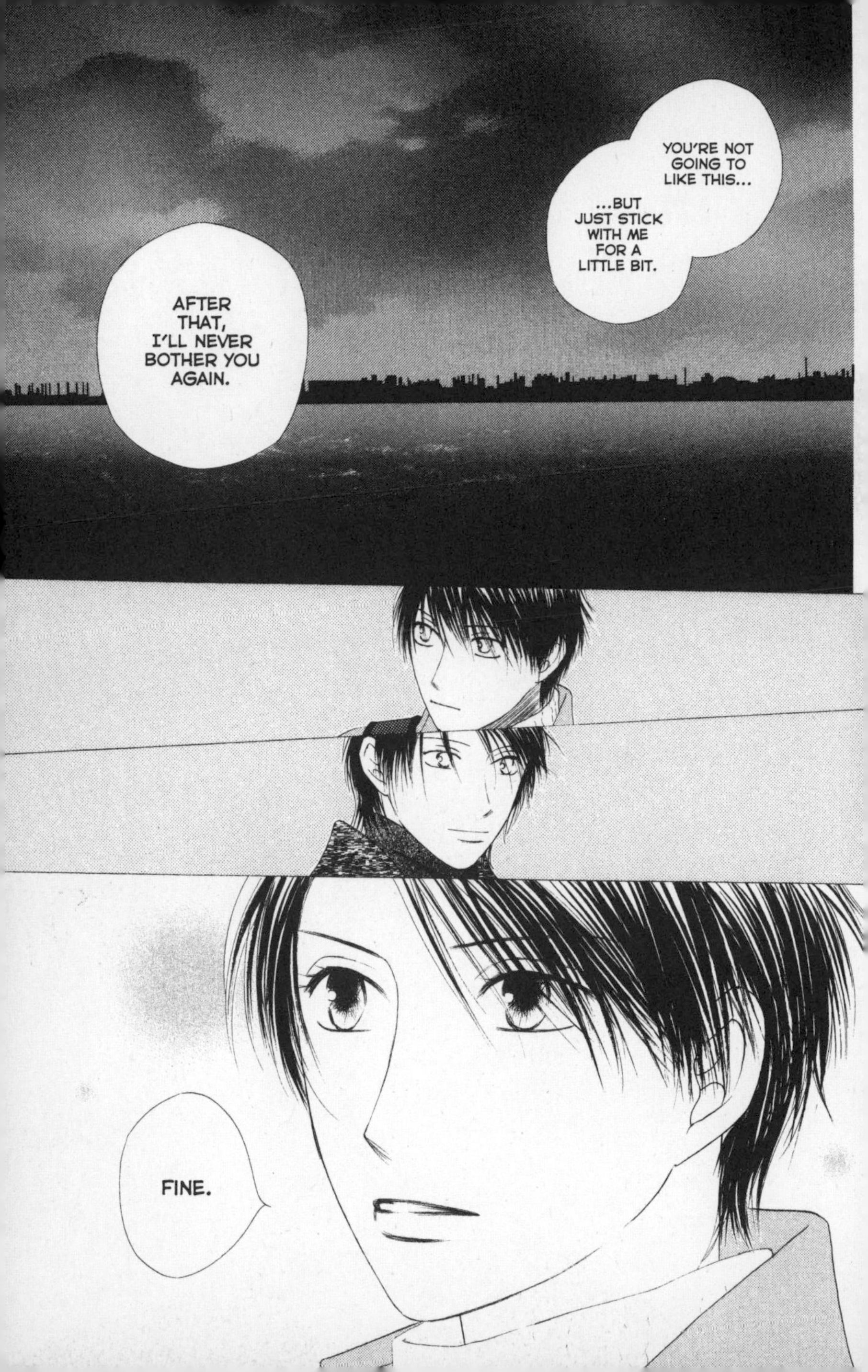
YOU'RE NOT GOING TO LIKE THIS...
...BUT JUST STICK WITH ME FOR A LITTLE BIT.
AFTER THAT, I'LL NEVER BOTHER YOU AGAIN.
FINE.

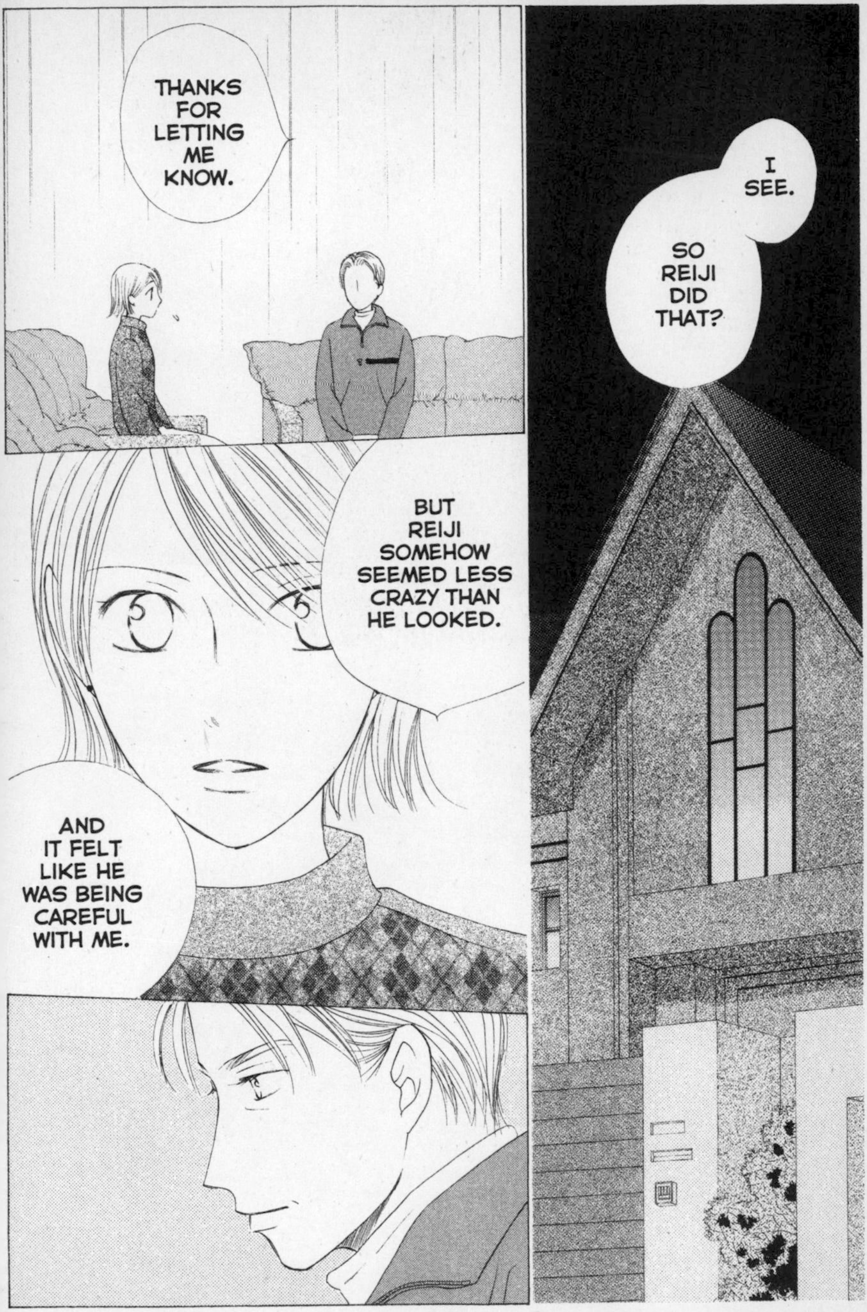
I SEE.
SO REIJI DID THAT?
THANKS FOR LETTING ME KNOW.
BUT REIJI SOMEHOW SEEMED LESS CRAZY THAN HE LOOKED.
AND IT FELT LIKE HE WAS BEING CAREFUL WITH ME.

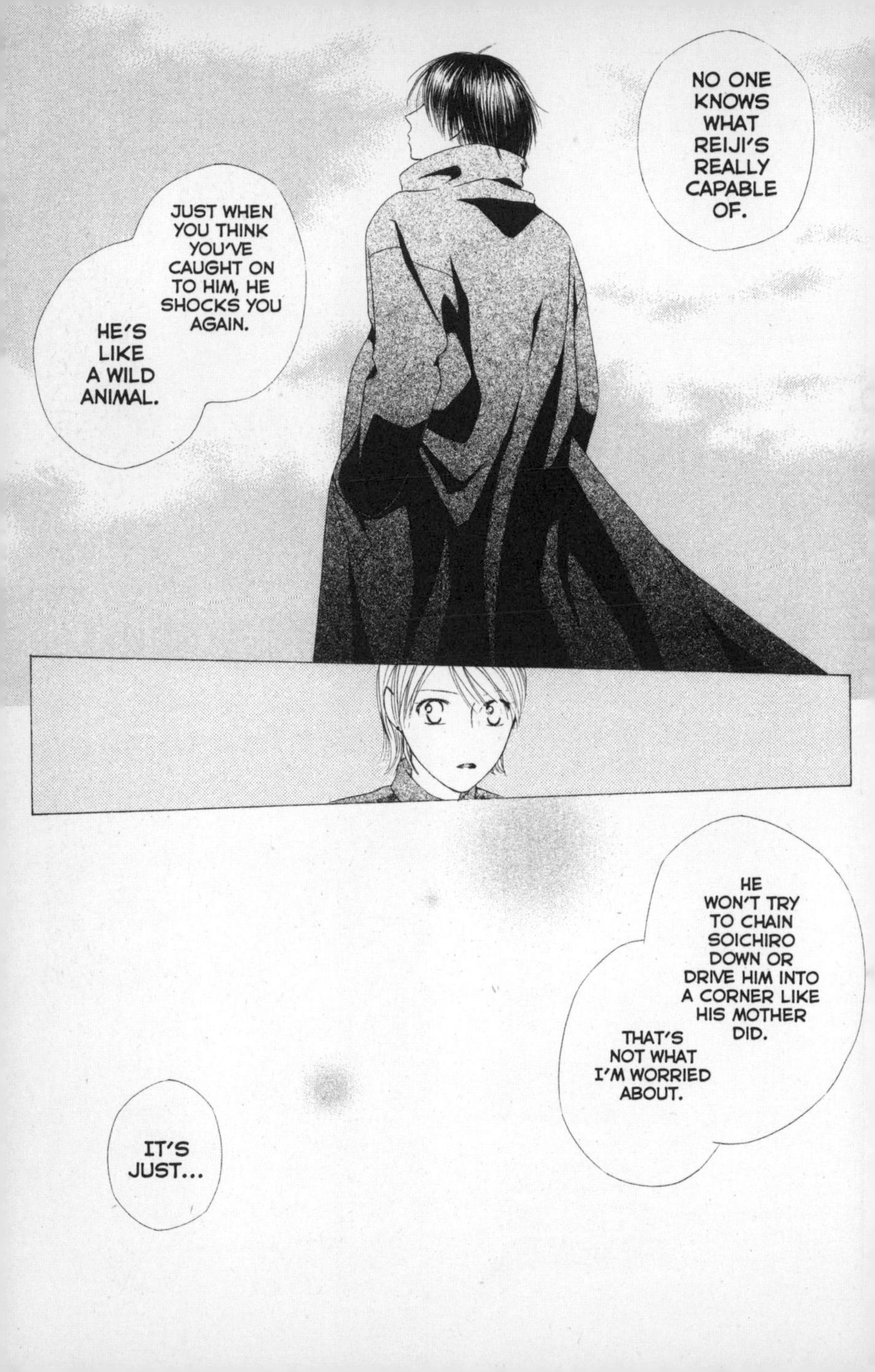
NO ONE KNOWS WHAT REIJI'S REALLY CAPABLE OF.
JUST WHEN YOU THINK YOU'VE CAUGHT ON TO HIM, HE SHOCKS YOU AGAIN.
HE'S LIKE A WILD ANIMAL.
HE WON'T TRY TO CHAIN SOICHIRO DOWN OR DRIVE HIM INTO A CORNER LIKE HIS MOTHER DID.
THAT'S NOT WHAT I'M WORRIED ABOUT.
IT'S JUST...

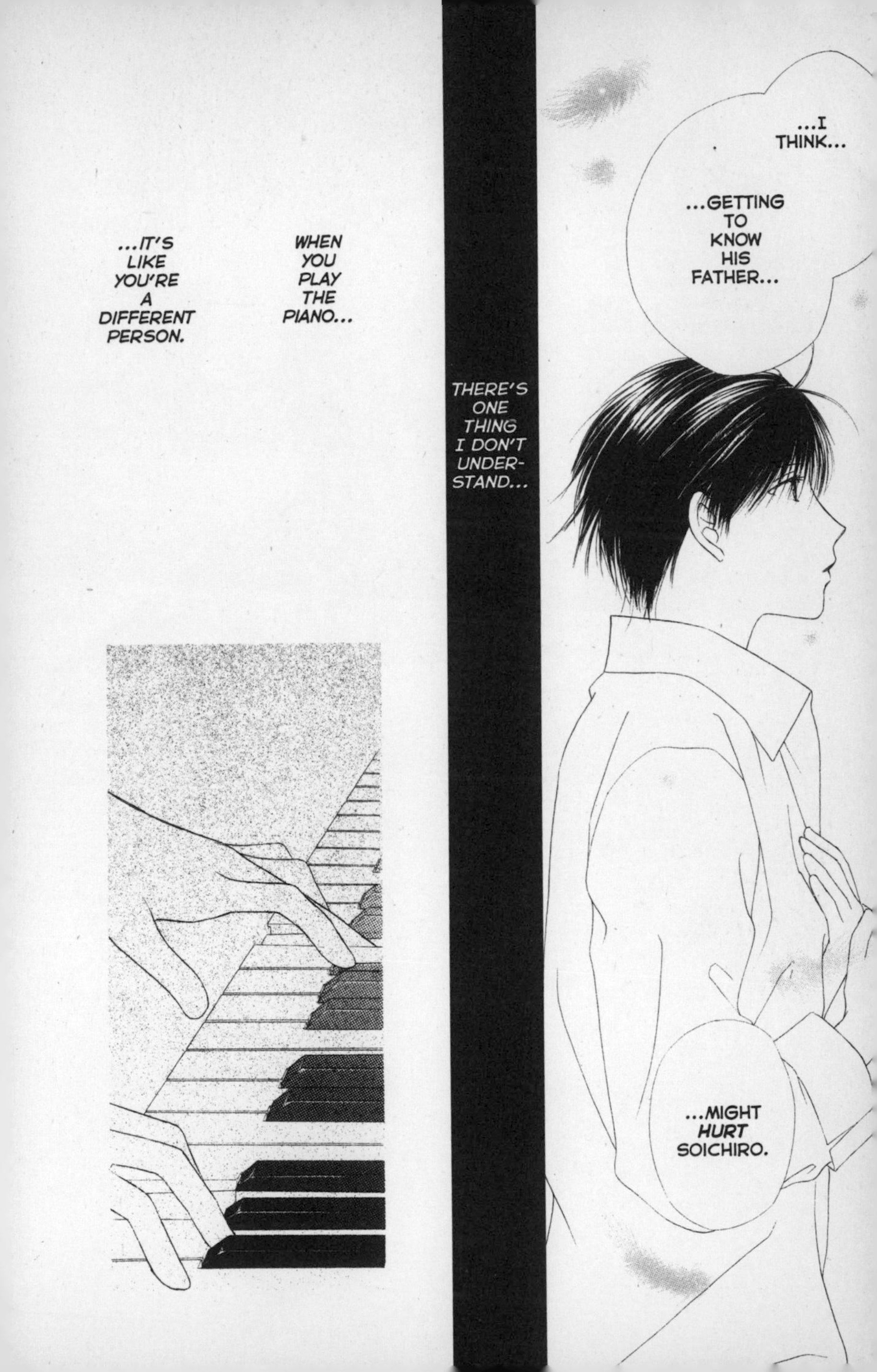
...I THINK...
...GETTING TO KNOW HIS FATHER...
...MIGHT *HURT* SOICHIRO.
THERE'S ONE THING I DON'T UNDER-STAND...
WHEN YOU PLAY THE PIANO...
...IT'S LIKE YOU'RE A DIFFERENT PERSON.

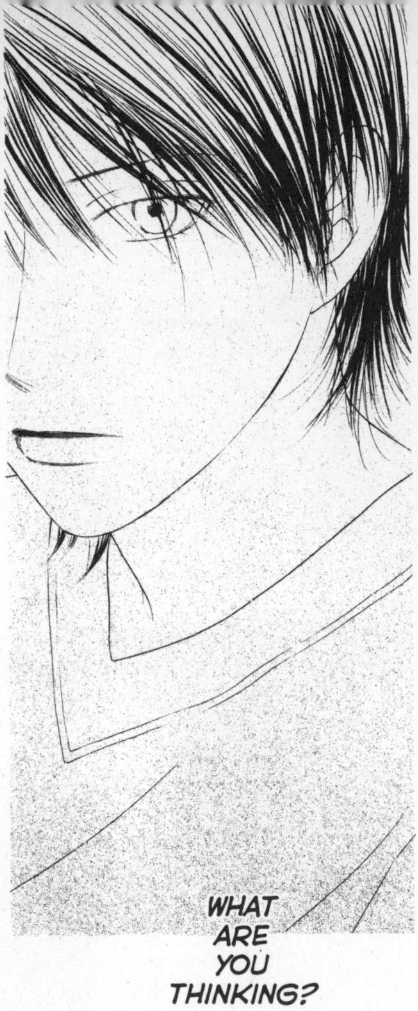
WHAT ARE YOU THINKING?

5

This is my last space to chat.

Writing this part was so much fun. A lot of mysteries have been unraveled!

By the time this is published you'll already know this, but this year was all about my work. So next year, I'm going to take time to do lots of things for myself! ♡ ♡ I can't wait! ♡ Of course, I'm still going to be working hard, so if you'd like, please take a look at the next volume, too!

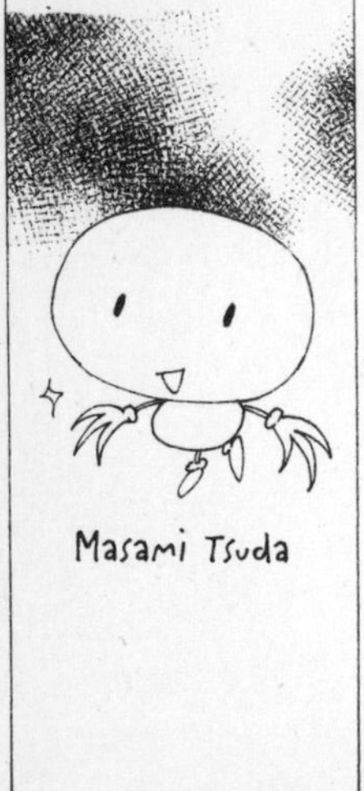

Masami Tsuda

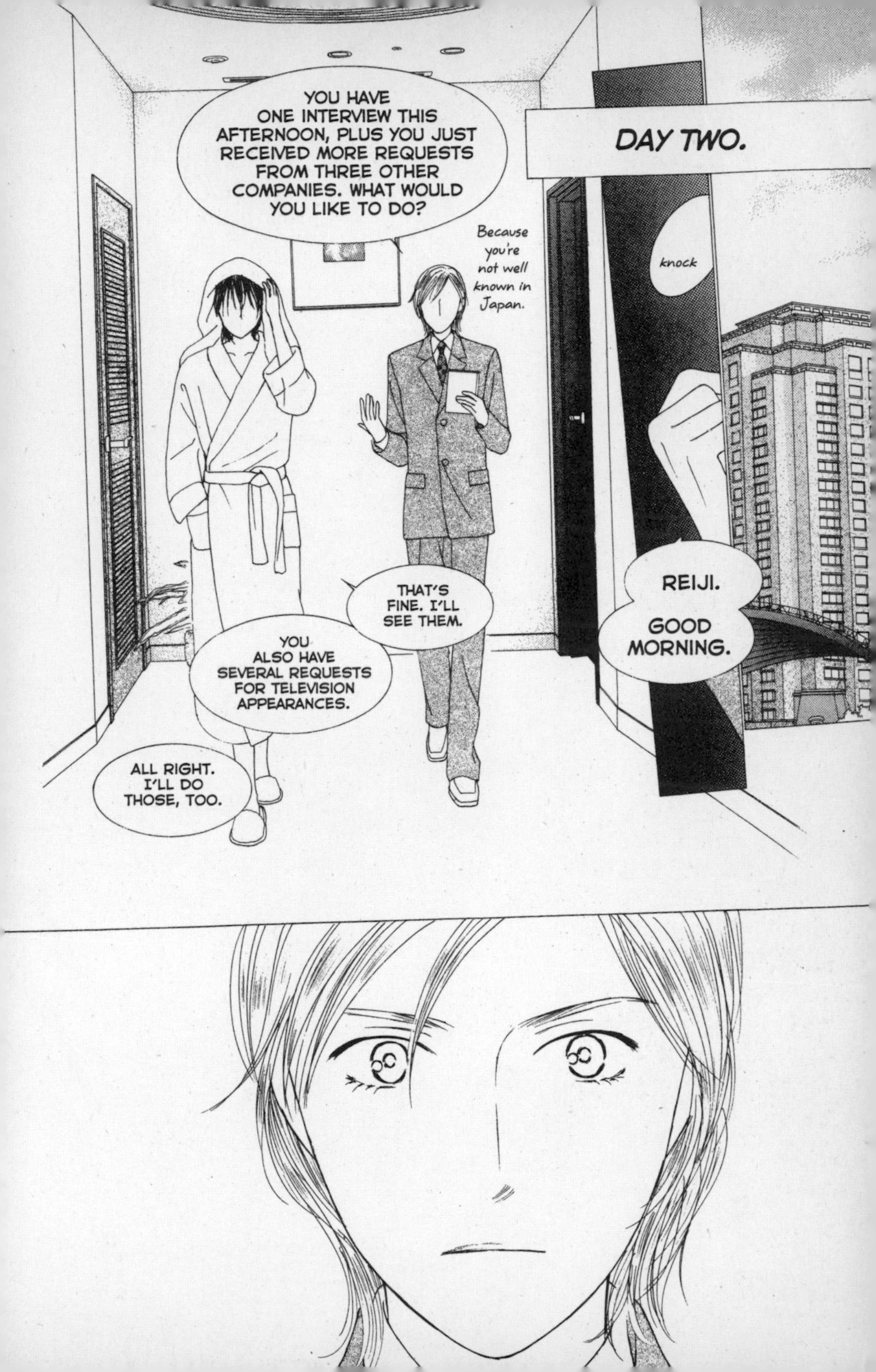
DAY TWO.
knock
REIJI.
GOOD MORNING.
YOU HAVE ONE INTERVIEW THIS AFTERNOON, PLUS YOU JUST RECEIVED MORE REQUESTS FROM THREE OTHER COMPANIES. WHAT WOULD YOU LIKE TO DO?
Because you're not well known in Japan.
THAT'S FINE. I'LL SEE THEM.
YOU ALSO HAVE SEVERAL REQUESTS FOR TELEVISION APPEARANCES.
ALL RIGHT. I'LL DO THOSE, TOO.

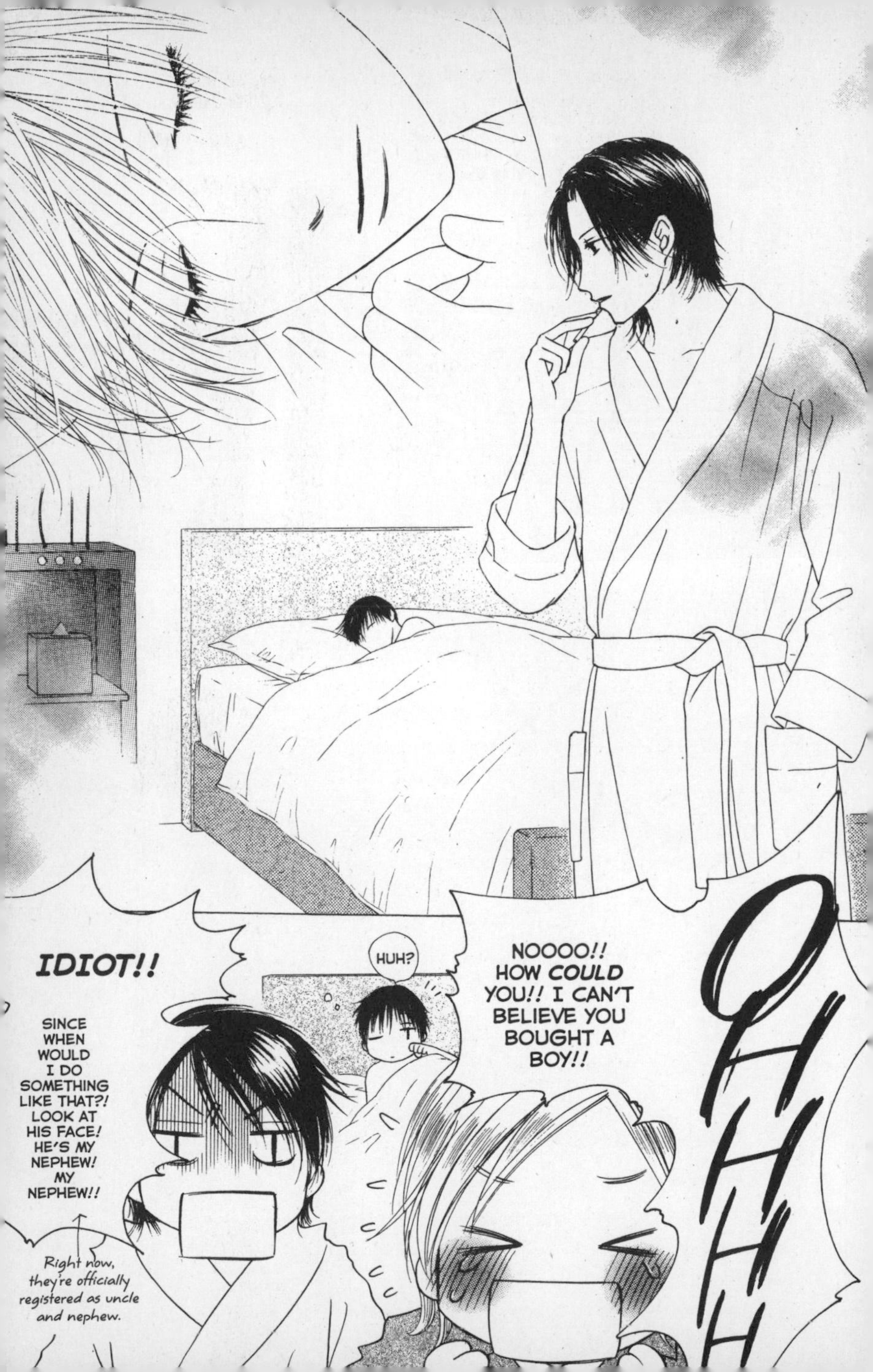
NOOOO!! HOW **COULD** YOU!! I CAN'T BELIEVE YOU BOUGHT A BOY!!
HUH?
IDIOT!!
SINCE WHEN WOULD I DO SOMETHING LIKE THAT?! LOOK AT HIS FACE! HE'S MY NEPHEW! MY NEPHEW!!
Right now, they're officially registered as uncle and nephew.

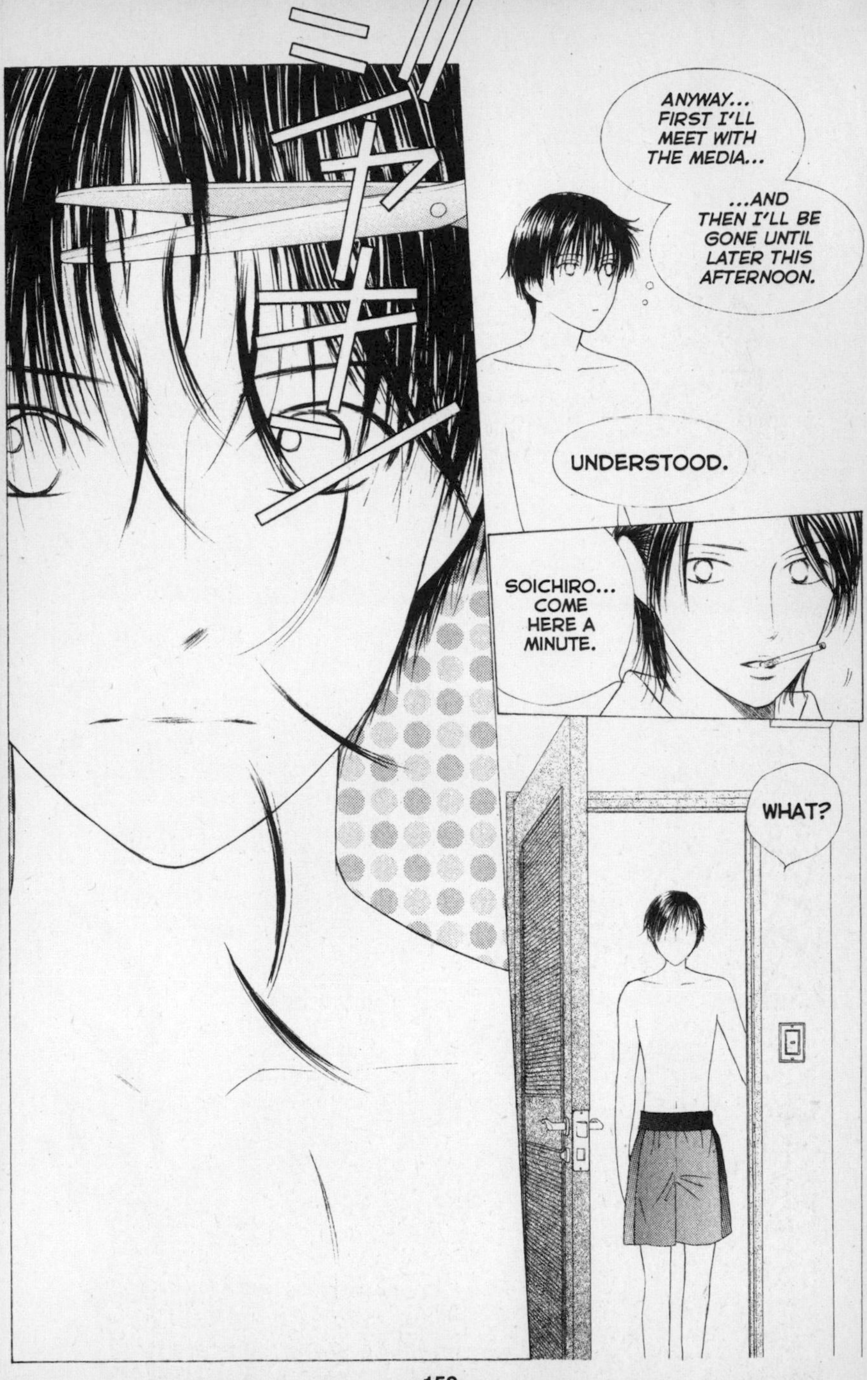
ANYWAY... FIRST I'LL MEET WITH THE MEDIA...
...AND THEN I'LL BE GONE UNTIL LATER THIS AFTERNOON.
UNDERSTOOD.
SOICHIRO... COME HERE A MINUTE.
WHAT?

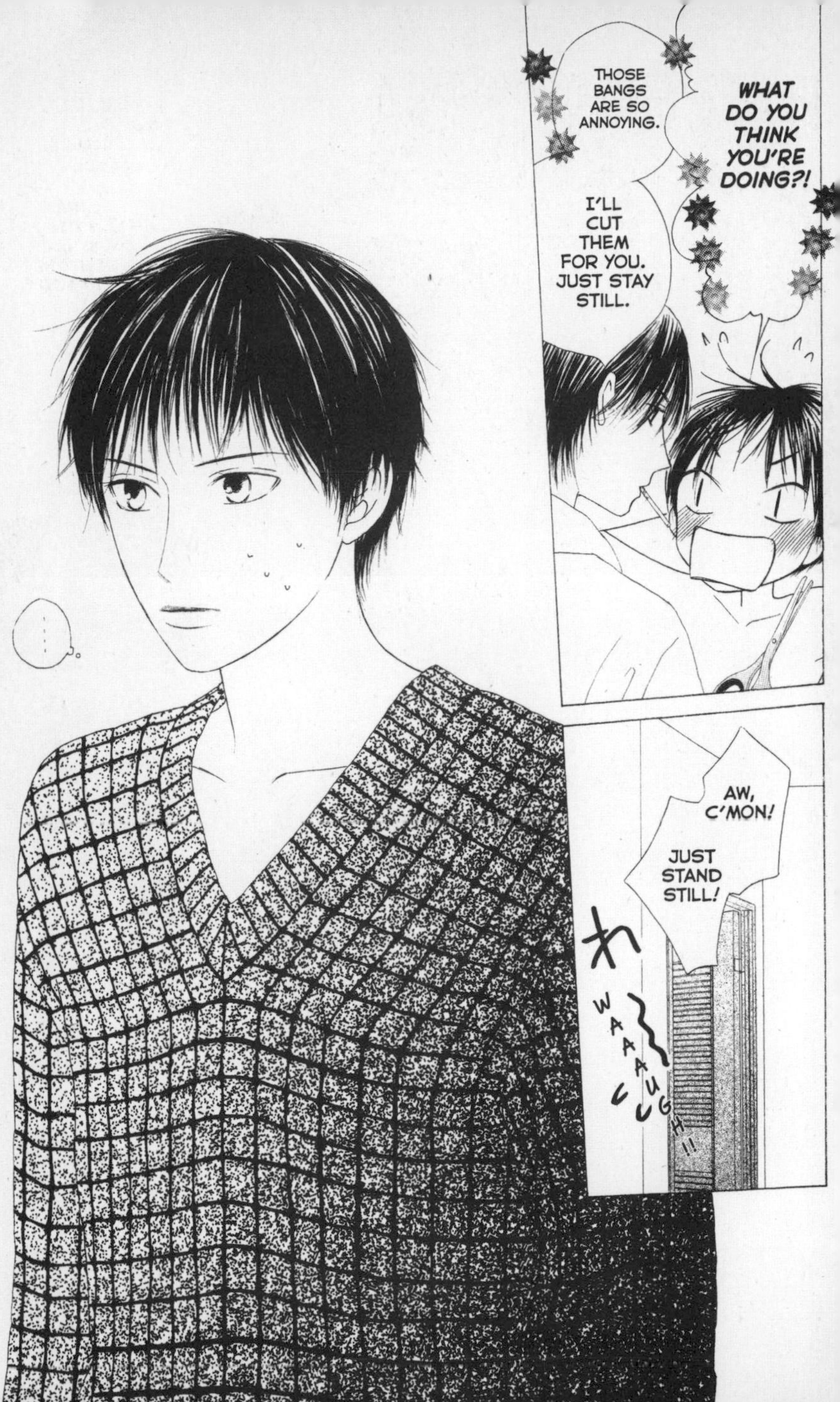
WHAT DO YOU THINK YOU'RE DOING?!
THOSE BANGS ARE SO ANNOYING.
I'LL CUT THEM FOR YOU. JUST STAY STILL.
AW, C'MON!
JUST STAND STILL!
わ
WAAAAUGH!!

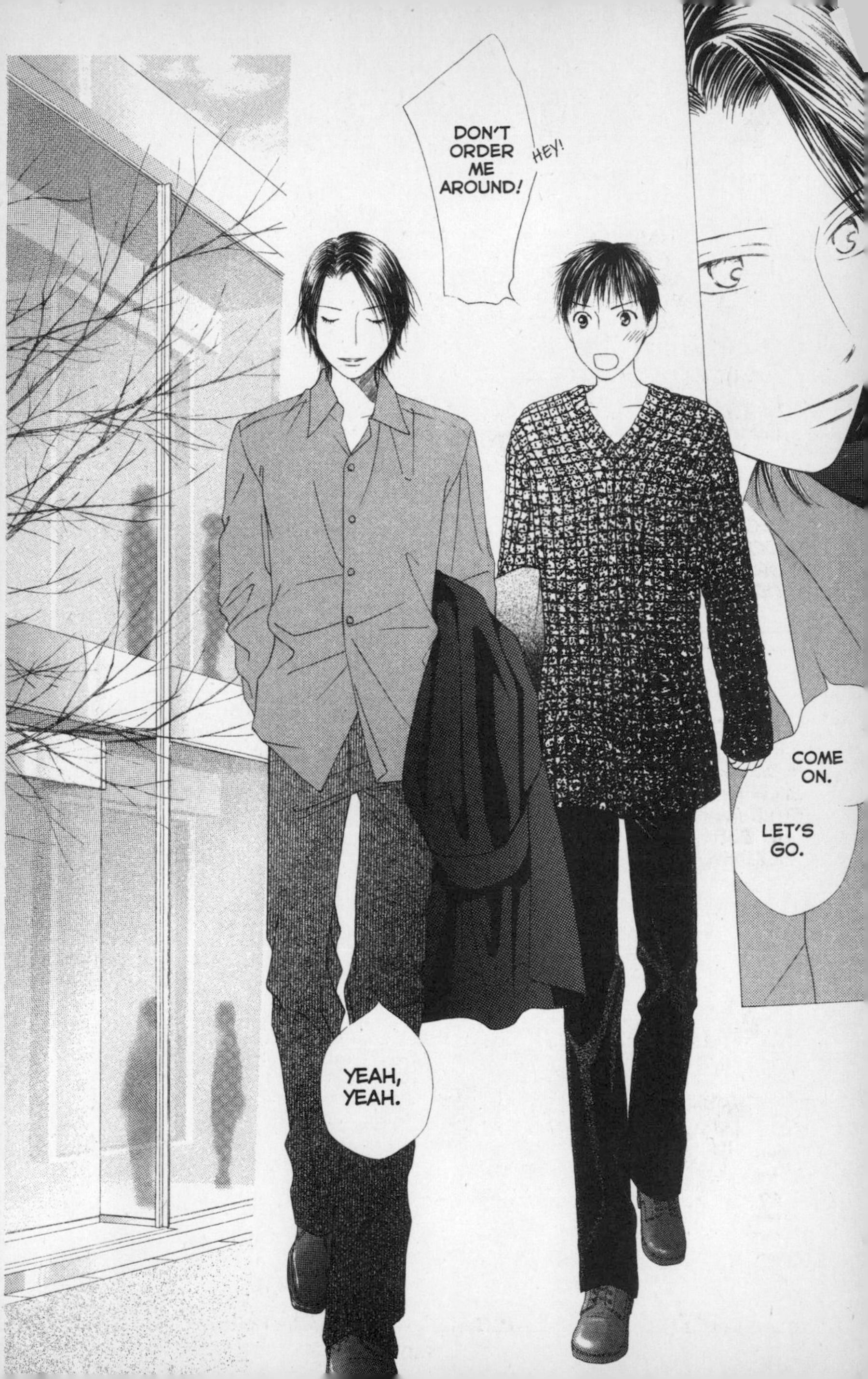
COME ON.
LET'S GO.
HEY!
DON'T ORDER ME AROUND!
YEAH, YEAH.

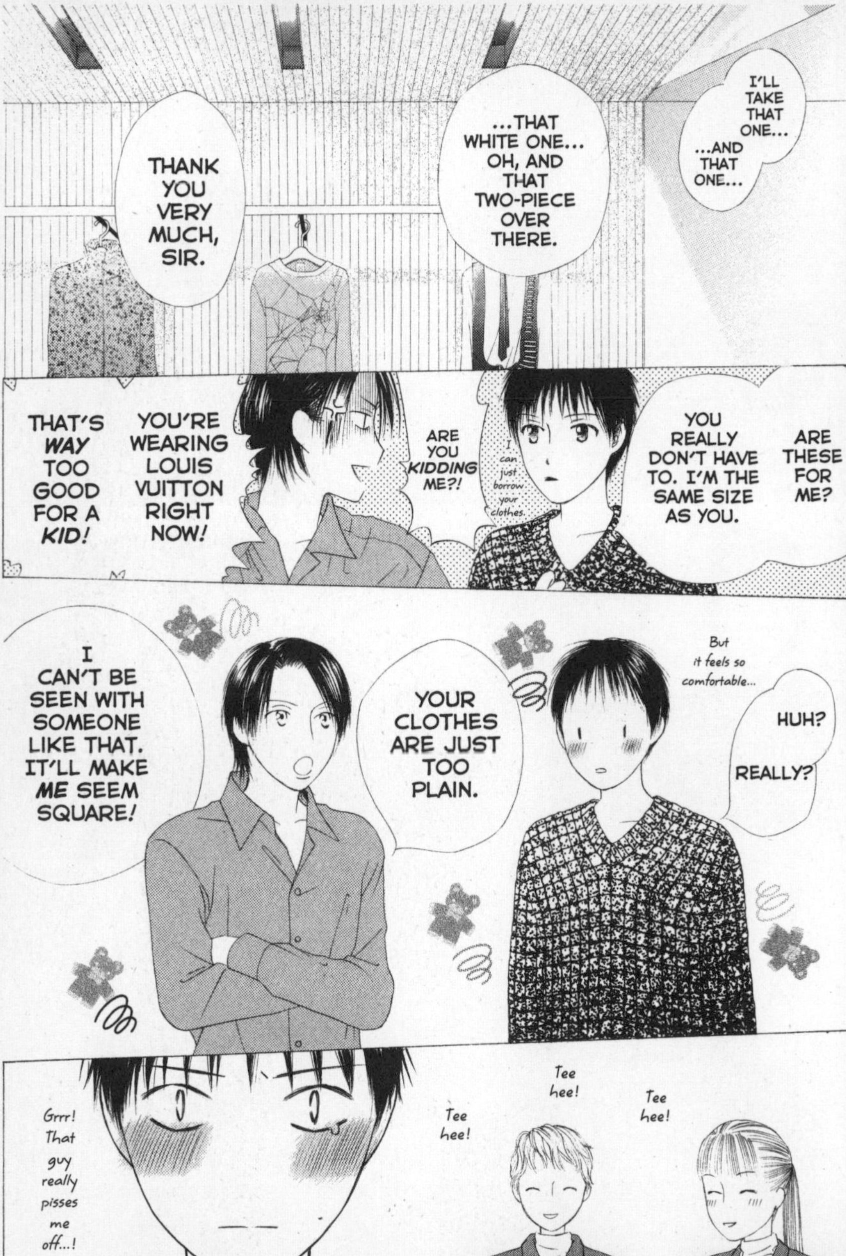
I'LL TAKE THAT ONE...
...AND THAT ONE...
...THAT WHITE ONE... OH, AND THAT TWO-PIECE OVER THERE.
THANK YOU VERY MUCH, SIR.
ARE THESE FOR ME?
YOU REALLY DON'T HAVE TO. I'M THE SAME SIZE AS YOU.
I can just borrow your clothes.
ARE YOU KIDDING ME?!
YOU'RE WEARING LOUIS VUITTON RIGHT NOW!
THAT'S WAY TOO GOOD FOR A KID!
But it feels so comfortable...
HUH?
REALLY?
YOUR CLOTHES ARE JUST TOO PLAIN.
I CAN'T BE SEEN WITH SOMEONE LIKE THAT. IT'LL MAKE ME SEEM SQUARE!
Tee hee!
Tee hee!
Tee hee!
Grrr! That guy really pisses me off...!

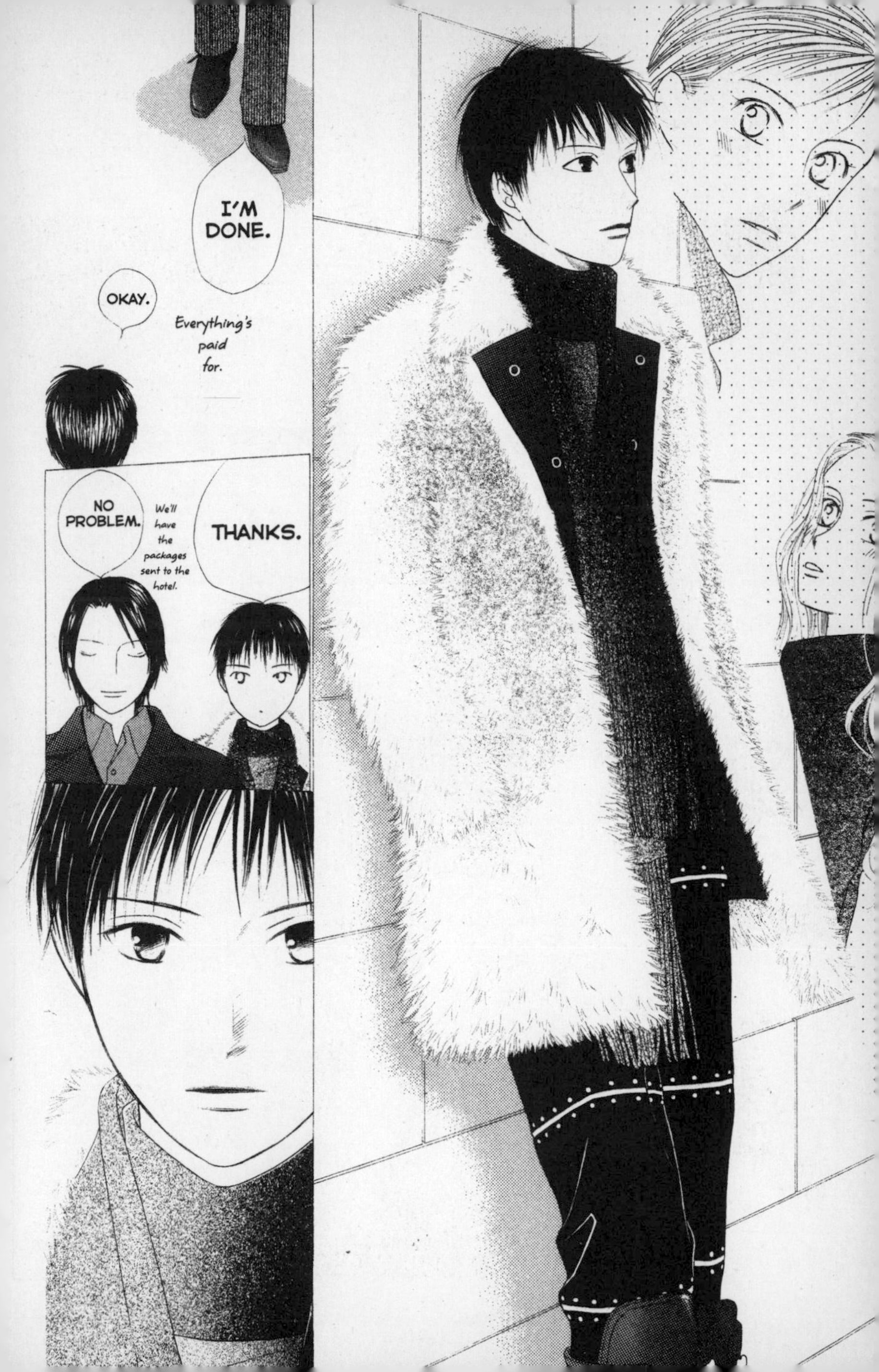
I'M DONE.
OKAY.
Everything's paid for.
THANKS.
NO PROBLEM.
We'll have the packages sent to the hotel.

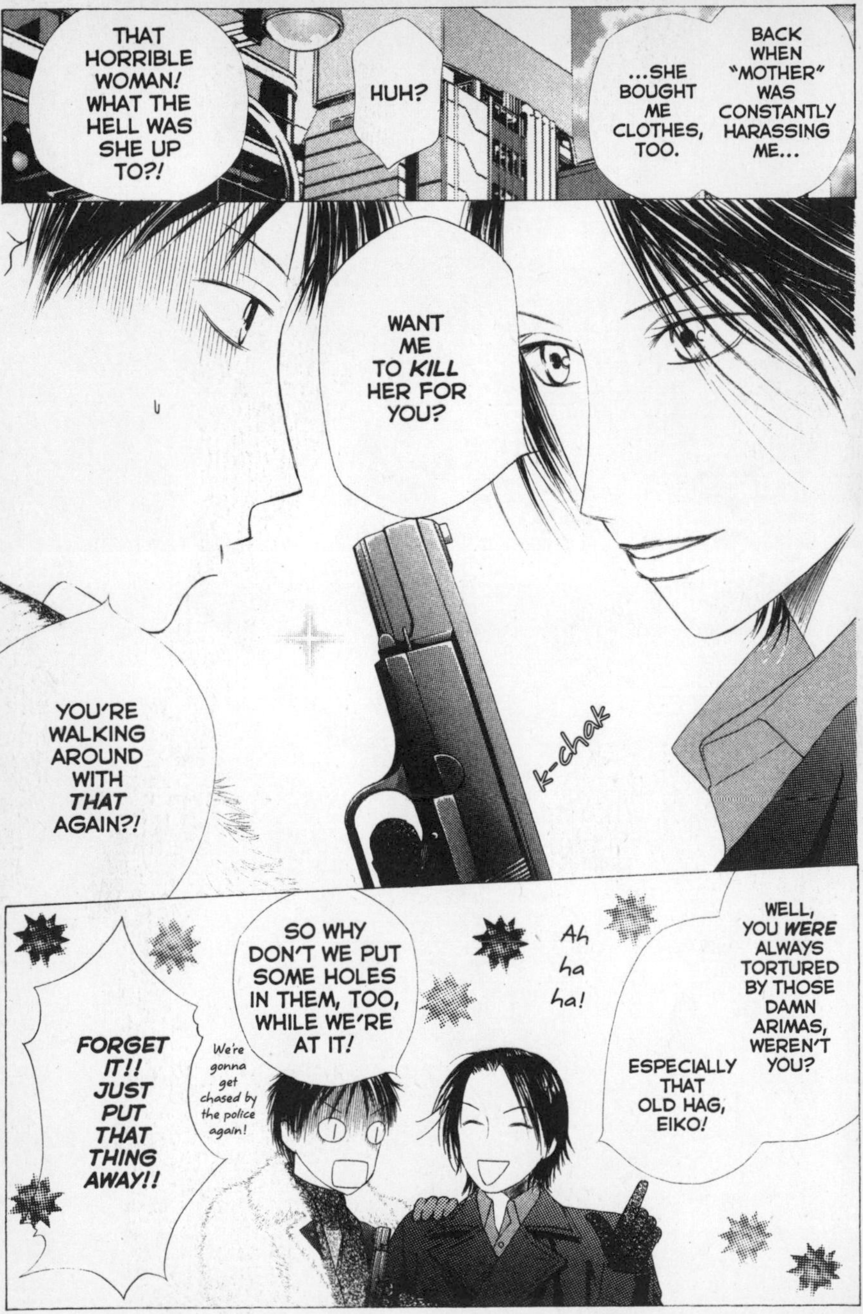
BACK WHEN "MOTHER" WAS CONSTANTLY HARASSING ME...
...SHE BOUGHT ME CLOTHES, TOO.
HUH?
THAT HORRIBLE WOMAN! WHAT THE HELL WAS SHE UP TO?!
WANT ME TO KILL HER FOR YOU?
k-chak
YOU'RE WALKING AROUND WITH THAT AGAIN?!
WELL, YOU WERE ALWAYS TORTURED BY THOSE DAMN ARIMAS, WEREN'T YOU?
ESPECIALLY THAT OLD HAG, EIKO!
Ah ha ha!
SO WHY DON'T WE PUT SOME HOLES IN THEM, TOO, WHILE WE'RE AT IT!
We're gonna get chased by the police again!
FORGET IT!! JUST PUT THAT THING AWAY!!

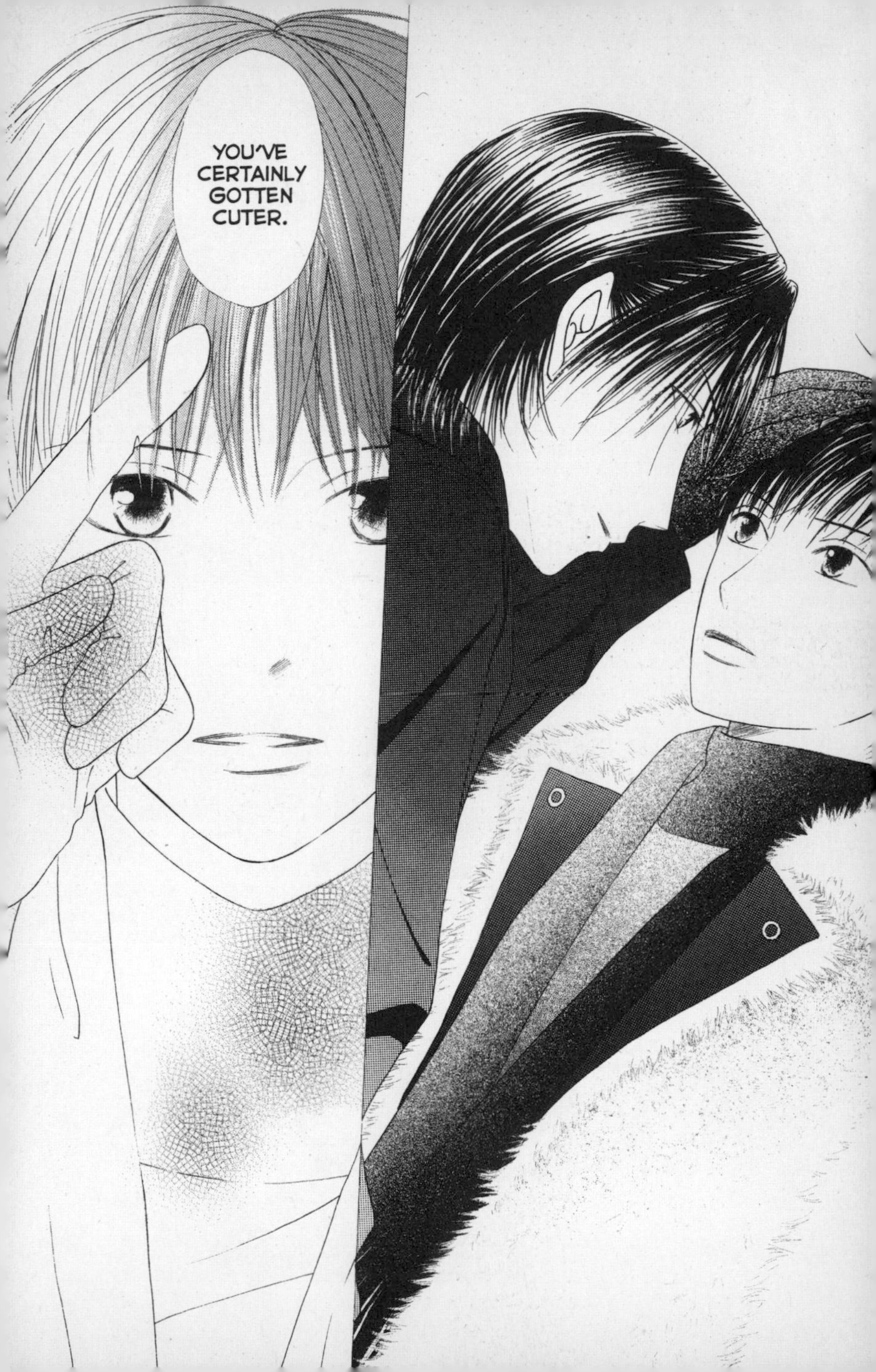
YOU'VE CERTAINLY GOTTEN CUTER.

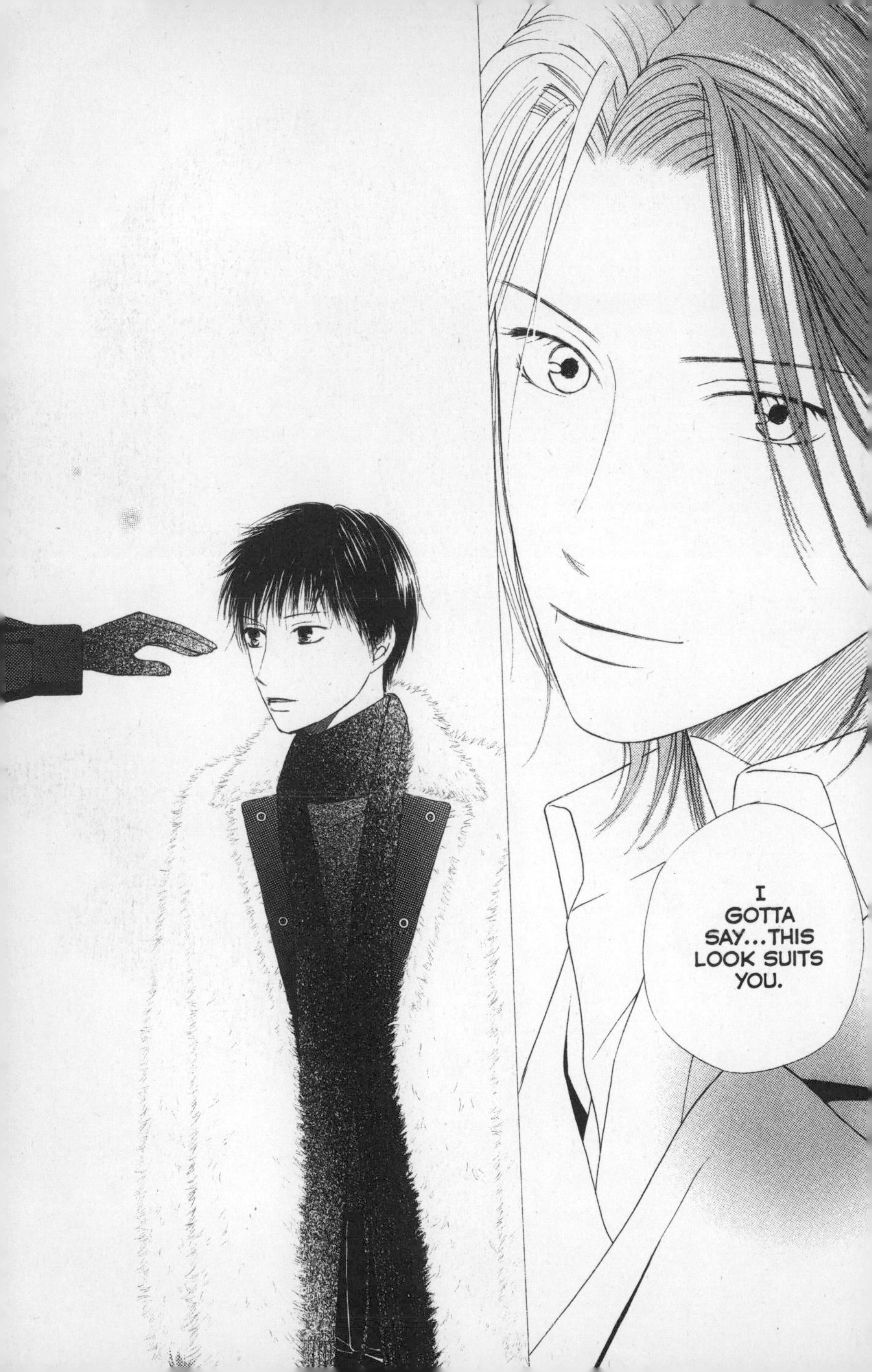
I GOTTA SAY...THIS LOOK SUITS YOU.

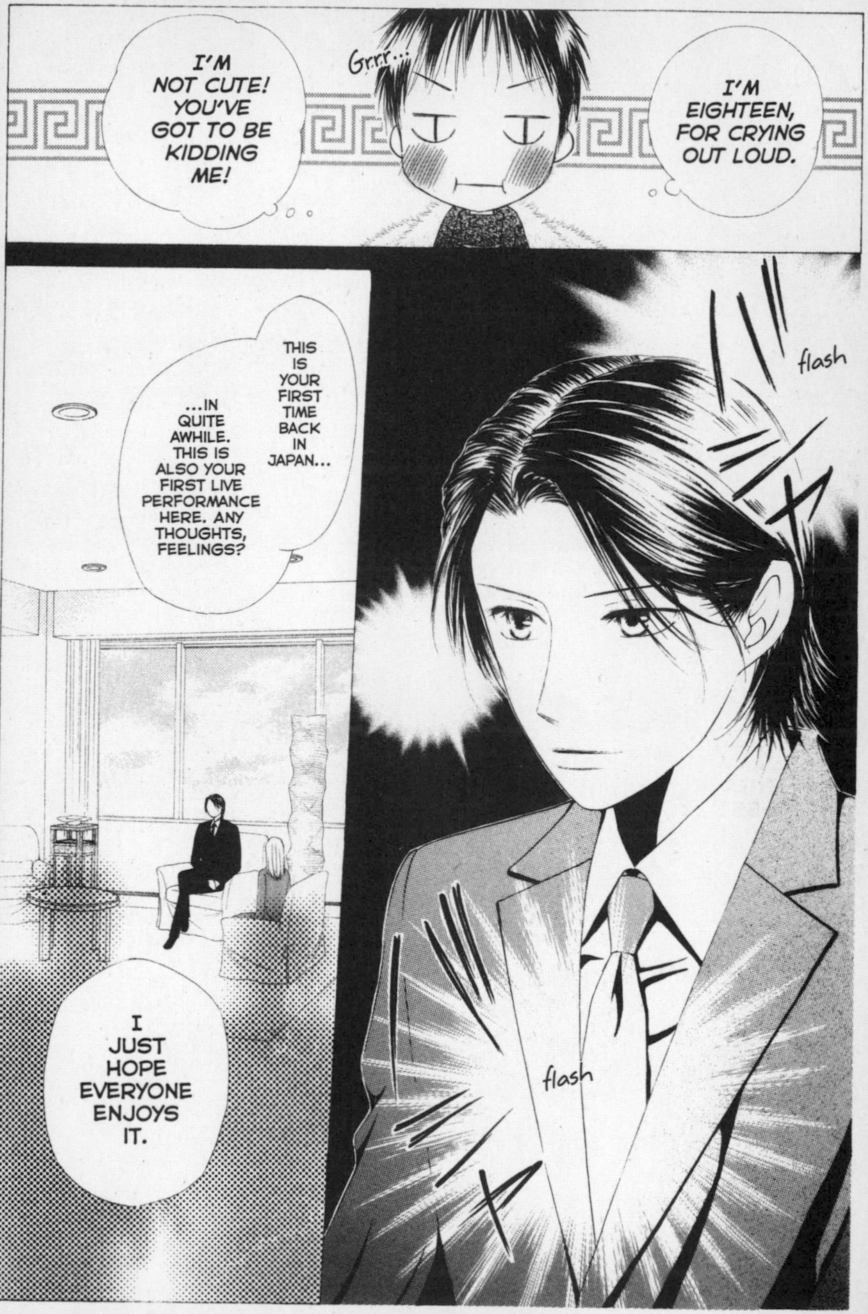
I'M EIGHTEEN, FOR CRYING OUT LOUD.
Grrr...
I'M NOT CUTE! YOU'VE GOT TO BE KIDDING ME!
flash
flash
THIS IS YOUR FIRST TIME BACK IN JAPAN...
...IN QUITE AWHILE. THIS IS ALSO YOUR FIRST LIVE PERFORMANCE HERE. ANY THOUGHTS, FEELINGS?
I JUST HOPE EVERYONE ENJOYS IT.

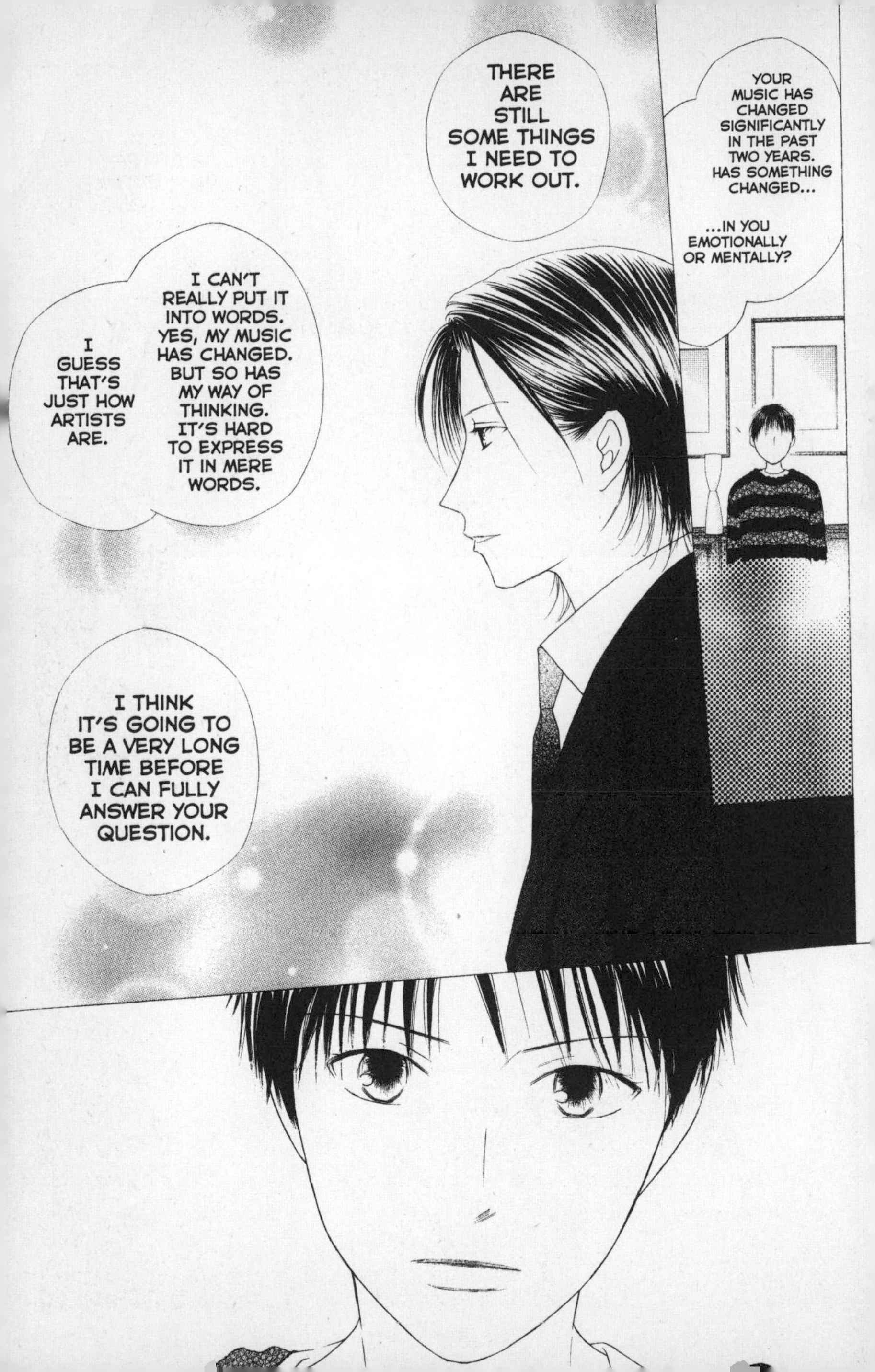
YOUR MUSIC HAS CHANGED SIGNIFICANTLY IN THE PAST TWO YEARS. HAS SOMETHING CHANGED...
...IN YOU EMOTIONALLY OR MENTALLY?
THERE ARE STILL SOME THINGS I NEED TO WORK OUT.
I CAN'T REALLY PUT IT INTO WORDS. YES, MY MUSIC HAS CHANGED. BUT SO HAS MY WAY OF THINKING. IT'S HARD TO EXPRESS IT IN MERE WORDS.
I GUESS THAT'S JUST HOW ARTISTS ARE.
I THINK IT'S GOING TO BE A VERY LONG TIME BEFORE I CAN FULLY ANSWER YOUR QUESTION.

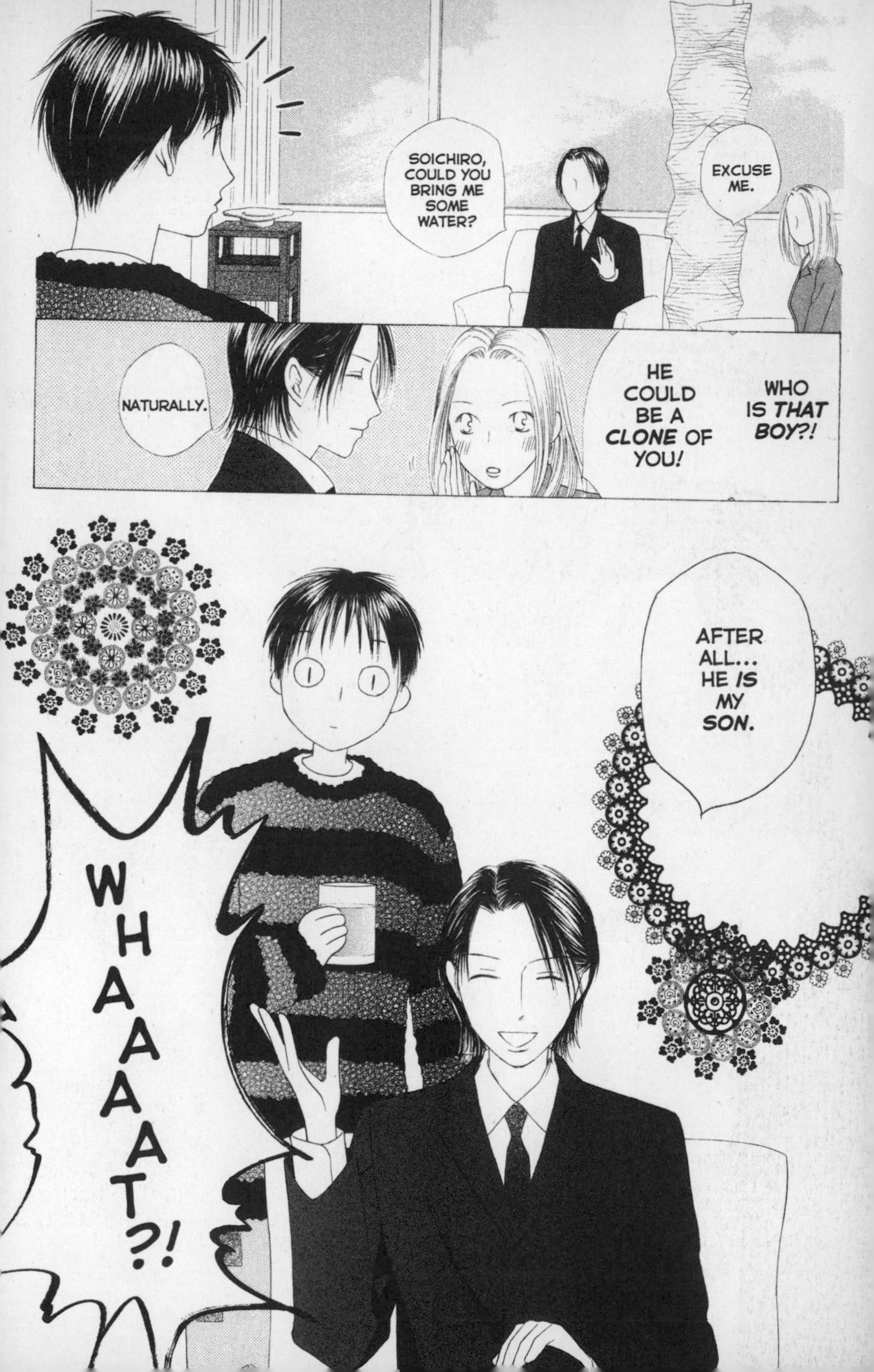
EXCUSE ME.
SOICHIRO, COULD YOU BRING ME SOME WATER?
WHO IS *THAT* BOY?!
HE COULD BE A *CLONE* OF YOU!
NATURALLY.
AFTER ALL... HE *IS* MY SON.
WHAAAAT?!

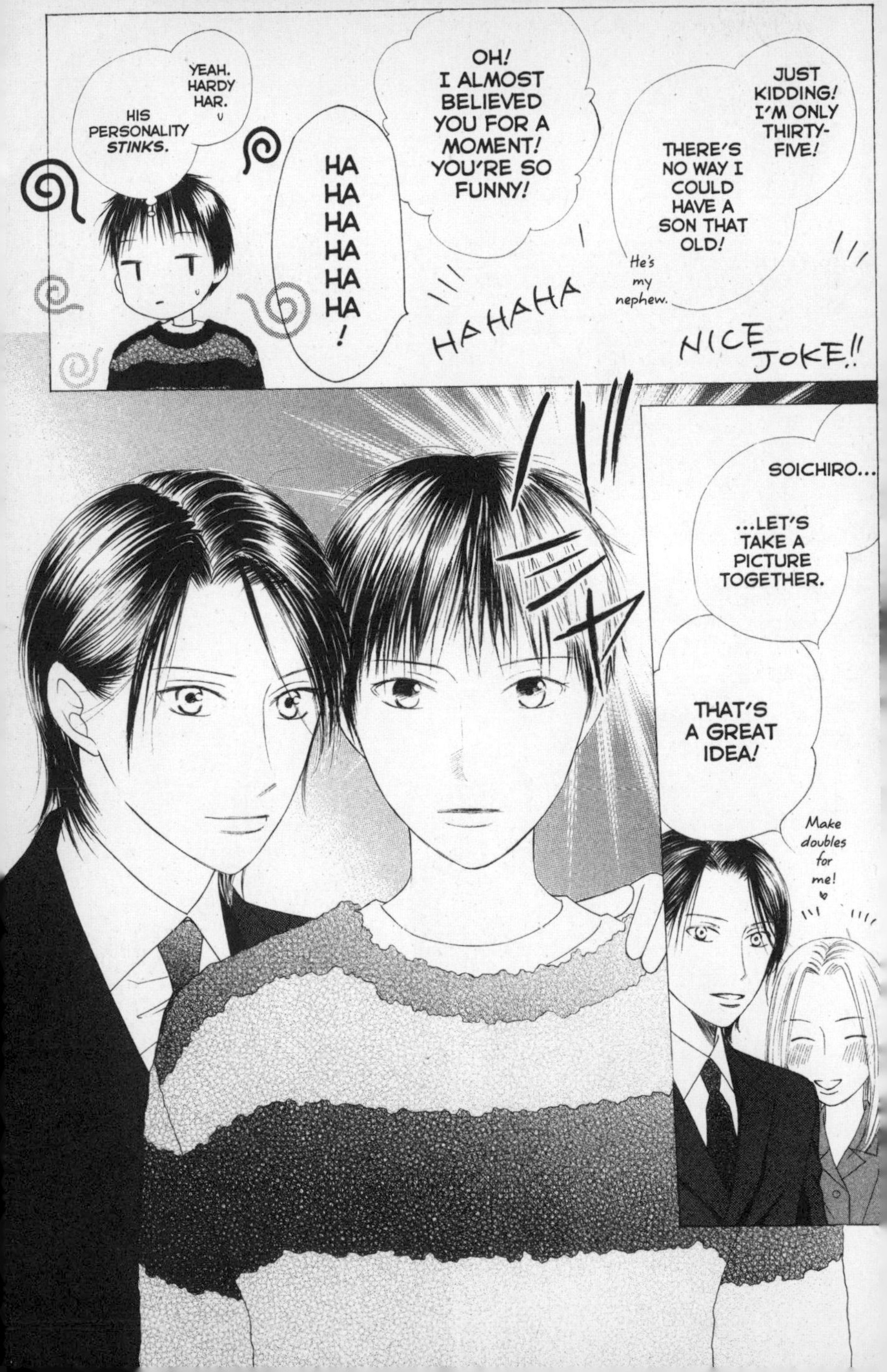
JUST KIDDING! I'M ONLY THIRTY-FIVE!
THERE'S NO WAY I COULD HAVE A SON THAT OLD!
He's my nephew.
NICE JOKE!!
OH! I ALMOST BELIEVED YOU FOR A MOMENT! YOU'RE SO FUNNY!
HAHAHA
HA HA HA HA HA HA!
YEAH. HARDY HAR.
HIS PERSONALITY STINKS.
SOICHIRO...
...LET'S TAKE A PICTURE TOGETHER.
THAT'S A GREAT IDEA!
Make doubles for me!

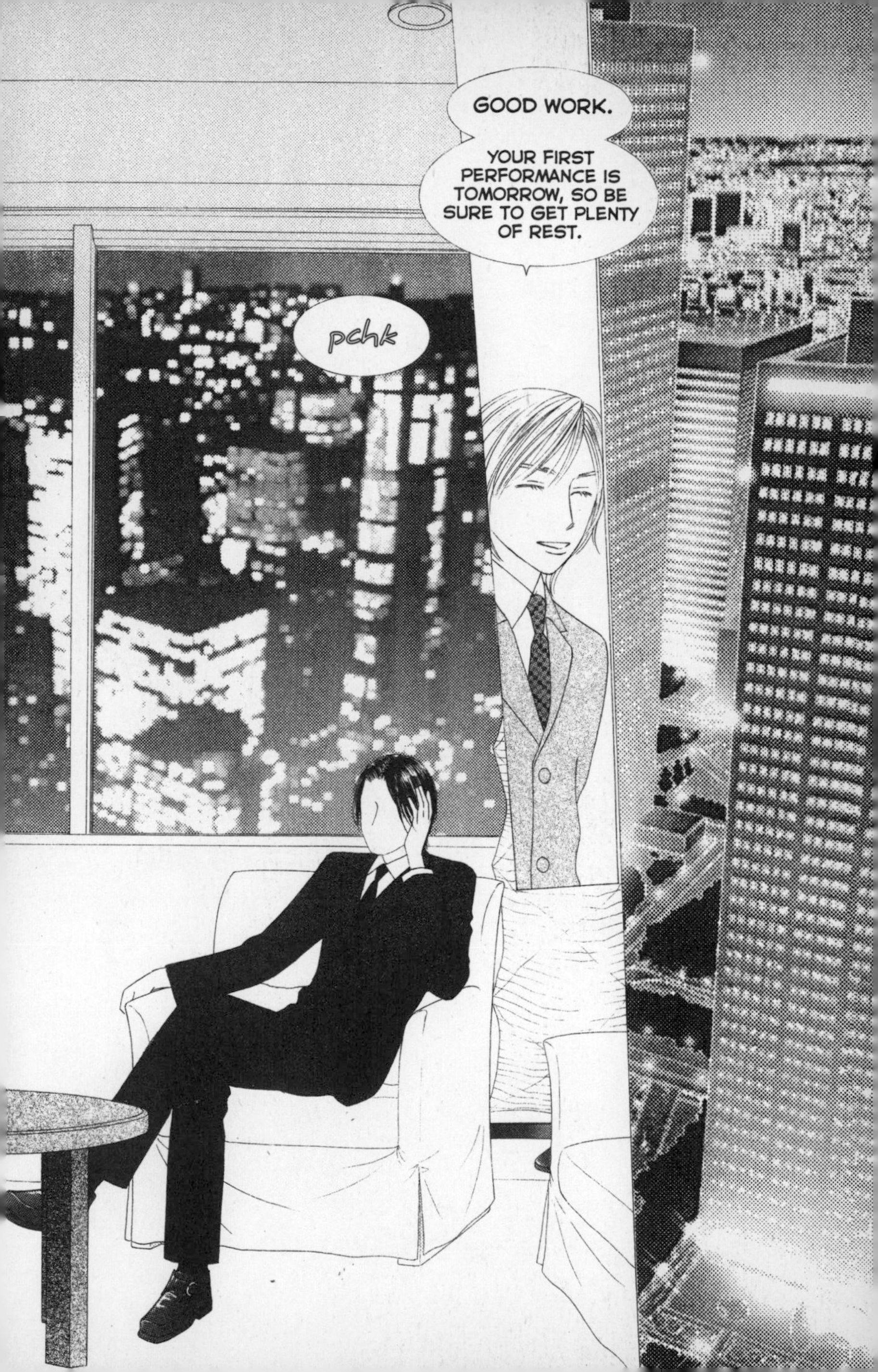
GOOD WORK.
YOUR FIRST PERFORMANCE IS TOMORROW, SO BE SURE TO GET PLENTY OF REST.
pchk

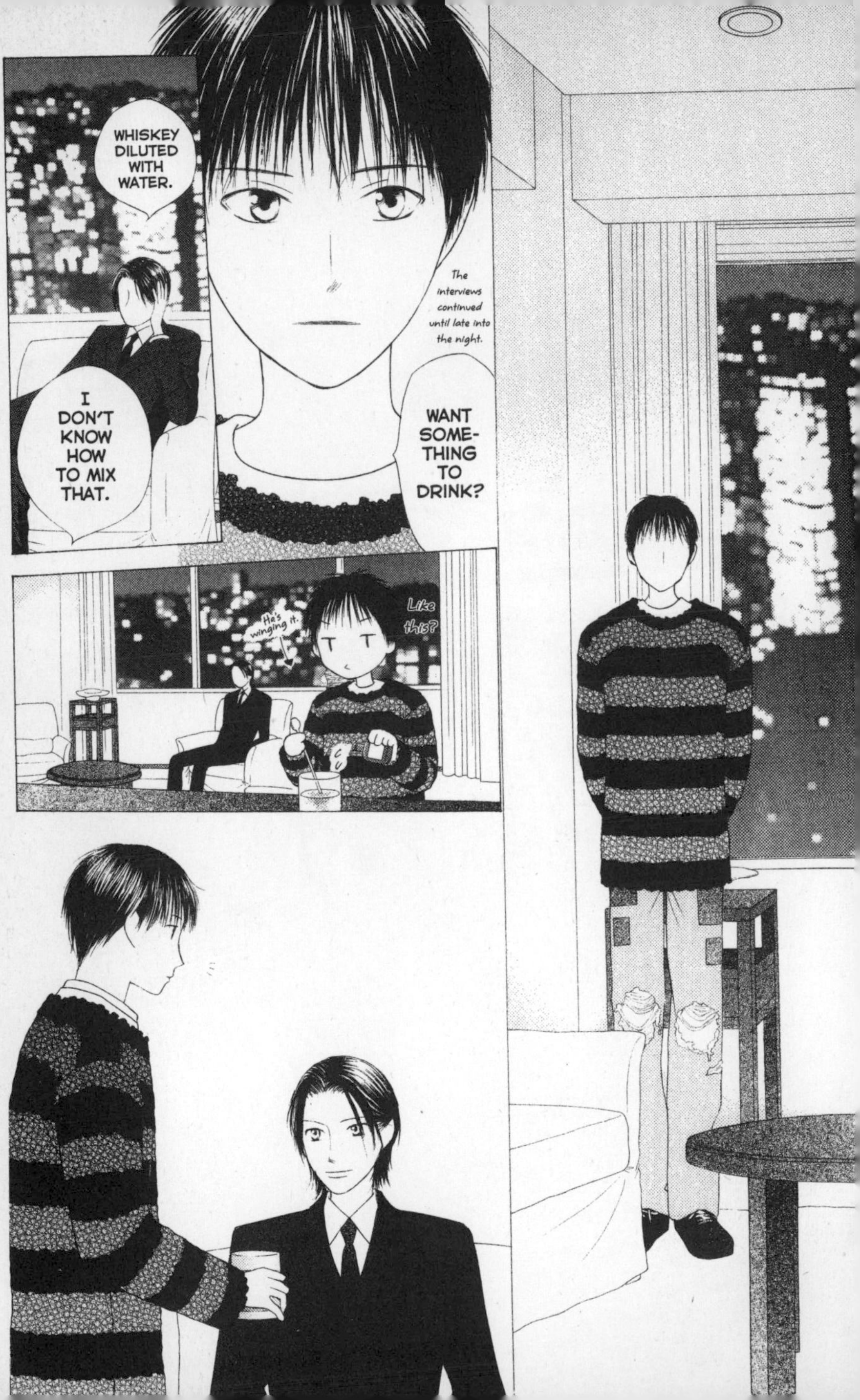
The interviews continued until late into the night.
WANT SOMETHING TO DRINK?
WHISKEY DILUTED WITH WATER.
I DON'T KNOW HOW TO MIX THAT.
Like this?
He's winging it.

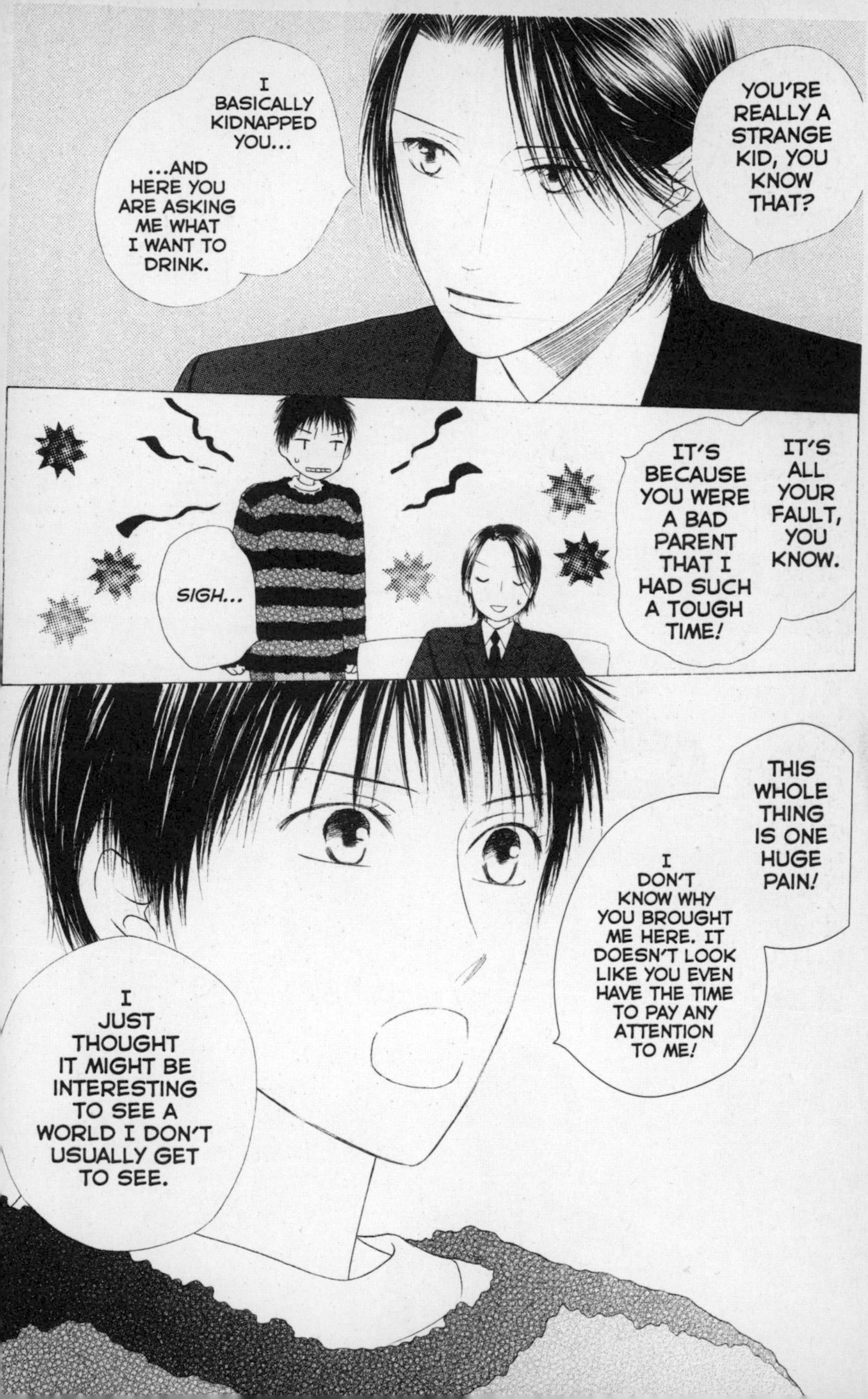
YOU'RE REALLY A STRANGE KID, YOU KNOW THAT?
I BASICALLY KIDNAPPED YOU...
...AND HERE YOU ARE ASKING ME WHAT I WANT TO DRINK.
IT'S ALL YOUR FAULT, YOU KNOW.
IT'S BECAUSE YOU WERE A BAD PARENT THAT I HAD SUCH A TOUGH TIME!
SIGH...
THIS WHOLE THING IS ONE HUGE PAIN!
I DON'T KNOW WHY YOU BROUGHT ME HERE. IT DOESN'T LOOK LIKE YOU EVEN HAVE THE TIME TO PAY ANY ATTENTION TO ME!
I JUST THOUGHT IT MIGHT BE INTERESTING TO SEE A WORLD I DON'T USUALLY GET TO SEE.

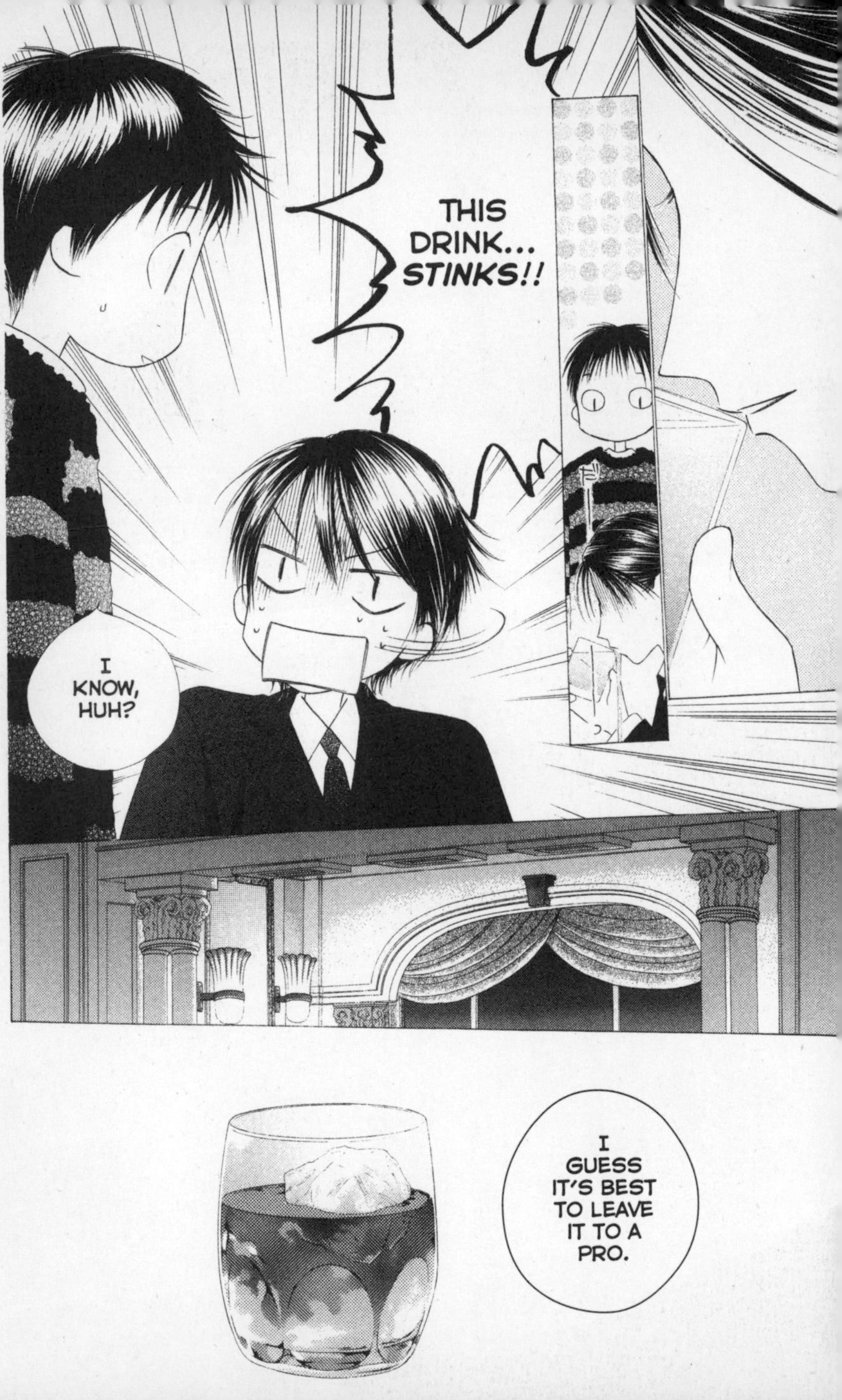
THIS DRINK... STINKS!!
I KNOW, HUH?
I GUESS IT'S BEST TO LEAVE IT TO A PRO.

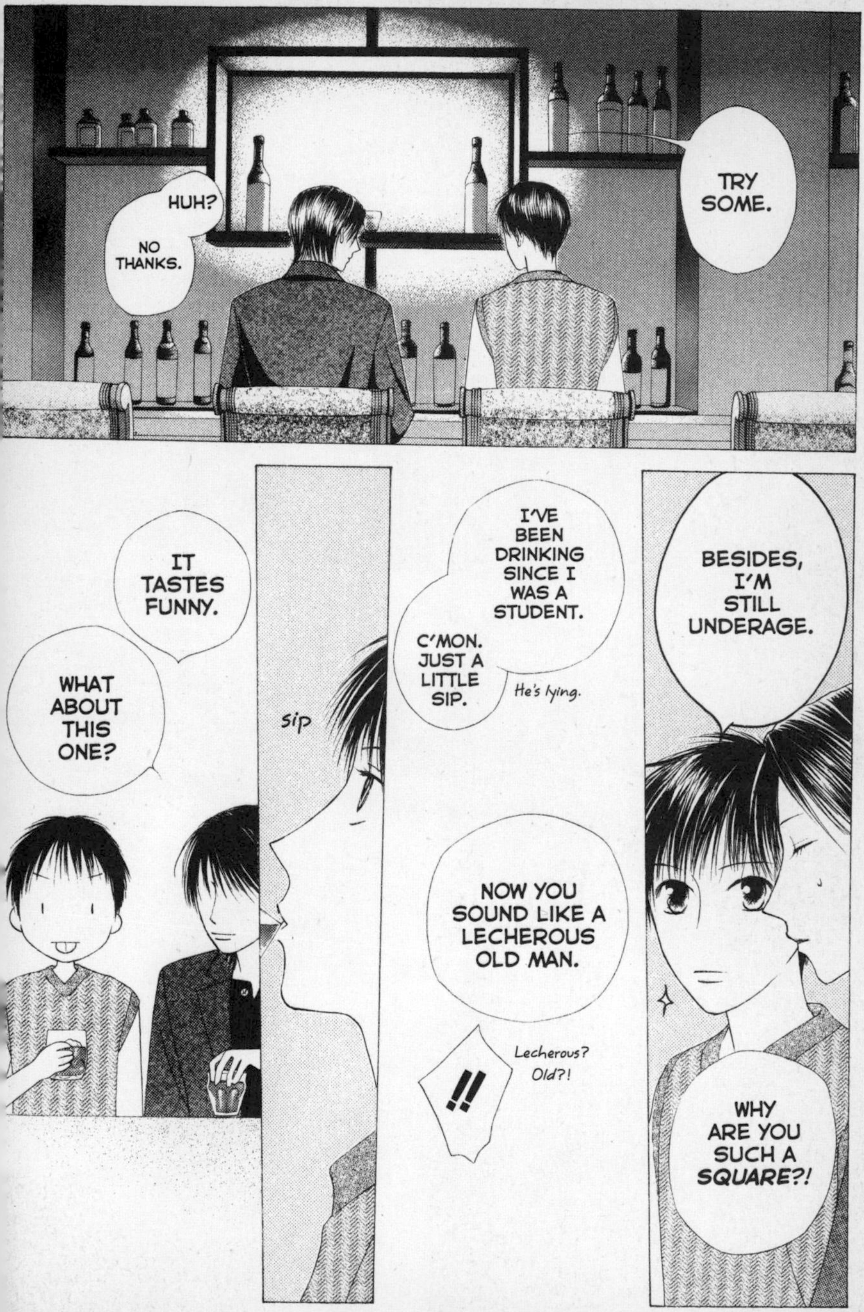
TRY SOME.
HUH?
NO THANKS.
BESIDES, I'M STILL UNDERAGE.
WHY ARE YOU SUCH A SQUARE?!
I'VE BEEN DRINKING SINCE I WAS A STUDENT.
C'MON. JUST A LITTLE SIP.
He's lying.
NOW YOU SOUND LIKE A LECHEROUS OLD MAN.
!!
Lecherous? Old?!
sip
IT TASTES FUNNY.
WHAT ABOUT THIS ONE?

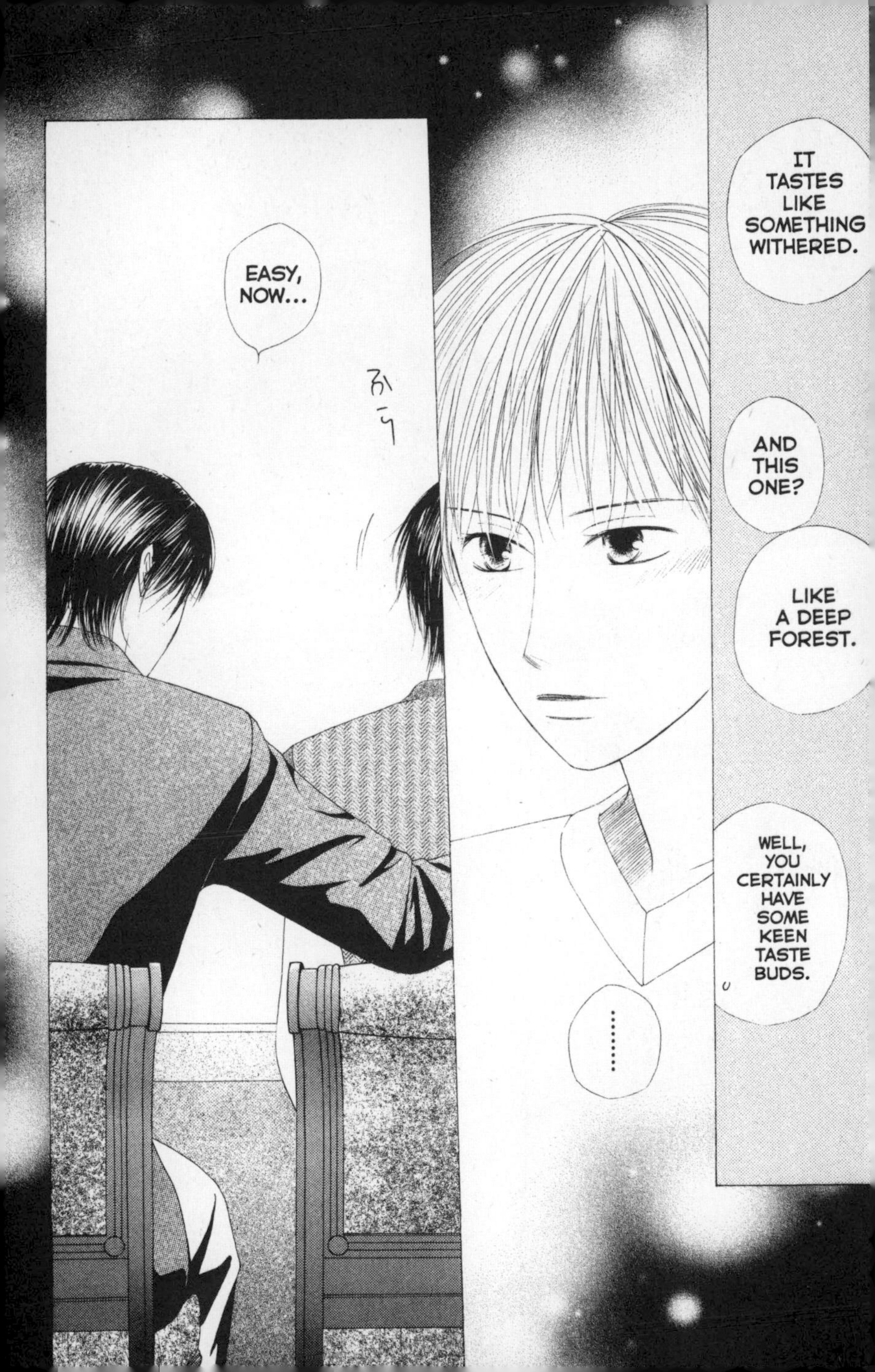
IT TASTES LIKE SOMETHING WITHERED.
AND THIS ONE?
LIKE A DEEP FOREST.
WELL, YOU CERTAINLY HAVE SOME KEEN TASTE BUDS.
......
EASY, NOW...

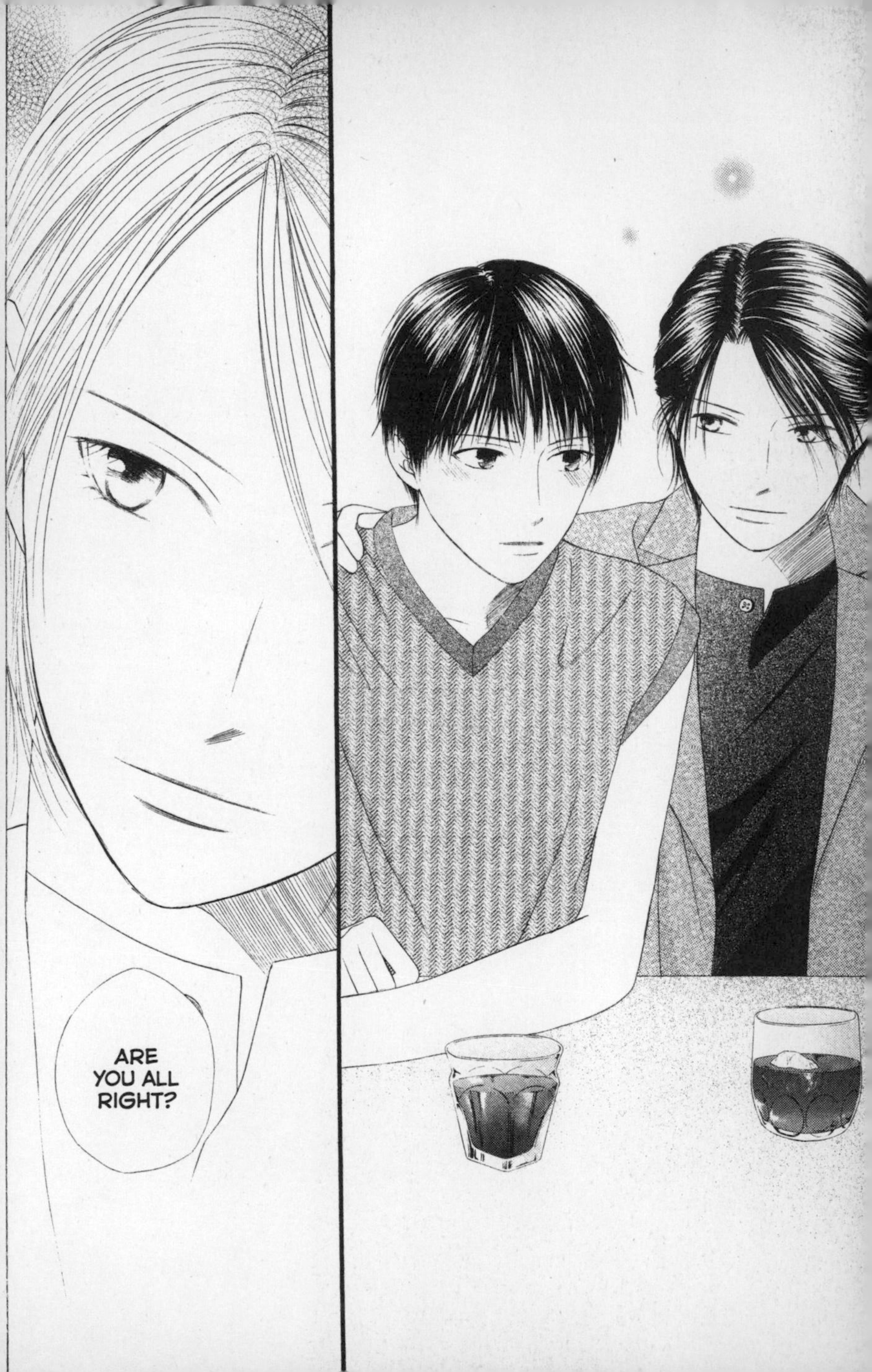
ARE YOU ALL RIGHT?

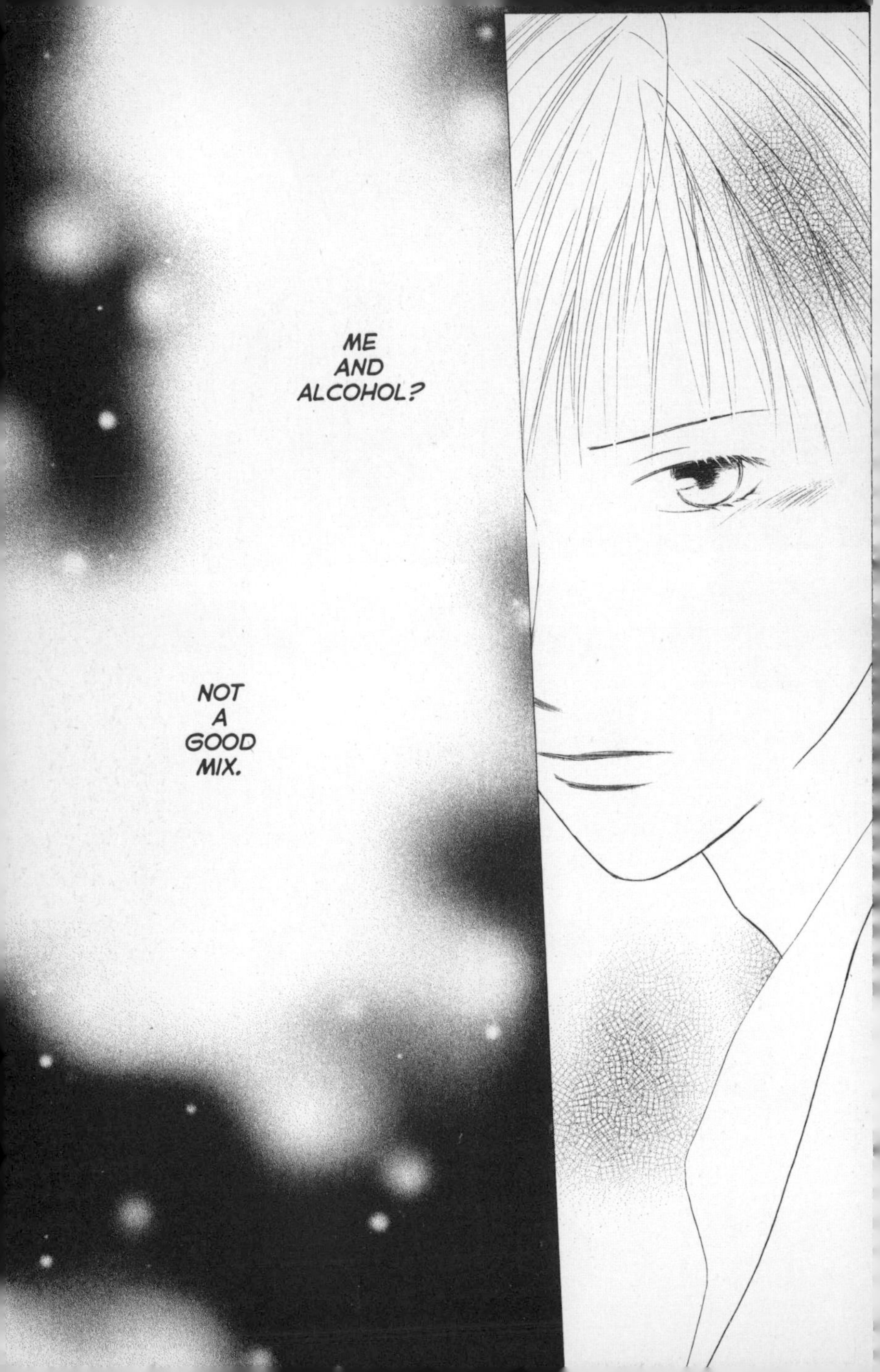
ME AND ALCOHOL?
NOT A GOOD MIX.

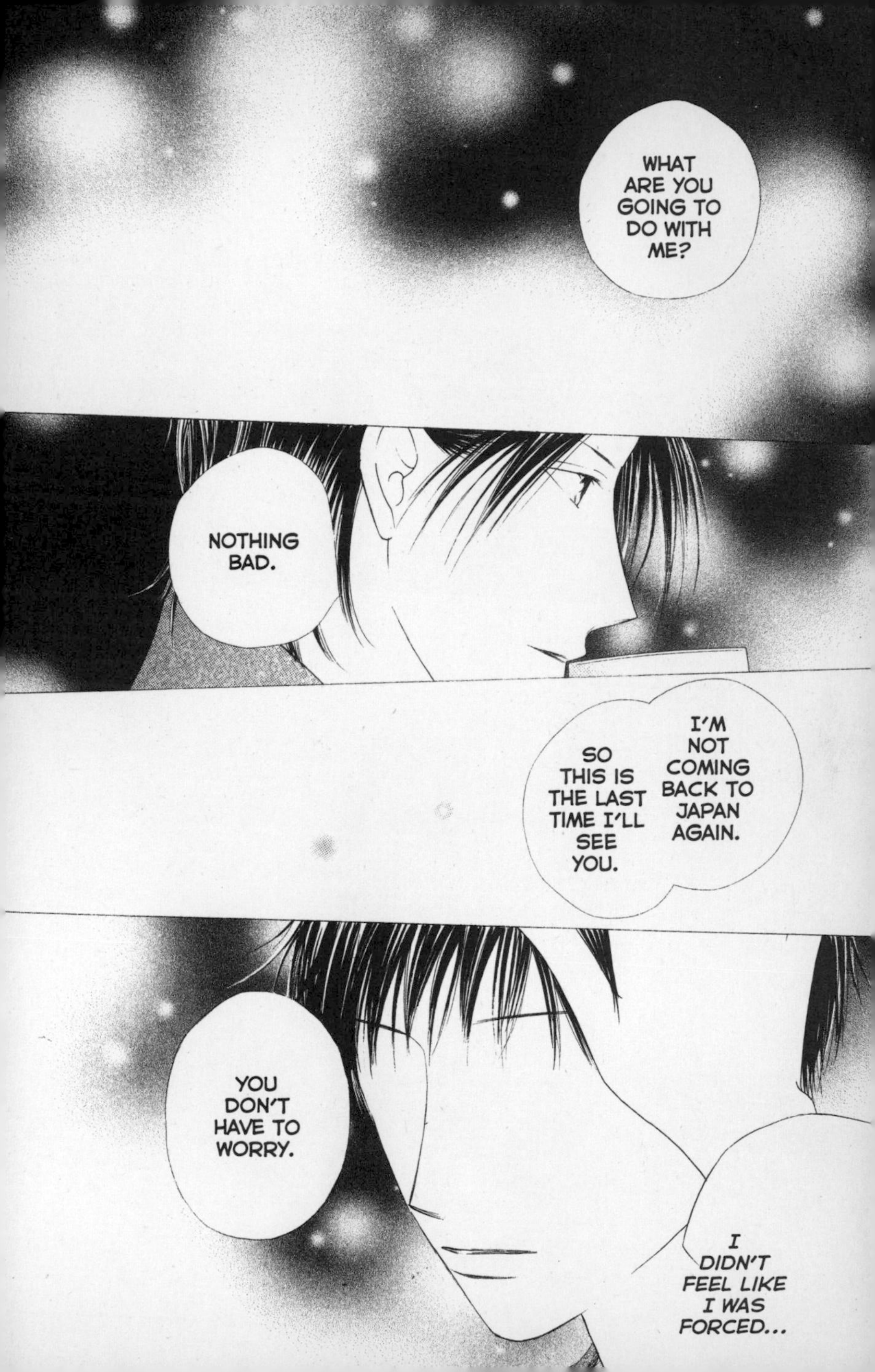
WHAT ARE YOU GOING TO DO WITH ME?
NOTHING BAD.
I'M NOT COMING BACK TO JAPAN AGAIN.
SO THIS IS THE LAST TIME I'LL SEE YOU.
I DIDN'T FEEL LIKE I WAS FORCED...
YOU DON'T HAVE TO WORRY.

...TO COME HERE.

I WAS HIDING MY FEELINGS
NOT ONLY FROM HIM...
BUT FROM MYSELF.

I REALLY LIKE THIS GUY.

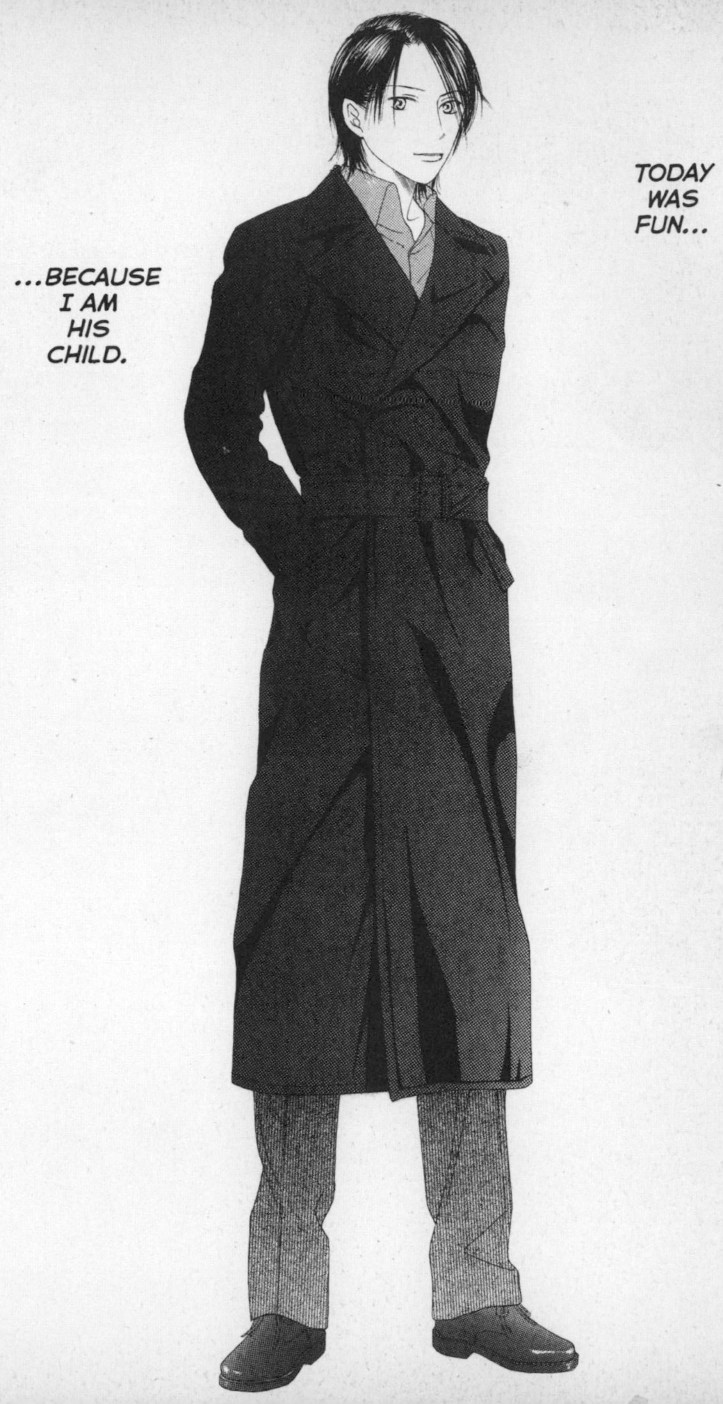
TODAY WAS FUN...
...BECAUSE I AM HIS CHILD.

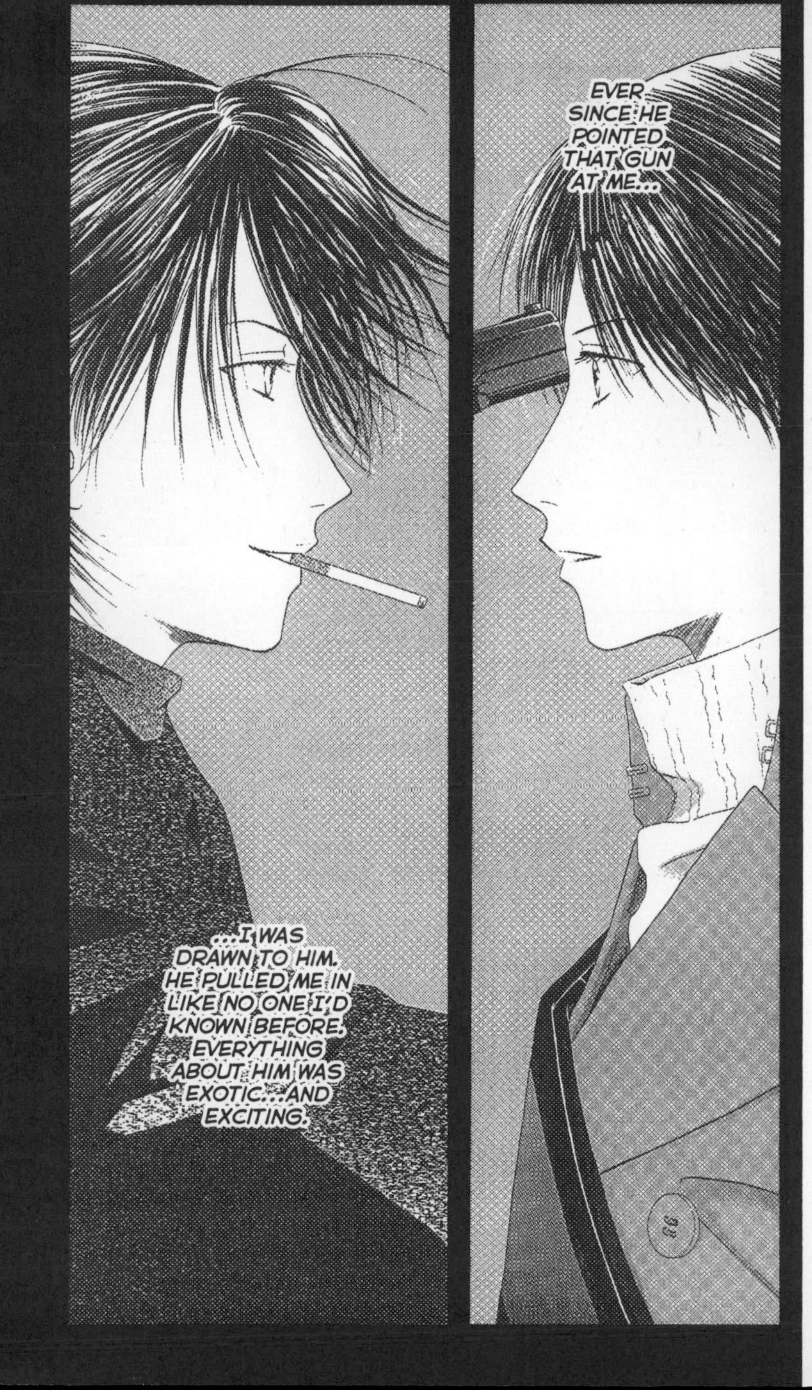
EVER SINCE HE POINTED THAT GUN AT ME...
...I WAS DRAWN TO HIM. HE PULLED ME IN LIKE NO ONE I'D KNOWN BEFORE. EVERYTHING ABOUT HIM WAS EXOTIC...AND EXCITING.

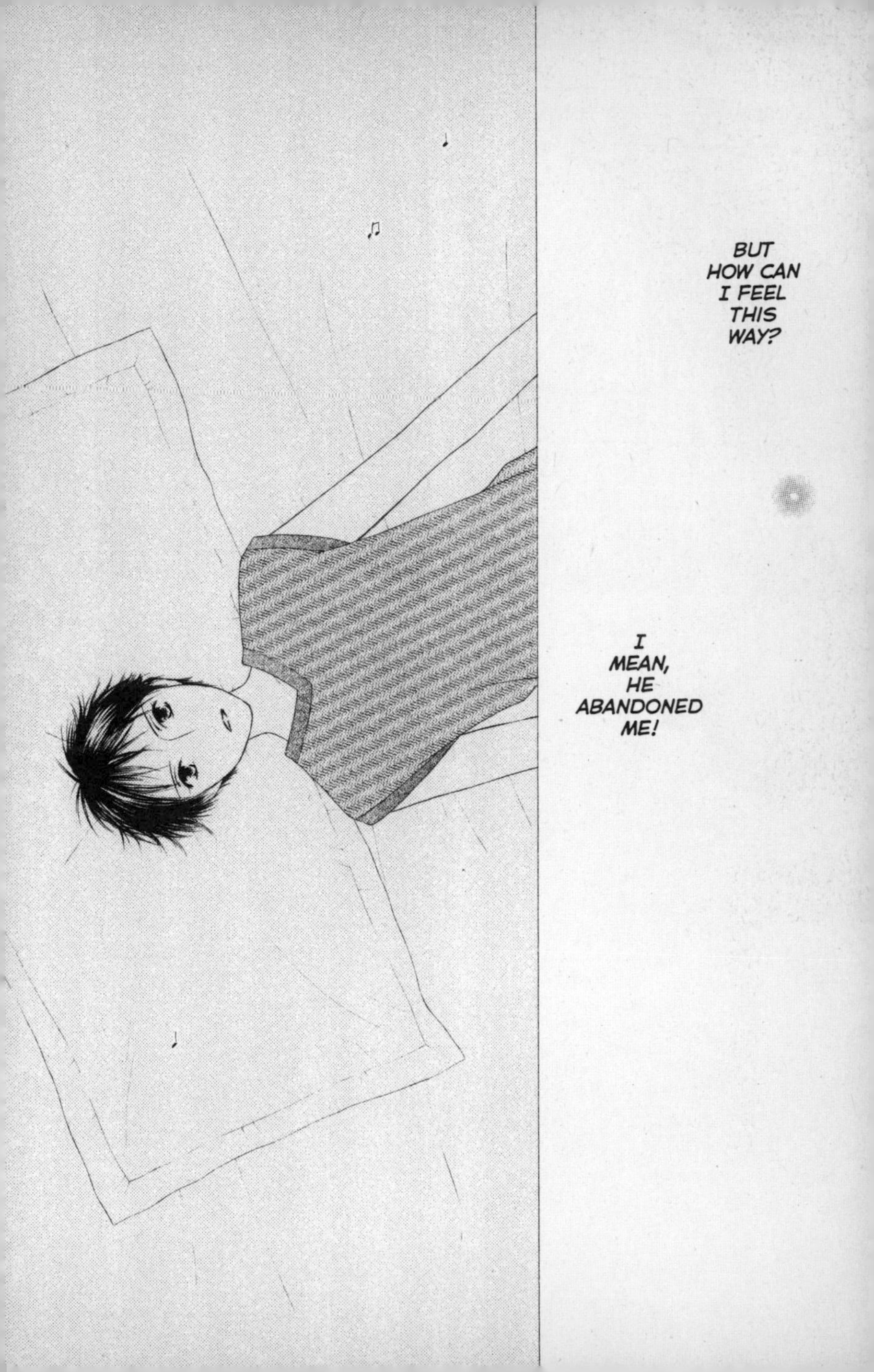
BUT HOW CAN I FEEL THIS WAY?
I MEAN, HE ABANDONED ME!

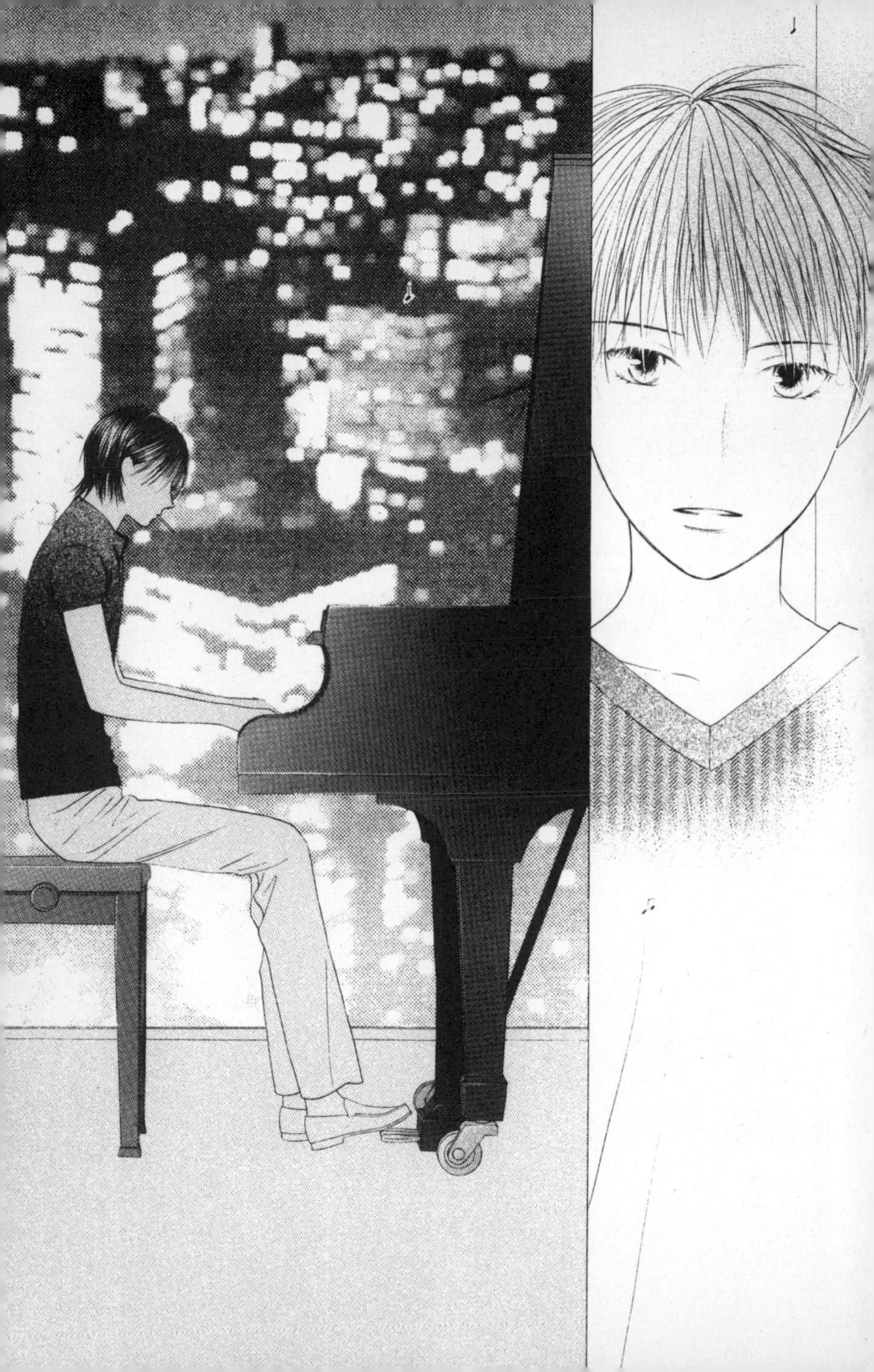

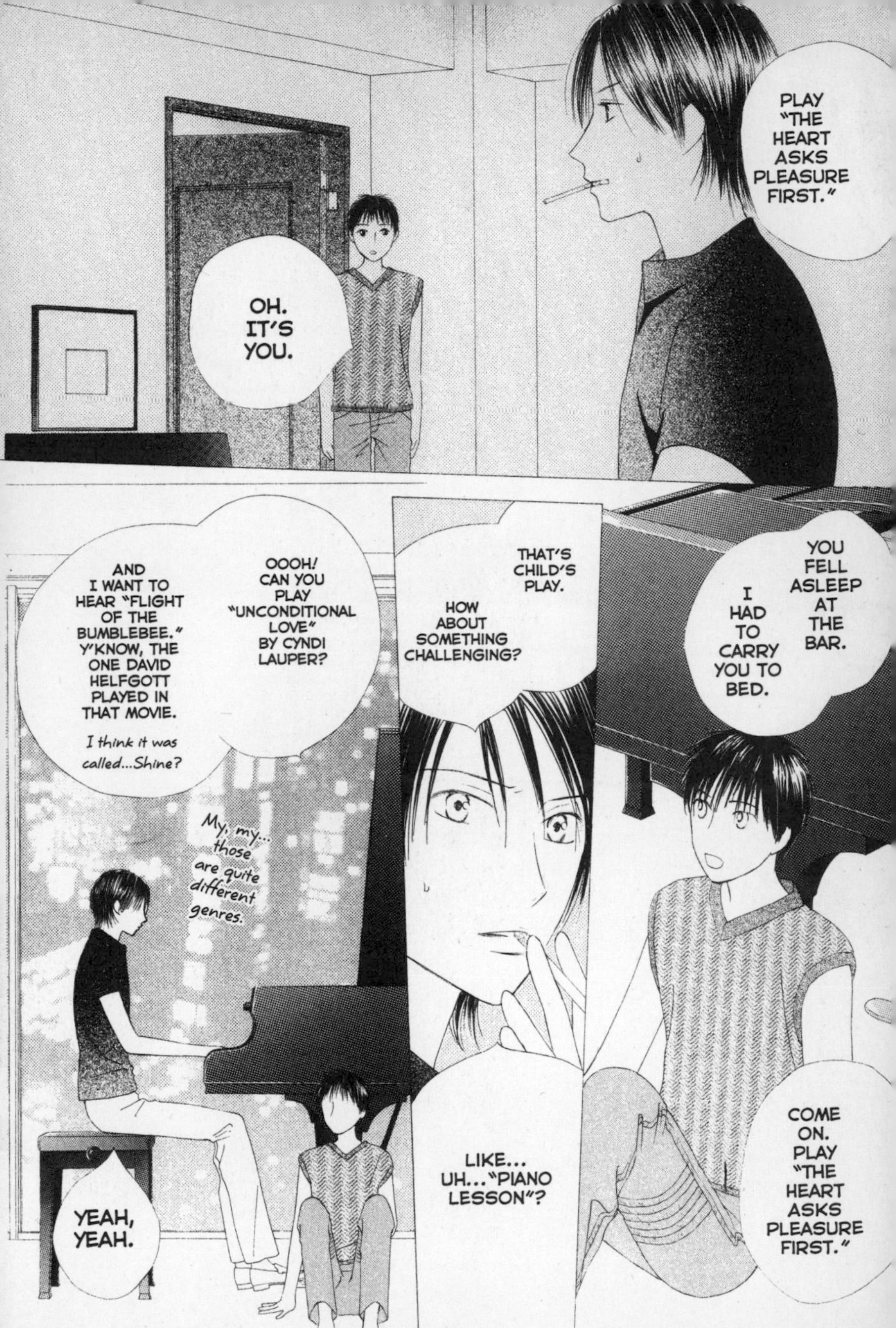
PLAY "THE HEART ASKS PLEASURE FIRST."
OH. IT'S YOU.
YOU FELL ASLEEP AT THE BAR.
I HAD TO CARRY YOU TO BED.
COME ON. PLAY "THE HEART ASKS PLEASURE FIRST."
THAT'S CHILD'S PLAY.
HOW ABOUT SOMETHING CHALLENGING?
LIKE... UH... "PIANO LESSON"?
OOOH! CAN YOU PLAY "UNCONDITIONAL LOVE" BY CYNDI LAUPER?
AND I WANT TO HEAR "FLIGHT OF THE BUMBLEBEE." Y'KNOW, THE ONE DAVID HELFGOTT PLAYED IN THAT MOVIE.
I think it was called...Shine?
My, my... those are quite different genres.
YEAH, YEAH.

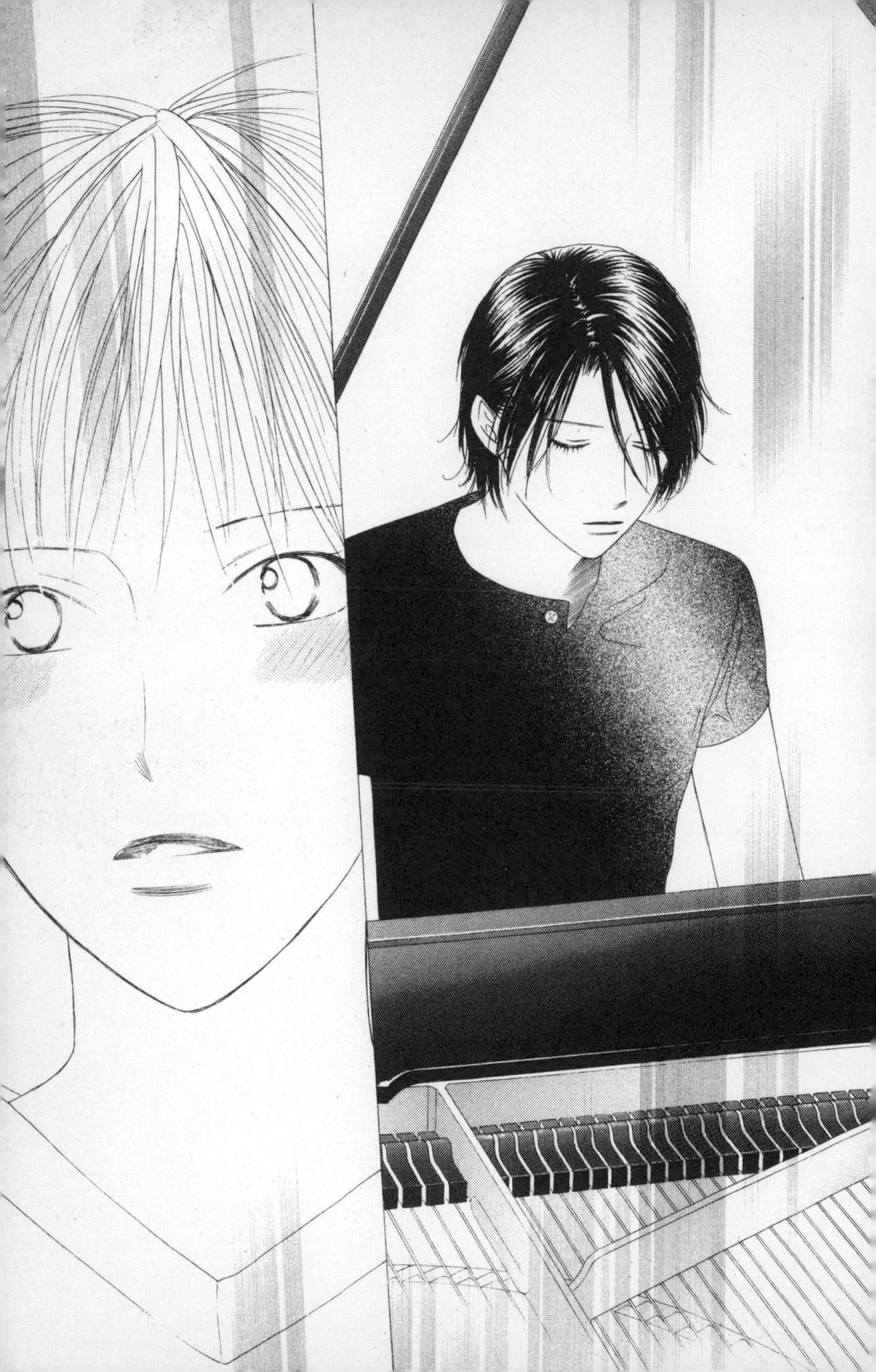

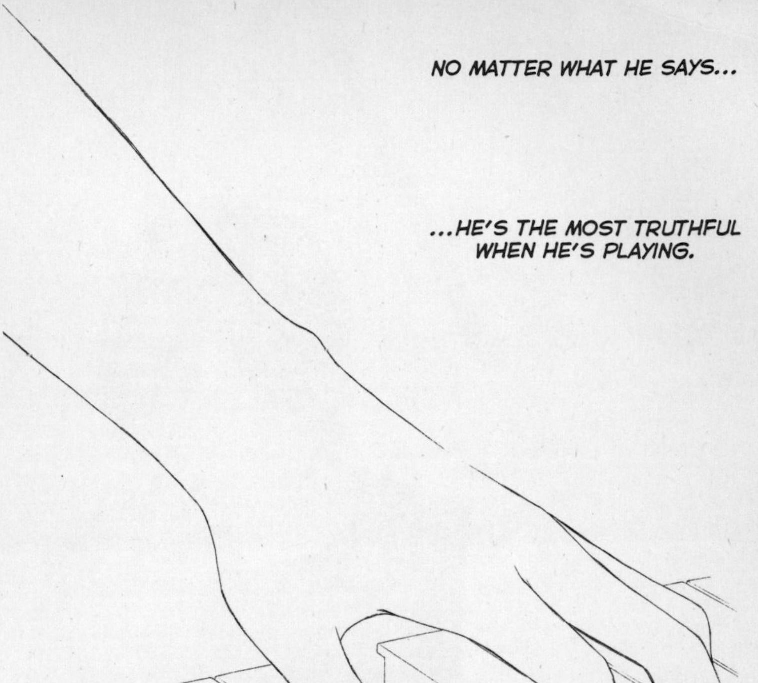
NO MATTER WHAT HE SAYS...
...HE'S THE MOST TRUTHFUL WHEN HE'S PLAYING.
IT'S IN THOSE MOMENTS THAT HE'S AS SHARP AS A KNIFE. IN THOSE MOMENTS, HE'S EVEN MORE BEAUTIFUL.

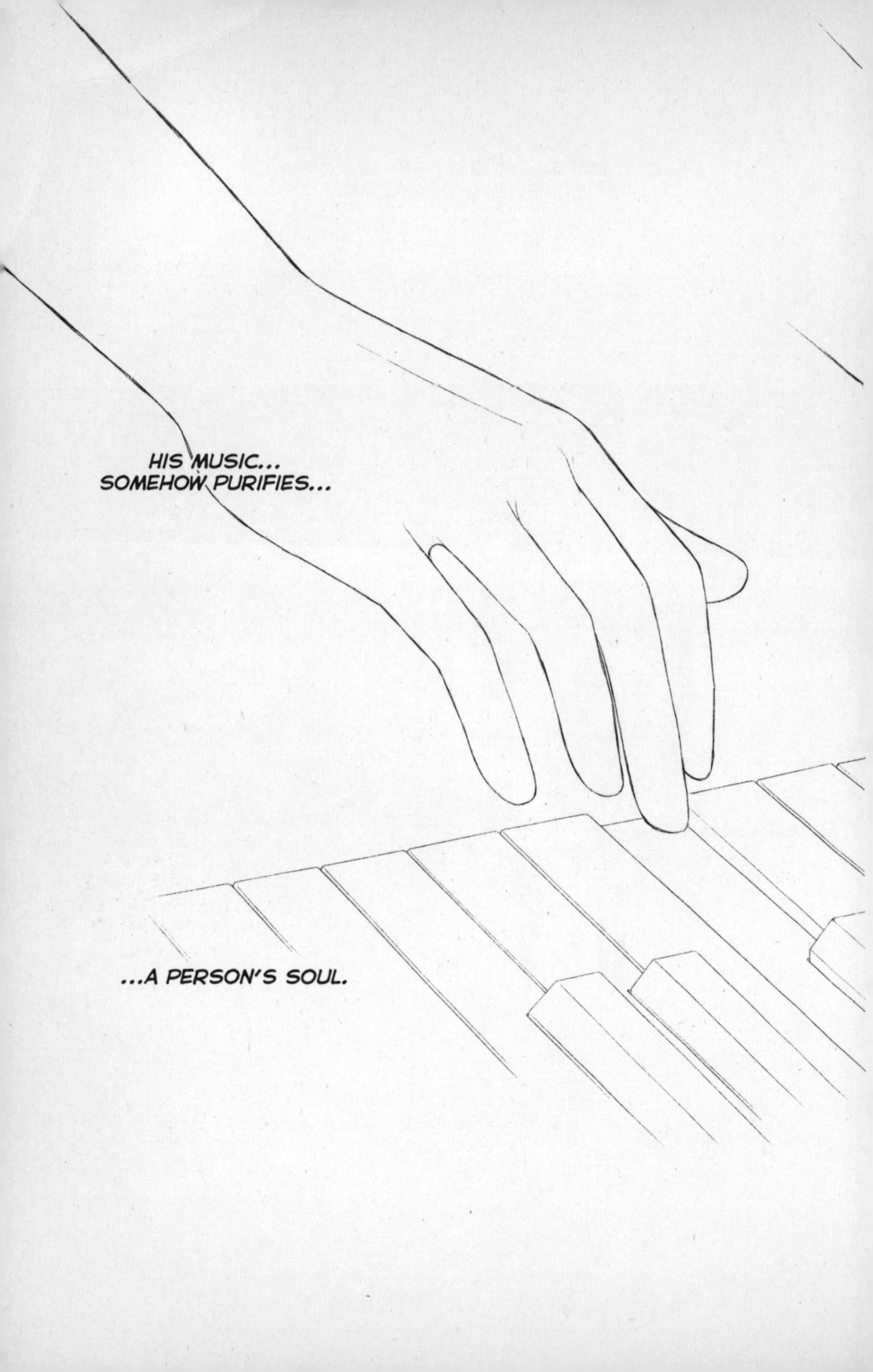
HIS MUSIC...
SOMEHOW PURIFIES...
...A PERSON'S SOUL.

NOTHING COMPLETELY EVIL CAN CREATE
SOMETHING SO RADIANT.

SO I'LL STAY WITH HIM...FOR NOW.

FOR NOW...I'LL ALLOW HIM
TO SOOTHE MY HEART.

ACT 83 ★ A BOY AND A MAN

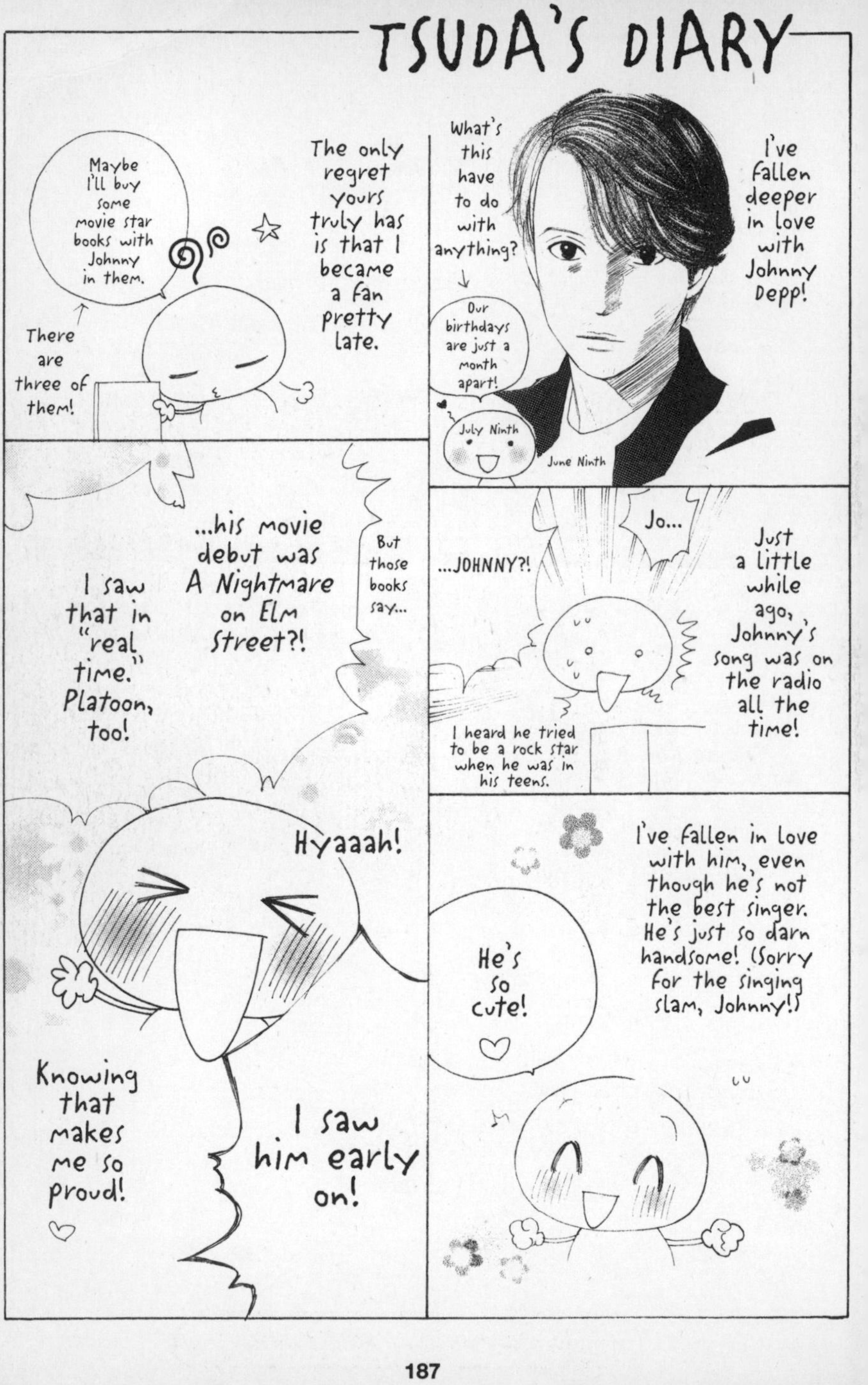
TSUDA'S DIARY
I've fallen deeper in love with Johnny Depp!
What's this have to do with anything?
Our birthdays are just a month apart!
July Ninth
June Ninth
The only regret yours truly has is that I became a fan pretty late.
Maybe I'll buy some movie star books with Johnny in them.
There are three of them!
Just a little while ago, Johnny's song was on the radio all the time!
Jo...
...JOHNNY?!
I heard he tried to be a rock star when he was in his teens.
I've fallen in love with him, even though he's not the best singer. He's just so darn handsome! (Sorry for the singing slam, Johnny!)
He's so cute!
But those books say...
...his movie debut was A Nightmare on Elm Street?!
I saw that in "real time." Platoon, too!
Hyaaah!
I saw him early on!
Knowing that makes me so proud!

MUSIC I'M INTO RIGHT NOW

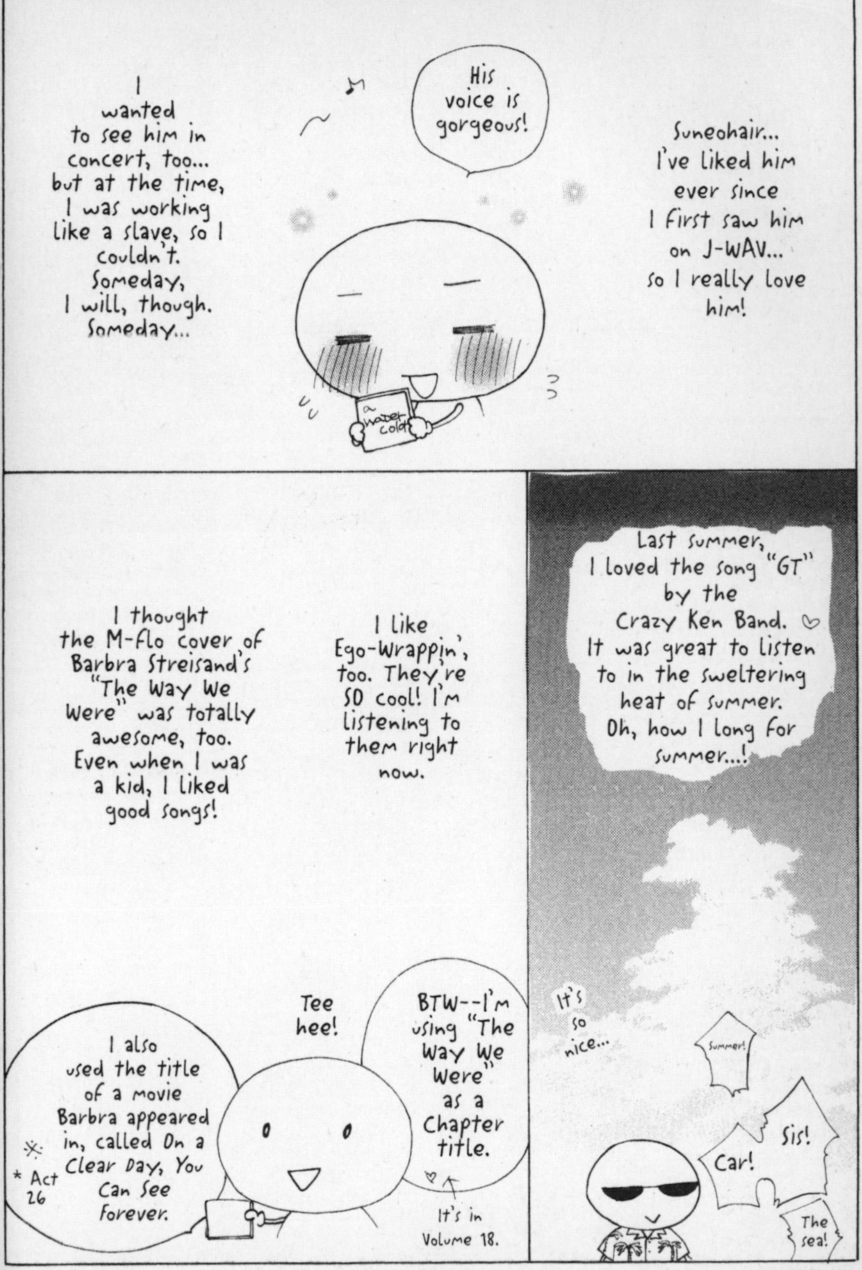
Suneohair... I've liked him ever since I first saw him on J-WAV... so I really love him!
His voice is gorgeous!
I wanted to see him in concert, too... but at the time, I was working like a slave, so I couldn't. Someday, I will, though. Someday...
Last summer, I loved the song "GT" by the Crazy Ken Band. ♡ It was great to listen to in the sweltering heat of summer. Oh, how I long for summer...!
It's so nice...
Summer!
Sis!
Car!
The sea!
I like Ego-Wrappin', too. They're SO cool! I'm listening to them right now.
I thought the M-flo cover of Barbra Streisand's "The Way We Were" was totally awesome, too. Even when I was a kid, I liked good songs!
BTW--I'm using "The Way We Were" as a Chapter title. ♡
It's in Volume 18.
Tee hee!
I also used the title of a movie Barbra appeared in, called On a Clear Day, You Can See Forever. ※
* Act 26

TSUDA'S GRADES

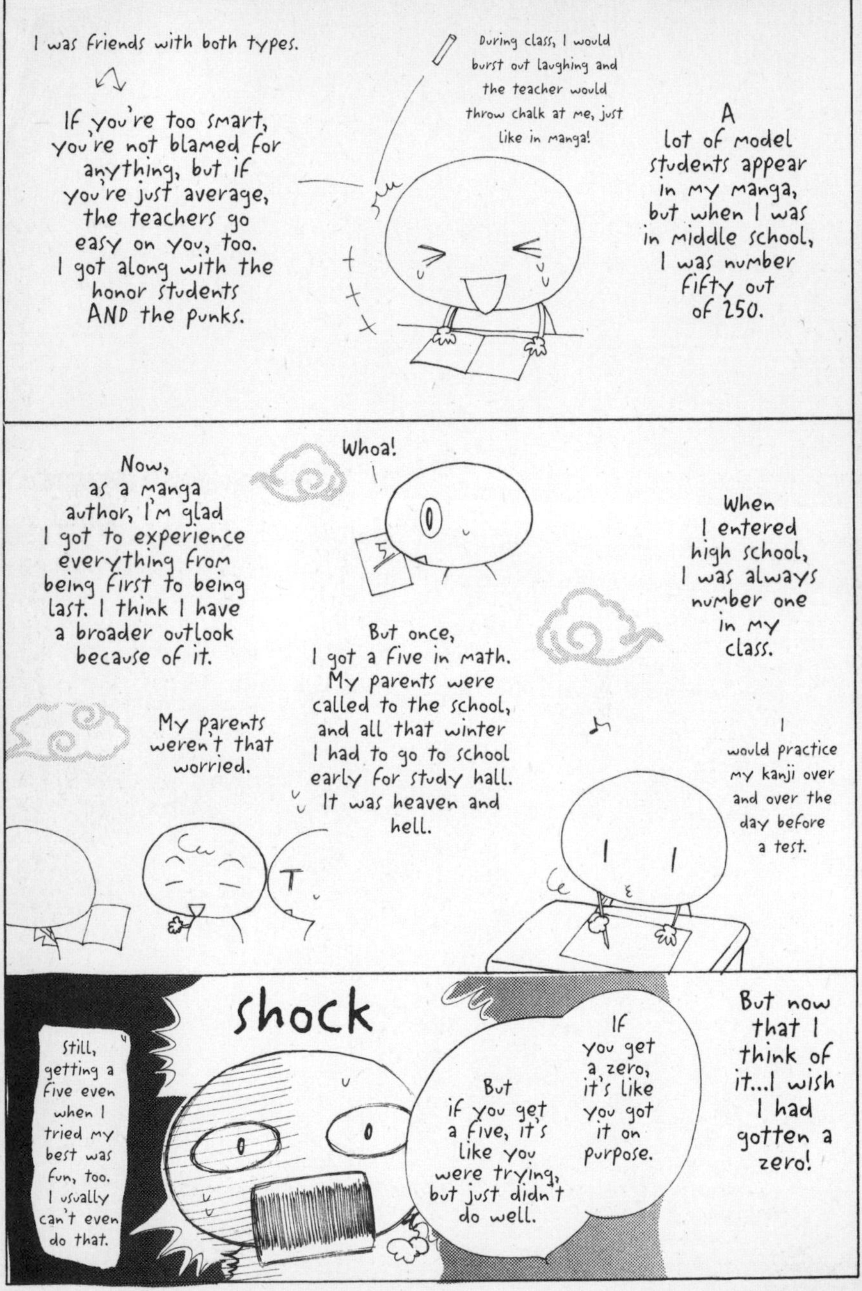
A lot of model students appear in my manga, but when I was in middle school, I was number fifty out of 250.
During class, I would burst out laughing and the teacher would throw chalk at me, just like in manga!
I was friends with both types.
If you're too smart, you're not blamed for anything, but if you're just average, the teachers go easy on you, too. I got along with the honor students AND the punks.
When I entered high school, I was always number one in my class.
Whoa!
I would practice my kanji over and over the day before a test.
But once, I got a five in math. My parents were called to the school, and all that winter I had to go to school early for study hall. It was heaven and hell.
My parents weren't that worried.
Now, as a manga author, I'm glad I got to experience everything from being first to being last. I think I have a broader outlook because of it.
But now that I think of it...I wish I had gotten a zero!
If you get a zero, it's like you got it on purpose.
But if you get a five, it's like you were trying, but just didn't do well.
shock
Still, getting a five even when I tried my best was fun, too. I usually can't even do that.

🌀 Thanks to the following people: 🌀

Editor	S. TAKEOKA
Staff	N. SHIMIZU
	R. OGAWA
	Y. ETŌ
	R. TAKAHASHI
AND	K. U

coming soon

kare kano

his and her circumstances

volume eighteen

With the encouragement of his
adoptive dad, Soichiro decides he should
get to know his birth father after all. And
when Reiji invites Soichiro to dinner, it
seems like the perfect opportunity. But
will Soichiro finally learn the whole truth
about his father's troubled past,
or will he just get burned?

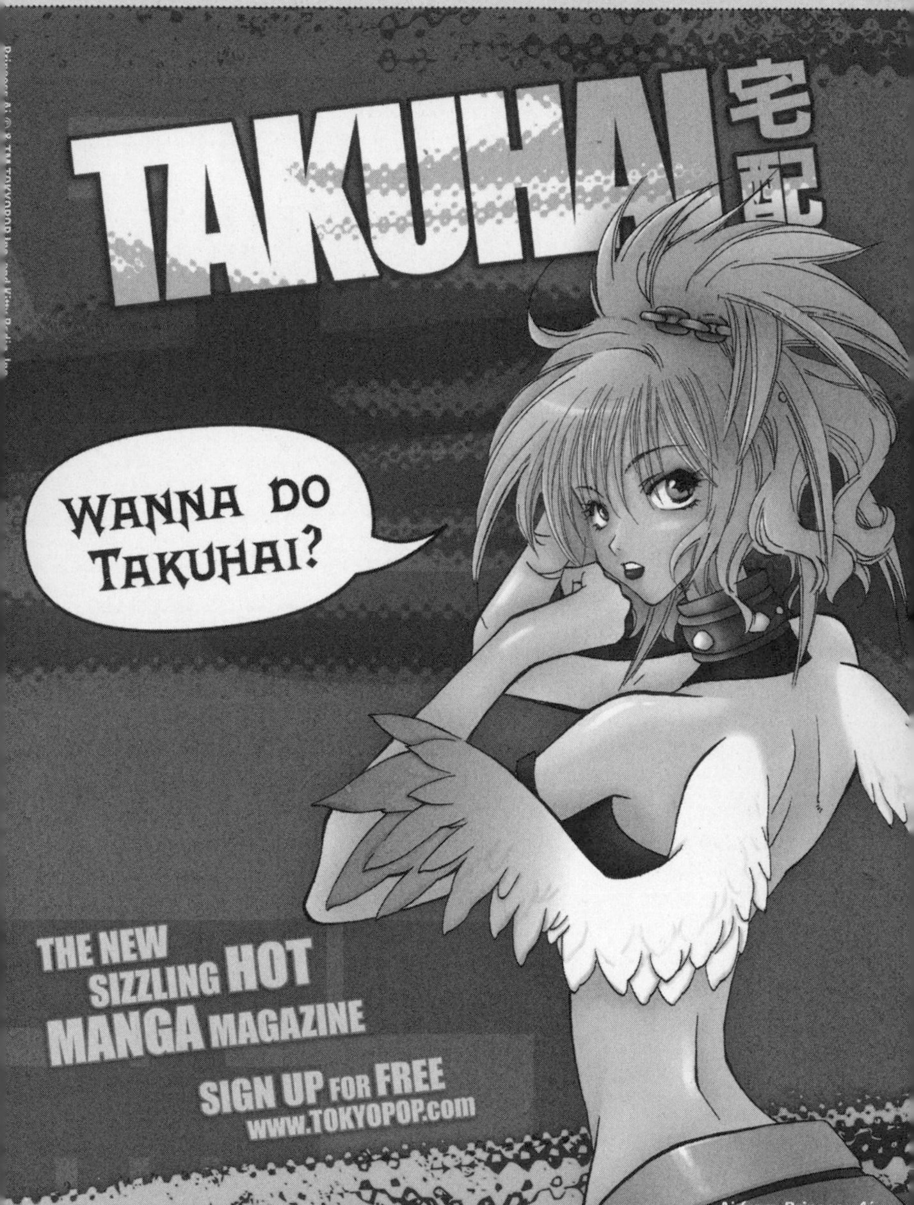
TAKUHAI 宅配
WANNA DO TAKUHAI?
THE NEW SIZZLING HOT MANGA MAGAZINE
SIGN UP FOR FREE
WWW.TOKYOPOP.com
Ai from *Princess Ai*
Princess Ai © & TM TOKYOPOP Inc. and Kitty Radio, Inc.

TOKYOPOP SHOP

WWW.TOKYOPOP.COM/SHOP

HOT NEWS!
Check out the TOKYOPOP SHOP! The world's best collection of manga in English is now available online in one place!

GIRLS BRAVO

RIZELMINE

WAR ON FLESH

War on Flesh and other hot titles are available at the store that never closes!

- LOOK FOR SPECIAL OFFERS
- PRE-ORDER UPCOMING RELEASES
- COMPLETE YOUR COLLECTIONS

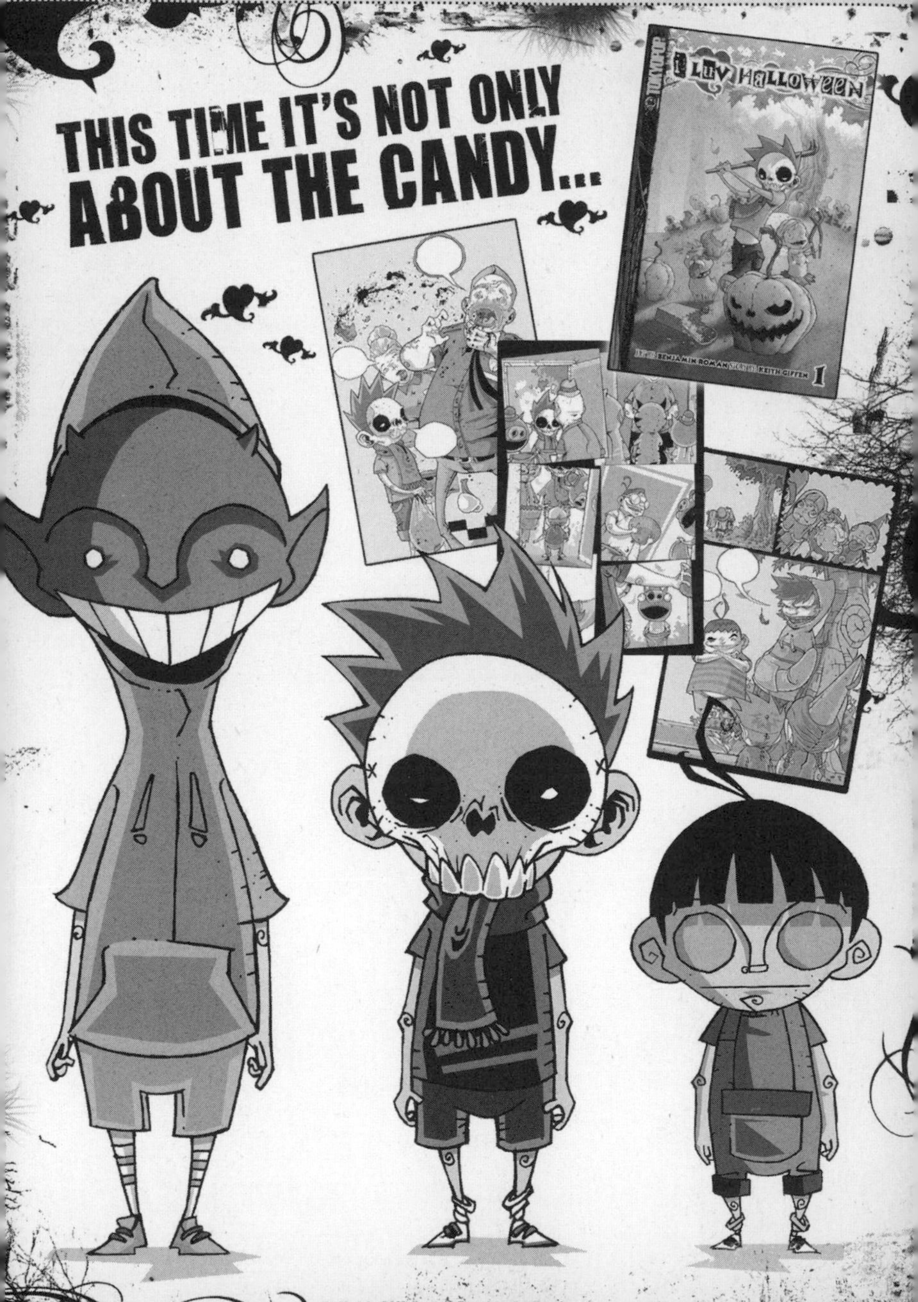
THIS TIME IT'S NOT ONLY ABOUT THE CANDY...
I LUV HALLOWEEN
BENJAMIN ROMAN
KEITH GIFFEN
1

Written by Keith Giffen, comic book pro and English language adapter of *Battle Royale* and *Battle Vixens*.

Join the misadventures of a group of particularly disturbing trick-or-treaters as they go about their macabre business on Halloween night. Blaming the apples they got from the first house of the evening for the bad candy they've been receiving all night, the kids plot revenge on the old bag who handed out the funky fruit. Riotously funny and always wickedly shocking—who doesn't *love* Halloween?

OT
OLDER TEEN
AGE 16+

SPOTLIGHT

TOKYOPOP MANGA SUPPLEMENT

SCRAPPED PRINCESS

BY GO YABUKI, ICHIRO SAKAKI, AND YUKINOBU AZUMI

HER BIRTH FORETOLD THE DESTRUCTION OF THE WORLD!

Fifteen years ago, a set of twins—a girl and a boy—was born to the king of Linevan. Shortly after their birth, a prophecy foretold that when the girl turned 16, she would bring about the end of humanity. To avoid this terrible fate, the king ordered the girl disposed of—scrapped! She miraculously survived and was raised away from the kingdom that would kill her. But now she has turned 15, the king's guards have caught wind that she's still alive...and they set out to finish the job!

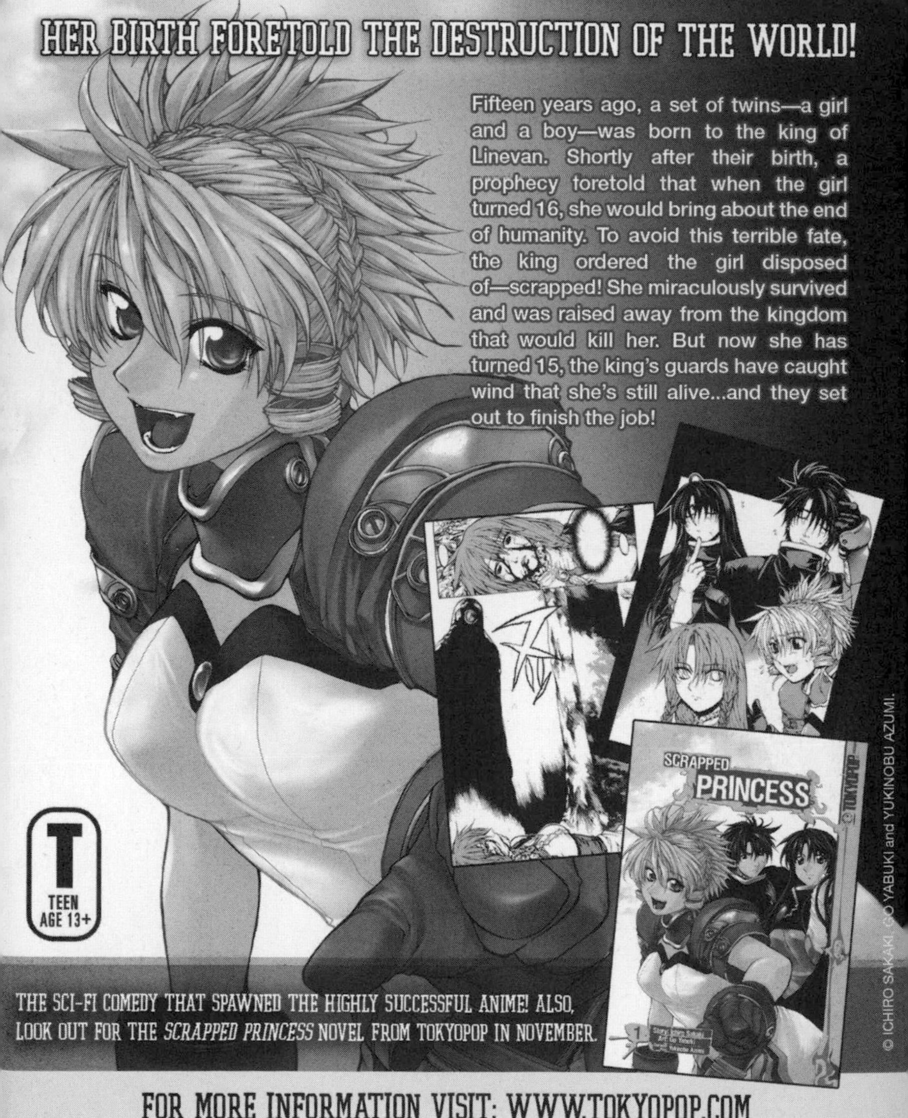
SCRAPPED PRINCESS
TOKYOPOP
1
T
TEEN
AGE 13+

THE SCI-FI COMEDY THAT SPAWNED THE HIGHLY SUCCESSFUL ANIME! ALSO, LOOK OUT FOR THE *SCRAPPED PRINCESS* NOVEL FROM TOKYOPOP IN NOVEMBER.

FOR MORE INFORMATION VISIT: WWW.TOKYOPOP.COM

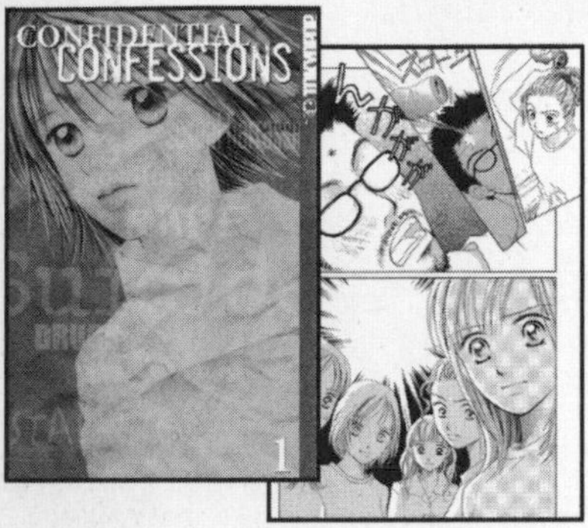
CONFIDENTIAL CONFESSIONS
1

BY REIKO MOMOCHI

CONFIDENTIAL CONFESSIONS

If you're looking for a happy, rosy, zit-free look at high school life, skip this manga. But if you're jonesing for a real-life view of what high school's truly like, *Confidential Confessions* offers a gritty, unflinching look at what really happens in those hallowed halls. Rape, sexual harassment, anorexia, cutting, suicide...no subject is too hardcore for *Confidential Confessions*. While you're at it, don't expect a happy ending.

~Julie Taylor, Sr. Editor

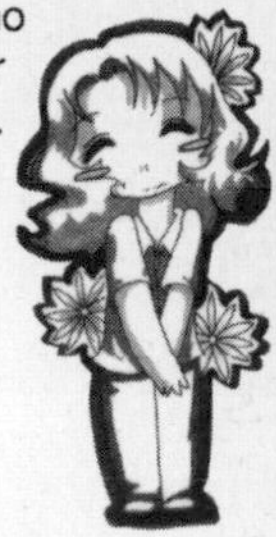

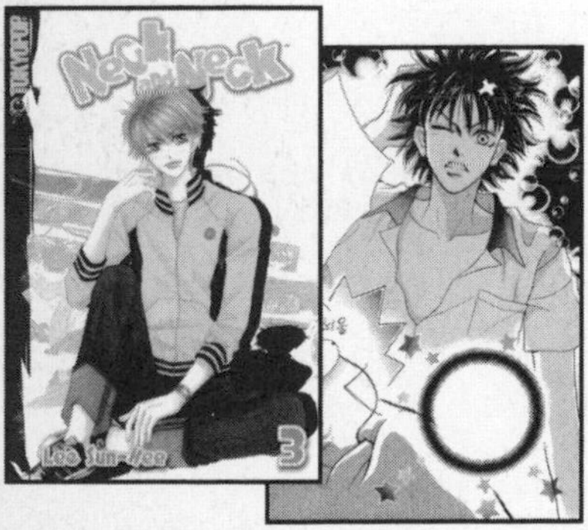
Neck and Neck
Lee Sun-Hee
3

BY LEE SUN-HEE

NECK AND NECK

Competition can bring out the best or the worst in people...but in *Neck and Neck*, it does both! Dabin Choi and Shihu Myoung are both high school students, both children of mob bosses, and each is out to totally humiliate the other. Dabin and Shihu are very creative in their mutual tortures and there's more than a hint of romantic tension behind their attacks. This book's art may look somewhat shojo, but I found the story to be very accessible and very entertaining!

~Rob Tokar, Sr. Editor

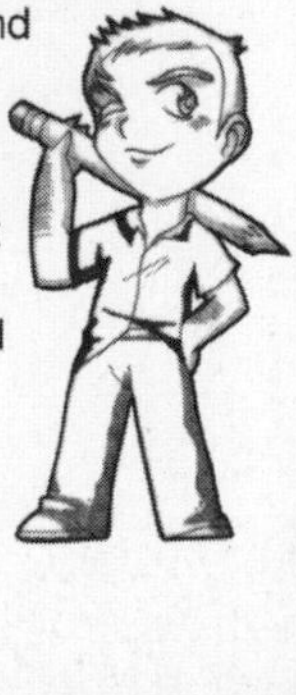

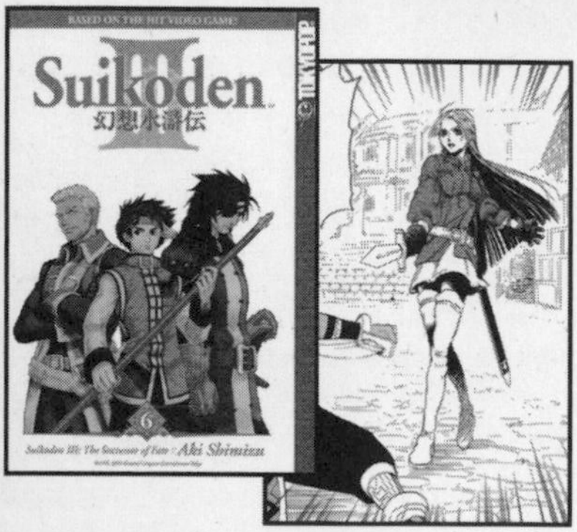
Suikoden
III
幻想水滸伝
6
Aki Shimizu

BY AKI SHIMIZU

SUIKODEN III

I'm one of those people who likes to watch others play video games (I tend to run into walls and get stuck), so here comes the perfect manga for me! All the neat plot of a great RPG game, without any effort on my part! Aki Shimizu, creator of the delightful series *Qwan*, has done a lovely, lovely job of bringing the world of Suikoden to life. There are great creatures (Fighting ducks! Giant lizard people!), great character designs, and an engaging story full of conflict, drama and intrigue. I picked up one volume while I was eating lunch at my desk one day, and was totally hooked. I can't wait for the next one to come out!

~Lillian Diaz-Przybyl, Editor

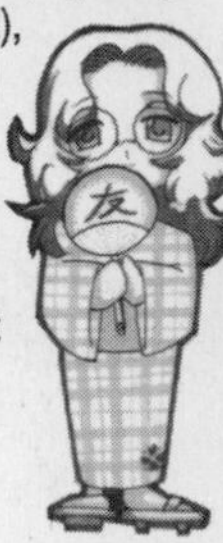

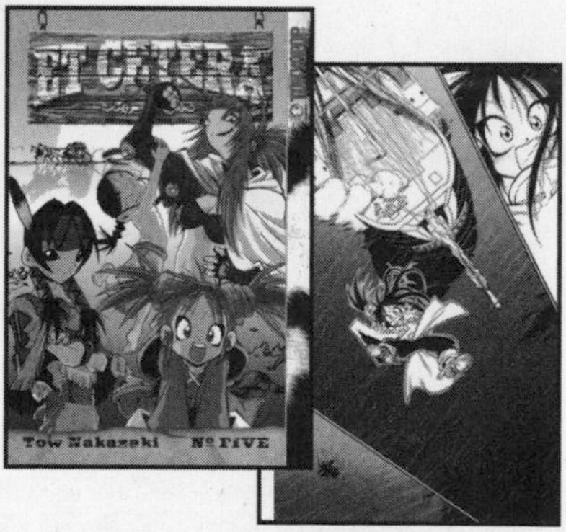
Tow Nakazaki
Nº FIVE

BY TOW NAKAZAKI

ET CETERA

Meet Mingchao, an energetic girl from China who now travels the deserts of the old west. She dreams of becoming a star in Hollywood, eager for fame and fortune. She was given the Eto Gun—a magical weapon that fires bullets with properties of the 12 zodiac signs—as a keepsake from her grandfather before he died. On her journey to Hollywood, she meets a number of zany characters...some who want to help, and others who are after the power of the Eto Gun. Chock full of gun fights, train hijackings, collapsing mineshafts...this East-meets-wild-West tale has it all!

~Aaron Suhr, Sr. Editor

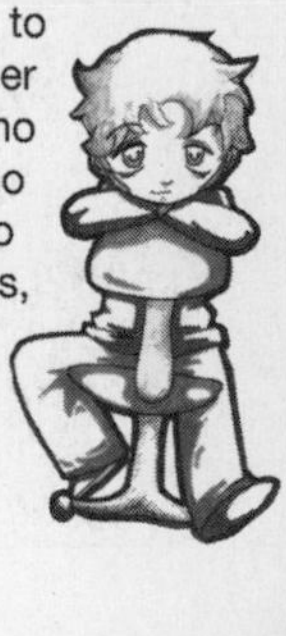

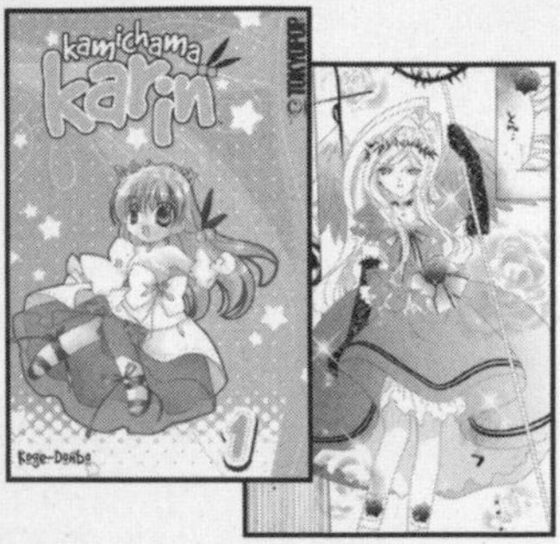
kamichama karin
Koge-Donbo
1

KAMICHAMA KARIN

BY KOGE-DONBO

Karin is an average girl...at best. She's not good at sports and gets terrible grades. On top of all that, her parents are dead and her beloved cat Shi-chan just died, too. She is miserable. But everything is about to change—little does Karin know that her mother's ring has the power to make her a goddess!

From the creator of *Pita-Ten* and *Digi-Charat!*

Y
YOUTH AGE 10+

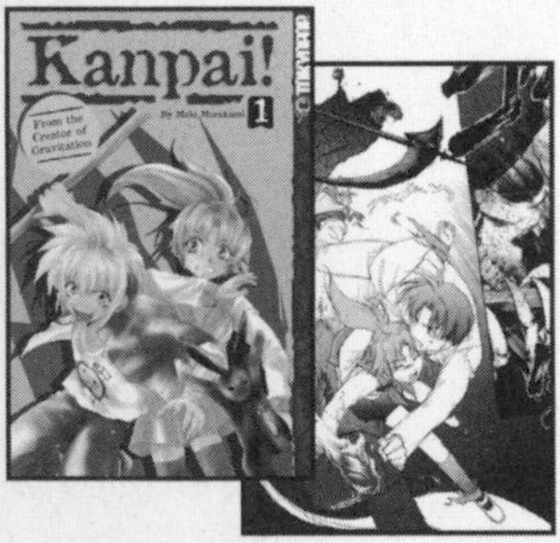
Kanpai!
From the Creator of Gravitation
By Maki Murakami
1

KANPAI!

BY MAKI MURAKAMI

Yamada Shintaro is a monster guardian in training—his job is to protect the monsters from harm. But when he meets Nao, a girl from his middle school, he suddenly falls in love...with her neckline! Shintaro will go to any lengths to prevent disruption to her peaceful life—and preserve his choice view of her neck!

A wild and wonderful adventure from the creator of *Gravitation!*

T
TEEN AGE 13+

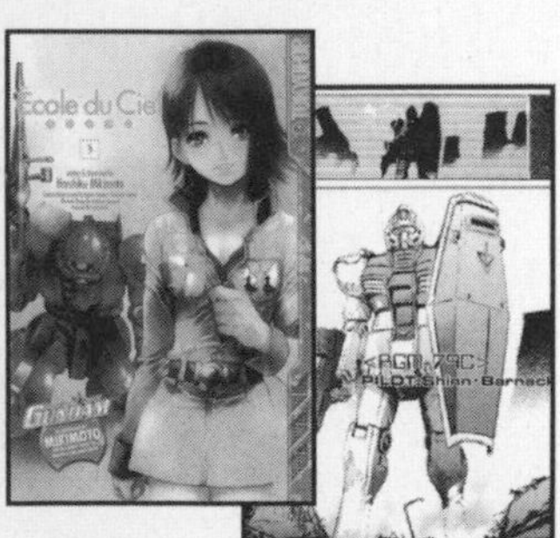
École du Ciel
GUNDAM
MIKIMOTO
PILOT Shian Barnach

MOBILE SUIT GUNDAM ÉCOLE DU CIEL

BY HARUHIKO MIKIMOTO

École du Ciel—where aspiring pilots train to become Top Gundam! Asuna, daughter of a brilliant professor, is a below-average student at École du Ciel. But the world is spiraling toward war, and Asuna is headed for a crash course in danger, battle, and most of all, love.

From the artist of the phenomenally successful *Macross* and *Baby Birth!*

T
TEEN AGE 13+

STOP!

This is the back of the book.
You wouldn't want to spoil a great ending!

This book is printed "manga-style," in the authentic Japanese right-to-left format. Since none of the artwork has been flipped or altered, readers get to experience the story just as the creator intended. You've been asking for it, so TOKYOPOP® delivered: authentic, hot-off-the-press, and far more fun!

DIRECTIONS

If this is your first time reading manga-style, here's a quick guide to help you understand how it works.

It's easy... just start in the top right panel and follow the numbers. Have fun, and look for more 100% authentic manga from TOKYOPOP®!